Financial Landscape Transformation

EMERALD STUDIES IN FINANCE, INSURANCE, AND RISK MANAGEMENT

Series Editor: Simon Grima

Books in this series collect quantitative and qualitative studies in areas relating to finance, insurance, and risk management. Subjects of interest may include banking, accounting, auditing, compliance, sustainability, behaviour, management, and business economics.

In the disruption of political upheaval, new technologies, climate change, and new regulations, it is more important than ever to understand risk in the financial industry. Providing high-quality academic research, this book series provides a platform for authors to explore, analyze and discuss current and new financial models and theories, and engage with innovative research on an international scale.

Previously published:

Uncertainty and Challenges in Contemporary Economic Behaviour
Ercan Özen and Simon Grima

New Challenges for Future Sustainability and Wellbeing
Ercan Özen, Simon Grima and Rebecca Dalli Gonzi

Insurance and Risk Management for Disruptions in Social, Economic and Environmental Systems: Decision and Control Allocations within New Domains of Risk
Simon Grima, Ercan Özen and Rebecca Dalli Gonzi

Public Sector Leadership in Assessing and Addressing Risk
Peter C. Young, Simon Grima, and Rebecca Dalli Gonzi

Big Data Analytics in the Insurance Market
Kiran Sood, B. Balamurugan, Simon Grima, and Pierpaolo Marano

Big Data: A Game Changer for Insurance Industry
Kiran Sood, Rajesh Kumar Dhanaraj, B. Balamurugan, Simon Grima and R. Uma Maheshwari

The Adoption and Effect of Artificial Intelligence on Human Resources Management, Part A
Pallavi Tyagi, Naveen Chilamkurti, Simon Grima, Kiran Sood, and B. Balamurugan

The Adoption and Effect of Artificial Intelligence on Human Resources Management, Part B
Pallavi Tyagi, Naveen Chilamkurti, Simon Grima, Kiran Sood, and B. Balamurugan

Contemporary Studies of Risks in Emerging Technology, Part A
Simon Grima, Kiran Sood, and Ercan Özen

Contemporary Studies of Risks in Emerging Technology, Part B
Simon Grima, Kiran Sood, and Ercan Özen

The Framework for Resilient Industry: A Holistic Approach for Developing Economies
Narinder Kumar, Kiran Sood, Ercan Özen, and Simon Grima

VUCA and Other Analytics in Business Resilience, Part A
Deepmala Singh, Kiran Sood, Sandeep Kautish, and Simon Grima

VUCA and Other Analytics in Business Resilience, Part B
Deepmala Singh, Kiran Sood, Sandeep Kautish, and Simon Grima

Finance Analytics in Business: Perspectives on Enhancing Efficiency and Accuracy
Sanjay Taneja, Pawan Kumar, Kiran Sood, Ercan Özen, and Simon Grima

Enterprise Risk Management in Today's World: Enterprise-Wide Risk Management and Strategy, Part A
Author: Jean-Paul Louisot; Editor: Simon Grima

Enterprise Risk Management in Today's World: A Current and Futuristic View of the Complexity, Resilience, Responsibility and Tools in ERM, Part B
Author: Jean-Paul Louisot; Editor: Simon Grima

Green Management: A New Paradigm in the World of Business
Swati Gupta, Sanjay Taneja, Ercan Özen, Kiran Sood and Simon Grima

Business Challenges and Opportunities in the Era of Industry 5.0
Simon Grima, Salih Serkan Kaleli, Mehmet Baygin, and Engin Boztepe

Financial Landscape Transformation: Technological Disruptions

EDITED BY

MANJIT KOUR
Chandigarh University, India

SANJAY TANEJA
Graphic Era Deemed to be University, India

ERCAN ÖZEN
University of Uşak, Turkey

KIRAN SOOD
Chitkara Business School, Chitkara University, Punjab, India

AND

SIMON GRIMA
University of Malta, Malta

emerald PUBLISHING

United Kingdom – North America – Japan – India – Malaysia – China

Emerald Publishing Limited
Emerald Publishing, Floor 5, Northspring, 21-23 Wellington Street, Leeds LS1 4DL.

First edition 2025

British Library Cataloguing in Publication Data
A catalogue record for this book is available from the British Library

ISBN: 978-1-83753-751-8 (Print)
ISBN: 978-1-83753-750-1 (Online)
ISBN: 978-1-83753-752-5 (Epub)

Printed and bound by CPI Group (UK) Ltd, Croydon, CR0 4YY

INVESTOR IN PEOPLE

Contents

About the Editors

Manjit Kour is a Professor at University Business School, Chandigarh University, Punjab, India. She completed her PhD in management from Punjab Technical University, India. Her research interests revolve around fintech, sustainable finance, and social marketing, where she has contributed significantly. Her dedication to research is evident through an impressive portfolio of 54 research papers published in renowned international and national journals, including SCOPUS, ABDC, WOS, and UGC indexed journals. She is entrusted with editorial responsibilities for several esteemed journals, including those indexed by ABDC and Scopus. As a reviewer, she plays a vital role in maintaining the quality and rigor of academic publications. She has also received International Researcher Award 2021 by International Institute of Organized Research (I2OR).

Sanjay Taneja, ICSSR Fellow, PhD MBA (University Topper) and ADBM. He is currently working as Associate professor in DOMS, Graphic Era Deemed to be University, Mohali, Punjab (India). His research areas of interest are finance, banking and insurance. He has published his dozen works in national and international journals (Scopus indexed/SCI indexed and UGC care listed) and two textbooks, two edited books on different areas of banking, social science and entrepreneurship. He received the awards from Indian University ICFAI and GKU towards the contribution in teaching and research. ORCID: 0000-0002-3632-4053

Ercan Özen, received his BSc in Public Finance (1994), MSc in Business-Accounting (1997), PhD in Business Finance (2008) from the University of Afyon Kocatepe. Now he is Associate Professor of Finance in Department of Banking and Finance, Faculty of Applied Sciences, University of Uşak, Turkey. His current research interests include different aspects of finance. He has (co-)authored 10 book chapters and more than 50 papers, more than 40 conferences participation. He is a member in International Program Committee of 3 conferences and workshops. He is chair of International Applied Social Sciences Congress. He is also certificated accountant, member of Asian Finance Association and member of TEMA (Turkey Combating Soil Erosion, for Reforestation and the Protection of Natural Resources Foundation).

Kiran Sood is a Professor at Chitkara Business School, Chitkara University, Punjab, India. She received her Undergraduate and Postgraduate degrees in Commerce from Panjab University, respectively, in 2002 and 2004. She earned her Master of Philosophy degree in 2008 and Doctor of Philosophy in Commerce with a concentration on Product Portfolio Performance of General Insurance Companies in 2017 from Panjabi University, Patiala, India. Before joining Chitkara University in July 2019, Kiran had served four organizations with a total experience of 18 years. She has published various journal articles and presented papers at various international conferences. She serves as an Editor of the refereed journal, particularly the *IJBST International Journal of BioSciences and Technology, International Journal of Research Culture Society,* and *The Journal of Corporate Governance, Insurance, and Risk Management (JCGIRM)*. Her research mainly focuses on regulations, marketing and Finance in insurance, insurance management, economics and management of innovation in insurance. She has edited more than 10 books with various international publishers such as Emerald, CRC, Taylor & Francis, AAP, WILEY Scrivener, IET, Rivers Publishers, and IEEE.

Prof. Simon Grima, is the the Deputy Dean of the Faculty of Economics, Management and Accountancy, Associate Professor and the Head of the Department of Insurance and Risk Management. Simon is also a Professor at the University of Latvia, Faculty of Business, Management and Economics a visiting Professor at UNICATT Milan and an Affiliate Professor at Haxhi Zeka University, Kosovo. He served as the President of the Malta Association of Risk Management (MARM) and was President of the Malta Association of Compliance Officers (MACO) between 2013 and 2015, and between 2016 and 2018 respectively. He is again the current President of MARM since 2023. Moreover, he is the Co-chair of the Scientific Education Committee of the Federation of European Risk Managers (FERMA) and is a member of the Strategic Risk Leaders Association (SRLA), previously the Public Risk Management Association (PRIMO). His research focus is on Governance, Regulations and Internal Controls and has over 30 years of experience varied between Financial Services, academia and public entities. He has acted as Co-chair and is a member of the scientific program committee on some international conferences and is a Chief Editor, Editor and Review Editor of some journals and book series. He has been awarded outstanding reviewer for *Journal of Financial Regulation and Compliance* in the 2017 and 2022 and the outstanding author contribution for the Book Series *Contemporary Studies in Economic and Financial Analysis* Emerald Literati Awards in 2024. Moreover, Simon acts as an Independent Director for Financial Services Firms, sits on Risk, Compliance, Procurement, Investment and Audit Committees and carries out duties as a Compliance Officer, Internal Auditor and Risk Manager. ORCID: 0000-0003-1523-5120.

About the Contributors

Dr Anshul Agrawal has a robust background encompassing 10 years of combined experience in academia and corporate sectors, along with a dedicated tenure in research. Her specialization lies in finance, econometrics, time series analysis, security and derivative markets, and financial modelling. She has published her work in SCOPUS Indexed and ABDC category journals. She is proficient in various analytical tools such as SPSS, E-Views, Minitab, Microsoft Project Planner, and Advanced Excel. Furthermore, she has been a valuable resource, sharing her knowledge through numerous workshops.

Dr Paiman Ahmad is an Assistant Professor at the University of Raparin, Rania-Kurdistan Region-Iraq. She has research interests in energy economics, sustainable development in developing economies, climate change, energy transition, SDGs, migration, and the public sector in the developing world. She holds a PhD in Public Administration from the National University of Public Service-Budapest-Hungary-2018. Her research works have been published in reputable journals such as *International Environmental Agreements, Politics, Law and Economics, Journal of Public Affairs, Sustainable Development Wiley, Journal of Cleaner Production, Gondwana Research, Renewable Energy, Environmental Science, and Pollution Research, Environmental Impact Assessment Review, Global Business Review, Public Policy and Administration, Economic Research-Ekonomska Istraživanja*, and top-tier academic publishers: Elsevier, Palgrave Macmillan, Sage, Springer, Taylor & Francis, Routledge, and Wiley.

Shakil Ahmad, Assistant Professor, School of Business, University of Creative Technology Chittagong. He is pursuing PhD in Business Management (Financial Technology). He completed MBA from the University of Chittagong, Bangladesh. He teaches finance, banking, and insurance. He has been teaching for more than 7 years. He has 36 research publications in several reputed national and international peer-reviewed journals. He presented research papers in more than 20 national and international conferences. He is the member of editorial board and reviewer of several international journals and PC member of conferences.

Muhammed Akin was born in 1993 in Ankara, Turkey. He completed his high school education at Ankara Atatürk High School and graduated with a degree in English Economics from Ankara Yıldırım Beyazıt University. He earned his

Master's degree in Banking and Finance from Karabük University. An innovative entrepreneur, Akin founded his own e-commerce firm, which operates in the print-on-demand sector, serving clients in the United States. His academic background and professional experience make him a proficient expert in banking, finance, and e-commerce, with a strong track record in the industry.

Franklin Akosa is a PhD student at the Edith Cowan Business and Law School, working on a project to investigate a career in the hotel industry. Previously, he was the Head of Research, Monitoring, and Evaluation at the Ghana Library Authority within the Ministry of Education. In this role, he led a team in streamlining the Ministry's research and evaluation practices. His expertise was further recognized through his involvement as a member of the technical working group at Ghana's Ministry of Education, where he played a crucial role in optimizing the operations of the education sector. Franklin also brings extensive academic experience, having lectured and served as a research assistant at the University of Ghana Business School, University of Cape Coast, and MountCrest University College, Accra.

Rozina Akter is an Assistant Professor, Department of Business Administration, Daffodil International University, Dhaka, Bangladesh. She completed MBA from the University of Dhaka, Bangladesh. She teaches Finance & Banking. She has been teaching for more than 9 years. She has been doing research for more than 9 years and has a strong knack for research. She has research publications in several reputed national and international peer-reviewed journals. She is the member of editorial boards of several international journals and conferences.

S. M. Ashraful Alam received his BBA and MBA degrees from the Department of Management Information Systems, Faculty of Business Studies from the University of Dhaka, Bangladesh, in 2013 and 2014, respectively. He has been working as an Assistant Professor in the Department of Management Information Systems, Faculty of Business Studies, Begum Rokeya University, Rangpur, Bangladesh, since December 2021. His major research interest is in the fields of technology adoption, fintech, digital economy, green tech, and e-health.

Dr Alhamzah Alnoor holds a PhD in Business Administration and is currently a Senior Lecturer of Strategic Management at the Management Technical College, Southern Technical University, Basrah, Iraq. Alnoor received a BSc degree with first-class honors from Southern Technical University in 2013. After completing his BSc in Operation Management, he was awarded a Master's degree in Business Administration from the University of Basrah, Iraq, in 2016. He obtained his PhD from the School of Management, Universiti Sains Malaysia, Malaysia 2022. His research interests lie in strategic management, business ethics, leadership, human resources management, organizational psychology, organizational sociology, innovation, entrepreneurship, SMEs, technology adaption, and social commerce. He has published numerous scientific journal articles and conference papers. He is a regular reviewer of numerous prestigious journals. He has many handbooks that were published under Springer publisher. During his career, he was engaged in more than 50 projects.

Tyrone De Alwis is a PhD student attached to the University of Colombo, Sri Lanka. He completed his Bachelor's degree, followed by a Postgraduate Diploma in Economic Development and a Master's in Economics from the University of Colombo, Sri Lanka. His work has been published in scholarly journals such as *Heliyon*, *PLOS One*, *Asian Economic and Financial Review*, *Sri Lanka Journal of Management Studies*, *International Journal of Food Science*, and *Journal of the Academy of Social Sciences*.

Prof Wasantha Athukorala holds a Doctorate in Economics from Queensland University of Technology, Australia, an MPhil, and a B.A. (Honours) in Economics from the University of Peradeniya, where he has been working as a Professor in Economics. He has over 50 research papers published in prestigious national and international journals. Wasantha Athukorala has been named the 2nd best Environmental Economist in Sri Lanka by the Global AD Scientific Index. Given his overall research profile, the University of Peradeniya has categorized him in the top research category (Tier 4*) in 2022. He also earned two presidential awards for scientific publication in 2023.

Neha Bansal is currently working as Research Scholar in the Department of Commerce, USB, Chandigarh University, India. Her research areas of finance, banking, and green finance. She has published her work in the national and international indexed journals and edited books.

Dr XinYing Chew received a PhD degree in Statistical Quality Control from Universiti Sains Malaysia. She is currently a Senior Lecturer at the School of Computer Sciences, Universiti Sains Malaysia. She is also a Certified Trainer with the Human Resources Development Fund (HRDF). She is also an Adjunct Research Fellow of the Swinburne University of Technology Sarawak Campus and the Professional Technologist with the Malaysia Board of Technologist (MBOT). Her research interests include advanced analytics and statistical quality/process control.

Adriana AnaMaria Davidescu is Full Professor in the Department of Statistics and Econometrics of the Bucharest Academy of Economic Studies and Senior Researcher at the National Institute for Scientific Research in Labour and Social Protection, with over 14 years of experience in socio-economic research and labour market analysis. Adriana has a PhD from the Bucharest University of Economic Studies and has been a Visiting Scholar at the University of Salerno (Italy). She has over 14 years of experience in the analysis of informal economy issues, coordinating or being a member of the research team of over 50 national and international projects. ORCID: 0000-0002-9847-1200

Dr Shweta Dewangan is an Assistant Professor at ICFAI University in Raipur, Chhattisgarh, where she has cultivated a 16-year career in academia, including 12 years post-PhD. Her expertise spans finance, human resources, economics, etc. Currently, she is working in different fields of research, such as blockchain technology, Metaverse, Fintech, and AI. She has a prolific publication record in UGC CARE, Scopus, Web of Science-recognized journals, peer-reviewed publications, and book and various book chapters. Additionally, Dr Dewangan has supervised four PhD scholars to completion and is an active member of the Indian Commerce Association and Commerce & Management Association.

Prof Dr Narayanage Jayantha Dewasiri is a Professor of Finance attached to the Department of Accountancy and Finance, Sabaragamuwa University of Sri Lanka. Furthermore, he serves as the Brand Ambassador at Emerald Publishing, UK, and the Vice President of the Sri Lanka Institute of Marketing. He is a pioneer in applying triangulation research approaches in the management discipline. He is currently serving as the Co-Editors-in-Chief of the *South Asian Journal of Marketing*, published by Emerald Publishing; Senior Associate Editor of the *FIIB Business Review*, published by SAGE Publishing; Managing Editor of the *Asian Journal of Finance*, and *South Asian Journal of Tourism and Hospitality*, published by the Faculty of Management Studies, Sabaragamuwa University of Sri Lanka.

Vlora Berisha Dranqolli is an accomplished Assistant Professor of Accounting and Finance at Business College – UHZ, with a PhD degree in Bank, Accounting and Finance from the University Hasan Prishtina, and a Fulbright Visiting Scholar post-doc degree from Northern Arizona University. She completed Postdoctoral Research in Managerial Accounting at the University of Malta. Vlora has contributed to several TEMPUS and ERASMUS + Projects, including CONSUS, T2P, and CTPE Projects. Her work has been published in numerous journals and presented at many conferences, and she is a member of the prestigious European Cooperation in Science and Technology (COST). ORCID: 0000-0002-1049-1742

Dr Mehmed Ganić, PhD, is a Full Professor of Economics specializing in Macro-Finance Theory, Applied Econometrics, and Financial Economics. He has over 12 years of academic background in the graduate and postgraduate level of various economic and finance courses and 11 years of professional experience in the finance industry. A specialist in East and Central European economics, he has published over 150 scholarly articles widely in reputable journals and has authored four books. The bulk of his research attempts to extend standard growth-finance theoretical models.

Dr Shubhangi Gautam is working as an assistant professor at Lovely Professional University. She has various publications in the field of behavioral finance, and cryptocurrency investments in different prestigious journals indexed in Scopus, ABDC listed, Web of Science, and UGC care. She is also serving as a reviewer for Scopus, ABDC-listed finance, and multidisciplinary journals. ORCID iD: 0000-0002-0236-0216.

Cristina Maria Geambasu is a PhD student at the Doctoral School of Cybernetics and Statistics and has an experience of over five years on data manipulation and analysis, currently occupying the position of senior data analyst at GfK Romania, aiming to bring innovative approaches and insightful visualizations to data collections and analysis. In the last year, she has focused on exploring the data science branch and machine learning techniques. The subject studied in the PhD is micro and macro approaches on the regional informal economy phenomenon and the main objective of the thesis is to explore the main determinants of informality and to estimate the dimension of the regional informal economy. ORCID: 0000-0003-0705-0476

Mohammad Osman Goni is a lecturer at the Department of Business Administration, Daffodil International University, Dhaka, Bangladesh. He pursued BBA and MBA from the Department of Finance, University of Chittagong. He has presented three papers at international conferences. His research area focuses on capital markets and instruments and digital financial technology.

Dr Munish Gupta, an Associate Professor at Chandigarh University's University School of Business, specializes in Behavioural Studies related to technology adoption. His research delves into the complex decisions made by individuals and organizations when encountering new technologies, blending insights from psychology, sociology, and economics. Central to his work is understanding the cognitive aspects that shape people's readiness to embrace technological tools. His multidisciplinary approach combines information systems, psychology, and marketing to offer a comprehensive view of the factors influencing technology adoption. His studies highlight the significance of usability, perceived benefits, and social influence in guiding technology adoption decisions, aiming to provide valuable insights for successful implementation. ORCID: 0000-0002-1982-4136

Dr Chabi Gupta, Christ University, India is an alumnus of Shri Ram College of Commerce Delhi University. She has over 21 years of rich teaching and industrial experience of working in reputable universities, banks, and financial institutions. To her credit, there are several national and international publications and presentations at conferences. Her research areas of interest are finance, banking, and analytics. She is presently affiliated to Christ University, Bengaluru, India.

Tasnim Ara Hossen pursued her MBA at the Department of Finance, University of Chittagong. She obtained her BBA from the University of Chittagong. Her research interests focus on microfinance and digital financial systems and instruments. She just started working as a Management Trainee Officer at Brac-Microfinance and is midway through her training. Soon, she will undertake project work on digital micro-financial transactions within Brac.

Dr Kshitiz Jangir is currently working as an Assistant Professor (Senior Scale), Department of Commerce, Manipal University Jaipur, Rajasthan. He received his PhD from the University of Rajasthan. His research areas are FinTech, behavioural finance, corporate governance, banking and insurance. He has published various articles and chapters in national and international peer-reviewed books and journals.

Dr Sanjeev Kadam is an Experienced Educator and Mentor with a demonstrated history of working in the management education industry. He did his PhD in Management from Symbiosis International (Deemed University), Pune, India. To his credit, he has 20 years of professional experience and has been into academics for the last 13 years. His research interests are multidisciplinary in nature specially focusing on operations. Dr Kadam is an Associate Member of The Institution of Engineers (India).

Hakan Kahyaoglu graduated from Marmara University's Department of Econometrics in 1993. He completed his Master's and Doctorate studies at Dokuz Eylul University and received his PhD in Economics in 2007. He is still working as an International Economics Professor at the same university. Prof Hakan contributes to the literature with his articles, books and publications in numerous refereed journals. His research interests focus on digital economy, financial economics, time series analysis, and international economics and political economy. ORCID: 0000-0002-6031-7494

Sezer Bozkus Kahyaoglu is currently Associate Professor at Izmir Bakircay University since 2018 to the present. Sezer has certifications in CIA, CFSA, CRMA, CICP, CFE and CPA. Her research interests mainly include applied econometrics, data analytics, financial markets and instruments, sustainability, corporate governance, risk management, fraud accounting, auditing, coaching, mentoring and NLP. Sezer has various refereed articles, books and book chapters published via international publishing companies. She has previously worked in a variety of management positions in the banking, audit, and risk sectors. ORCID: 0000-0003-2865-3399

Rejaul Karim is an Assistant Professor of Finance and Banking in the Department of Business Administration at Varendra University, Rajshahi, Bangladesh. He completed the Bachelor of Business Administration and Master of Business Administration in Finance and Banking from the Pabna University of Science and Technology, Pabna, Bangladesh. He is pursuing PhD in Corporate Finance from the Institute of Bangladesh Studies, University of Rajshahi, Bangladesh. Karim has teaching and research experience for over eight years in undergrad and Master's level tertiary education. He has published more than 14 research papers in reputed national and international peer-reviewed journals in relevant fields.

Sadia Noor Khan is an Assistant Professor in the Department of Banking and Insurance, University of Dhaka. She is a PhD student in the finance section of

Kobe University, Japan. She has several research publications in national and international journals. One of her research papers was awarded as the best paper at an international conference held in UAE, 2016. Her research areas focus on finance and banking.

Prof Dr Sanjeev Kumar is an Accomplished Expert in Food and Beverage. He currently holds the position of Professor in Lovely Professional University, Punjab, India. With over a decade of experience in the field, Food Service Industry, his research focuses on alcoholic beverages, event management and sustainable management practices, metaverse and artificial intelligence. He has published more than 45 research papers, articles, and chapters in Scopus Indexed, UGC Approved and peer-reviewed journals and books. Dr Sanjeev Kumar participated and acted as a resource person in various national and international conferences, seminars, research workshops and industry talks and his work has been widely cited.

Dr Pardeep Kumar is working as an Associate Professor at the University School of Business, Chandigarh University, India. He is a versatile educator, researcher, and trainer with more than 14 years of professional experience in the areas of professional teaching. He has published two books and several research papers in various international and national journals, and he has presented papers at several international and national conferences and seminars in the field of management. He is a life member of the Indian Society of Technical Education (ISTE).

Reshma Pervin Lima is an Assistant Professor, Department of Accounting, Faculty of Business Studies, Mawlana Bhashani Science and Technology University, Bangladesh. She obtained BBA and MBA degrees in Finance from Chittagong University, Bangladesh. She has been working as a Faculty Member from 2015. Her research interests focus on the areas of finance, financial instruments, financial institutions and markets, financial technology, etc. She has published some research papers in renowned national and international journals.

Eduard Mihai Manta is a PhD student at the Doctoral School of Cybernetics and Statistics and has over seven years of experience in model risk management, holding various positions in data teams. In the last few years, he focused on machine learning and data science. The subject studied in the PhD is the COVID pandemic - 19 - an accelerator of the implementation of sustainable development concepts, resilience, green and inclusive of the global economy. He has experience working with one of the principal NGOs in the field of education, working on reports that underlie decision-making within the organization. ORCID: 0000-0001-9693-8607

Akansha Mer is an Assistant Professor in the Department of Commerce and Management, Banasthali Vidyapith, Rajasthan, India. She has earned her Doctorate on Work Engagement in NPOs from Banasthali Vidyapith. She has 2.5 years of corporate and about a decade of academic work experience. Her research interests include work engagement, adoption of technology by consumers, mindfulness, workplace spirituality, working patterns of non-profit organizations and

Artificial Intelligence in HRM and marketing. She has published research papers and book chapters with leading publishers like Taylor and Francis (Routledge), Sage, Wiley & Scrivener, Inderscience, etc.

Dr Md Imtiaz Mostafiz is an Associate Professor in Strategy and International Business at the University of Leicester School of Business, University of Leicester, UK. Before joining ULSB, he was a Reader in Business the Founding Director of the Centre for Global Business and Enterprise, and the Lead for UoA -17 (knowledge and understanding) – REF 2029 at Greater Manchester Business School, University of Bolton, UK. He was also a Senior Lecturer of International Business and Strategy at Sheffield Business School, Sheffield Hallam University, United Kingdom. He also served at Taylor's Business School, Taylor's University, Malaysia, as a Lecturer in International Business. He is a Fellow of the Higher Education Academy, UK. Dr Imtiaz received the Global Talent Award from the British Academy. He leads Early Career Research Development at ENT SIG at the British Academy of Management. He is also a Peer Review College member of the British Academy of Management, as well as the Economics and Social Research Council in the UK Research and Innovation. He won several best paper awards from the Academy of International Business Conference, the British Academy of Management Conference, and others. He also serves on several Editorial Review Boards, such as *Entrepreneurship Research Journal*, *Journal of Business and Industrial Marketing*, *Business Strategy and Development*, and *Journal of Entrepreneurship in Emerging Economy*. He also acted as a Chief Guest Editor in Special Issues in the *International Journal of Entrepreneurial Behaviour & Research* and the *Canadian Journal of Administrative Science*. He won the Best Reviewer Award from the *Journal of World Business* in 2023.

Shwan Mohammed Mustafa is an Orthopaedic Surgeon m.B.ch.B, F.I.C.M.S, who works in Erbil-Kurdistan Region-Iraq. An Orthopedic Medical Doctor, who has in-depth experience in the health-care system in the Iraqi Kurdistan Region and many years as a practitioner who has been experiencing and serving many different cases so far. He has been taking part in many global trainings in his specialty and health care services in Dubai, UK, and Italy.

Ram B. Ramachandran is a Professor and Vice Dean at the Jindal School of Banking & Finance, O.P. Jindal Global University. Ram teaches and conducts research in the interdisciplinary areas of emerging technologies like FinTech/Blockchain and artificial intelligence, management, leadership, and entrepreneurship. Ram is an accomplished hands-on senior executive with over 35 year's track record of building and leading global consulting practices in the financial services sector. Most recently, he was the Managing Director at Ernst & Young, New York responsible for transformative technology solutions for his clients. His articles have been published in reputed International and Indian industry magazines.

Blake Rayfield is an Assistant Professor of Finance at the University of North Florida, boasting a robust background in higher education. He has published over ten peer-reviewed journal articles and book chapters, including works in the *Journal of Financial Research* and the *Quarterly Review of Economics and Finance.* His research spans financial technology, corporate finance, and investments, reflecting his deep engagement with the evolving finance field and community focus. He has served as a Visiting Professor at the University of Strasbourg in France and as a guest Lecturer for FGV. Blake holds a BS in Finance from Florida International University, as well as a Master's and PhD in Financial Economics from the University of New Orleans. ORCID: 0000-0003-0390-1587

Dr Goran Ridic is a Strategy Lecturer at the Frankfurt School of Finance and Management. Dr Ridic studied Economics at Trinity College in Connecticut (USA), holds a Master of Business Administration degree in Finance from the University of Connecticut School of Business, as well as a Doctorate in Public Policy from Northeastern University in Boston, Massachusetts, USA. He worked as Consultant for several Fortune 500 companies including General Electric (GE), United Technologies – Pratt & Whitney, ING Group, The Hartford Investment Management Co. (HIMCO) and the United States Agency for International Development (USAID). In addition, Dr Ridic was a Senior Lecturer at Northeastern University in Boston (USA) and Professor at the University Sarajevo School of Science and Technology (University of Buckingham, UK) and the International University of Sarajevo (IUS).

Vikas Sharma is an associate professor at the University School of Business at Chandigarh University, holding an MBA in Finance and a Ph.D. in Management, with a focus on Finance and Accounting. With 16 years of academic and professional experience, Dr. Sharma specializes in the research areas of fintech and behavioral intention. He has published papers in Q1 and Q2 journals and has served as an editor and reviewer for several reputed publications. Additionally, he has developed expertise in administrative support and data analysis. He is actively seeking opportunities in the finance sector to further apply and expand his knowledge.

Nargis Sultana was born in Chattogram, Bangladesh. Presently, she occupies a position of an Assistant Professor in the Department of Finance and Banking, Comilla University, Cumiila, Bangladesh. Besides, she is the moderator of the Finance and Banking Debating Association and advisor of the Finance and Banking Club. She is a responsible faculty conducting all the academic activities on time which made her get a 'Letter of Appreciation' from the university. She completed a Bachelor of Business Administration in Finance and Banking as well as a Masters of Business Administration in Finance from Chittagong University, Chattogram, Bangladesh. Nargis has teaching and research experience of almost seven years in undergraduate and master's level of tertiary education. She is found competent in teaching a plethora of subjects in English on multidisciplinary subjects related to finance, banking, development studies, statistics and economics. As per the research activities considered, she is found to be highly engaged in conducting her academic activities. She has numerous publications in international peer-reviewed journals having sound impact factors. She received research grants many times from the university authority. She frequently writes for English dailies on manifold issues. She aims to play a vital role in the community in building a nation with the aid of her versatile teaching.

S. M. Sohrab Uddin is a Professor at the Department of Finance, Faculty of Business Administration (FBA), University of Chittagong, Bangladesh. He also served the Bureau of Business Research, FBA, University of Chittagong as Director. He obtained a BBA and MBA from the University of Chittagong and an MBA and PhD from Ritsumeikan Asia Pacific University, Oita, Japan. His research area focuses on financial markets, institutions, and instruments with particular emphasis on banking sector development, including Islamic finance in developing countries.

Amarpreet Singh Virdi is an Assistant Professor at the Department of Management Studies, Kumaun University Bhimtal Campus, Nainital (Uttarakhand). He has corporate experience of working with a software company dealing with share market software based on Oracle database and forms. His research interests include the self-service technologies in banking, green products/marketing, adoption of technology by consumers, working patterns of NGOs, design thinking, Fintech, Artificial Intelligence in marketing and HR, etc. He has published papers and book chapters with leading publishers like Sage, Inderscience, Wiley & Scrivener, etc.

Muhammed Ali Yetgin is an Assistant Professor at the University of Karabük which is a State University in Türkiye. He earned his Bachelor of Science in Computer Science from the State University of New York in the USA, and Master's in Business Administration at Istanbul Bilgi University, and PhD in Business Administration at Turkish Aeronautical Association University (Ankara). He worked in the Ministry of Interior of Türkiye for many years and has been working as an academician since 2019. He teaches undergraduate and graduate (master's and PhD classes) related to Business Administration. His research interests include digitalization in businesses, the organizational structure of institutions, and technological innovations in companies. ORCID: 0000-0002-8120-4704

Foreword

This collection of academic papers explores the complex relationship between technological progress and economic occurrences in the fast-changing financial environment of the current day. The convergence of finance and technology, commonly called 'Fintech', has enabled groundbreaking advancements and substantial transformations in the financial sector. The authors do a comprehensive examination of the relationship between the expansion of the insurance sector and foreign direct investment (FDI) through a panel cointegration analysis. They highlight the crucial role that robust insurance markets play in fostering a conducive environment for foreign investments.

The influence of artificial intelligence (AI) on personal and business finance is a noteworthy topic of concern in this compilation. The authors comprehensively analyze the available literature to assess the present status of AI implementations in the banking sector. They meticulously assess and debate the prospective benefits and challenges predicted. This extensive inquiry provides the groundwork for future research to use the potential of AI in revolutionizing financial decision-making, risk management, and consumer contact.

An in-depth comprehension of significant price fluctuations and alterations in volatility factors is essential in financial markets. The authors employ a thorough case study on Borsa Istanbul, examining the atypical price swings and their underlying causes. Examining extraordinary events enables market participants to develop essential inferences that aid in predicting and mitigating risks linked to financial trading and investing.

Digitalization has dramatically transformed the consumer experience, notably affecting customer happiness and loyalty. This book analyses digital banking services to explore the crucial factors that impact customer involvement in the digital era. A thorough comprehension of these dynamics allows financial institutions to develop more effective strategies to enhance service delivery and foster long-lasting customer relationships.

Stock market investors are perpetually concerned about inflation and abrupt fluctuations in oil prices. This compilation employs empirical research to elucidate the intricate interrelationships between macroeconomic factors and stock market results. The authors offer crucial guidance for investors and policymakers to create more robust investment portfolios and adopt creative economic policies to address macroeconomic volatility.

This report does a comparative analysis of the regulatory frameworks in Central and Eastern Europe for fintech startups. The article highlights the different approaches countries use to overcome the regulatory challenges posed by breakthroughs in fintech. The book offers valuable perspectives on how various regulatory frameworks can either support or hinder the progress and development of fintech.

Innovation is the primary focus of the future of fintech, uncovering new opportunities and challenges. Understanding the potential of blockchain technology is crucial for enhancing the efficiency and security of fintech firms. It is essential to thoroughly analyze the significant possibilities of blockchain and develop a clear plan for integrating it into the financial ecosystem.

The advent of virtual currencies and decentralized metaverse introduces unprecedented financial dynamics and user interaction patterns. The authors examine the analytical systems present in the metaverse and uncover innovative approaches to creating and exchanging value, which have the potential to revolutionize the future of finance.

The analysis of cognitive biases in decision-making about bitcoin investments is under serious scrutiny. This study focuses on comprehending behavioural finance principles when developing investment strategies and regulatory frameworks for digital assets.

A significant field of research focuses on the impact of currency devaluation on inflation, specifically in Sri Lanka. By comprehending this association, economists and policymakers can augment their capacity to moderate inflationary forces and promote stability within their economies.

Regulatory Technology (RegTech) can revolutionize compliance and regulatory operations entirely. This book explores the policies and practices that impact the developing field of RegTech in Bangladesh. The comprehensive examination centres on the digital revolution of the insurance industry, referred to as InsurTech, and the broader financial transformation commonly known as FinTech.

Enjoy your reading!

Prof Dr Ibish Mazreku
Faculty of Business
University Haxhi Zeka
www.unhz.eu

Preface

Financial Technology has emerged as the new disruption in the world of finance. Finance technology is evolving and expanding rapidly with innovations. The scope of technology in finance is growing across the world. The integration of technology into the financial process is referred to as fintech. Fintech has enhanced the degree of automation in the financial services sector. Financial applications thrive to enhance outcomes for various stakeholders, including consumer firms, by leveraging tailor-made algorithms and computing applications. Financial technology is being employed to enhance the efficiency of operations, streamline processes, and reduce costs for the firms and ease of use for consumers. Smartphones' rapid penetration and expansion have been instrumental in adopting financial technology.

Financial technology is a bigger umbrella, which includes machine learning, AI, blockchain, cryptocurrencies, and core banking solutions. It includes applications run on mobiles and technologies that offer automation and enhance the traditional banking financial services and insurance sector processes. The traditional approach to financial services has gone through a paradigm shift with the evolution of technology in finance. Technology has overcome the barriers of time and distance for customers by enhancing the satisfaction of financial services with better speed, convenience, and access and integrating financial transactions with other transactions across the sectors.

This book culminates discussions and interactions between finance experts, bankers, academicians, researchers, technocrats and entrepreneurs. It was observed that it is paramount to navigate and assess the developments in financial technology to explore new avenues, improve existing practices, and develop solutions for the challenges concerning fintech usage by the various stakeholders. The intention of coming out with this book is to compile and share critical insights after evaluating them for academic rigour and assessing them for the feasibility of implementation by the organizations. This book attempts to bridge the gap between theory and practice. Every chapter focuses on a specific domain and aspect of financial technology, exploring stakeholders' understanding and experiences. The book provides a comprehensive framework for better application of technology for current usage and for addressing the needs of future generations.

We are grateful for the efforts of researchers from across the world who have shared deep insights with readers. This book will guide individuals and firms willing to explore integrating technology with financial wisdom to achieve better outcomes. The book could not have reached the final shape without the efforts of peer reviewers and stakeholders to evaluate the contributions and provide input for improvement thoroughly. We express our gratitude to all reviewers and experts.

The book will be useful for students, academicians, practitioners, and policymakers. We urge the readers to explore the insights and share their experiences after implementing them in their respective firms. Financial technology is evolving and offering opportunities and challenges. The opportunities can be converted into useful outcomes, and challenges can be overcome by precision planning, analytics debate, comprehensive evaluation, and assimilation of new ideas. The journey of fintech can be revolutionary for developing sustainable solutions for stakeholders.

Thank you for embarking on this journey with us.

Sanjay Taneja
Department of Management Studies, Graphic Era,
is deemed to be a university in Dehradun, India

Kiran Sood
Chitkara Business School, Chitkara University, Punjab, India

Simon Grima
Faculty of Economics, Management and Accountancy, Department of
Insurance and Risk Management, University of Malta, Malta
Faculty of Economic and Social Sciences, University of Latvia, Latvia

Chapter 1

A Panel Cointegration Analysis of Insurance Development and FDI Nexus

Mehmed Ganić[a] *and Goran Ridic*[b]

[a]*International University of Sarajevo, Department of Economics and Management, Bosnia and Herzegovina*
[b]*SRH University Heidelberg, Germany*

Abstract

Introduction: The possible role of foreign direct investments (FDIs) in the insurance services industry has not received much research compared to the banking industry. The FDI inflows are seen as crucial to the general economic growth of these emerging European transition countries because the insurance sector is still growing and integrating.

Purpose: This chapter explores whether the increase in FDI inflows leads to higher life and non-life insurance penetration in different groups of European transition countries and European post-transition countries.

Methodology: The study employs annual data between 1995 and 2021 using dynamic ordinary squares (DOLS) estimator and Dumitrescu and Hurlin (2012) panel causality methods.

Findings: The study found evidence about the link between FDI and life and non-life insurance penetration, where their gains are marginal and very weak when controlling the effect of Gross Domestic Product per capita (GDPPC) in the long run. More specifically, the effect of FDI on insurance development is greater in the European post-transition countries with higher GDPPC and FDI inflows than in the European transition countries.

These discrepancies may be attributed to the various stages at which their development policies have advanced as well as the overall execution of

Financial Landscape Transformation: Technological Disruptions, 1–16

doi:10.1108/978-1-83753-750-120251001

reforms within the insurance industry. The findings suggest affirmative action programs should be put in place to attract FDI inflows in general and insurance in particular.

Keywords: Life insurance; non-life insurance; FDI flows; transition countries; panel cointegration analysis; Granger causality; DOLS estimator

JEL Codes: F21; G22; E22

Introduction

Numerous profitable industries, including manufacturing, services, real estate, and insurance, are impacted by flows of foreign direct investment (FDI). The amount and value of assets can be significantly impacted by FDI in the insurance sector. It is crucial to make sure that the quality, dependability, and insurance costs of domestic businesses are not jeopardized because different strategies can have varied effects. Insurance rates for domestic enterprises could increase if there is no foreign reinsurance. However, in contrast to other economic ventures, insurance underwriting is highly volatile. In this situation, FDI inflows can support a fair sharing of risks among nations.

The communist era had a profound impact on every area of the economy, and the protracted shift from communism to capitalism necessitated extensive systemic changes. In the transition period of the early 1990s, each country had a distinct level of economic development and implemented various reforms that attracted varying degrees of FDI. The insurance markets in developing countries experience varying phases of development, and the overall amount of premiums collected is directly correlated with the overall state of those markets (Beck et al., 2000). Along with other financial services, the insurance industry has grown in significance since the mid-1980s as part of the overall growth of financial markets and institutions. In the belief that FDI would spur economic growth, most nations at this time substantially relaxed limits on FDI and actively offered tax advantages and subsidies to attract foreign capital (Javorcik, 2004). However, during the 1990s, the expansion of global trade, the liberalization of financial markets, and the growing influence of FDI have also contributed to the expansion of financial institutions' roles and the globalization of insurance services (Outreville, 2021).

Due to a dearth of data, no specific empirical study on FDI in the insurance services sector has been done, even though numerous studies have been done on FDI flows in general and the operations of foreign banks in transitioning nations. Many countries' policy makers are interested in the role that FDI plays in the growth process, and they are working to increase the competitiveness and productivity of their home industries by luring FDI in. By contrast, very limited research has looked at FDI's possible impact on the insurance services industry. Since the insurance sector in these transitional European countries is still developing and building integration, FDI inflows are seen as essential to the countries' overall economic growth. In contrast, not much research has examined how FDI inflows might affect the insurance development. The FDI inflows are seen as crucial to the general economic growth of these emerging European countries because the insurance sector is still growing and integrating.

Life and non-life insurance businesses serve as important financial intermediaries that help secure long-term financial needs and enhance risk management. Deposit insurance and setting aside funds for unforeseen circumstances also boost the efficiency of other financial sectors, such as banking and the capital market. Despite sharing a common history, being in proximity, and belonging to the same region, these countries differ in terms of macroeconomic performances and how FDI affects them. In a sample of 18 European transition and post-transition nations, the life cycle hypothesis (LCH) was investigated (Ganić & Mamuti, 2020). The results shed light on the effects that lifestyle modifications and the gradual process of economic transformation have on European transition and post-transition nations. It also exposes a special and very fascinating relationship that shapes gross national savings between demographic patterns, transition processes, and economic advancement levels. Empirical research findings indicate that variations exist among the countries in the area regarding the influence of FDI on economic expansion (Mahmoodi & Mahmoodi, 2016; Simionescu, 2016). While much research has been done on FDI inflows into European transition countries, less research has been done on how these inflows affect the insurance industry in these countries.

This research paper aims to empirically investigate the existence of a positive relationship between FDI and insurance development, and to analyze whether this relationship differs among different groups of countries that differ in their level of development and degree of European economic integration. More preciously, the study investigates whether the increase in FDI leads to higher life and non-life insurance penetration in emerging Europe countries.

Finding a long-term link between FDI and insurance development is the first novel aspect of our research. Using a panel of emerging European countries with dynamic ordinary least squares (DOLS) analyses and Granger causality analysis, our work improves on the previous very limited research for European transition countries. The second novel suggests that the gross domestic product per capita may indicate weaker economic conditions and modest FDI inflows, which could be the cause of the relative underdevelopment of the insurance sector in transitioning nations. More specifically, the effect of FDI on insurance development is greater in the European post-transition countries with higher GDPPC and FDI inflows than in the European transition countries. The conditions for the further development of life and non-life insurance are better in countries under the study with comparatively higher GDP per capita and FDI inflows.

Literature Review

The relationship between the financial sector and economic growth has been thoroughly examined in the literature on finance and growth, with frequently contradictory findings in time-series or cross-sectional studies (Beck et al., 2000; Pradhan et al., 2015, 2017). The FDI flows into emerging Europe's countries are insufficient due to the poor quality of institutions in their own markets (Ganić,2022). Evidence on the impact of FDI is varied, and macro-level analysis investigates whether countries that attract more FDI experience faster economic growth. Some empirical studies in transition countries confirm this positive relationship between FDI flows and growth (Asteriou et al., 2005; Ganić et al., 2016; Kinoshita & Campos, 2002; Nath, 2005), while other studies have failed a positive relationship (Carkovic & Levine, 2005; Lyroudi et al., 2004; Topxhiu & Radoniqi, 2018).

Finally, the banking literature has also investigated the link between FDI, financing, and development – the findings have been conflicting (Yerpude et al., 2022). The possible role of foreign FDI in the insurance services industry has not received much research compared to the banking industry. These studies, like the banking literature, examine the elements that lead to foreign corporations entering a nation or identify the best places for FDI.

According to economic theory and insurance literature, a host country's economic development can be facilitated by the free flow of insurance services across national borders, as it increases competition and improves the social welfare of the domestic market (Carris, 1990; Skipper, 1996; for example; Smith, 1970). However, there has been inconsistent application of this idea. There are plenty of studies that focus on the insurance sector and FDI separately. However, research that has investigated insurance-related aspects of FDI is quite limited. Because of this, some extremely interesting research on this issue has been discovered and presented below.

The factors affecting FDI in Germany, the United Kingdom and the US insurance industry are examined (Moshirian, 1997, 1999). His findings suggest that the growth of international insurance companies is influenced by both insurance premiums and the GDP of the host nation. Due to insufficient cross-sectional data, this research has up to now been restricted to time series analyses of specific nations. Furthermore, the real involvement of foreign insurance companies through FDI in these local markets has not been examined in these researches, which have typically concentrated on the financial resource investment. OECD countries with higher gross domestic product (GDP) and reduced trade barriers are more likely to attract more international insurance companies (Ma & Pope, 2003).

The size of the insurance market influences greater FDI in the insurance industry in source countries as well as the degree of financial development in host countries (Li & Moshirian, 2004). Additionally, studies indicate that FDI in the insurance industry is discouraged by the comparatively high cost of capital in host nations. In a panel analysis, one study examined the direct connection between FDI and the life insurance industry in 28 developing nations between 1992 and 2011 (Carson et al., 2014). The study also considers the significance of financial development and a country's specific factors, like governance and human capital. The findings show that countries that have greater FDI inflows typically have higher volumes of insurance services, particularly in the financial sector. However, the analytical model's inclusion of financial development determinants and country-specific variations reduces the significance of FDI.

Additionally, FDI inflows affected the uptake of non-life insurance in 76 developing nations between 1996 and 2011 (Sawadogo et al., 2018). Their research is predicated on two well-established concepts from the literature: FDI raises per capita income, and higher per capita income fosters the growth of insurance, especially non-life insurance. The authors claim that the influence of FDI inflows on the insurance industry extends beyond GDP per capita performance. In fact, FDI may result in a rise in the consumption of insurance services at a particular GDP per capita level.

Another study investigated the relationship between foreign capital insurance market, FDI, and economic growth in China (Wang & Li, 2019). Through the analysis of data from 1984 to 2015, they used tests such as the unit root test, least squares regression, and Granger causality test. Their findings showed that the development of the foreign capital insurance market in China did not contribute to economic growth in China, while FDI was found to have a positive impact on economic growth. They also noted that China's general economic growth encouraged the development of the foreign capital insurance market, although the insurance market channels were not efficient enough for foreign capital in China, emphasizing the applicability to China's domestic insurance market (Ansi et al., 2024; Novarlić & Đurić, 2024).

Carson et al. (2021) focused on the life insurance industry while building a panel of 29 rising emerging countries. The authors find that higher rates of life insurance penetration are also found in nations with larger levels of FDI, particularly in the banking sector.

Dragotă et al. (2023) explored the impact of new elements in the financial and economic environment on the demand for life insurance in 29 OECD member nations between 2005 and 2017. Regardless of the degree of old age dependency, their findings show that the development of the life insurance market accelerates in nations with high rates of FDI and high scores in investment flexibility. They also concluded that the demand for life insurance products is positively impacted by GDP per capita.

Research on the effect of FDI on the growth of the insurance sector in all transitioning European countries was lacking. Nevertheless, certain research that has considered many countries from that sample has generally demonstrated a strong correlation between FDI inflows and the growth of the insurance industry. For example, for the region of the Western Balkans, we found one study done recently (Berisha & Sopi, 2023). The authors used panel data analysis to examine the effects of FDI inflows into the insurance sector between 2004 and 2021. According to their analysis, the econometric model's behavior of three independent variables – the gross written premium, the insurance asset, and the penetration rate – indicate that FDI inflows have a favorable impact on the growth of the insurance industry.

Data and Methodology

The study employs data sourced from the World Bank's Financial Development and Structure Dataset database for 14 emerging European countries between

1990 and 2021. The countries are divided into two groups: European transition countries (Albania, Bosnia and Herzegovina, North Macedonia, Moldova, Serbia, and Georgia) and European post-transition countries (Bulgaria, Croatia, Czech Republic, Hungary, Poland, Romania, Slovakia, and Slovenia). The degree of economic integration and economic development between these two groups of people varies. The European transition economies are less developed countries than those that have already passed the transition and belong to the newest members of the EU. The following variables are used in our research: the life insurance premium volume to GDP (%), the non-life insurance premium volume to GDP (%), GDP per capita (in constant 2015 dollars), and the inflows of FDI as a percentage of GDP. The availability of data on the observed variables was taken into consideration when choosing the countries for the study.

The long-term impacts of increased FDI on the insurance development are empirically explored in this research study, with a focus on life and non-life insurance in European transition and post-transition countries. To ascertain their long-term association, the analysis employs fully modified ordinary least squares (FMOLS) and dynamic ordinary least squares (DOLS) dynamic panel analysis. The DOLS estimator is normally distributed and asymptotically unbiased even in the presence of endogenous regressors. This indicates that the DOLS estimates tend to resemble the genuine model parameters and have a normal distribution under optimal conditions with large enough samples. Because endogeneity can skew the regression results, it is crucial that we account for the potential endogeneity of FDI flows through this feature.

The study estimates the following model:

$$LINS/NLINS_{it} = \beta_0 + \alpha_1 FDI_{it} + \alpha_2 LnGDPPC + \varepsilon_{it} \qquad (1)$$

where α stands for the parameters that need to be evaluated; ϵ indicates the model error term; and β is a constant. The dependent variables are: LINS measured by the life insurance premium volume to GDP (%) denotes life insurance penetration and NLINS measured by the life insurance premium volume to GDP (%) denotes non-life insurance penetration for country i during period t. FDI as a percentage of GDP represents an explanatory variable, and GDPPC denotes GDP per capita expressed in constant 2015 dollars (in logarithm form), as a control variable to examine the impact of insurance development independently of the income effect. To appreciate the effects of FDI inflows on the economy, it can be helpful to separate the effects of FDI from the effects of overall economic development. Therefore, we can more accurately evaluate the unique effects of FDI on development, independent of the overall state of the nation's economy, by including GDP per capita in the model (1).

Panel root analysis is used to investigate whether the variables are stationary at the start of the analysis. The panel cointegration technique is used to establish cointegration relationships between variables when non-stationarity has been determined.

The set of panel unit root tests is used to assess the stationarity of the employed variables. Because it assists in identifying erroneous correlations, this study is significant. To account for the various ways that trends could manifest themselves and the seasonality of the data, the series is considered to have intercept as well as constant and trend. To guarantee accurate modeling and result interpretation, these tests enable researchers to ascertain whether a data series is stationary. Cointegration tests, such as the Pedroni test (1999, 2004), the Johansen test (1988, 1991), and the Kao test (1999), are methodologies used to reveal the existence of a long-term relationship among variables that have long-run characteristics. This method makes it possible to verify whether all the analysis's variables have a sustained link with one another.

Furthermore, estimations of cointegration equations include the application of the DOLS approach (Kao & Chiang, 2000). These methods are used with the aim of estimating or quantifying the long-term relationship between variables. The DOLS technique addresses endogeneity issues and eliminates serial correlation that occurs in the standard ordinary least squares (OLS) method. Furthermore, panel causality methods will be applied to analyze causality between selected variables in equation 1 (Dumitrescu & Hurlin, 2012).

Empirical Results

Table 1 provides information on the probabilities at the 0.05 significance level for testing the stationarity of the employed dependent and independent variables, both in the intercept and trend models and in the intercept models. The output presented in Table 1 shows that the probabilities for those variables are greater than 0.05, which indicates the presence of unit roots for the variable LINS and GDPPC (Intercept and trend as well as Intercept). Since the null hypothesis implies the presence of unit roots, we consider the first-order differences of these variables. It is clearly visible that all employed variables are stationary after applying first-order differences, indicating their stationarity at $I(1)$.

As shown in Table 1, the unit root test output satisfies the requirements needed for cointegration analysis. We first perform a cointegration test to make sure the employed variables are stationary after applying the proper transformations, and then we investigate any potential long-term relationships between them. Then, we can determine whether there are long-term linkages between variables and whether there may be long-term equilibrium links between them by using the cointegration test. The understanding of the long-term impact interplays between FDI inflows and other economic variables encompassed in the study is contingent upon this examination. Once the variables had reached stationarity, we methodically examined the cointegration of FDI, LINS, NLINS, and Log of GDP per capita (LNGDPPC). First, the Pedroni test (1999, 2004) was used to determine whether the variables showed signs of cointegration. Table 2 presents a summary of estimates of Pedroni's residual cointegration tests. The null hypothesis of no cointegration for the most of models can be rejected because most of the statistical tests (Group Phillips–Perron (PP)-Statistic, Group Augmented Dickey-Fuller (ADF)-Statistic, Panel PP-Statistic, and Panel ADF-Statistic) revealed statistical significance. In fact, the variables are cointegrated at statistically significant levels.

As indicated in Table 3, the Kao panel cointegration test results for each model coincide with the Pedroni's panel cointegration test findings. In other words, these

Table 1. Stationarity Tests.

Variables	Intercept and Trend							
	I(0)				*I*(1) First difference			
	ADF – Fisher	PP – Fisher	Levin, Lin, and Chu (LLC)	Im, Pesaran, and Shin (IPS)	ADF – Fisher	PP – Fisher	LLC	IPS
FDI	41.79**	57.44***	−2.51***	−2.47***	127.20**	81.43***	−7.42***	−9.34***
LINS	27.09	44.05**	−0.45	0.23	68.11***	262.17***	−2.14**	−4.41***
NLINS	43.37**	42.12**	−1.81**	−2.05**	86.00***	139.17***	−5.42***	−6.15***
LnGDPPC	23.82	282.35***	2.69	0.20	87.65***	387.22***	−5.05***	−6.28***
	Intercept							
	I(0)				*I*(1) First difference			
	ADF – Fisher	PP – Fisher	LLC	IPS	ADF – Fisher	PP – Fisher	LLC	IPS
FDI	59.00***	83.57***	−3.12***	−4.04***	167.50***	308.01***	−8.62***	−11.54***
LINS	30.12	61.40***	−1.59*	−0.74	74.38***	188.32***	−3.08***	−4.94***
NLINS	49.19***	50.43***	−2.71***	−2.29**	114.72***	177.92***	−7.45***	−8.10***
LnGDPPC	8.86	33.22	−1.45*	2.86	111.43***	178.76***	−6.16***	−7.92***

Source: Authors' calculations.

Note: *, **, ***means significance of the tested variables at 10%, 5%, 1% levels. Standard errors are in brackets.

Table 2. Pedroni Residual Cointegration Tests.

Alternative hypothesis: common Autoregressive Processes (AR) coeffs. (within-dimension)				
	Statistic	**Prob.**	**Statistic**	**Prob.**
Panel v-Statistic	−1.722446	0.9575	−0.375415	0.6463
Panel rho-Statistic	0.035588	0.5142	−1.405162	0.0800
Panel PP-Statistic	−13.93783	0.0000	−6.937681	0.0000
Panel ADF-Statistic	−15.76460	0.0000	−6.288624	0.0000

Alternative hypothesis: individual AR coeffs. (between-dimension)		
	Statistic	**Prob.**
Group rho-Statistic	−0.269551	0.3938
Group PP-Statistic	−8.737774	0.0000
Group ADF-Statistic	−6.236214	0.0000

Source: Authors' calculations.

Table 3. Kao Panel Cointegration Test.

	***t*-Statistic**	**Prob.**
ADF	−4.207092	0.000
Residual variance	100.8045	
Heteroskedasticity and Autocorrelation Consistent Variance (HAC) variance	15.27434	

Source: Authors' calculations.

tests confirm that the GDPPC, FDI, life insurance penetration (LINS), and non-life insurance penetration (NLINS) have a long-term cointegration connection.

The number of cointegration vectors can be ascertained from the results of the largest eigenvalue test (λ_{max}-test) and the eigenvalue matrix trace test (λ_{trace}-test). Based on the data in Table 4, which indicates that there is no cointegration relationship between the variables as shown by the max eigenvalue, the null hypothesis of the trace test is rejected. FDI, LINS, NLINS, and GDPPC can all be identified as having long-term cointegration, according to the Johansen cointegration test.

All three applied cointegration tests (Tables 2–4) confirmed the presence of a long-run relationship in our model, which gives us a basis for estimating the DOLS model. The DOLS model's results are displayed in Table 5. As shown in Table 5, column 1 displays DOLS results at constant values, column 2 displays an estimate of the same model assuming a linear trend, and the DOLS estimates for quadratic trends are displayed in column 3. To confirm that the estimated models were accurate, some diagnostic tests were performed. First and foremost,

Table 4. Johansen Cointegration Test.

Hypothesized	**Fisher Stat.**[a]		**Fisher Stat.**[a]	
The number of cointegrating equations (CEs)	**(from trace test)**	**Prob.**	**(from max-eigen test)**	**Prob.**
None[a]	183.4	0	146.3	0
At most 1[a]	68.98	0	56.3	0.0005
At most 2	34.22	0.1295	32.88	0.1657
At most 3	28.94	0.314	28.94	0.314

[a]Probabilities are computed using asymptotic Chi-square distribution.

Source: Authors' calculations.

all three models showed better *R*-squared and adjusted *R*-squared values, across all three models for both regions suggesting that the computed regression models fit reasonably well.

The DOLS findings indicate that there is a link between FDI and LINS at the 5% (M1) and 10% (M2) significance level, in two out of three models for European post-transition countries and in Model 1 for European transition countries. This suggests that an increase in FDI inflows of 1% is associated with an increase in LINS for 0.01% (Model 1) and 0.001% (Model 2) in the long run. Table 5 indicates that the long-term estimates anticipated for the link between the link between FDI and LINS in all three models for European transition countries are statistically insignificant and negative. It is in line with the studies done by Carson et al. (2021), Dragotă et al. (2023), and Sawadogo et al. (2018) where higher rates of life insurance penetration are associated with levels of FDI and GDP per capita.

Long-run elasticities can also be derived from the coefficients determined for European post-transition nations and European transition countries. In addition, Table 6 reveals that the estimated long-run coefficients for NLINS are negative and statistically insignificant in all three models for European post-transition countries. In European transition countries, for NLINS, a 1% increase in FDI increases NLINS by 0.03% (Model 1).

Granger causality analysis is a technique used to investigate the potential impact of one indicator on another. Tables 7 and 8 provide an overview of all test findings for the variables for both regions. It should be mentioned that the Akaike and Schwarz information criteria were used to estimate the ideal number of lags. In our case, we employed the Dumitrescu and Harlin (2012) panel causality tests to find the directions of the causal relationship among the variables for Granger causality.

If the study uses LINS as a dependent variable, the findings reveal that FDI causes LINS in both regions at 1% and 10% level of significance, respectively and LNGDPPC causes LINS at 1% as well as in both regions. FDI causes LNGDPPC at a 5% level of significance in EU transition countries (Table 7). Furthermore, the findings provided in Table 7 for EU post-transition nations, failed to identify a causal association between FDI and LNGDPPC.

Table 5. Panel Dynamic Least Squares (DOLS) – Dependent Variable LINS.

Variables	European Post-Transition Countries			European Transition Countries		
	M1. Constant level	M2. Linear trend	M3. Quadratic trend	M1. Constant level	M2. Linear trend	M3. Quadratic trend
FDI	0.014991**	0.001244*	0.001519	−0.005306	−0.002089	−0.000694
LNGDPPC	2.211325**	2.043399***	2.165722***	0.123403***	0.066049	0.076902
R-squared	0.661511	0.708117	0.722814	0.919060	0.986439	0.992477
Adjusted *R*-squared	0.517527	0.557543	0.551335	0.873265	0.976946	0.986011
S.E. of regression	0.480588	0.460227	0.463445	0.050111	0.021373	0.016649
Long-run variance	0.132852	0.105257	0.095470	0.003521	0.000373	0.000159

Source: Authors' calculations.

Table 6. Panel Dynamic Least Squares (DOLS) – Dependent Variable NLINS.

Variables	European Post-Transition Countries			European Transition Countries		
	M1. Constant level	M2. Linear trend	M3. Quadratic trend	M1. Constant level	M2. Linear trend	M3. Quadratic trend
FDI	0.008336	−0.005392	0.005327	0.036005*	0.011838	0.003705
LNGDPPC	0.387449**	2.345403***	0.365272	−0.093061	0.058664	1.260971**
R-squared	0.804574	0.850043	0.960421	0.807152	0.935288	0.978945
Adjusted *R*-squared	0.721444	0.772684	0.935936	0.703496	0.892438	0.961915
S.E. of regression	0.287115	0.259367	0.137692	0.282535	0.170172	0.101260
Long-run variance	0.124267	0.089044	0.015998	0.095036	0.027039	0.006568

Source: Authors' calculations.

Table 7. Results of Pairwise Dumitrescu–Hurlin Panel Causality Tests – Dependent Variable LINS.

	European Post-Transition Countries		European Transition Countries	
Null Hypothesis:	**Zbar-Stat.**	**Decision**	**Zbar-Stat.**	**Decision**
FDI does not homogeneously cause LINS	2.80105***	Unidirectional causality	1.88602*	Unidirectional causality
LINS does not homogeneously cause FDI	−1.21695		0.59707	
LNGDPPC does not homogeneously cause LINS	7.01956***	Unidirectional causality	3.27076***	Unidirectional causality
NLINS does not homogeneously cause LNGDPPC	0.14960		−0.12782	
LNGDPPC does not homogeneously cause FDI	0.09396	No causality	0.44888	Unidirectional causality
FDI does not homogeneously cause LNGDPPC	−0.23798		2.45075**	

Source: Authors' calculations.

Table 8. Results of Pairwise Dumitrescu–Hurlin Panel Causality Tests – Dependent Variable NLINS.

	EU Post-Transition Countries		**EU Transition Countries**	
Null Hypothesis:	**Zbar-Stat.**	**Decision**	**Zbar-Stat.**	**Decision**
FDI does not homogeneously cause NLINS	1.26640	Unidirectional causality	3.36669***	Unidirectional causality
NLINS does not homogeneously cause FDI	2.03678**		−0.64683	
LNGDPPC does not homogeneously cause NLINS	0.56936***	Bidirectional causality	4.16260***	Bidirectional causality
NLINS does not homogeneously cause LNGDPPC	2.11659**		4.75257***	
LNGDPPC does not homogeneously cause FDI	2.73973	No causality	0.14746	Unidirectional causality
FDI does not homogeneously cause LNGDPPC	1.73383		1.97368**	

Source: Authors' calculations.

In the second case, when the study employs NLINS as a dependent variable, we found unidirectional causality between FDI and NLINS in European post-transition countries and unidirectional causality between NLINS and FDI (Table 8). The study concludes that there is bidirectional causality between LNGDPPC and NLINS at 1% and 5% for both regions. It indicates that the null hypothesis – that there is no causality – is rejected. Also, there is unidirectional causality running from FDI to economic growth (Table 8).

Conclusion

The study examined the impact of FDI inflows on the development of the life and non-life insurance industry in 14 emerging European countries divided into two regions between 1995 and 2021. In European transition countries, from our three models, we could not find evidence that FDI is significantly associated with life insurance penetration when controlling the effect of GDPPC while that link is found in two out of three models in European post-transition countries. Also, we could not find evidence that FDI is significantly associated with non-life insurance penetration when controlling the effect of GDPPC in European post-transition countries as in European transition countries except in Model 1. Although we found some evidence about the link between FDI and life and non-life insurance penetration, their gains are marginal and very weak when controlling the effect of GDPPC in the long run. However, with the point of causality, the study finds a positive causal effect run from FDI to life insurance penetration for both European regions and a positive causal effect run from FDI to non-life insurance penetration in European transition countries. This demonstrates that life and non-life insurance are still a relatively underdeveloped type of insurance service in the nations under study.

The gross domestic product per capita may indicate weaker economic conditions and modest FDI inflows, which could be the cause of the relative underdevelopment of the insurance sector in transitioning nations. The conditions for the further development of life and non-life insurance are better in countries under the study with comparatively higher GDP per capita and FDI inflows.

Despite having a specific focus on the markets of emerging European countries, the research's conclusions have relevance for emerging markets as they grow and become more integrated into the EU economy. Because they imply that insurance should be seen as an alternative to banking and the securities market rather than merely as another industry, the study's findings are especially significant for policymakers. The study's conclusions can also assist policymakers in identifying critical elements that should be considered when developing financial regulations and laws, particularly those pertaining to the insurance industry, and in developing strategies to attract FDI flows.

References

Asteriou, D., Dassiou, X., & Glycopantis, D. (2005). FDI and growth: Evidence from a panel of European Transition countries. *Spoudai, 55*(1), 9–30.

Al-Ansi, A. M., Garad, A., & Ryabtsev, V. (2024). Intelligent risk analysis of investment projects in the extractive industry. *Journal of Industrial Intelligence, 2*(1), 42–53. http://dx.doi.org/10.56578/jii020104

Beck, T., Levine, R., & Loayza, N. (2000). Financial intermediation and growth: Causality and causes. *Journal of Monetary Economics, 46*(1), 31–77.

Berisha, S., & Sopi, X. (2023, December). The effects of foreign direct investment in the insurance industry in the Western Balkan countries – A panel data analysis. *International Journal of Sustainable Development and Planning, 18*(12), 373–378. http://dx.doi.org/10.18280/ijsdp.181209

Carkovic, M., & Levine, R. (2005). *Does foreign direct investment accelerate economic growth, in Institute for International Economics.* [Working Paper, University of Minnesota Department of Finance].

Carson, J., Chen, P. H., & Outreville, J. F. (2014). *Does foreign direct investment affect the supply of life insurance in developing countries?* The American Risk and Insurance Association Annual Meeting, August 3-6, Seattle, WA.

Carson, J. M., Chen, P.-H., & Outreville, J. F. (2021). Foreign direct investment and the supply of life insurance in emerging countries. *Journal of Insurance Issues, 44*(1), 38–64.

Carris, R. (1990). The production possibilities: Curve and international insurance. *CPCU Journal, 43*, 107–111.

Dragotă, I. M., Cepoi, C. O., & Ştefan, L. (2023). Threshold effect for the life insurance industry: Evidence from OECD countries. *Geneva Pap Risk Insurance Issues*

Practical, 48, 799–820. https://doi.org/10.1057/s41288-022-00272-8 http://dx.doi.org/10.1057/s41288-022-00272-8

Dumitrescu, E. I., & Hurlin, C. (2012). Testing for Granger non-causality in heterogeneous panels. *Econometric Model, 29*, 1450–1460.

Ganić, M. (2022). Does institutional quality matter for the IDP hypothesis? Evidence from emerging Europe. *Croatian Economic Survey, 24*(1), 83–113. https://doi.org/10.15179/ces.24.1.3

Ganić, M., Ismić, B., & Sarajcic, S. (2016). Does financial deepening spur economic growth? Evidence from Bosnia and Herzegovina (June 7, 2016). *Journal of Economic Cooperation and Development, 37*(1), 131–158. Available at SSRN: https://ssrn.com/abstract=2805896

Ganić, M., & Mamuti, A. (2020). A re-examination of the validity of the life cycle hypothesis (LCH): Evidence from emerging Europe. *Croatia Economic Survey, 22*(2), 73–99. https://doi.org/10.15179/ces.22.2.3

Im, K. S, Pesaran, M. H., & Shin, Y. (2003). Testing for unit roots in heterogeneous panels. *Journal of Econometrics, 115*, 53–74. http://dx.doi.org/10.1016/S0304-4076(03)00092-7

Javorcik, B. S. (2004). Does Foreign Direct Investment increase the productivity of domestic firms? In search of spillovers through backward linkages. *American Economic Review, 94*(3), 605–627. http://dx.doi.org/10.1257/0002828041464605

Kao, C., & Chiang, M. H. (2000). On the estimation and inference of a cointegrated regression in panel data. In B. Baltagi (Ed.), *Nonstationary panels, panel co-integration, and dynamic panels (Advances in Econometrics)*. (pp. 161–178). JAI Press. http://dx.doi.org/10.1016/S0731-9053(00)15007-8

Kinoshita, Y., & Campos, N. F. (2002). *Foreign direct investment as technology transferred: Some panel evidence from the transition economies*. Center for Economic and Policy Research (CEPR) Discussion Paper no. 3417, 2.

Levin, A., Lin, C. F., & Chu, C. S. (2002). Unit root tests in panel data: Asymptotic and finite sample properties. *Journal of Econometrics, 108*, 1–24. http://dx.doi.org/10.1016/S0304-4076(01)00098-7

Li, D., & Moshirian, F. (2004). International investment in insurance services in the US. *Journal of Multinational Financial Management, 14*(3), 249–260. http://dx.doi.org/10.1016/j.mulfin.2003.04.001

Lyroudi, K., Papanastasiou, J., & Vamvakidis, A. (2004). Foreign direct investment and economic growth in transition economies. *South-Eastern Europe Journal of Economics, 2*(1), 97–110.

Ma, Y. L., & Pope, N. (2003). Determinants of international insurer's participation in foreign non-life markets. *Journal of Risk and Insurance, 70*(2), 235–248. http://dx.doi.org/10.1111/1539-6975.00058

Mahmoodi, M., & Mahmoodi, E. (2016). Foreign direct investment, exports, and economic growth: Evidence from two panels of developing countries. *Economic Research-Ekonomska Istrazivanja, 29*, 938–949. http://dx.doi.org/10.1080/1331677X.2016.1164922

Moshirian, E. (1997). Foreign direct investment in insurance services in the United States. *Journal of Multinational Financial Management, 7*, 159–173. http://dx.doi.org/10.1016/S1042-444X(97)00010-8

Moshirian, E. (1999). Sources of growth in international insurance services. *Journal of Multinational Financial Management, 9*, 177–194. http://dx.doi.org/10.1016/S1042-444X(98)00054-1]

Nath, H. (2005). *Trade of direct Investment and growth: Evidence from transition economies*. Working Paper Sam Houston State University.

Novarlić, B., & Đurić, P. (2024). Enhancing comprehensive waste management in transition economies through green logistics: A case study of Bosnia and Herzegovina. *Journal of Intelligent Management Decision, 3*, 42–55. http://dx.doi.org/10.56578/jimd030104

Outreville, J. F. (2021). Insurance and foreign direct investment: A review (or lack) of evidence. *Geneva Papers on Risk and Insurance. Issues and Practice 46*, 236–247. https://doi.org/10.1057/s41288-021-00218-6

Pedroni, P. (1999). Critical values for co-integration tests in heterogeneous panels with multiple regressors. *Oxford Bulletin of Economics and Statistics, 61*, 653–667. http://dx.doi.org/10.1111/1468-0084.0610s1653

Pedroni, P. (2004). Panel co-integration: Asymptotic and finite sample properties of pooled time series tests with an application to the PPP hypothesis. *Econometric Theory, 20*, 597–625. http://dx.doi.org/10.1017/S0266466604203073

Phillips, P., & Moon, H. (1999). Linear regression limit theory for nonstationary panel data. *Econometrica, 67*, 1057–1111. http://dx.doi.org/10.1111/1468-0262.00070

Phillips, P. C. B., & Perron, P. (1988). Testing for a unit root in time series regressions. *Biometrika, 75*, 335–346. http://dx.doi.org/10.2307/2336182

Pradhan, R. P., Arvin, M. B., Bahmani, S., Bennett, S. E., & Hall, J. H. (2017). Insurance-growth nexus and macroeconomic determinants: Evidence from Middle-income countries. *Empirical Economics, 52*(4), 1337–1366. http://dx.doi.org/10.1007/s00181-016-1111-7]

Pradhan, R. P., Arvin, M. B., & Norman, N. R. (2015). Insurance development and the finance-growth nexus: Evidence from 34 OECD countries. *Journal of Multinational Financial Management, 31*(1), 1–22. http://dx.doi.org/10.1016/j.mulfin.2015.02.001

Sawadogo, R., Guérineau, S., & Ouedraogo, M. I. (2018). Foreign direct investment and insurance in developing countries: Beyond the income effect. *Revue Deconomie du Developpement, 26*(4), 69–97. https://doi.org/10.3917/edd.324.0069

Simionescu, M. (2016). The relation between economic growth and foreign direct investment during the economic crisis in the European Union. *Zbornik radova Ekonomskog fakulteta u Rijeci: Časopis za ekonomsku teoriju i praksu, 34*, 187–213.http://dx.doi.org/10.18045/zbefri.2016.1.187

Smith, A. (1970). *The Wealth of Nations*. Dent.

Skipper, H. D., Jr., (1996). The role of foreign insurers in transition economies and developing countries. *International Insurance Monitor, 49*, 18–20.

Topxhiu, R. M., & Radoniqi, D. K. (2018). Foreign direct investment and economic growth: Empirical evidence from the West Balkan countries. *Journal of Academic Research in Economics, 10*(2), 315–334.

Wang, D., & Li, Y. (2019). The development of foreign capital insurance market, FDI and economic growth in China. *Modern Economy, 10*(3), 872–885. http://dx.doi.org/10.4236/me.2019.103058

Yerpude, S., Sood, K., & Grima, S. (2022). Blockchain-augmented digital supply chain management: A way to sustainable business. *Journal of Risk and Financial Management, 16*(1), 7. http://dx.doi.org/10.3390/jrfm16010007

Chapter 2

A Bibliometric Analysis of Artificial Intelligence in the Financial Journals

Eduard Mihai Manta[a], *Adriana AnaMaria Davidescu*[b,c] *and Cristina Maria Geambasu*[a]

[a]*Doctoral School of Cybernetics and Statistics, Bucharest University of Economic Studies, Bucharest, 010374, Romania*
[b]*Bucharest University of Economic Studies, Department of Statistics and Econometrics, Bucharest, 010374, Romania*
[c]*National Scientific Research Institute for Labour and Social Protection, Bucharest, Romania*

Abstract

Purpose: This study presents a comprehensive bibliometric analysis to explore the evolving role of artificial intelligence (AI) in the financial sector, emphasizing the breadth and depth of research in this dynamic field through science mapping.

Need for the Study: The advancement of AI within the financial sector heralds a significant transformation, altering the traditional methodologies financial entities utilize to confront industry-specific hurdles and seize opportunities.

Methodology: The investigation spans articles from the Web of Science databases, covering a total of 295 documents indexed in WoS from 1997 to 2023, highlighting the rapid growth in scholarly output particularly in recent years. This growth mirrors the technological advancements in AI and its expanding applications in financial domains such as risk management, decision-making, and auditing.

Findings: The chapter aims to identify leading researchers, journals, organizations, and countries in AI finance research, investigate geographical research focuses,

Financial Landscape Transformation: Technological Disruptions, 17–35

doi:10.1108/978-1-83753-750-120251002

uncover key keywords and research clusters, and delve into the conceptual, social, and intellectual foundations of primary research publications.

Practical Implications: Despite its strengths, the study provides valuable insights and a foundation for future research to explore alternative metrics and qualitative content analyses, aiming to offer deeper insights into the impact of AI on finance.

Keywords: Artificial intelligence; AI; financial sector; Web of Science; bibliometric analysis; biblioshiny; finance

JEL Code: G00

1. Introduction

The advancement of artificial intelligence (AI) within the financial sector heralds a significant transformation, altering the traditional methodologies financial entities utilize to confront industry-specific hurdles and seize opportunities. Initially, the introduction of AI in finance served primarily to automate mundane tasks and enhance the management of expansive datasets with greater efficiency than conventional approaches. However, as AI technology has progressed, its deployment has broadened to encompass more sophisticated and pivotal functions, including enhancing cybersecurity measures, refining fraud detection capabilities, and improving risk management processes. These developments have had a profound effect on the operational dynamics of the financial sector, signaling a shift toward more innovative and efficient practices.

This transformative journey within the finance industry commenced with AI's capacity to streamline simple, repetitive operations, thereby minimizing the likelihood of human errors and bolstering operational productivity. Early implementations of AI, such as algorithmic trading systems, customer service chatbots, and elementary tools for analyzing market trends, laid the groundwork for its potential. These initial forays into AI demonstrated the technology's capability to not only augment the efficiency of financial operations but also significantly improve the quality of customer interactions and service delivery. These advancements serve as the cornerstone, illustrating AI's capacity to revolutionize the financial landscape, propelling it toward a future marked by enhanced efficiency, accuracy, and customer satisfaction. In this context, this chapter aims to understand the AI role in the financial sector through a bibliometric analysis emphasizing the variability of the literature and prospective following research paths using science mapping, which allows for the analysis of scientific knowledge. To further explain the temporal growth terms of publications, we gathered articles from the Web of Science databases, investigating a total of 295 documents indexed in WoS.

This chapter focuses to provide explanations for the following research questions: RQ1: Who are the leading researchers investigating the AI in the finance, and what are the leading journals, organizations, and countries in this field? RQ2: Does research have a geographic focus, and if so, how is it connected? RQ3: What are the top keywords and important research clusters connected to them? RQ4: What is the conceptual, social, and intellectual underpinning of the primary research publications?

The research is structured into six sections. The first section consists of outlining the significance of the subject. The next section focuses on theoretical considerations around the objective of the study. Data and the methodology are presented in the third section, and the empirical findings are shown in the following section. The fifth section focuses on the study's conclusions.

2. Literature Review

The evolution of AI applications in the financial sector marks a paradigm shift in how financial institutions approach challenges and opportunities within the industry. Initially, AI technologies laid the groundwork for automating routine tasks and processing large datasets more efficiently than traditional methods. As AI technologies have advanced, their applications have expanded into more complex and critical areas such as cybersecurity, fraud detection, and risk management, significantly impacting the sector's operational dynamics. This progression from foundational uses to addressing intricate challenges underscores the transformative role AI is set to play in revolutionizing the financial sector. The journey began with AI's ability to automate simple, repetitive tasks, thereby reducing human error and increasing operational efficiency. Early applications included algorithmic trading, customer service chatbots, and basic data analysis for market trend prediction. These applications served as the foundation, demonstrating AI's potential to enhance productivity and customer interaction (Fernández, 2019).

The integration of AI into finance, as highlighted by Almutairi and Nobanee (2020) and Fernández (2019), illustrates a dynamic and ongoing transformation. Financial institutions that leverage these advanced AI capabilities can navigate the complexities of the modern financial landscape more effectively, ensuring resilience, competitiveness, and innovation in their operations.

The application of AI in the financial sector has transcended beyond mere experimental phases, embedding itself as a cornerstone in several critical operational areas, notably in financial failure prediction, portfolio management, market analysis, and stock price estimation. These areas represent the core of financial decision-making and strategy, where the accuracy and timeliness of insights can significantly influence outcomes. AI, through its sophisticated algorithms and data-processing capabilities, has introduced a new era of precision and efficiency in handling these complex tasks. Yildirim et al. (2023) highlight the particular promise of optimization algorithms like Artificial Bee Colony and Differential Evolution in these financial applications. These algorithms stand out for their ability to find optimal solutions in complex, multidimensional spaces, simulating processes observed in nature to solve real-world financial problems efficiently. The use of such sophisticated algorithms underscores the potential of AI to not only enhance existing financial processes but also to innovate and create new methodologies for financial analysis and decision-making.

The intricate landscape of AI and machine learning (ML) research within the financial sector has been meticulously mapped through the lens of co-citation and bibliometric coupling analyses, as elucidated by (Goodell et al., 2021). This comprehensive exploration, spanning from 1986 to 2021, has not only categorized the vast body of research into coherent clusters but has also illuminated the prevailing trends and potential avenues for future inquiry. These clusters – portfolio construction, financial fraud, financial distress, and sentiment analysis – each represent a significant domain of AI and ML applications in finance, reflecting both the historical evolution of the field and its current frontiers.

AI and ML systems, despite their computational prowess, are not inherently impartial. The biases present in training data or algorithmic design can lead to skewed or unfair outcomes, especially in sensitive applications like credit scoring or fraud detection (Halvaiee & Akbari, 2014). Such biases not only compromise the fairness of financial services but also risk exacerbating social inequalities. The challenge lies in developing methodologies for identifying, measuring, and correcting these biases, ensuring that AI-driven financial systems operate equitably and justly (Sadok et al., 2022).

The ethical implications of AI and ML extend beyond bias to encompass questions of privacy, transparency, and accountability. As financial institutions leverage AI to analyze consumer behavior and personalize services, the ethical handling of personal data becomes paramount (Aldboush & Ferdous, 2023). Moreover, the opaque nature of some ML models raises concerns about transparency and the ability of users to understand and challenge automated decisions. Establishing ethical guidelines that prioritize consumer rights and welfare is crucial in fostering trust and acceptance of AI technologies (Zhang & Zhou, 2019).

The rapid pace of AI and ML development poses a challenge to existing legal and regulatory frameworks, which often struggle to keep up with technological advancements. The lack of clear regulations can lead to uncertainty and inhibit the responsible adoption of AI in finance (Cao, 2022; Cath, 2018; Lee, 2020; Maple et al., 2023; Price, 2018). There is a pressing need for regulatory bodies to collaborate with technologists and industry experts to develop regulations that ensure the safe, fair, and ethical use of AI, while also promoting innovation (Boni, 2021; Huang & Rust, 2022; Molitorisová et al., 2022; Wang et al., 2020).

The recognition of these challenges has led to a call for balanced approaches that leverage the benefits of AI and ML while mitigating potential risks. This entails a multifaceted strategy encompassing the development of bias-free algorithms, the establishment of ethical standards, and the creation of robust legal and regulatory frameworks (Rana et al., 2023; Srinivasan & Chander, 2021). Such strategies should aim to promote transparency, fairness, and accountability in AI applications, ensuring that these technologies serve the public good and contribute to a more equitable financial system (Gerdes, 2022; Taddeo & Floridi, 2018).

3. Data and Methodology

The term "bibliometric methodology" refers to the application of quantitative processes (bibliometric analysis-citation analysis) to bibliometric data (citation and units of publication) (Davidescu et al., 2022). With an average of 1,021 in the preceding decade, bibliometrics-based publications have grown over time, which may be attributed to the expansion of scientific research. On the other hand, because of the enormous bibliographic databases, traditional review procedures have grown laborious and impractical (Ramos-Rodríguez & Navarro, 2004).

It is important to note that the development of bibliometric software, such as Gephi, Leximancer, and VOSviewer, has led to a recent rise in scholarly interest in bibliometric analysis. Scientific databases like Scopus and Web of Science have made it relatively simple to obtain large quantities of bibliometric data, and these databases also allow for the effective analysis of such data. A number of domains and areas, including business, e-commerce (Donthu et al., 2021), finance (Xu et al., 2018), management (Zupic & Cater, 2015), marketing (Donthu & Gustafsson, 2020) and human resources (Andersen, 2019), have emphasized the use of bibliometric techniques. The topics covered in the bibliometric analysis articles range from examining publications to compiling trends and examining the conceptual, intellectual, or social structure of the research subject.

In a broader context, it has been demonstrated that Google Scholar discovered 88% of all citations while evaluating journal coverage through citations utilizing various platforms, with Microsoft Academic coming in second and being followed by Scopus and WoS (Martín-Martín et al., 2021).

The data was extracted from the Web of Science (WoS) database to examine the publications around the subject of AI in financial journals. The WoS platform's 1997–2023 time frame was chosen. The WoS platform was selected for the research because it supports high-calibre research that can be measured by ISI-indexed publications having an impact factor. In addition, by considering the publications included in international databases or conferences with ISI indices. As a result, the search turned up 61,487 documents in the initial stage.

Fig. 1 highlights the approach used in selecting the documents for the analysis. Out of the total number of 61,487 documents containing the keyword "AI," 2,843 documents are part of the category core economics journals. A further filter was

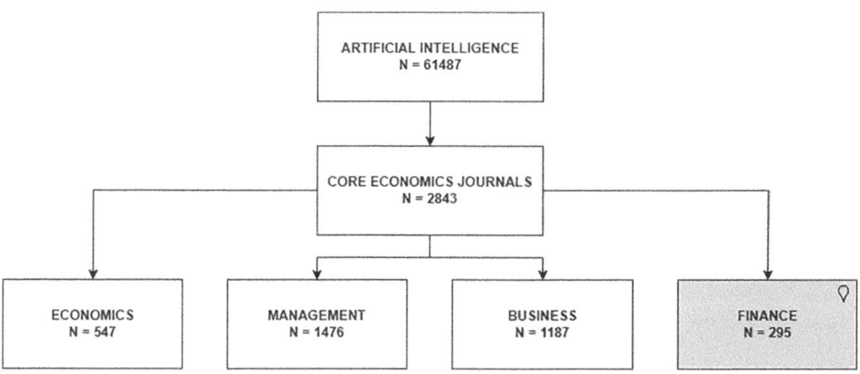

Fig. 1. Documents Included in the Bibliometric Analysis. *Source*: Authors' own creation.

applied to the core economics journals in order to get only the research papers present in the financial journals, adding up to 295 documents.

4. Empirical Results

The bibliometric analysis of the intersection between AI and financial journals over the timespan from 1997 to 2023 has yielded several notable findings. According to Fig. 2, the field has seen a substantial increase in activity, as evidenced by the annual growth rate of 15.13%. This indicates a rapid expansion of interest and research output in the integration of AI within financial studies or applications. A total of 295 documents have been produced, signifying a moderate body of literature. There are 719 authors contributing to the field, suggesting a wide and diverse research community. However, with 51 authors having single-authored documents, this also indicates that there is a certain degree of individual contribution that is not uncommon in the field. The rate of international co-authorship stands at 29.49%, which demonstrates a significant level of global collaboration, reflecting the international relevance of the research area.

The research is spread across 113 sources, showing that the findings and discussions related to AI in financial journals are disseminated through a variety of journals and conference proceedings. This implies a multidisciplinary interest and the applicability of AI in different financial contexts. With 1,007 author's keywords, researchers explored a wide array of subtopics and themes within AI in journals of finance. Additionally, the 13,672 references cited across these documents illustrate the rich and extensive groundwork upon which current research is built, indicating a mature domain with a substantial foundational literature.

The average age of documents is 2.95 years, suggesting recent research is actively cited and the field is rapidly evolving. Furthermore, the average number of citations per document is 8.6, which can be interpreted as a moderate to high impact within the scholarly community, assuming that citations correlate with the influence and recognition of the work. An average of 2.7 co-authors per document indicates a tendency toward collaborative research efforts rather than solitary endeavors, which is common in fields that are interdisciplinary and technically complex.

The line graph presented in Fig. 3 depicts the annual scientific production in the field of AI in the financial journals from 1997 to 2023. The graph shows a relatively flat trend in the number of articles published annually up until around 2014, with a modest increment that does not exceed 10 articles per year.

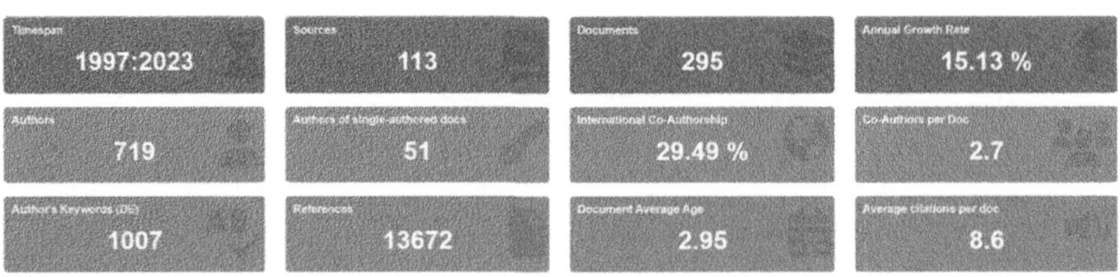

Fig. 2. Main Information of the Documents. *Source*: Authors' own creation,

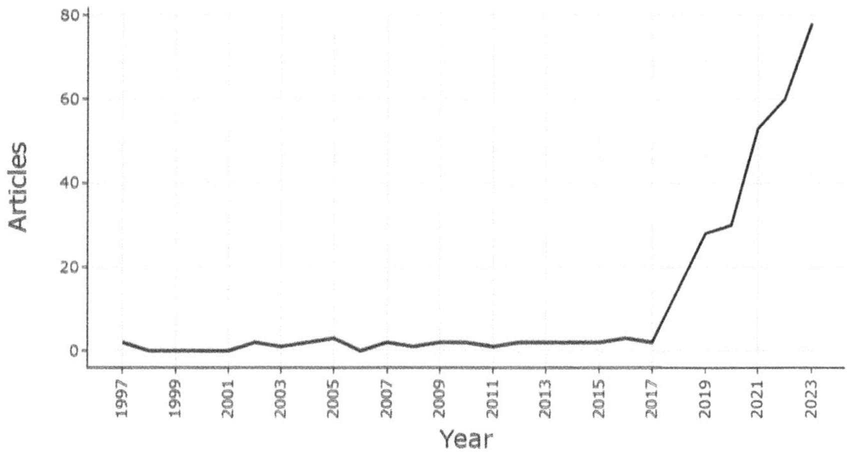

Fig. 3. The Evolution of the Number of Articles Published Per Year.
Source: Authors' own creation.

This indicates that the field was in a nascent or early development stage, with gradual accumulation of research.

From approximately 2014 onwards, there is a noticeable inflection point where the number of articles begins to increase at a more rapid pace, with the most striking growth occurring after 2019. This uptrend continues through to 2023, reaching a peak that suggests a surge of interest and research activity in recent years. In the last full year depicted, the graph shows that the number of articles exceeds 70, which could be aligned with the previously mentioned annual growth rate of 15.13%. This pattern of growth in academic output is characteristic of a field experiencing a boom in both theoretical and practical interest. The most recent years, particularly, suggest that the domain of AI in financial publications has become a hotbed for research, likely due to its increasing relevance and potential for impact on the financial industry.

The Sankey diagram from Fig. 4 illustrates the bibliometric landscape of research in AI in the specific financial journals, detailing the relationship between publication venues, contributing authors, and the thematic focus of their work from 1997 to 2023. Journals such as *Journal of Risk Finance* and *International Journal of Accounting Information Systems* are prominent, with the width of the bands indicating the volume of research output. The central column of authors, linked to these journals, reflects individual and collective contributions, with some authors showing a diverse range of publications across multiple sources.

The rightmost section of the diagram highlights the prevalent keywords within the field, such as "AI," "ML," and "fintech," pointing to core technological advancements being explored. Simultaneously, terms like "accounting," "auditing," and "risk management" underscore the practical application areas in finance. The interplay between authors and keywords suggests areas of thought leadership and research focus. Overall, the diagram encapsulates a dynamic,

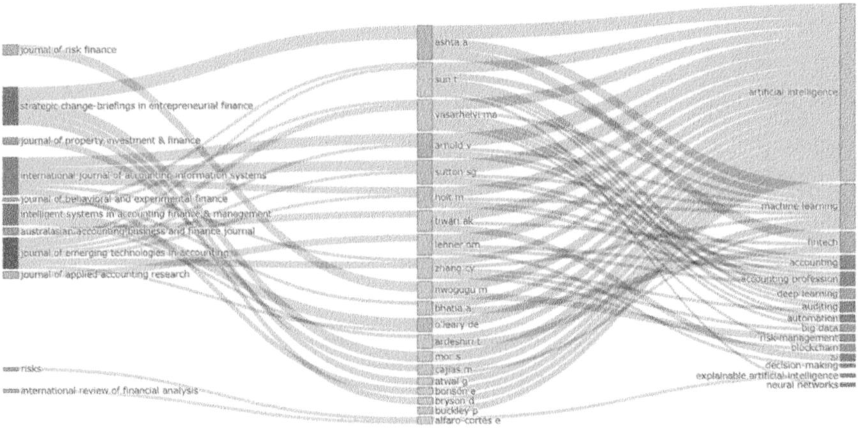

Fig. 4. Sankey Diagram. *Source*: Authors' own creation.

interdisciplinary field characterized by a fusion of high-tech AI methodologies and their practical implications in the financial world.

Table 1 lists the most relevant sources in the domain of AI in financial journals, ranked by the number of articles published. The source with the highest output is the *Journal of Risk and Financial Management*, with a total of 20 articles, indicating that this journal is a key outlet for research at the intersection of risk management and the application of AI in finance. Following closely is the *Journal of Emerging Technologies in Accounting* with 18 articles, which underscores the importance of new technologies in reshaping accounting practices.

Finance Research Letters ranks third with 15 articles, suggesting its significant role in disseminating short and impactful research notes or findings in the field of finance that may include AI applications. The *Strategic Change-Briefings in Entrepreneurial Finance* and *Intelligent Systems in Accounting Finance & Management* journals also feature prominently with 13 and 12 articles, respectively. This indicates a strong interest in strategic and intelligent systems within the entrepreneurial finance sector, where AI plays a critical role in strategic decision-making and financial management.

Overall, the distribution of articles among these top sources reflects a diverse but focused research interest, encompassing risk management, accounting technologies, and strategic financial decision-making. The prominence of these journals also suggests they are influential platforms for scholars and practitioners interested in the latest AI advancements and their implications for finance and accounting.

Table 2 provides a list of the most relevant authors in the AI and finance literature, along with the number of articles they have published and their fractionalized article count. The fractionalized count is a measure of the individual contribution to multi-authored papers, providing a more nuanced view of each author's impact.

Table 1. The Most Relevant Sources.

Sources	Articles
Journal of Risk and Financial Management	20
Journal of Emerging Technologies in Accounting	18
Finance Research Letters	15
Strategic Change-Briefings in Entrepreneurial Finance	13
Intelligent Systems in Accounting Finance & Management	12
International Journal of Accounting Information Systems	8
Journal of Revenue and Pricing Management	8
Financial and Credit Activity-Problems of Theory and Practice	7
International Journal of Financial Studies	7
Journal of Property Investment & Finance	7
Research in International Business and Finance	7

Source: Authors' own creation.

Table 2. The Most Relevant Authors.

Authors	Articles	Articles Fractionalized
Arnold V	4	1.20
Ashta A	4	1.67
O'leary DE	4	4.00
Sutton SG	4	1.20
Holt M	3	1.00
Lehner OM	3	0.95
Mor S	3	1.08
Nwogugu M	3	3.00
Sun T	3	1.83
Tiwari AK	3	0.65
Vasarhelyi MA	3	1.03
Zhang CY	3	1.53

Source: Authors' own creation.

The table indicates that authors such as Arnold V., Ashta A., O'Leary D.E., and Sutton S.G. are leading contributors with four articles each. Notably, O'Leary D.E. has a fractionalized article count of 4.00, suggesting that their contributions were either sole-authored or that they had a dominant role in co-authored publications. In contrast, Arnold V. and Sutton S.G. have a fractionalized count of 1.20, which reflects substantial collaborative efforts with other scholars.

The presence of these authors across publications in the field signifies that they are key thought leaders, potentially driving the research agenda and contributing significant knowledge to the intersection of AI in financial journals. Their work spans various topics within the domain, contributing to the development of the field through both theoretical and applied research. The fractionalized article count serves as a valuable metric for assessing individual research input, which, when combined with the total article count, provides insight into both productivity and collaborative practices in academia.

Table 3 details the affiliations most frequently associated with publications in the realm of AI in the financial journals. The Ministry of Education and Science of Ukraine appears at the top of the list with 12 counts, which could indicate multiple departments or teams within the ministry contributing to the field. The University of Central Florida is also a prominent contributor with seven articles, denoting a significant academic focus on the intersection of AI and finance at this institution.

Rutgers New Brunswick and the State University System of Florida are each credited with six articles, underscoring their roles as active research hubs in this domain. The presence of educational institutions and governmental departments on this list illustrates a strong institutional backing for research in AI applications within finance, potentially indicating areas where academic and governmental interests align.

Table 4 ranks documents in the field of AI presented in the business finance journals by their global citation impact, providing insights into the most influential research papers. The document at the top, by Moll J. (2019) in the *British Accounting Review*, holds a significant lead with 143 total citations and a high annual citation rate of 28.60, indicating its strong influence and relevance in the field. Its high normalized citation count (10.51) suggests that it has been particularly impactful relative to other works published in the same period.

Following this, the work of Goodell J.W. (2021) in the *Journal of Behavioural and Experimental Finance* also shows a substantial citation footprint with 131 total citations, an even higher annual citation rate of 43.67, and a normalized citation count of 12.62, highlighting its prominence and possibly its contribution

Table 3. The Most Relevant Affiliations.

Affiliation	**Articles**
Ministry of Education and Science of Ukraine	12
University of Central Florida	7
Rutgers New Brunswick	6
State University System of Florida	6
Universiti Malaya	5

Source: Authors' own creation.

Table 4. The Most Cited Documents.

Paper	Total Citations	TC per Year	Normalized TC
Moll J, 2019, ***Brit Account Rev***	143	28.60	10.51
Goodell JW, 2021, ***J Behav Exp Financ***	131	43.67	12.62
Kokina J, 2017, ***J Emerg Technol Acco***	129	18.43	1.95
Issa H, 2016, ***J Emerg Technol Acco***	101	12.63	1.80
Berg A, 2018, ***J Monetary Econ***	82	13.67	3.39
Mhlanga D, 2020, ***Int J Financ Stud***	70	17.50	5.53
Sutton SG, 2016, ***Int J Account Inf Sy***	67	8.38	1.20
Preece A, 2018, ***Intell Syst Account***	61	10.17	2.52
Dowling M, 2023, ***Financ Res Lett***	59	59.00	29.13
Tiberius V, 2019, ***J Int Account Audit***	55	11.00	4.04

Source: Authors' own creation.

to newer, behaviorally oriented research streams in finance. Kokina J. (2017) in the *Journal of Emerging Technologies in Accounting* and Issa H. (2016) in the same journal represent earlier but influential works with 129 and 101 total citations respectively, showcasing their sustained relevance over time.

Lastly, the paper by Berg A. (2018) in the *Journal of Monetary Economics* with 82 total citations and a normalized citation count of 3.39 reflects interdisciplinary interest, bridging AI with monetary economics. The citation metrics, especially the total citations and citations per year, reflect the impact and ongoing relevance of these documents in shaping the discourse and research trajectory in AI applications within financial studies.

The word cloud you provided in Fig. 5 visualizes the key terms associated with the field of AI in the financial publications. The most prominent terms, such as "explainable artificial intelligence," (XAI) "deep learning," "blockchain," and "big data," highlight the cutting-edge technologies and concepts that are currently at the forefront of research and discussion within this domain. These terms are substantially larger than others, indicating their frequency and significance in the literature.

Terms like "credit risk," "risk management," "neural networks," "auditing," and "accounting" are also featured prominently, suggesting that a significant portion of the research focuses on applying AI to assess and manage financial risk, and to improve the efficiency and accuracy of accounting and auditing processes. The presence of words such as "ethics," "ESG (Environmental, Social, and Governance) algorithms," and "deskilling psychology" suggests that the field is not only engaged with the technical and financial aspects but also concerned with the ethical, social, and psychological implications of integrating AI into finance.

In Fig. 6, the term "AI" is central and significantly larger than other terms, which indicates that it is the most frequently occurring and likely the core subject

Fig. 5. Keywords Word Cloud. *Source*: Authors' own creation.

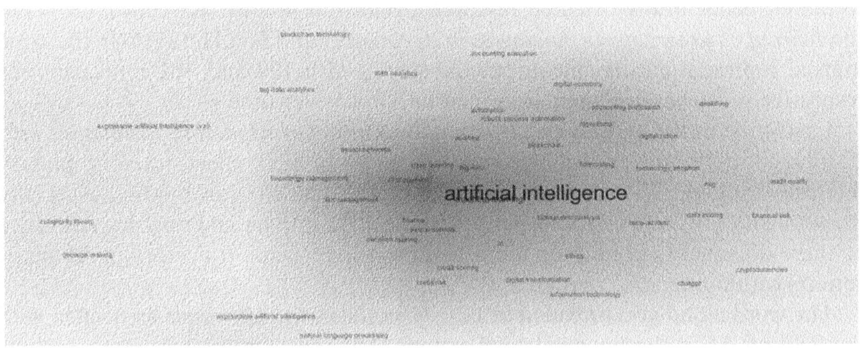

Fig. 6. Keywords Co-Occurrence Network. *Source*: Authors' own creation.

of the research in this dataset. Surrounding it, terms like "deep learning," "neural networks," "big data," and "blockchain" are prominent, suggesting these are key technologies closely associated with AI in the research corpus.

Secondary terms such as "risk management," "credit risk," and "financial risk" imply a focus on the application of AI for managing and assessing risk within finance. "XAI" and "ethics" are also visible, indicating a conscious integration of transparency and ethical considerations in AI research. "Data analytics," "data mining," and "natural language processing" reflect specific methods or branches of AI that are prevalent in the field.

Fig. 7 depicts the authors' co-citation network, which visualizes the relationships between authors based on how frequently their work is cited together in the

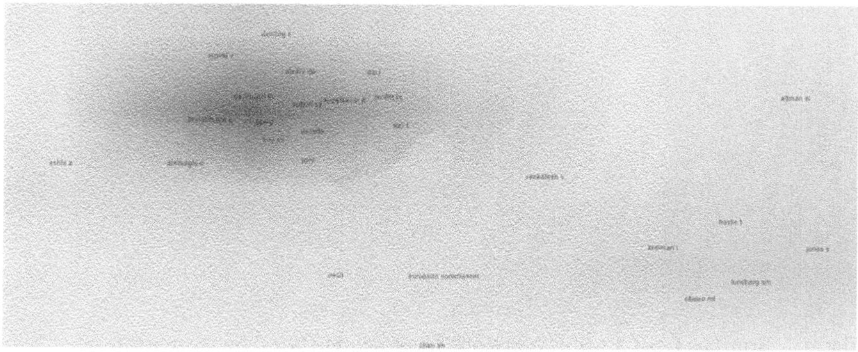

Fig. 7. Authors Co-Citation Network. *Source*: Authors' own creation.

literature. In such a network, each author is a node, and the area between them represents co-citations. The intensity of the grey color or the proximity of nodes often indicates the strength of the co-citation relationship.

In this network, certain authors appear to be more central and heavily cited, as indicated by the deeper grey color and central positioning. These authors are likely to be influential in the field, and their work may be foundational or particularly relevant to current research. The presence of consulting firms like KPMG, Deloitte, PwC, and entities like the OECD (Organisation for Economic Co-operation and Development) and the European Commission suggests that the research is not only academically oriented but also of practical and policy relevance.

Fig. 8 illustrates the papers co-citation network, where nodes represent individual papers, and the connections indicate how often each pair of papers is cited together across a body of literature. In this visualization, the most prominent nodes – such as those representing works by "Kokina J. 2017," "Issa H. 2016," and "Sutton SG. 2016" – likely signify highly influential papers within the field, as evidenced by their central positioning and the intensity of the grey.

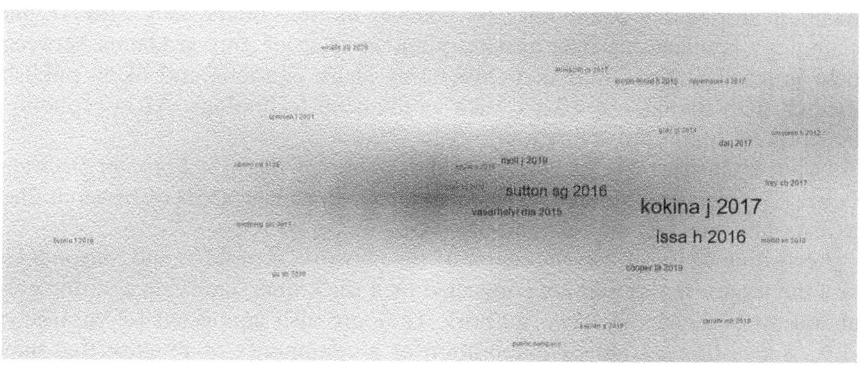

Fig. 8. Papers Co-Citation Network. *Source*: Authors' own creation.

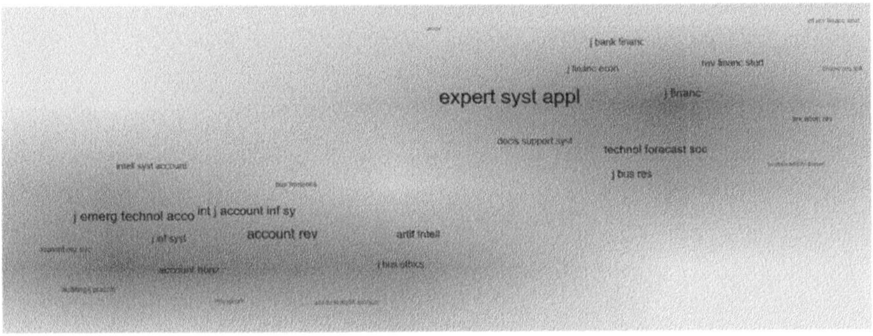

Fig. 9. Sources Co-Citation Network. *Source*: Authors' own creation.

The network reveals several clusters of research, with the intensity of the black and white gradients reflecting the frequency and strength of co-citations among these papers. This suggests thematic or methodological similarities that prompt researchers to cite these works together. For instance, the cluster around "Kokina J. 2017" and "Issa H. 2016" represent a specific area of AI application in finance or a particular technological development within the field, such as ML or blockchain.

Papers that are positioned on the periphery and are connected by fainter lines to the central nodes may represent more specialized or emerging areas of research. The dates attached to each author also provide a temporal context, indicating the period in which these papers have contributed to the discourse in the field.

Fig. 9 represents the sources co-citation network, which displays the relationships between different journals or publication venues based on the frequency with which they are cited together in the literature. At the core of this network is "Expert Systems with Applications," indicating that it is a central and highly cited source within the field. Its prominence suggests that it publishes influential research that is often cited in conjunction with work from other key journals.

Around this central node, other important journals such as *Journal of Financial Economics*, *Journal of Banking and Finance*, *Review of Financial Studies*, and *American Economic Review* form a cluster, which indicates their significant role in the financial research community, particularly in areas intersecting with AI and technology applications. The proximity and overlap of grey gradients between these journals suggest that they commonly share citations and likely publish research with thematic overlaps, such as financial technology, AI in economic modeling, or quantitative finance.

Lesser intensity areas, like those around *Journal of Business Ethics* or *Decision Support Systems*, might indicate more specialized or niche areas of research that occasionally intersect with AI and finance.

According to Fig. 10, in the center of the network, Arnold V. and Sutton S.G. have the largest nodes and are connected by a thick line, signifying a strong collaboration between these two authors. They are also connected to Vasarhelyi M.A., suggesting a triadic collaboration or a community of practice that may have co-authored multiple works together. Holt M is also a central figure with

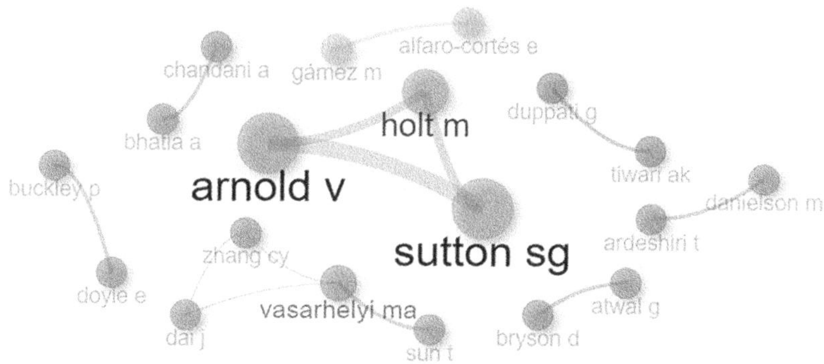

Fig. 10. Authors Collaboration Network. *Source*: Authors' own creation.

connections to several other authors, indicating their role as a key collaborator within this network.

The varying sizes of the nodes suggest the number of collaborations each author has, with larger nodes like Arnold V. and Sutton S.G. indicating a higher number of collaborations. The different sub-networks represent different clusters or groups of authors who tend to collaborate more frequently with each other, pointing to potential subfields or specialized areas of research within the broader field.

According to Fig. 11, the State University System of Florida and the University of Central Florida are prominently featured with large nodes, suggesting they are central hubs of collaboration, possibly reflecting a high volume of joint research output. The Rutgers system, including Rutgers Newark and Rutgers

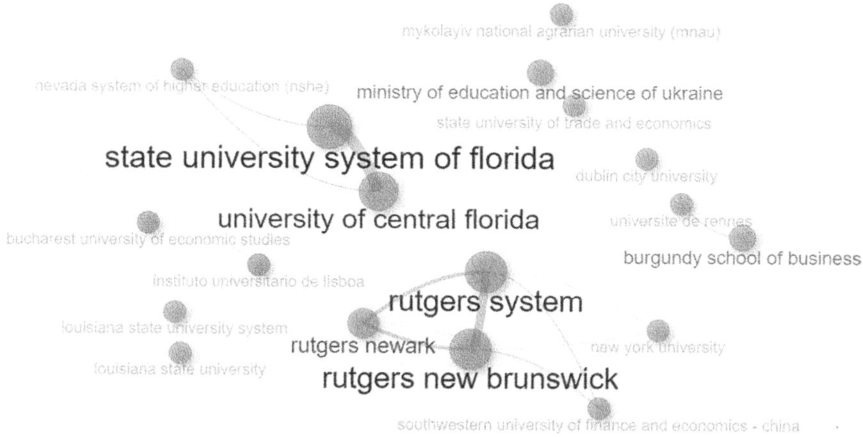

Fig. 11. Institutions Collaboration Network. *Source*: Authors' own creation.

Fig. 12. Countries Collaboration Network. *Source*: Authors' own creation.

New Brunswick, also appears as a significant cluster, indicating robust internal collaboration as well as external partnerships.

Other nodes, such as the Nevada System of Higher Education, Ministry of Education and Science of Ukraine, and various international institutions like the Université de Rennes and the Burgundy School of Business, indicate the global nature of these collaborations. The varying sizes of the nodes may represent the relative volume of collaborative output, while the lines suggest direct relationships between institutions.

According to Fig. 12, the United States is a central hub, with multiple lines connecting it to various countries across the globe, reflecting its significant role in international research collaborations. The lines span to Europe, Asia, Australia, and within North America, emphasizing a widespread network of partnerships. Countries such as USA-UK-Spain-China have the strongest collaboration within the dataset.

This map provides a visual representation of how interconnected the global research community is, with collaboration occurring across continents. It underscores the importance of international cooperation in advancing knowledge and innovation.

5. Conclusion

Throughout the analysis of the bibliometric data in the field of AI published in financial journals, several clear trends and insights emerge that underscore the dynamism and interdisciplinary nature of this research area. The data spans from 1997 to 2023, and it reveals a remarkable growth in scholarly output, particularly evident from the sharp increase in publications in recent years. This surge is reflective of the rapid technological advancements in AI and its increasing applications in financial domains such as risk management, decision-making, and auditing. The analysis indicates that the field is not only expanding rapidly but is also gaining considerable academic and practical significance.

The authorship patterns demonstrate a robust and collaborative scientific community, with a notable presence of international co-authorship. This suggests a widespread recognition of the importance of diverse perspectives and expertise in advancing the state of research. Authors from a variety of academic and professional backgrounds contribute to a rich tapestry of knowledge, with certain key individuals and institutions emerging as thought leaders and central hubs of collaboration. The presence of consulting firms and government entities in the co-citation networks indicates that the research is highly relevant to practical, real-world applications and policy formulation.

The subject matter tackled within AI and finance is broad and multifaceted, as evidenced by the diverse range of keywords like "deep learning," "blockchain," and "credit risk," which points to both the technical focus and the practical financial applications being explored. Ethical considerations, transparency in AI decision-making, and the social implications of technological integration are also prominent themes, highlighting a conscientious approach to the adoption of AI in finance. This suggests that the field is not only technologically progressive but also socially responsible and attuned to the broader impacts of its applications.

Institutional collaborations, both within and across borders, form an integral part of the research landscape. Universities and academic systems such as the State University System of Florida, the University of Central Florida, and the Rutgers System are particularly prominent, indicating their significant contributions to research and the fostering of academic partnerships. The international collaboration map further reveals a global research network with active participation from various countries, emphasizing the importance of cross-border knowledge exchange in advancing AI applications in finance.

The bibliometric analysis, while extensive, is not without limitations that should be acknowledged and addressed in future research. One key limitation is that the analysis may not capture the full scope of informal collaborations and knowledge sharing that occurs outside of published literature, such as through conferences, workshops, and industry collaborations. Moreover, bibliometric data often lag behind the most current research trends, given the time it takes for studies to be published and subsequently cited. Additionally, citation counts and publication metrics, while indicative of influence and productivity, do not measure the quality or impact of research directly. They may also bias toward older publications that have had more time to accumulate citations. Furthermore, the analysis may be skewed by the inclusion criteria of databases, language biases, and the accessibility of certain journals, potentially overlooking significant contributions from lesser-known sources or non-English publications.

Future research directions should aim to incorporate alternative metrics of impact, such as altmetrics, which account for the broader influence of research in online environments and social media. Additionally, qualitative analyses of the content could provide deeper insights into the evolution of ideas and the emergence of new research themes. The exploration of grey literature, including technical reports and white papers, could also enrich the understanding of the field's practical advancements. Future studies should also consider longitudinal approaches to track the progression of research impact over time, as well as network analyses that delve into the nature of collaborative ties. As AI technology progresses, research should increasingly focus on real-world applications, ethical considerations, regulatory responses, and the societal implications of AI in finance to ensure that the field develops in a manner that is both innovative and responsible.

In conclusion, the bibliometric analysis paints a picture of a field that is at the forefront of technological innovation, with a strong and growing global community of researchers. The trends suggest that the integration of AI in finance is not only a rich area of academic inquiry but also a crucial aspect of the future of the financial industry. The interdisciplinary collaborations and the ethical considerations present within the literature point toward a comprehensive and holistic approach to research that is likely to drive significant developments in the coming years. As AI continues to evolve, its symbiotic relationship with finance is expected to deepen, leading to transformative changes in how financial services operate and are consumed.

Acknowledgments

The research study was conducted within the Data Science Research Lab for Business and Economics of the Bucharest University of Economic Studies, within the project ID 585 PERFECTIS, entitled "Increasing institutional performance through the development of the infrastructure and research ecosystem of transdisciplinary excellence in the socio-economic field," contract number and date: 42PFE, 30.12.2021.

References

Aldboush, H. H., & Ferdous, M. (2023). Building trust in Fintech: An analysis of ethical and privacy considerations in the intersection of Big Data, AI, and Customer Trust. *International Journal of Financial Studies*, *11*(3), 90.

Almutairi, M., & Nobanee, H. (2020). Artificial intelligence in financial industry. *SSRN Electronic Journal*. https://doi.org/10.2139/ssrn.3578238

Andersen, N. (2019). Mapping the expatriate literature: A bibliometric review of the field from 1998 to 2017 and identification of current research fronts. *The International Journal of Human Resource Management*, *32*, 4687–4724.

Boni, M. (2021). The ethical dimension of human–artificial intelligence collaboration. *European View*, *20*(2), 182–190.

Cao, L. (2022). AI in finance: Challenges, techniques, and opportunities. *ACM Computing Surveys (CSUR)*, *55*(3), 1–38.

Cath, C. (2018). Governing artificial intelligence: Ethical, legal and technical opportunities and challenges. *Philosophical Transactions of the Royal Society A: Mathematical, Physical and Engineering Sciences*, *376*(2133), 20180080.

Davidescu, A. A., Florescu, M. S., Mosora, L. C., Mosora, M. H., & Manta, E. M. (2022). A bibliometric analysis of research publications of the Bucharest University of Economic Studies in time of pandemics: Implications for teachers' professional publishing activity. *International Journal of Environmental Research and Public Health*, *19*(14), 8779. https://doi.org/10.3390/ijerph19148779

Donthu, N., & Gustafsson, A. (2020). Effects of COVID-19 on business and research. *Journal of Business Research*, *117*, 284–289.

Donthu, N., Kumar, S., Mukherjee, D., Pandey, N., & Lim, W. (2021). How to conduct a bibliometric analysis: An overview and guidelines. *Journal of Business Research, 133*, 285–296.

Fernandez, A. (2019, April 5). Artificial intelligence in financial services. *Banco de Espana Article 3/19*, Available at SSRN: https://ssrn.com/abstract=3366846 or http://dx.doi.org/10.2139/ssrn.3366846

Gerdes, A. (2022). A participatory data-centric approach to AI ethics by design. *Applied Artificial Intelligence, 36*(1), 2009222.

Goodell, J. W., Kumar, S., Lim, W. M., & Pattnaik, D. (2021). Artificial intelligence and machine learning in finance: Identifying foundations, themes, and research clusters from bibliometric analysis. *Journal of Behavioral and Experimental Finance, 32*, 1.

Halvaiee, N. S., & Akbari, M. K. (2014). A novel model for credit card fraud detection using Artificial Immune Systems. *Applied Soft Computing, 24*, 40–49.

Huang, M. H., & Rust, R. T. (2022). A framework for collaborative artificial intelligence in marketing. *Journal of Retailing, 98*(2), 209–223.

Lee, J. (2020). Access to finance for artificial intelligence regulation in the financial services industry. *European Business Organization Law Review, 21*(4), 731–757.

Maple, C., Szpruch, L., Epiphaniou, G., Staykova, K., Singh, S., Penwarden, W., Wen, Y., Wang, Z., Hariharan, J. & Avramovic, P. (2023). The AI revolution: Opportunities and challenges for the finance sector. *ArXiv*, abs/2308.16538.

Martín-Martín, A., Thelwall, M., Orduna-Malea, E., & Delgado López-Cózar, E. (2021). Google scholar, microsoft academic, scopus, dimensions, web of science, and opencitations' COCI: A multidisciplinary comparison of coverage via citations. *Scientometrics, 126*, 871–906.

Molitorisová, A., Purnhagen, K., & Šístek, P. (2022). Techno-regulation: Technological collaboration between EU administrations. *Law, Innovation and Technology, 14*(2), 421–446.

Price, E. (2018). The core challenges of financial regulation. *Global Policy, 9*(3), 432–433.

Ramos-Rodríguez, A.-R., & Navarro, J. (2004). Changes in the intellectual structure of strategic management research: A bibliometric study of the Strategic Management Journal, 1980–2000. *The Strategic Management Journal, 25*, 981–1004.

Rana, S. A., Azizul, Z. H., & Awan, A. A. (2023). A step toward building a unified framework for managing AI bias. *PeerJ Computer Science, 9*, e1630.

Sadok, H., Sakka, F., & El Maknouzi, M. E. (2022). Artificial intelligence and bank credit analysis: A review. *Cogent Economics & Finance, 10*(1), 2023262.

Srinivasan, R., & Chander, A. (2021). Biases in AI systems. *Communications of the ACM, 64*(8), 44–49.

Taddeo, M., & Floridi, L. (2018). How AI can be a force for good. *Science, 361*(6404), 751–752.

Wang, D., Churchill, E., Maes, P., Fan, X., Shneiderman, B., Shi, Y., & Wang, Q. (2020). From human-human collaboration to human-AI collaboration: Designing AI systems that can work together with people. In *Extended abstracts of the 2020 CHI confer.*

Xu, X., Chen, X., Jia, F., Brown, S., Gong, Y., & Xu, Y. (2018). Supply chain finance: A systematic literature review and bibliometric analysis. *International Journal of Production Economics, 204*, 160–173.

Yildirim, F. M., Burçin, O. N., & Kunduraci, S. Ö. (2023). Artificial intelligence optimization algorithms in the finance sector. *Uluslararası Akademik Birikim Dergisi, 6*(2), 281–289.

Zhang, Y., & Zhou, L. (2019). Fairness assessment for artificial intelligence in financial industry. *arXiv preprint arXiv:1912.07211.*

Zupic, I., & Cater, T. (2015). Bibliometric methods in management and organization. *Organizational Research Methods, 18*, 429–472.

Donthu, N., Kumar, S., Mukherjee, D., Pandey, N., & Lim, W. M. (2021). How to conduct a bibliometric analysis: An overview and guidelines. *Journal of Business Research*, [illegible]

[illegible]

Chapter 3

An Analysis of Abnormal Extreme Price Movements within the Context of Volatility Parameter Shifts: A Case Study of Borsa Istanbul

Sezer Bozkus Kahyaoglu[a,b,c] *and Hakan Kahyaoglu*[d]

[a]*Izmir Bakircay University, Management Department, Türkiye*
[b]*University of Johannesburg, Department of Commercial Accounting, College of Business & Economics, South Africa*
[c]*University of South Africa (UNISA), Department of Financial Governance, South Africa*
[d]*Dokuz Eylül University, Izmir, Türkiye*

Abstract

Introduction: In this study, approaches based on right-tail unit root tests are used to analyze high-frequency time series. Although these approaches successfully capture unusually extreme price movements (bubbles) in financial markets, they can be biased in policymaking and forecasting. Testing the parameter stability enables the detection of both unusual price behavior and possible change points within the framework of the volatility approach. The break dates that cause the parameter change on the return series can be obtained, and the differentiation in the period can be seen.

Purpose: In this study, the analysis of periods that differ from the "changing parameter values" of the volatility process that emerged after November 2018 in the Borsa Istanbul (BIST) is made by using a new econometric approach in terms of change dates, parameter stability, and explosiveness characteristics. In this way, starting from determining periods with stable parameter values, the volatility process is tested to decide whether or not it shows an explosive feature.

Financial Landscape Transformation: Technological Disruptions 37–50

doi:10.1108/978-1-83753-750-120251003

Methodology: This study's mainstay was published in February 2023. The findings reached within the framework of the knowledge provided by the technique in question will be the first in the applied literature. We used a uniform test for a mildly explosive GARCH process with double supreme statistics for BIST.

Findings: BIST is significantly affected by social and political events. This result implies that the "semi-efficient" market hypothesis for BIST needs to be re-examined in this context.

Keywords: Abnormal volatility; explosive behavior; point of change analysis; uniform test; GARCH Supreme Richter-Wang-Wu (GSRWW) test

JEL Codes: G10; F65; C58

Introduction

Within the dynamic structure of financial markets and technological developments that cause them to become more complex daily, the need for quality information required by investors is gaining importance. In this context, it is necessary to investigate whether market data are indicative and to estimate whether sudden price movements and bubbles in the market are permanent. For this purpose, applied research on market risk and return, volatility analysis, and shock determination is quite comprehensive in the literature (Harvey et al., 2016, 2017, 2019). Analysis of the exploiting return series view of markets based on structural breaks and bubbles is gaining importance as a solution to market conditions where conventional volatility, risk, and return modeling are insufficient in investors' market predictions (Richter et al., 2023).

Our work aims to develop a generalized uniform test for GARCH models that can detect exuberant behavior periods, i.e., periods with integrated or mildly explosive parameter values, associated with the empirical phenomenon of mild explosiveness in the second moment. We used a "double-supreme test" for the existence of breaks and then provided an algorithm to identify the periods of change. Ignoring parameter change leads to biased analysis in policymaking and forecasting. This issue is essential for the financial market risk assessment and policy generation.

The organization of the work is given in Fig. 1.

In this study, a new approach is put forward to contribute to the literature within the framework of the subject discussed in the empirical findings part and based on a comprehensive literature review regarding the method used. After presenting the data and method, the necessary data analysis, parameter constancy test, diagnostic tests, and estimation results were tabulated and interpreted in the order shown in Fig. 1. The conclusion section presents policy recommendations within the framework of the critical empirical findings regarding the Borsa Istanbul BIST100 index return series.

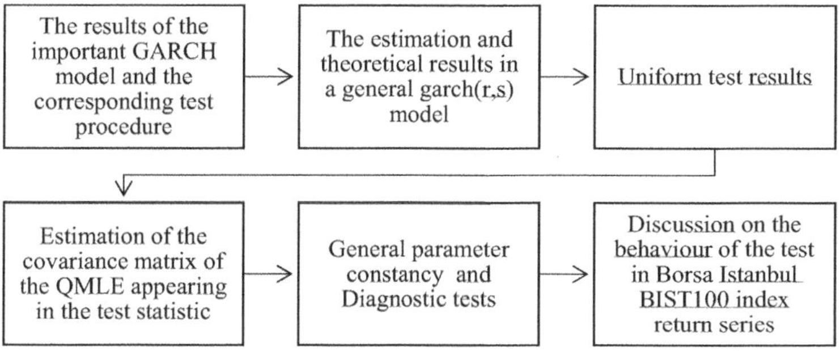

Fig. 1. The Organization of the Empirical Work. *Source*: Prepared by the authors.

Literature Review

The bubble observed in financial markets indicates the part of the price that deviates from the fundamental price realized in the market and is expressed as an explosive autoregressive process (Blanchard & Watson, 1982; Diba & Grossman, 1988). In this respect, a bubble is part of the deviated price that can be predicted and modeled (Evans, 1991).

Generally, a bubble can form for all financial assets, and it is necessary to group the frequently encountered bubbles in the literature into four classes. These are, respectively: "Asset bubbles," "Commodity bubbles," "Stock bubbles," and "Credit bubbles" (Talin, 2022). It is critical to closely monitor bubbles that emerge in financial markets, understand their root causes, and make investment decisions accordingly. The main reason for this is that the emergence of bubbles causes market instability, collapses in asset prices, and, occasionally, economic recessions (Harvey et al., 2016, 2017, 2019). However, the literature has different opinions regarding monitoring and forecasting bubbles. Evans (1991) reveals and defends that periodically collapsing bubbles cannot be easily detected with a simple unit root test. According to the author, a price bubble with a periodic collapse can be more like a unit root, and in some cases, it even behaves like a stationary process (Evans, 1991).

Within the framework of technological advancements and new approaches emerging in financial markets, especially in the last two decades, significant research and empirical efforts have been made to develop new strategies aimed at improving the detection capabilities of price bubbles and achieving early detection (Harvey et al., 2017, 2019; Homm & Breitung, 2012; Hu & Oxley, 2017; Pang et al., 2021; Phillips et al., 2011; Phillips & Shi, 2020; Phillips & Yu, 2011; Shi & Phillips, 2022; Skrobotov, 2023).

Pioneering among these in the literature, successful and effective testing procedures are the approaches proposed by Phillips et al. (2011). Critical approaches reveal the process of the formation and termination of bubbles beyond the traditional Augmented Dickey-Fuller (ADF) test by predicting breaks in the time dimension (Richter et al., 2023).

In this context, this study presents the empirical findings obtained from new approaches and test techniques through Borsa Istanbul (BIST) return data to determine the bubble structure via analysis of the behavior of abnormal extreme price movements in the framework of volatility parameter change. Below, we present information on the data and methodology used in the study for the corresponding period.

Data and Methodology

This study analyzes the Borsa Istanbul BIST100 index return series using a new approach to predict bubbles and change points. The data and methodology are introduced briefly in this section.

Data

The information used in this study was gathered from BIST 100, the most inclusive index in BIST, and its return series. Specifically, we utilized the Borsa Istanbul BIST100 Return Series, covering the years 2017–2023 daily. The descriptive statistics for both the normal series and the return series are presented in Table 1, respectively.

Table 1. Descriptive Statistics Normal Series and Return Series of BIST 100 (2017–2023).

A. Normal Series of BIST100		**B. Return Series of BIST100**	
Parameters	**Descriptive Statistics Results**	**Parameters**	**Descriptive Statistics Results**
nobs	1.712	nobs	1711
NAs	0.000	NAs	0.000
Minimum	7.614	Minimum	−0.103
Maximum	8.513	Maximum	0.094
1. Quartile	9976	1. Quartile	−0.006
3. Quartile	2038	3. Quartile	0.009
Mean	2004	Mean	0.001
Median	1156	Median	0.001
Sum	3432	Sum	2.268
SE Mean	4280	SE Mean	0.000
LCL Mean	1920	LCL Mean	0.000
UCL Mean	2088	UCL Mean	0.002
Variance	3.370	Variance	0.000
Std. dev	1.771	Std. dev	0.016
Skewness	**2.027**	**Skewness**	**−0.719**
Kurtosis	**3.239**	**Kurtosis**	**5.284**

95% Confidence Interval.

Source: Prepared by the authors.

According to the descriptive statistics of the normal series in the BIST data shown in Table 1, the skewness value, an indicator of the market, is 2.027. This indicates a right-tailed distribution and the explosive nature of the upward trend in the normal series.

The data's kurtosis value is 3.239, which indicates a fat-tailed structure. Table 1 shows that the coefficients of the return series in BIST have a negative skewness value of −0.719. This suggests that the market is sensitive to negative news because of its explosive nature and that negative news has a more significant impact on changes. The kurtosis value of the return series in BIST's data, which is 5.284, indicates a fat-tailed structure.

The Jarque-Bera (JB) test is a widely used statistical tool for checking data normality. It evaluates the skewness and kurtosis and provides valuable information about how much the data deviates from a normal distribution. This can be helpful in statistical analysis of financial market data (Khadka, 2023).

The JB test assumes that the sample distribution is normally distributed. However, since the JB test result is significant, it suggests that the data distribution is not normally distributed. Specifically, the BIST Return Series data is not normal, with a value of 2146.3 and a *p*-value of less than 2.2e-16. The histogram in Fig. 2 illustrates the fat-tailed and skewed structure of the return series at BIST.

The return series of the Borsa Istanbul BIST100 index shows features such as fat-tailed, right-skewed, upward explosive, and sensitivity to negative news and abnormal events (as shown in Fig. 2).

The ADF test and the Kwiatkowski–Phillips–Schmidt–Shin (KPSS) test were conducted to determine whether the return series has a unit root.

Table 2 presents the test results. The two test results indicate no unit root; thus, the data is stationary. We can now proceed with estimating the empirical model in the next section.

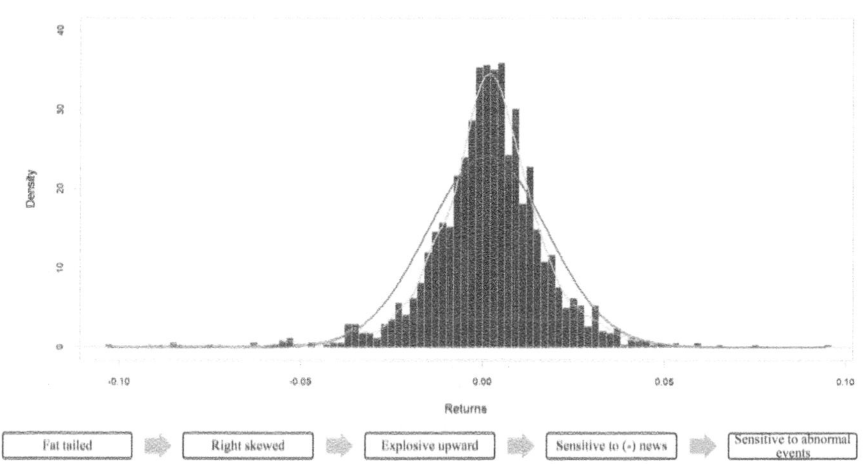

Fig. 2. Histogram of BIST Return Series (2017–2023) and Key Features of Data. *Source*: Prepared by the authors.

Table 2. Unit Root Test Results of BIST100 Return Series (2017–2023).

ADF Test Result	KPSS Test Result
−11.971	0.58035
p-value = 0.01	*p*-value = 0.02442

95% Confidence Interval.

Source: Prepared by the authors.

Methodology

The study aimed to analyze the duration of a possible bubble effect and its impact in the presence of potential risks. To achieve this, we used the methods for estimating GARCH models to select the most appropriate GARCH model, considering the asymmetric situation. The "rugarch" package in the R program was utilized for this purpose (Galanos Alexios, 2023).

Generalized Autoregressive Conditional Heteroskedasticity (GARCH) models are generally used in volatility forecasting and are also defined as the "GARCH family" in the literature due to the wide variety of GARCH models used depending on their assumptions based on symmetry or asymmetry conditions (Bollerslev, 1986; Engle, 1982; Engle & Bollerslev, 1986).

The original GARCH model was introduced and formally defined by Bollerslev (1986). Equation 1 as GARCH(p,q) can be expressed in the following form:

$$\sigma_t^2 = a_0 + \sum_{i=1}^{q} a_i e_{t-i}^2 + \sum_{i=1}^{p} b_i \sigma_{t-i}^2 \tag{1}$$

where

σ_t^2 is defined as the "variance at time t"

e_{t-i}^2 represents "the squared residuals from previous periods"

σ_{t-i}^2 is defined as "the variance from the previous time periods"

To determine GARCH and ARCH terms, the "p and q" values play a crucial role in the model specification. GARCH models are divided into two main types, namely, "1-symmetrical" and "2-asymmetrical" models. A symmetrical model is one where the impact of positive and negative movements on the returns is equal. This situation arises due to the use of "quadratic past residuals," which is a constraint on the model, as explained by Harrison and Moore (2011).

Our study was based on an article that utilized the symmetric GARCH model to predict possible market bubbles. Our research discovered that the adverse effects in BIST are more significant and severe than the positive effects. This was indicated by the negative skewness in the return series distribution for the BIST100 index.

We aim to test whether or not the GARCH process with constant parameters is globally stable. We do this by testing the null hypothesis against the alternative hypothesis, which suggests an abnormal period with changed parameter values at Borsa Istanbul BIST100 Return Series. This test motivates us to develop a general method for testing parameter constancy for volatility models for BIST. The estimation process is done in three stages as follows:

1. We conduct a uniform test to determine if there is any change.
2. We identify the duration of the change and estimate the corresponding parameters.
3. We would like to make inferences on our estimated parameters. We use the GARCH Supreme Richter-Wang-Wu (GSRWW) test, which depends on some tuning parameters. We have experimented with various choices.

Empirical Findings and Discussion

We have used a standardized test to detect and date the integrated or mildly explosive behavior of a strictly stationary GARCH process. To estimate volatility, we have utilized a method that considers the asymmetry according to the parameter of the Standard Student's *t*-distribution, which provides information about the existence of an asymmetric effect and assumes the presence of tail effects in the volatility model. We have analyzed the period during which the impact of potential bubbles persists in the presence of asymmetric effects. To this end, we have estimated the GARCH model to demonstrate the bubble effects in the BIST market.

The GARCH volatility models were evaluated using different information criteria such as Akaike (AIC) (−5.630), Bayesian (BIC) (−5.614), Shibata (SIC) (−5.630), and Hannan-Quinn (HQC) (−5.624). Among these, the GARCH (1,1) Student *t* model with the lowest AIC value (−5.630) was selected as the most appropriate model for Student *t* prediction. The estimation results for the robust GARCH (1,1) Student *t* model are presented in Table 3.

We apply the Ljung-box and Lagrange multiplier (LM) tests to our GARCH model of the BIST100 index return series to test for the presence of stationarity and ARCH effects in the return series's residuals. These diagnostic tests are used to determine the presence of ARCH effects in the data, and the results are given in

Table 3. GARCH Model Robust Estimation of BIST100 Return Series (2017–2023).

Mu	Omega	Alpha1	Beta1	Shape
0.001	0.000008	0.086	0.890	4.675
(5.931) *	(2.537) *	(13.138) *	(66.248) *	(9.187) *

*: 95% Confidence Interval, AIC: −5.630, LogLikelihood: 4821.879.

Source: Prepared by the Authors based on "rugarch" package in the R program.

Appendices 1A, 1B, and 2, respectively. In this respect, based on the test results in related appendices, there is no autocorrelation between error terms of the BIST100 index return series.

In addition, we apply the Sign Bias test, Pearson Goodness-of-Fit test, and Nyblom Stability test in Appendices 3–5, respectively. In this respect, the Sign Bias Test results of the BIST100 index return series show no model specification error. The Adjusted Pearson Goodness-of-Fit Test result indicates that the conditional probability distribution of the model is statistically fit and correct for the BIST100 index return series.

The Nyblom stability test analyzes the structural breaks in the BIST100 index return series. According to the individual and joint test statistics of the Nyblom stability test results, there is a structural break in the BIST100 index return series, and the stability of the parameters over time cannot be achieved.

We should focus on one aspect of the parameter: parameter changes driving the volatility over time. Our method does not claim to directly identify the cause of this behavior.

Test Statistic Based on Supremes

Assuming that no information on the period and the change itself is available, we develop a test statistic based on supreme, which searches for all possible sub-windows of the data. We prove asymptotic consistency and provide a limited distribution of our test statistic.

It is essential that the test is not of unit-root type since the hypothesis and the alternative are still in the regime where the GARCH process is strictly stationary. The theoretical contributions extend the existing theoretical results on GARCH QML estimators to uniform consistency statements over an arbitrary observation period.

This period has two breaks for the Borsa Istanbul BIST100 index Return Series. The break values are estimated as 0.903 and 0.855. The significant break periods and change points are shown as, i.e. (January 02, 2027–October 18, 2017) and (October 17, 2019–August 06, 2020) in Table 4 and Fig. 3, respectively.

It was found that the markets were impacted by certain events that occurred during a period under analysis. This information has been compiled based on simultaneous disclosures in all press media during the relevant period. Therefore, specific references to single news items have been avoided.

Regarding the first break period, a terrorist attack took place at a nightclub in Istanbul on New Year's Eve between January 02, 2017 and October 18, 2017, which had a significant impact on the business world and foreign investors. During the same period, the Turkish Army carried out the Euphrates Shield operation to prevent a possible terrorist attack. This operation ended in March 2017 and influenced the Borsa Istanbul BIST100 index returns. In April 2017, Turkey held a referendum on constitutional amendments. However, even after this period, the state of emergency regulations continued. During this time, the alpha and beta parameters (In2+In3= 0.213+0.823=1.036) were higher than the value of out1 (0.95), which is the general volatility parameter. This indicates that there

Table 4. Break periods of BIST100 Return Series (2017–2023).

Time1	Time2	In1	In2	In3	Out1	Out2	Out3	Sig.Level
January 02, 2017	October 18, 2017	**1.036**	0.213	0.823	0.95	0.046	**0.903**	5.975***
October 17, 2019	August 06, 2020	**1.002**	0.063	0.938	0.95	0.094	**0.855**	4.311***

***: significant at 1% confidence interval.

Source: Prepared by the Authors based on "rugarch" package in the R program.

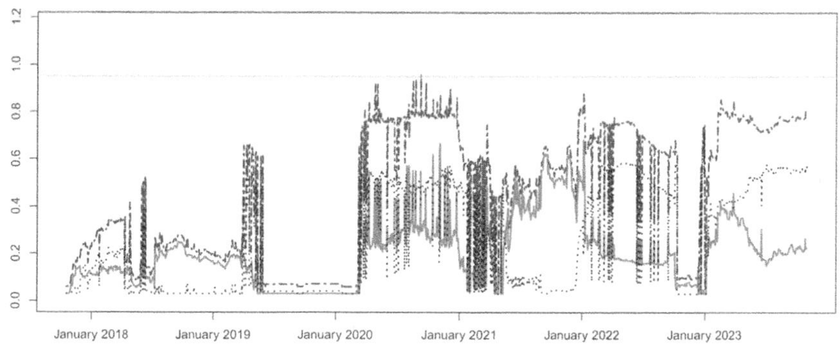

Fig. 3. Break Periods of BIST100 Return Series (2017–2023). *Source*: Prepared by the authors based on "rugarch" package in the R program.

was abnormal volatility during this period. The forecasting approach used in this study identified four significant events as the main reasons for this abnormal volatility. This approach contributed significantly to the GARCH (1, 1) estimation result and offers a precise approach to detecting changes in volatility.

Between October 17, 2019 and August 06, 2020, news agencies reported that a virus had emerged in China that could have a significant impact similar to Ebola and SARS. BIST reacted quickly to this news, as evidenced by the alpha and beta values (In2+In3= 0.063+0.938=1.002) during this period. These values were more significant than 0.95, indicating an abnormal period. This was the period when the impact of the coronavirus began to be at its highest. As a result, a Scientific Board was established for the Ministry of Health to combat COVID-19, and the expectation that the virus could also reach Turkey increased. During this same period, significant events occurred in Turkey, such as the Elazığ earthquake on January 24, 2020, and the Idlib attack by the Syrian Government on February 27, 2020. In response, Türkiye launched the Spring Shield operation on March 1, 2020. The first death in Turkey due to COVID-19 occurred, and comprehensive measures were taken. In June 2020, Türkiye launched the Claw Eagle operation in Northern Iraq. It has been determined that BIST responds to these significant events. Therefore, we analyzed this period using a hypothesis testing approach that Richter et al. (2023) developed in the GARCH process against the alternative of an abnormal period with changing parameter values.

Conclusion

This chapter used a uniform test for a mildly explosive GARCH process with double supreme statistics for BIST. Our test is easy to implement and can help effectively identify mildly explosive periods with suitable sizes and power. In sum, we used a change-point test to detect the possible unstable behavior of a strictly stationary GARCH (1, 1) process in the Borsa Istanbul BIST100 index return series. The null hypothesis is a GARCH process with globally constant parameters, while the alternative is the existence of a period in which the parameter values change to other (higher) values. This increase potentially leads to a period of mildly explosive volatility.

It has been discovered that a particular approach to analyzing market data produces more accurate results in capturing the impact of events on the market than other tools. This approach also helps to identify time intervals of abnormal volatility in the period under consideration. Applying this approach has revealed that BIST is significantly affected by social and political developments, which the stock exchange reacts to instantly. This result implies that the "semi-efficient" market efficiency analysis findings of BIST need to be re-examined and analyzed in this context.

The study has indicated that BIST is influenced by all events that can impact the market's expectations and financial indicators. The research also suggests that the available information can affect the country's economy regarding its impact on stock exchange volatility. Furthermore, the empirical model has detected that potential events can explosively impact Stock Market volatility. Such studies are significant in generating derivatives of financial instruments and analyzing new price dynamics. The method used in the study indicates that BIST responds very quickly to social and political events.

Within the scope of this study, the existence of an effect on BIST's volatility in the context of the possible effects we mentioned is analyzed. The finding still shows the situation at BIST based on the region of parameters corresponding to the case that the volatility process is non-covariance stationary but still strictly stationary (integrated or mildly explosive). Whether or not the volatility parameter is estimated consistently is essential in determining the general future values of all derivative financial market indicators and prices.

At this point, not considering the changes occurring in the spot markets, especially the effect of temporary explosive bubbles, may reveal market anomalies. This approach can be used as a solution to market anomaly detection and as a tool to examine the asymmetry between futures and spot markets.

This work may be extended based on the algorithm to online risk assessment procedures, allowing for real-time detection of breaks in financial markets to capture market anomalies. This situation can be stated as the source of the anomalies that occur occasionally, especially in future markets, when the conjuncture is not exposed to any effect in the financial markets.

References

Blanchard, O. J., & Watson, M. W. (1982). *Bubbles, rational expectations and financial markets*. NBER Working Paper No. 0945.

Bollerslev, T. (1986). Generalized autoregressive conditional heteroscedasticity. *Journal of Econometrics*, *31*, 307–327.

Brooks, C. (2008). *Introductory econometrics for finance* (2nd ed.). Cambridge University Press.

Diba, B. T., & Grossman, H. I. (1988). Explosive rational bubbles in stock prices? *The American Economic Review*, *78*(3), 520–530.

Engle, R. F. (1982). Autoregressive conditional heteroscedasticity with estimates of the variances of United Kingdom inflation. *Econometrica*, *50*, 987–1007.

Engle, R. F., & Bollerslev, T. (1986). Modelling the persistence of conditional variances. *Econometric Reviews*, *5*(1), 50.

Evans, G. W. (1991). Pitfalls in testing for explosive bubbles in asset prices. *The American Economic Review*, *81*(4), 922–930.

Fryzlewicz, P., & Subba Rao, S. (2014). Multiple-change-point detection for auto-regressive conditional heteroscedastic processes. *Journal of the Royal Statistical Society: Series B*, *76*(5), 903–924.

Galanos Alexios (2023). Package 'rugarch'. Version 1.5-1. Retrieved April 28, 2024, from https://cran.r-project.org/web/packages/rugarch/rugarch.pdf

Hafner, C. M. (2020). Testing for bubbles in cryptocurrencies with time-varying volatility. *Journal of Financial Econometrics*, *18*(2), 233–249.

Harrison, B., & Moore, W. (2011). Forecasting stock market volatility in Central and Eastern European Countries. *Journal of Forecasting*. https://doi.org/10.1002/for.1214

Harvey, D. I., Leybourne, S. J., & Sollis, R. (2017). Improving the accuracy of asset price bubble start and end date estimators. *Journal of Empirical Finance*, *40*, 121–138.

Harvey, D. I., Leybourne, S. J., Sollis, R., & Taylor, A. R. (2016). Tests for explosive financial bubbles in the presence of non-stationary volatility. *Journal of Empirical Finance* *38*, 548–574.

Harvey, D. I., Leybourne, S. J., & Zu, Y. (2019). Testing explosive bubbles with time-varying volatility. *Econometric Reviews*, *38*(10), 1131–1151.

Homm, U., & Breitung, J. (2012). Testing for speculative bubbles in stock markets: A comparison of alternative methods. *Journal of Financial Econometrics*, *10*(1), 198–231.

Hu, Y., & Oxley, L. (2017). *Exuberance, bubbles or froth? Some historical results using long run house price data for Amsterdam, Norway and Paris*. [Technical report, Working Paper, University of Waikato.]

Khadka, N. (2023). *Jarque-Bera Test: Guide to testing normality with statistical accuracy*. Dataasprant. Retrieved April 28, 2024, from https://dataaspirant.com/jarque-bera-test/#:~:text=The%20Jarque%2DBera%20test%20is%20a%20test%20that%20assesses%20normality,data%20is%20not%20normally%20distributed

Nelson, D. B. (1991). Conditional heteroskedasticity in asset returns: A new approach. *Econometrica*, *59*(2) (March 1991), 347–370.

Pang, T., Du, L., & Chong, T. T. L. (2021). Estimating multiple breaks in nonstationary autoregressive models. *Journal of Econometrics*, *221*(1), 277–311.

Phillips, P. C. B., & Shi, S. (2020). Real time monitoring of asset markets: Bubbles and crises. In H. D. Vinod & C. R. Rao (Eds.), *Handbook of statistics* (Vol. 42, pp. 61–80). Elsevier.

Phillips, P. C., Wu, Y., & Yu, J. (2011). Explosive behavior in the 1990s nasdaq: When did exuberance escalate asset values? *International Economic Review*, *52*(1), 201–226.

Phillips, P. C., & Yu, J. (2011). Dating the timeline of financial bubbles during the subprime crisis. *Quantitative Economics*, *2*(3), 455–491.

Richter, S., Weining, W., & Wu, W. B. (2023). Testing for parameter change epochs in GARCH time series. *Econometrics Journal*, *00*, 1–25. https://doi.org/10.1093/ectj/utad006

Shi, S., & Phillips, P. C. (2022). *Econometric analysis of asset price bubbles*. Cowles Foundation Discussion Papers 2331, Cowles Foundation for Research in Economics, Yale University. https://ideas.repec.org/p/cwl/cwldpp/2331.html

Skrobotov, A. (2023). Testing for explosive bubbles: A review. *Dependence Modeling*, *11*(1), 20220152.

Talin, B. (2022). *Economic bubbles and financial bubbles explained – Definition, Types and 5 Stages, More Than Digital*. Retrieved April 28, 2024, from https://morethandigital.info/en/economic-bubble-definition-types-and-5-stages-of-financial-bubbles/

Appendix 1A. Weighted Ljung-Box Test on Standardized Residuals of BIST100 Return Series

Lag	Statistic	*p*-value
Lag[1]	0.154	0.694
Lag[2*(*p*+*q*)+(*p*+*q*)-1][2]	2.800	0.158
Lag[4*(*p*+*q*)+(*p*+*q*)-1][5]	7.770	0.0336

Notes: *H*0: No serial correlation, d.o.f.: 0.

Prepared by the Authors based on "rugarch" package in the R program.

Appendix 1B. Weighted Ljung-Box Test on Standardized Squared Residuals of BIST100 Return Series

Lag	Statistic	*p*-value
Lag[1]	0.127	0.720
Lag[2*(*p*+*q*)+(*p*+*q*)-1][5]	1.204	0.811
Lag[4*(*p*+*q*)+(*p*+*q*)-1][9]	2.161	0.884

Notes: *H*0: No serial correlation, d.o.f.: 2.

Prepared by the Authors based on "rugarch" package in the R program.

Appendix 2. Weighted ARCH LM Tests of BIST100 Return Series

Lag	Statistic	Shape	Scale	*p*-Value
ARCH Lag[3]	1.354	0.500	2.000	0.244
ARCH Lag[5]	1.599	1.440	1.667	0.566
ARCH Lag[7]	2.217	2.315	1.543	0.671

Note: Prepared by the Authors based on "rugarch" package in the R program.

Appendix 3. Sign Bias Test of BIST100 Return Series

Sign	*t*-value	Prob Sig
Sign Bias	1.108	0.267
Negative Sign Bias	0.479	0.631
Positive Sign Bias	0.625	0.531
Joint Effect	6.025	0.110

Note: Prepared by the Authors based on "rugarch" package in the R program.

Appendix 4. Adjusted Pearson Goodness-of-Fit Test of BIST100 Return Series

Group	Statistic	*p*-value (*g*-1)
1 20	12.80	0.848
2 30	23.55	0.750
3 40	33.50	0.718
4 50	46.95	0.556

Note: Prepared by the Authors based on "rugarch" package in the R program.

Appendix 5. Nyblom stability test of BIST100 Return Series

Parameters	Statistics
Mu	1.180
Omega	1.476
Alpha1	0.803
Beta1	0.816
Shape	0.414
Joint Statistic	13.208

Notes: Asymptotic Critical Values (10% 5% 1%).

Joint Statistic: 1.28 1.47 1.88.

Individual Statistic: 0.35 0.47 0.75.

Prepared by the Authors based on "rugarch" package in the R program.

Chapter 4

The Impact of the Customer Experience Offered to Customers Through Digital Banking Applications on Customer Loyalty and Customer Satisfaction*

Muhammed Akin[a] *and Muhammed Ali Yetgin*[b]

[a]*Master of Science in Banking & Finance, E-Trade Expert, Ankara, Turkey*
[b]*Social Science Voc. School of University of Karabuk, Karabük, Turkey*

Abstract

Introduction: The difficulties and restrictions faced during the pandemic have led various organizations to offer online services. Organizations with the necessary infrastructure have adapted more seamlessly to this shift, while unprepared organizations have faced significant challenges. Recognizing the increasing importance of digital transformation, the banking sector, as a critical player in this process, has been widely examined in the literature.

Purpose: The digitization of banking has enabled faster and more convenient access to banking services. It is crucial to investigate how customer experience, shaped by the services provided by customer-centric banking institutions, impacts customer loyalty and satisfaction. This study focuses on data collected in Ankara, the capital city of Turkiye.

Methodology: Data were collected from 564 participants through a face-to-face, online survey. Fifty-four participants were excluded from the study due to non-use of digital banking or being under 18.

*This study was produced from Muhammed Akin's Master's thesis with the same title, who was a graduate student at Karabuk University.

Financial Landscape Transformation: Technological Disruptions, 51–65

doi:10.1108/978-1-83753-750-120251004

Findings: We found that money transfer was the most frequent digital banking transaction. As a result of the research, we understood that there is a statistically significant relationship between customer experience and customer loyalty and satisfaction, and there was no statistically significant relationship between gender and these values.

Keywords: COVID-19; digital banking; customer experience; customer loyalty; customer satisfaction

JEL Codes: M10; M15; M21

1. Introduction

Banks hold a significant position in financial markets as one of the most essential institutions. The development and institutionalization of banks from the past to the present, their establishment in geographically large areas, their appeal to broad masses in the social field, and their ability to quickly adapt to technological developments are essential for economies worldwide (Başar & Coşkun, 2006, p. 15). Over time, banking and banking transactions, which emerged as a natural need with the development of trade and industry, have become an indispensable part of today's societies' economic and social lives (Bakkal & Aksüt, 2011). The digitalization process "*in the banking sector*" began with the invention of the Internet.

The COVID-19 pandemic in 2020 showed that digitalization was crucial in the banking sector, as in all industries. Digital banking has increased access to banking services and made banking transactions easier. The Internet's growing use and widespread availability have enabled banking services to be accessed outside branches (Karataş & Çetinkaya Bozkurt, 2020, p. 227). Banking transactions can now occur rapidly through the Internet and mobile banking. Mobile banking is important because it can use innovations to create new markets and develop financial products and services that will replace existing business models (Nicoletti, 2014). Digital banking provides uninterrupted service, while accessibility has increased with mobile banking (Akın & Karaboga, 2011, p. 310; Grima et al., 2021). Consumers and customers have accepted digitalization. Marketing goals in the digital environment created by banks have reached a critical point. Banks reducing the number of branches and increasing the service quality and products offered in digital/mobile applications is the most important indicator that this competition has moved to the digital environment. Through these services provided to customers, customers can perform their personal and commercial banking transactions in their environments without leaving the comfort of their homes or offices (Munusamy et al., 2010, p. 401). Customers can save on travel expenses and time spent at bank branches using the Internet and mobile banking applications. Digital banking's 24-hour service has allowed individuals to transfer money, pay bills, check their Internet account balances, and make online purchases whenever they desire. The developments experienced during digitalization have decreased banking costs, and banks are increasing their investments in Internet and mobile banking applications (Omari, 2020). Therefore, when calculating the profits from their services, they consider the ease of use for customers and the benefits Customers will provide.

2. Literature Review

The number of studies conducted in digital banking has recently increased. Innovations in technology enable new products and services to emerge in the banking sector. As competition between banks moves into the digital realm, customer experience, loyalty, and satisfaction are becoming increasingly crucial for banks. During the pandemic period in which "*the COVID-19*" began in Turkey, banks' frequency of using digital banking applications increased, reducing the adverse effects that the banking sector would experience. As a result of the digital services offered by banks during this period and the investments made in the infrastructure beforehand, problems were reduced, and there was an increase in the orientation toward digital banking channels (Demirel, 2021). Increasing competition in digital banking has led to improved services offered through competition, thus highlighting service quality. "*Customer satisfaction and loyalty*" have become increasingly important for organizations since the day the financial benefits they provide were understood (Hill & Alexander, 2017). The positive reception of digital banking applications by customers has made it necessary for banks to improve the customer experience, loyalty, and satisfaction in this area by providing better services.

Mengülerek (2021) researched the impacts of "*customer experience dimensions on customer loyalty in the banking sector's*" digital applications, which have become part of our lives with the development of technology. People who used digital channels participated in the online survey and responded to the questions about their perceptions of customer experience. The analysis of the responses revealed that customer experiences affected loyalty in digital banking, and "*a significant and positive relationship*" was observed between "*customer experience and loyalty*" in digital banking.

Gümüş et al. (2020) examined using "*artificial intelligence*" in the banking system. The beginning of artificial intelligence in mobile applications presents significant opportunities such as cost reduction, faster processing times, and ease of accessibility. In this research, 500 participants responded to the survey on their experience with artificial intelligence. The study found variations in how users interacted with artificial intelligence based on demographic characteristics. Increased age, income, and education levels increased trust in artificial intelligence. The active utilization of "*artificial intelligence in the financial sector*" has significantly benefited users.

Paçan Özcan et al. (2019) conducted a study on "the factors that influence individual customers' intentions to use mobile banking, based on the Technology Acceptance Model (TAM)." In addition to the variables of intention, attitude, "perceived usefulness, and perceived ease of use" included in the model, "subjective norm, trust, and perceived risk" were also incorporated into the study's model. "Structural Equation Modeling (SEM)" was applied to the data collected from "736 participants" through a survey. The data assay showed that attitude was the essential variable affecting individuals' intention to use digital banking. When the factors influencing individuals' attitudes were ranked, "perceived usefulness," "trust," and "perceived ease of use" were the top three factors.

Kaplan and Gürbüz (2021) executed a research study on the intentions of individuals in Turkiye to use digital banking applications and the effects on user behavior. According to the study results, 315 individuals said they did not use mobile applications among 1,053 people. However, 684 respondents answered the questionnaire. The analysis of the collected data showed that 68.4% of the participants used mobile banking while 31.5% did not. The study found that the intention to utilize "*digital banking*" is influenced by trust, "*performance expectations,*" social impact, facilitating conditions, price value, and habits. The study also revealed that habits and trust affect user behavior and behavioral intentions.

Ling et al. (2016) conducted a study on customer loyalty in Internet banking using a survey technique and collected data from 200 people. The study pointed out that

> the factors affecting customer satisfaction in Internet banking were investigated, and five factors that could affect customer satisfaction in Internet banking were identified as service quality, website design and content, security, privacy, convenience, and speed. The study showed that website design and content, convenience, and speed were the top three factors influencing customer satisfaction in Internet banking.

Yoon's (2010) study investigated how customer experience perceptions influenced "*customer satisfaction*" in online banking in China. The study found that "*design, transaction speed, security, information content, and customer support*" services significantly impacted customer satisfaction in both "*high and low experience*" groups, "*but the ease*" of use did not have a significant effect. Additionally, the study found that "*the impact of design, security, transaction speed, and information content on customer satisfaction was significantly higher in the high-experience group, while the impact of customer support service on customer satisfaction was higher in the low-experience group.*"

Wang et al. (2003) used a telephone survey technique to collect data through a questionnaire, and "*the sample*" included a representative section of "*the Taiwanese adult population.*" The respondents answered the questionnaire if they performed banking transactions, and out of the 154 participants, 123 responded positively and continued with the survey. All interviewers had previous experience with conducting telephone surveys. 55% of the participants were male, and the majority (87%) were between 20 and 40. While 88% of the participants had completed high school, the remaining 12% were university graduates. The study "*strongly*" supports the appropriateness of using the extended TAM to understand people's intention to adopt "*Internet banking applications.*" The study found that "*perceived usefulness, perceived ease of use, and perceived trustworthiness significantly affect behavioral intention.*" Perceived ease of use had a "*stronger impact on behavioral intention than perceived usefulness and perceived trustworthiness.*"

3. Methodology

This research investigated the effects of digital banking services on customer satisfaction and loyalty. A customer experience, loyalty, and satisfaction survey were used to collect data for this study. The Likert scale survey ranges from "*(1) strongly disagree, (2) disagree, (3) neutral, (4) agree, and (5) strongly agree.*" We obtained demographic data from the participants.

Based on a literature review, the study observed eight sub-dimensions of customer experience, one sub-dimension of customer satisfaction, and one sub-dimension of customer loyalty. These sub-dimensions are described as design, "*ease of use, information content, transaction speed, security, customer support, customer loyalty, and customer satisfaction.*" In this context, the effect of digital banking usage on "*customer experience, customer loyalty, and customer satisfaction*" is the subject of this research, and the model of the study is presented in Fig. 1.

The study's main question was to examine the impact of digital banking applications of banks on "*customer experience, loyalty, and satisfaction,*" as well as "*the effect of demographic characteristics*" on customer experience and loyalty. In this context, the research hypotheses and sub-hypotheses developed to examine the relationships between the variables considered are listed as follows:

H1. Customer experience has a direct effect on customer loyalty.

H1a. Ease of use has a direct effect on customer loyalty.

H1b. Security has a direct effect on customer loyalty.

H1c. Transaction speed has a direct effect on customer loyalty.

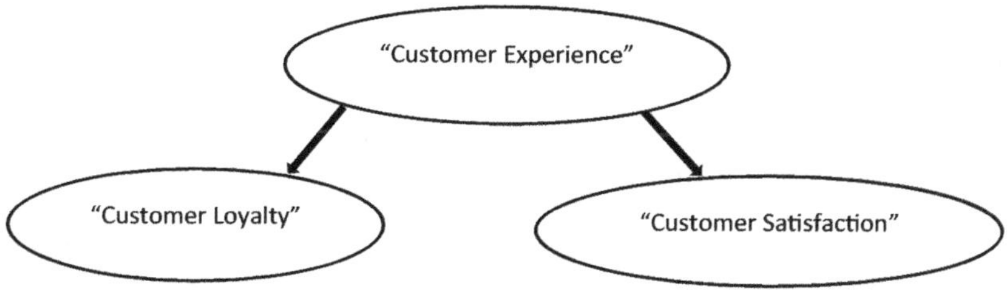

Fig. 1. The Main Model of the Study. *Source*: Authors' compilations.

H2. Customer experience has a direct effect on customer satisfaction.

H2a. Ease of use has a direct effect on customer satisfaction.

H2b. Security has a direct effect on customer satisfaction.

H2c. Transaction speed has a direct effect on customer satisfaction.

H3. Demographic variables have a direct effect on customer experience.

H3a. Gender has a direct effect on customer experience.

H3b. Age has a direct effect on customer experience.

H3c. Education level has a direct effect on customer experience.

H3d. Employment status has a direct effect on customer experience.

H3e. Income level has a direct effect on customer experience.

H4. Demographic variables have a direct effect on customer loyalty.

H4a. Gender has a direct effect on customer loyalty.

H4b. Age has a direct effect on customer loyalty.

H4c. Education level has a direct effect on customer loyalty.

H4d. Employment status has a direct effect on customer loyalty.

H4e. Income level has a direct effect on customer loyalty.

The study population consists of individuals 18 or older living in Turkiye using at least one digital banking application. In determining the sample, we defined the population and identified the relevant group for the research. The sample for the study was formed through the voluntary participation of individuals residing within the boundaries of Ankara province and using at least one digital banking application. Participants were included in the study using an appropriate "*sampling method*" from the selected population to determine the sample. The appropriate sampling method was the selection of easily accessible and applicable units due to time, money, and workforce limitations. The sample size is an important factor in studies, and various opinions exist in the literature. De Winter et al. (2009) stated that the sample size for exploratory factor analysis "*should be at least 50 people*." However, "*the number of participants*" required to measure all variables is determined by ratios such as 3:1, 5:1, or 20:1 (Gorsuch, 1983; Pett et al., 2003; Tabachnick & Fidell, 2014). In addition, while Tabachnick and Fidell (2014) consider the ideal sample size to be 300, Comrey and Lee (1973) consider 200 to be sufficient and 500 to be very good. Like Comrey and Lee's view, Gorsuch (1983) considered a sample size of 50 and below inadequate and 200 and above adequate. McCallum et al. (1999) stated that a sample size between

100 and 200 would be sufficient. We obtained permission to conduct the research from the Ethics Committee of Karabuk University. Karabuk University Ethics Committee approved it on November 15, 2022. We conducted surveys face-to-face and online between October 13, 2022, and November 13, 2022. We prepared the survey through Google Forms to collect online data and shared it with relevant participants. The customer experience scales were developed by Yi-Shun et al. (2001), Lee (2009), and Yoon (2010), while customer loyalty and customer satisfaction scales were developed by "Klaus and Maklan" in 2013. The customer experience scale consists of six sub-dimensions and 28 statements. Design has five statements (DSG1, DSG2, DSG3, DSG4, DSG5), ease of use has six statements (EOU1, EOU2, EOU3, EOU4, EOU5, EOU6), security has six statements (SEC1, SEC2, SEC3, SEC4, SEC5, SEC6), information content has four statements (INF1, INF2, INF3, INF4), transaction speed has four statements (SPD1, SPD2, SPD3, SPD4), and customer support has three statements (CSS1, CSS2, CSS3). Customer loyalty consists of one dimension with five statements (LOY1, LOY2, LOY3, LOY4, LOY5), and customer satisfaction consists of one dimension with five statements (SAT1, SAT2, SAT3, SAT4, SAT5) (Fernando et al., 2023; Pajic et al., 2023).

A total of 564 individuals from Ankara participated in the study. Screening questions such as "Are you over 18 years old?" and "Do you use digital mobile banking?" were asked of these participants, and 54 individuals were excluded from the study as they did not pass the screening questions. Respondents consist of 49% men and 51% women. When examining the demographic information, we have seen that the highest participation is among individuals aged 26–35, with a participation rate of 55.9%. According to the education level, the highest participation is among university graduates. "*Factor analysis*" was applied to determine the validity of the scales used in the study. It is a statistical tool that has two main applications. "Exploratory Factor Analysis (EFA)" is to "explore and uncover" the underlying factor structure of a newly developed scale that may differ culturally, socially, or dynamically in a region.

On the contrary, "*Confirmatory Factor Analysis (CFA)*" is used to validate whether a previously developed and tested scale conforms to its original factor structure and is appropriate for use in current research (Suhr, 2006, p. 77). According to Noar (2003), while EFA investigates the factors of loaded items, CFA aims to validate the model the researcher created using the data. We analyzed the CFA using "SPSS 26 and AMOS" programs.

4. Findings of the Study

"*KMO*" values are considered "*excellent if they are between 0.90-1.00*," very good if they are between 0.80 and 0.89, and good if they are between 0.70 and 0.79 (Kaiser & Rice, 1974, p. 111). In this study, the KMO value was calculated as 0.959, indicating an excellent level of factor analysis. To determine the suitability of the collected data for factor analysis, the results of "Bartlett's Test of Sphericity" were also examined in addition to the KMO test. "*The Bartlett Test of Sphericity*" assesses whether the correlation between variables is sufficient and a "*p-value < 0.01*" is considered suitable for factor analysis. The chi-square value compares the expected frequency with the resulting frequency in data consisting of variables with multiple categories to clarify the relationship between them. The result of the Bartlett Sphericity Test given in Table 1 (chi-square = 26253.347 and $p < 0.01$) was statistically significant. The results of the "*Exploratory Factor Analysis*" are presented below.

We examined the level of perception of sub-dimensions according to factor analysis. Five items in the design and customer loyalty factors have the highest value and a reliability coefficient of $\alpha = 0.945$. The lowest reliability coefficient of $\alpha = 0.909$ belongs to the customer support factor, which has three values. The reliability coefficients of the remaining values are as follows: The reliability coefficient of the customer satisfaction factor with five values is $\alpha = 0.941$; the reliability coefficient of the transaction speed factor with four values is $\alpha = 0.936$; the reliability coefficient of the information content factor with four values is $\alpha = 0.935$; the reliability coefficient of the ease of use factor with six values is $\alpha = 0.931$, and finally, the reliability coefficient of the security factor with six values is $\alpha = 0.928$.

We calculated the "*Cronbach's Alpha Coefficient*" of the study for the reliability analysis. "*Cronbach's Alpha coefficient*" is considered reliable if it is more significant than 0.8, and the closer it is to 1, the higher the "*internal consistency*" of the items in the scale. At the same time, subjective judgments carried by "*Cronbach's Alpha coefficient*" are limited (Kula Kartal & Mor Dirlik, 2016, p. 1870). "*Cronbach's Alpha coefficient*" was calculated as 0.986. "Cronbach's Alpha coefficient" of 0.8 and above is reliable according to the literature. We formed statistical hypotheses by taking correlation values between the dimensions of the research in the correlation analysis of the study. The "*correlation coefficient*" (see Table 2) takes variables "*between +1 and −1. This value cannot be less than −1 and greater than +1*" (Taylor, 1990, p. 36). It is important to interpret the numerical data and its direction in the correlation coefficient interpretation. The two variables increase together in the positive correlation; in the negative correlation coefficient, one variable increases, and the other decreases. A positive coefficient indicates "*a direct relationship, while a negative coefficient indicates an inverse relationship,*" and if the "correlation coefficient is 0.00, there is no relationship between the variables" (Taylor, 1990, p. 36). When interpreting the Pearson "*correlation coefficient,*" values "*between 0.00–0.25 are considered very weak, 0.26–0.49 weak, 0.50–0.69 Moderate, 0.70–0.89 high, and 0.90–1.00 very high*" (Mukaka, 2012, p. 71). The highest correlation is 0.921, and the lowest correlation is 0.714. This result indicates that the factors in this study are positively and highly correlated.

Table 1. KMO Test Result.

The measure of Sampling Adequacy for Kaiser-Meyer-Olkin		0.959
"Bartlett's Test of Sphericity"	"Approximate Chi-Square"	26253.347
	df	703
	p	0.000

Source: Authors' compilations.

Table 2. Correlation Analysis.

	DSG	EOU	SEC	INF	SPD	CSS	LOY	SAT
DSG	1	0.848	0.718	0.762	0.766	0.714	0.764	0.784
EOU	0.848	1	0.750	0.811	0.797	0.738	0.829	0.791
SEC	0.718	0.750	1	0.821	0.764	0.800	0.773	0.803
INF	0.762	0.811	0.821	1	0.847	0.815	0.839	0.851
SPD	0.766	0.797	0.764	0.847	1	0.830	0.838	0.857
CSS	0.714	0.738	0.800	0.815	0.830	1	0.771	0.843
LOY	0.764	0.829	0.773	0.839	0.838	0.771	1	0.921
SAT	0.784	0.791	0.803	0,851	0.857	0.843	0.921	1

Source: Authors' compilations.

After conducting the EFA analysis, we found it necessary to perform a CFA analysis to test whether the model was compatible with the "*Structural Equation Modeling.*" The model and hypotheses were continuously updated using "*Structural Equation Modeling*" through the "*Amos program.*" The aim is to ensure that the test becomes stable. This process is continued until a stable structure is formed and the hypotheses are accepted. Providing general definitions before the model evaluation stage ensures that the interpretations and statistical evaluations in the model evaluation process are understandable. Although several fit indices exist in the literature, a standard method has not been established. Different opinions have been expressed on this issue (Gerbing & Anderson, 1992; Mulaik, 1989).

The result of the CFI value calculation is 0.906 in the study (see Table 3). Research has shown that the CFA is reliable since the CFI value exceeds 0.90 (CFI > 0.90). We had initially found the CFI value as 0.869, but literature research has emphasized that it must be 0.90 or above. There are methods to adjust the CFI. The first method involves establishing a correlation connection between the first items, while the second method involves removing items with factor loads less than 0.70 and reestablishing the correlation. In this study, we removed some questions to establish a correlation between items and reach a conclusion to ensure the validity of the CFA. When we removed some questions, we realized the establishment of a correlation of values. The "*p-value*" of the other item in the table is 0.000. A "*p-value*" less than 0.01 "*($p < 0.01$)*" indicates that we accepted the hypothesis. We stated that an RMSEA and TLI value of 0.90 or higher would fit the CFA analysis well. In this study, the program calculated the RMSEA value as 0.103, and we considered it a good fit. The calculation of the TLI value is 0.886, indicating sufficient fit in this study. We removed some questions to ensure the fit of the "Structural Equation Model (SEM)" prepared in the AMOS program. We removed the DSG3, EOU4, EOU5, SEC3, and SEC4 values during the study. We reached the establishment of correlations between the remaining items to achieve a "structural equation model" fit. The revised model of the study in the AMOS program is presented in Fig. 2.

Table 3. Research Findings and Model Fit Indices.

Indicator	Research Finding	References
x^2	2284.697	Good Fit = $0 \leq \chi^2$ /sd ≤ 2 Acceptable Fit = $2 \leq \chi^2$ /sd ≤ 3 (Kline, 2011)
Df	358	$0 \leq x^2/sd \leq 2$ (Hooper et al., 2008; Kline, 1998; Tabachnick & Fidell, 2014)
P	0.000	($p < 0.01$)
CFI	0.906	"Acceptable Fit = 0.90 ≤ CFI ≤ 0.95"
		"Good Fit = 0.95 ≤ CFI ≤ 1.00" (Hair et al., 2010; Tabachnick & Fidell, 2014)
TLI	0.886	"Perfect Fit = TLI ≥ 0.95 (Hu & Bentler, 1999) Good Fit = TLI ≥ 0.90 (Hair et al., 2010) Adequate Fit = TLI ≥ 0.80 (Forza & Filippini, 1998)"
RMSEA	0.103	Good Fit = RMSEA ≤ 0.06 (Hu & Bentler, 1999)
IFI	0.906	"Perfect Fit = IFI ≥ 0.95 (Hu & Bentler, 1999) Good Fit = IFI ≥ 0.90 (Hair et al., 2010; Tabachnick & Fidell, 2014)"

Source: Authors' compilations.

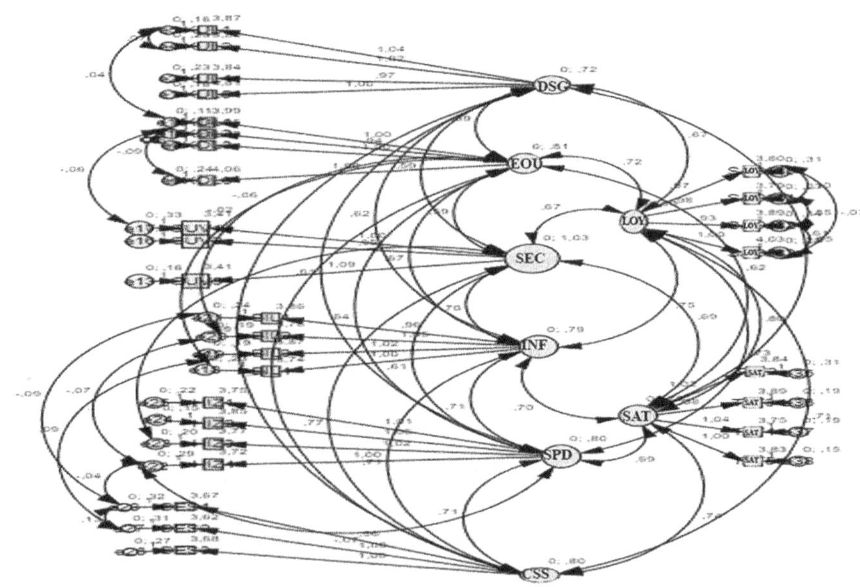

Fig. 2. Results of Structural Equation Model. *Source*: Research Model Revised by the authors in AMOS Program.

Path analysis in "*structural equation modeling*" tests "*hypotheses*" about the relationship between customer experience, customer loyalty, and customer satisfaction. "*The model fit*" indices for the basic model show a "*good fit*" ($\chi^2 = 2284.697$, "*p-value*" = 0.00; CFI = 0.906; RMR = 0.05; RMSEA = 0.103; IFI = 0.906). The path analysis shows the connection between variables, and we evaluated according to the "SEM"; however, the results are in Table 4. When assessing the "*hypotheses*" established in the study according to the path analysis, *H1: "There is a direct effect of customer experience on customer loyalty."* The hypothesis investigating the "effect of customer experience on customer loyalty" and we found it significant ($p < 0.01$); however, the result supported the *H1* hypothesis. *H1a: "Ease of use directly affects customer loyalty."* In the hypothesis where the relationship between "*ease of use and customer loyalty*" in digital banking applications we tested, the effect of "*ease of use on customer loyalty*" is significant ($p < 0.01$). The *H1a* hypothesis is supported. *H1b: "Security has a direct effect on customer loyalty."* In the hypothesis where the relationship between "*security and customer loyalty*" in digital banking applications was tested, the effect of security on customer loyalty is "significant" ($p < 0.01$). *H1b* hypothesis is supported. *H1c: "There is a direct effect of transaction speed on customer loyalty."* In the hypothesis testing, the relationship between "*transaction speed and customer loyalty*" in digital banking applications, "the effect of transaction speed on customer loyalty was found to be significant ($p < 0.01$)." The *H1c* hypothesis is supported. *H2: "There is a direct effect of customer experience on customer satisfaction."* The hypothesis testing the "effect of customer experience on customer

Table 4. Path Analysis.

			Estimate	S.E.	C.R.	*p*	Standard Estimates (*β*)
DSG	<-->	L	0.669	0.052	12.905	0.000	0.831
CSS	<-->	L	0.708	0.056	12.63	0.000	0.833
EOU	<-->	L	0.722	0.056	12.918	0.000	0.846
SPD	<-->	L	0.735	0.055	13.325	0.000	0.865
SEC	<-->	L	0.673	0.058	11.533	0.000	0.702
INF	<-->	L	0.755	0.057	13.277	0.000	0.894
SEC	<-->	SAT	0.689	0.055	12.493	0.000	0.785
SPD	<-->	SAT	0.692	0.05	13.743	0.000	0.890
EOU	<-->	SAT	0.616	0.049	12.635	0.000	0.788
CSS	<-->	SAT	0.744	0.054	13.805	0.000	0.956
DSG	<-->	SAT	0.615	0.047	13.134	0.000	0.833
INF	<-->	SAT	0.698	0.051	13.559	0.000	0.903

Source: Authors' compilations.

satisfaction has been found significant ($p < 0.01$)," and *H2* is supported. In *H2a*, we tested "Ease of use directly impacts customer satisfaction." According to the result ($p < 0.01$), we accepted the hypothesis.

H2b: "Security has a direct impact on customer satisfaction." In the hypothesis testing the relationship between "security and customer satisfaction" in digital banking applications, the effect of "security on customer satisfaction" has been found to be significant ($p < 0.01$). The *H2b* hypothesis is supported. *H2c:* "There is a direct effect of transaction speed on customer satisfaction." In the hypothesis testing the relationship between "transaction speed and customer satisfaction" in digital banking applications, the effect of "transaction speed on customer satisfaction" has been found significant ($p < 0.01$). The *H2c* hypothesis is supported. Path Analysis results are shown in Table 4.

We used a *T*-test for demographic data. We found "*p*-values" more excellent than 0.05 when we tested the relationship between gender and factors. The *p*-values of the factors we calculated by following: design 0.068, ease to use 0.728, security 0.104, information content 0.121, transaction speed 0.641, customer support 0.476, customer loyalty 0.857, and customer satisfaction 0.890. Therefore, there is "*no significant relationship between gender and factors.*" When we examined the age, *p* was 0.003. Thus, we found the result a "significant relationship between the age characteristic and the design factor." According to the findings, ease of use had a "*p-value*" of 0.340, reliability was "a *p-value*" of 0.481, information was "a *p-value*" of 0.131, "transaction speed" was "a *p-value*" of 0.804, support was "a *p-value*" of 0.212, loyalty was "*p-value*" of 0.177, and satisfaction was a "*p-value*" of 0.101. Since the "*p-values*" of these factors were not less than 0.05, there is "*no significant*" relationship between them and age. According to the findings of education level in demographic characteristics, its impact on design and ease of use factors are significant with "a *p-value*" of 0.000, information factor with "*p-value*" of 0.002, transaction speed with "*p-value*" of 0.028, loyalty with a "*p-value*" of 0.012, and satisfaction with a "*p*-value" of 0.008. Thus, a "significant relationship" exists between education level and the design, "ease of use," information, transaction speed, loyalty, and satisfaction factors. The impact of education level on the reliability factor was 0.141, and the effect on the support factor was 0.122. According to these results, there is "*no significant*" relationship between the education level and the reliability and support factors. According to the findings of the employment status from demographic characteristics, the effect on the design factor is 0.023, and the impact on the information factor is 0.013. Thus, "*there is a significant relationship*" between income level and design and information factors since the "*p-value*" is less than 0.05. The effect of income level on ease to use was 0.236, reliability was 0.67, transaction speed was 0.398, customer support was 0.387, customer loyalty was 0.71, and customer satisfaction was 0.302. According to this result, "no significant relationship" exists between "*income level*" and ease to use, reliability, transaction speed, customer support, customer loyalty, and customer satisfaction. According to the hypothesis status of the relationships between the dimensions of the research and "*demographic characteristics,*" the results obtained hypotheses *H3*,

H3b, H3c, H3d, H3e, H4, and *H4c* were accepted, while hypotheses *H3a, H4a, H4b, H4d*, and *H4e* were rejected.

5. Conclusion and Recommendations

The banking sector constitutes the main structure of financial markets. Banks with corporate networks offer their products and services in line with customers' needs while trying to increase their profit margins. To achieve this, digital transformation in the banking sector has become prominent in competition among banks, and we observed it to have a "*positive impact*" on customers. In the study, which aims to prove this effect scientifically, we reached 564 people and determined that 510 people use digital banking applications. According to the data, we found that there was a usage rate of 90.42%. The ratio of men and women among the participants was similar, and the age group of 26–35 was the most frequent users. High school-educated people have high use of digital banking applications all with a rate of 91.1%. The study is consistent with Mengülerek's (2021) study, which found that customer experiences affect customer loyalty in digital banking, and Aydın and Onaylı's (2020) study, which found that ease of use has a positive and significant impact on "*customer loyalty and satisfaction.*"

Demographics have a direct impact on customer experience and satisfaction. However, no "significant" relationship exists between gender and customer experience, customer loyalty, and customer satisfaction. There is no significant relationship between the reliability dimension of the customer experience and demographic characteristics such as "gender, age, education level, employment status, and income level." There is no relationship between individuals' income levels, education levels, employment status, age, gender, and trust in digital banking. Age factor has a significant relationship with the design perception of customer experience.

As a result, no significant relationship could be established between the other dimensions of ease of use, reliability, information, transaction speed, support, customer loyalty, and customer satisfaction. Education level directly affects "*customer experience, customer satisfaction, and customer loyalty.*" While work status and income level directly affect "customer experience," they do not directly affect "*customer satisfaction and loyalty.*"

In contrast, there is no significant relationship between the other dimensions of ease of use, reliability, information, transaction speed, support, customer loyalty, and customer satisfaction. The design stands out regarding demographic characteristics, while a significant relationship could not be established with the perception of reliability. It would be beneficial for banks to improve their applications on design. As a recommendation, "*factors that affect the intention*" not to use digital banking applications can be studied for bank clients who do not use digital banking applications. Increasing the "*loyalty and satisfaction*" of digital banking customers is essential for the banking sector, and services can be provided to non-users by considering how they can be persuaded to use the applications.

References

Akin, F., & Karaboga, K. (2011). Bireysel müşterilerin şubesiz bankacılık hizmetlerini kullanma kararına etki eden faktörlerin belirlenmesi üzerine bir araştırma: Bilecik örneği. *İktisadi ve İdari Bilimler Dergisi*, *30*(1), 301–320.

Aydın, S., & Onaylı, E. (2020). Bankacılıkta dijital dönüşümle değişen müşteri deneyimi: Müşteri sadakati, memnuniyeti ve tavsiye eğilimine yansımaları. *Yönetim ve Ekonomi Dergisi*, *27*(3), 645–663.

Bakkal, M., & Aksüt, U. (2011). *Türk bankacılık sisteminde elektronik bankacılık uygulamaları* (Vol. 32). Hiperlink Eğit. Ilet. Yay. San. Tic. Ve Ltd. Sti.

Başar, M. & Coşkun, M. (2006). *Bankacılık Uygulamaları*. Anadolu Üniversitesi, Eskişehir.

Comrey, A. L., & Lee, H. (1973). *A first course in factor analysis*. Academic Press.

De Winter, J. C., Dodou, D., & Wieringa, P. A. (2009). Exploratory factor analysis with small sample sizes. *Multivariate Behavioral Research*, *44*(2), 147–181. https://doi.org/10.1080/00273170902794206

Demirel, S. (2021). *The effect of digital banking applications of banks on customer loyalty and customer satisfaction* [Doctoral Dissertation, Beykent University].

Fernando, K. D. U. D., Tharanga, T. M. N., Dewasiri, N. J., Sood, K., Grima, S., & Thalassinos, E. (2023). Insurance penetration and ınstitutional spillover on economic growth: A dynamic spatial econometric approach on the Asian and Europe Region. *Journal of Risk and Financial Management*, *16*(8), 365.

Forza, C., & Filippini, R. (1998). TQM impact on quality conformance and customer satisfaction: A causal model. *International Journal of Production Economics*, *55*(1), 1–20. https://doi.org/10.1016/S0925-5273(98)00007-3.

Gerbing, D. W., & Anderson, J. C. (1992). Monte Carlo Evaluations of Goodness of Fit Indices for Structural Equation Models. *Sociological Methods & Research*, *21*(2), 132–160.

Gorsuch, R. L. (1983). *Factor analysis*. Erlbaum.

Grima, S., Kizilkaya, M., Sood, K., & ErdemDelice, M. (2021). The perceived effectiveness of blockchain for digital operational risk resilience in the European Union Insurance Market Sector. *Journal of Risk and Financial Management*, *14*, 363. https://doi.org/10.3390/jrfm14080363

Gümüş, E., Medetoğlu, B., & Tutar, S. (2020). Finans ve Bankacılık Sisteminde Yapay Zekâ Kullanımı: Kullanıcılar Üzerine Bir Uygulama. *Bucak İşletme Fakültesi Dergisi*, *3*(1), 28–53.

Hill, N., & Alexander, J. (2017). *The Handbook of Customer Satisfaction and Loyalty Measurement*. Routledge.

Hooper, D., Coughlan, J., & Mullen, M. R. (2008). Structural equation modelling: Guidelines for determining model fit. *The Electronic Journal of Business Research Methods*, *6*, 53–60.

Hu, L.-t., & Bentler, P. M. (1999). Cutoff criteria for fit indexes in covariance structure analysis: Conventional criteria versus new alternatives. *Structural Equation Modeling*, *6*(1), 1–55.

Kaiser, H. F., & Rice, J. (1974). Little Jiffy, Mark IV. *Educational and Psychological Measurement*, *34*(1), 111–117.

Kaplan, H. E. & Gürbüz, E. (2021). An extended UTAUT2 perspective-determinants of mobile banking use intention and use behavior. *Ömer Halisdemir Üniversitesi İktisadi ve İdari Bilimler Fakültesi Dergisi*, *14*(1), 207–227.

Karataş, Ö., & Çetinkaya Bozkurt, Ö. (2020). Mobil Bankacılık Hizmetlerinde Müşteri Memnuniyeti Üzerine Bir Araştırma. *International Social Mentality and Researcher Thinkers Journal*, *6*(29), 223–234. (ISSN: 2630-631X)

Klaus, P. P., & Maklan, S. (2013). Towards a better measure of customer experience. *International Journal of Market Research*, *55*(2), 227–246.

Kline, R. B. (1998). *Principles and practice of structural equation modeling in methodology in the social sciences*. Guilford Press.

Kline, R. B. (2011). *Principles and practice of structural equation modeling* (3rd ed.). Guilford Press.

Kula Kartal, S. & Mor Dirlik, E. (2016). Geçerlik Kavramının Tarihsel Gelişimi Ve Güvenirlikte En Çok Tercih Edilen Yöntem: Cronbach Alfa Katsayısı. *Abant İzzet Baysal Üniversitesi Eğitim Fakültesi Dergisi*, *16*(4), 1865–1879.

Lee, M. C. (2009). Factors influencing the adoption of Internet banking: An integration of TAM and TPB with perceived risk and perceived benefit. *Electronic Commerce Research and Applications*, *8*(3), 130–141. https://doi.org/10.1016/j.elerap.2008.11.006

Ling, G. M., Fern, Y. S., Boon, L. K., & Huat, T. S. (2016). Understanding customer satisfaction of Internet banking: A case study in Malacca. *Procedia Economics and Finance*, *37*, 80–85.

McCallum, R. C., Widaman, K. F., Zhang, S., & Hong, S. (1999). Sample size in factor analysis. *Psychological Methods*, *4*(1), 84–99.

Mengülerek, İ. E. (2021). *Dijital bankacılıkta müşteri deneyiminin müşteri sadakatine etkisi* [Yüksek Lisans Tezi, Maltepe Üniversitesi, İstanbul].

Mukaka M. M. (2012). Statistics Corner: A guide to the appropriate use of correlation coefficient in medical research. *Malawi Medical Journal: Medical Association of Malawi*, *24*(3), 69–71.

Mulaik, S. A. (1989). Evaluation of goodness-of-fit indices for structural equation models. *Psychological Bulletin*, *105*(3), 430–445. https://doi.org/10.1037/0033-2909.105.3.430

Munusamy, J., Chelliah, S., & Mun, H. W. (2010). Service quality delivery and its impact on customer satisfaction in the banking sector in Malaysia. *International Journal of Innovation, Management, and Technology*, *1*(4), 398–404.

Nicoletti, B. (2014). *Mobile Banking – Evolution or Revolution?* Palgrave Macmillan.

Noar, M. S. (2003). The role of structural equation modeling in scale development. *Structural Equation Modeling: A Multidisciplinary Journal*, *10*(4), 622–647.

Omari, K. (2020). *Determinants of the Adoption of Internet Banking Project in Kenya Commercial Banks-a Case of KCB Bank, Nairobi County* [Doctoral dissertation, University of Nairobi, Kenya].

Paçan Özcan, H., Sabah Çelik, Ş., & Özer, A. (2019). Bireysel Müşterilerin Mobil Bankacılık Kullanım Niyetini Etkileyen Faktörler. *Çankırı Karatekin Üniversitesi İktisadi ve İdari Bilimler Fakültesi Dergisi*, *9*(2), 475–506. https://doi.org/10.18074/ckuiibfd.590493

Pajic, V., Andrejic, M., & Sternad, M. (2023). FMEA-QFD approach for effective risk assessment in distribution processes. *Journal of Intelligent Management Decision*, *2*(2), 46–56.

Suhr, D. (2006). Exploratory or confirmatory factor analysis? *31st Annual SAS Users Group International Conference Proceedings* (pp. 200–231). SAS Institute Inc.

Tabachnick, B. G., & Fidell, L. S. (2014). *Using multivariate statistics*. Pearson Education Limited.

Taylor, R. (1990). Interpretation of the correlation coefficient: An introductory review. *Journal of Diagnostic Medical Sonography*, *6*(1), 35–39.

Wang, Y. S., Wang, Y. M., Lin, H. H., & Tang, T. I. (2003). Determinants of user acceptance of Internet banking: An empirical study. *International Journal of Service Industry Management*, *14*(5), 501–519.

Yi-Shun, W., Tang, T., & Tang, J. E. (2001). An instrument for measuring customer satisfaction toward websites that market digital products and services. *Journal of Electronic Commerce Research*, *2*(3), 89–102.

Yoon, C. (2010). Antecedents of customer satisfaction with online banking in China: The effects of experience. *Computers in Human Behavior*, *26*, 1296–1304.

Chapter 5

The Influence of Inflation and Oil Price Shocks on Stock Market Returns: A Bibliometric Analysis

Munish Gupta[a], *Vikas Sharma*[a] *and Kshitiz Jangir*[b]

[a]*University School of Business, Chandigarh University, Mohali, India*
[b]*Manipal University Jaipur, Rajasthan, India*

Abstract

Purpose: This study investigates the influence of inflation and oil price fluctuations on stock prices and returns. A thorough bibliometric analysis of research articles published in the last 22 years has been conducted to achieve this objective.

Need for the Study: Inflation and oil prices are critical macroeconomic variables that significantly impact the economy, including the stock market. It is crucial for investors and policymakers to understand the complex relationship between these economic variables and the stock market.

Methodology: The study employed a bibliometric analysis to identify the most influential authors, institutions, and research themes related to the impact of inflation and oil prices on stock prices.

Findings: The study identified that the fluctuations of the stock market are significantly influenced by both inflation and oil prices. This relationship has been extensively studied in the literature, with several key research themes identified. These themes include the effects of inflation and oil prices on various sectors and industries, the role played by monetary and fiscal policy, and the impact of international trade and global economic conditions.

Financial Landscape Transformation: Technological Disruptions, 67–102

doi:10.1108/978-1-83753-750-120251005

Practical Implications: The insights that have emerged have significant implications for investors and policymakers. It highlights the need for risk management strategies and mitigation of macroeconomic factors' impact on stock prices.

Keywords: Stock prices; inflation; oil price volatility; macroeconomic variables; stock market fluctuations; monetary policy; bibliometric analysis

JEL Code: O16

Introduction

The nexus between macroeconomic factors and stock prices has long been a topic of interest among economists, investors, and policymakers. Inflation and oil price volatility are two key drivers of stock market fluctuations. Inflation is the escalating rate at which aggregate price levels for commodities and services inflate within an economic system. Conversely, oil price shocks refer to sudden and significant changes in the price of oil due to factors such as supply disruptions or geopolitical tensions. The stock market is a vital component of a country's economy, and fluctuations in stock prices and returns have significant implications for investors and the overall financial system. The impact of inflationary pressures and oil price shocks on stock prices and returns has been a subject of interest for researchers and policymakers for several decades. While some studies have the viewpoint that inflation has a negative impact on stock prices and returns, others espouse a more optimistic view, positing a positive correlation between the two. Similarly, the impact of oil price shocks on the stock market is also ambiguous, with some studies showing a positive relationship and others a negative one.

This chapter aims to augment the existing literature through the execution of a bibliometric analysis, examining the impact of inflation and oil price shocks on stock prices and returns. A bibliometric analysis is a quantitative method that is designed to analyze and map the literature of a particular research field. In this chapter, we will employ the bibliometric analysis technique to earmark the most influential studies in this field, the most frequently used methodologies, and the gaps in the literature that require further research.

The chapter is structured as follows. The subsequent segment embarks on an evaluative review of the relevant literature focusing on the impact of inflation and oil price shocks on stock prices and returns, followed by a description of the methodology used for the bibliometric analysis. After that, the analysis results are presented, prefacing an in-depth discussion of the implications of the findings for researchers and policymakers. Finally, the paper concludes with a summary of the key findings and suggestions for future research.

Inflation

Inflation refers to the temporal escalation in the aggregate pricing structures for goods and services within an economic structure. Such inflationary dynamics often occur from an imbalance between the supply and demand of goods and services in an economy, leading to an increase in the cost of production and wages. This, in turn, leads to a rise in the price of goods and services. The aftershocks of inflationary episodes significantly impact stock market returns, and the direction and magnitude of the impact can depend on several factors, including the level and persistence of inflation, the sector and industry of the company, and the response of central banks and investors to the inflation shock. Inflation shocks can affect company earnings by increasing the cost of production and wages. Companies that cannot pass on these increased costs to consumers may experience a decrease in profits, leading to a decline in stock market returns. Furthermore, inflation possesses the potential to erode the purchasing power of money, making it more expensive for companies to borrow and invest, leading to a decrease in stock prices.

Conversely, inflationary conditions can elevate the nominal value of assets and revenues, increasing stock prices manifest heterogeneously across different sectors and industries. Some sectors, such as consumer staples and utilities, may be less affected by inflation shocks as they provide essential goods and services that consumers will continue to purchase regardless of the inflation level (Xie, 2020). In contrast, technology and financial services sectors often demonstrate heightened susceptibility to inflationary shocks as their earnings are more sensitive to interest rate oscillations. During the deflationary period in 2021, the stock market experienced volatility as investors tried to assess the impact of inflation on corporate earnings. However, overall, the market has continued to perform well, with the S&P 500 index delivering a return of around 27% (Philips et al., 2022). Inflation possesses the dual capacity to increase the nominal value of assets and revenues, increasing stock prices. The impact of inflation shocks is not uniformly distributed across different sectors and industries. Sectors, such as consumer staples and utilities, are less affected by inflation shocks as they provide essential goods and services that consumers will continue purchasing regardless of the inflation level (Xie, 2020). Conversely, technology and financial sectors may be more sensitive to inflation shocks as their earnings are more sensitive to interest rate fluctuations. During the deflationary period in 2021, the stock market experienced volatility as investors tried to assess the impact of inflation on corporate earnings. However, overall, the market has continued to perform well, with the S&P 500 index delivering a return of around 27%.

Oil Price Shocks

An oil price shock is characterized by a sudden and significant increase or decrease in the price of crude oil. Oil price shocks can have significant economic impacts, as crude oil is an essential raw material for many industries and is closely tied to transportation costs and energy. This significantly impacted the stock prices of energy companies, which saw their profits decline and stock prices fall. When oil prices rise, companies that use much oil may experience decreased profits, leading to lower stock returns. In mid-2014, global oil prices fell sharply due to a supply glut, reaching a low of around $30 per barrel in early 2016 (Hanieh, 2020). Between 2007 and mid-2008, global oil prices rose sharply, reaching a record high of over $140 per barrel in July 2008. This significantly impacted the stock market, as increasing energy costs led to lower profits for companies in other sectors and reduced consumer spending (Hamilton, 2009). However, oil production companies may benefit from higher profits, leading to higher stock returns.

Conversely, when oil prices decrease, companies that rely on oil and gas may experience lower production costs, increasing their profitability and potentially boosting their stock prices. Due to Western sanctions on Russia during the Ukraine–Russia war, Crude oil prices surged by 5%, exceeding $121 per barrel, while futures for natural gas exhibited a parallel uptick. This inflation in oil prices proves advantageous for equities in the energy sector yet imposes a financial burden on consumers and many enterprises. According to Joshipura and Lamba (2022), the S&P 500's energy segment advanced by 1.7%, and utilities inched up by 0.2%, even as other predominant sectors within the S&P 500 experienced a decline for the day. Many variables, including the magnitude and persistence of the price shift, broader economic landscapes, geopolitically-driven events, and legislative frameworks influence the ramifications of oil price fluctuations on equity markets.

The Procedure of Bibliometric Analysis

The procedure defined by Zupic and Čater (2015) and Bashir (2022) has been followed for bibliometrics analysis. The five steps followed to investigate bibliometrics analysis have been represented in Fig. 1. The figure shows a framework for conducting bibliometric analysis involving several vital steps. These include defining the research question, identifying data collection sources and techniques, selecting appropriate visualization tools and techniques for analysis, conducting the bibliometric analysis using suitable software, and finally interpreting the results to derive explanations and findings.

The process flow depicted in the figure suggests an iterative and comprehensive approach to bibliometric analysis. It starts with conceptualizing the research

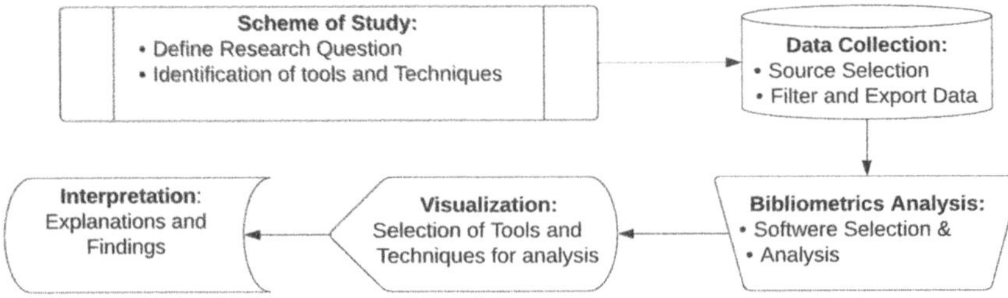

Fig. 1. Bibliometrics Analysis Procedure. *Source*: Self-developed by Authors.

problem, followed by data extraction, analysis, visualization, and ultimately, arriving at meaningful interpretations and conclusions.

Scheme of Study

The relationship between inflation, oil prices, and stock prices has been widely studied in the literature, and the results are often mixed. In this study, we have analyzed the literature on this topic by examining the frequency of publications, authors, journals, and keywords. The study will also identify the most cited articles and the most influential authors. The research question we seek to answer is: How do inflation and oil price shocks impact stock prices and returns? The study provides insights into the literature on this topic and identifies the key factors that drive the relationship between inflation, oil prices, and stock prices (Al-Ansi et al., 2024; Novarlić & Đurić 2024).

Moreover, applying Bradford's rule, we have split the sampled studies into three unique zones to identify core sources; zone 1 is titled "Nuclear zone" because it contains highly productive sources. Zone 2 comprises moderately productive sources, whereas Zone 3 encompasses low-production sources (Wardikar & Gudadhe, 2013). Samuel C. Bradford published how information is scattered for a particular theme in 1934 (Von Ungern-Sternberg, 2000).

Our main goal is to determine the most influential institutions and nations based on total citations and publication frequency. Future research directions can be identified by exploring overarching themes and pivotal areas. With reference to this, we rely on the thematic map, theme evolution, and Co-Occurrence Map. We have used the "biblioshiny" R package to extract research topics from the 22 years of publications for bibliometric analysis. Compared to the author's keywords, more descriptive trends are provided by keywords, which is useful for effectively conveying research subjects (Tripathi et al., 2018). For analysis, we add keywords to identify and link various study fields and analyze the thematic framework of current research (Sharifi, 2020).

Research Objectives and Analytical Techniques

The present research seeks to comprehensively review existing studies on the relationship between inflation and oil price fluctuations and their effects on stock market valuations. This study, applying the "biblioshiny" interface within the "bibliometrix 4.0" software, aims to uncover major contributing institutions, geographic locations, authors, and seminal works. Furthermore, this investigation will employ science mapping methodologies such as co-occurrence and co-citation analyses to pinpoint prevailing research themes and discern unexplored areas in the current body of literature (Yerpude et al., 2022).

Selection of Dataset

We employ a two-step approach in gathering bibliometric data for our ongoing investigations. Initially, we source our scholarly articles from Scopus, which

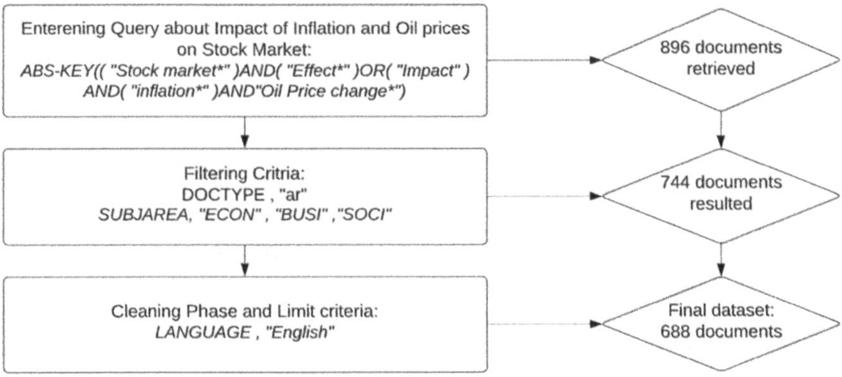

Fig. 2. Data Collection Flow. *Source*: Self-developed by authors.

serves as a comprehensive digital repository of published research. Following the establishment of a specific search query, we further refine the resultant dataset by applying a series of filters, as depicted in Fig. 2. This process ensures alignment with our overarching research objectives. Consequently, the search yielded a total of 688 relevant articles for our study.

As we do bibliometric analysis, we restrict our search to 2000 through 2022; finally, we manually review the research articles and discard 48 publications to fulfill the current study's objectives. Our final sample size is 640 articles.

Bibliometric Analysis and Visualization

We used "biblioshiny" from the Bibliometrics R package to conduct the bibliometric analysis. This tool is designed to disseminate bibliometric and scientometric analysis tools considering intellectual and conceptual structure constituents concerning authors, documents, and sources. Biblioshiny distinguishes itself from other bibliometric tools by allowing us to create various conclusions using graphs and tables. Table 1 provides descriptive statistics essential to understand before continuing the study. We reviewed 640 research papers authored by 1,369 researchers, with 138 single-authored research publications suggesting a higher degree of collaboration.

The average number of documents per author is 0.467, suggesting that no author has produced more than one research article, and the major chunk of research articles are published in collaborations. Figs. 1 and 2 represent yearly publication and citation trends. Annual publication patterns may split into two time- frames: before 2011, when research activity was low, and after 2012, when there was a significant increase in research output. The yearly citation pattern also shows over 1,000 citations in 2001, 2009, 2013, and 2014, coinciding with a spike in the literature regarding the impact of inflation and oil prices on stock market prices. Finally, we examine the major research themes and influential publications from different countries to broaden the investigation's scope. Fig. 4

Table 1. Descriptive Information.

Description	Information
MAIN INFORMATION	Timespan (2000:2022), Sources (280), Documents (640)
	Avg years from publication (7.1), Avg citations per document (18.46)
	Avg citations per year per doc (1.961), References (24,826)
DOCUMENT TYPES	Article (640)
DOCUMENT CONTENTS	Keywords Plus (ID) (617), Author's Keywords (DE) (1,606)
AUTHORS	Authors (1,369), Author Appearances (1,506)
	Authors of single-authored docs (127), Authors of multi-authored docs (1,242)
AUTHORS COLLABORATION	Single-authored documents (138), Documents per Author (0.467),
	Authors per Document (2.14), Co-Authors per Documents (2.35),
	Collaboration Index (2.47)

Source: Biblioshiny using data from Scopus.

shows a three-dimensional analysis of inflation and stock market prices, with major research issues in the center, countries on the right, and research journals to the left. According to the figure, the key research areas include monetary policy, inflation, oil prices, and stock returns, with most contributions coming from the United States, India, Pakistan, and China.

The graph in Fig. 3 illustrates the yearly trend in articles published from 2000 to 2022, using Scopus data to focus on "stock market," "inflation," and "oil price." Early years saw few publications (4 to 13 annually), with a significant increase in 2006 onwards. Publications peaked at 72 in 2021 but declined to 28 in 2022, reflecting fluctuating academic interest in these interconnected topics over two decades.

Fig. 4 displays the yearly trend of citations for research topics identified over the past 22 years, using data from Scopus. It illustrates the changes in citation counts, reflecting the academic impact of these topics over time. The early years saw variable citation counts, with peaks and declines. From 2008 to 2013, there was a stable yet high-impact trend, reflecting increased scholarly engagement. However, from 2019 onwards, there was a noticeable decline in citation counts, possibly indicating a shift in research focus or changes in academic priorities. The graph highlights the evolving interest and impact of research on the stock market, inflation, and oil prices within the academic community over the past two decades.

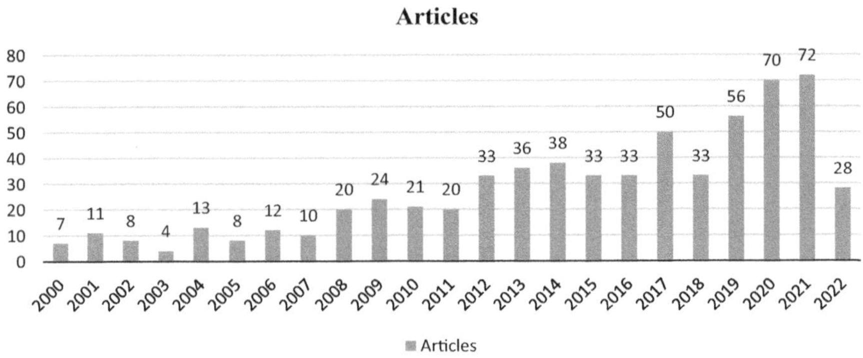

Fig. 3. Annual Publications Trend Shows the Number of "Articles" Over Several Years, Ranging from 2000 to 2021. *Source*: Own elaboration using data from Scopus.

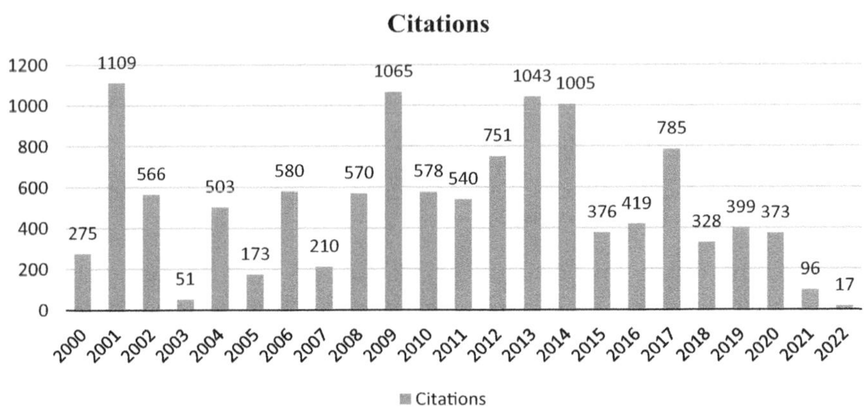

Fig. 4. Annual Citations Trend Shows the Citation History for the Research Subject Over the Past 22 Years, Highlighting the Changes in Citation Counts Over Time. *Source*: Own elaboration using data from Scopus.

The Sankey diagram in Fig. 5 illustrates the intricate relationships between economic research sources, thematic keywords, and their geographic focus. It depicts how journals such as "*Energy Economics*," "*Applied Economics*," and "*Applied Financial Economics*" contribute to a wide array of keywords, including "stock market," "inflation," "financial market," and "monetary policy." These themes are then linked to various countries, mostly the USA, China, and India. For instance, research on the "stock market" is significantly associated with the USA and China, indicating these markets' prominence in economic studies. The diagram also highlights how "inflation" and "interest rate" are common themes across different journals, reflecting their critical importance in economic research. This visualization effectively demonstrates the diverse thematic coverage of

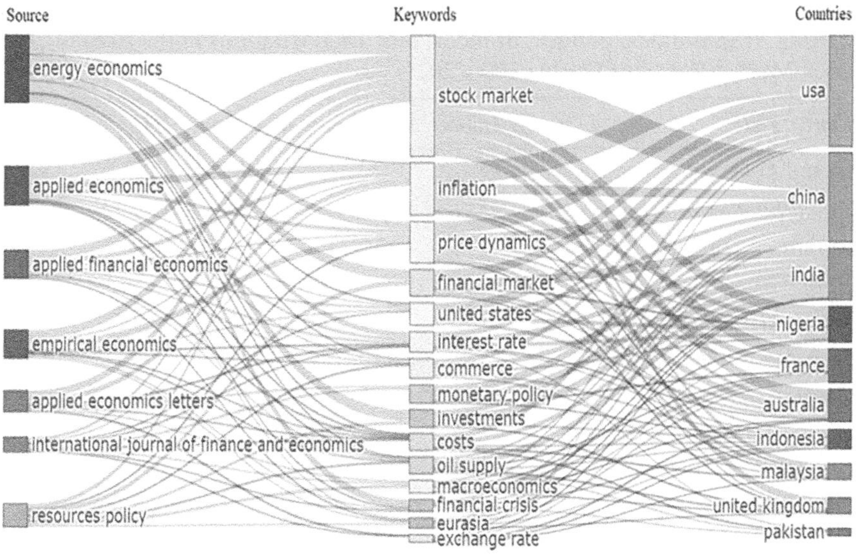

Fig. 5. Three-Dimensional Analyses of Theoretical Literature. This network visualization or map displays relationships between research keywords from 2000 to 2021. This visualization illustrates the global interconnectedness and interdependence of research in areas like business, finance, economics, and energy across the world. *Source*: Biblioshiny using data from Scopus.

economic journals and the broad geographic distribution of research topics, underscoring the global interconnectedness and regional focus within the field of economics.

Influential Aspects of Economic Literature

Most Influential Research Journals

Between 2000 and 2022, 640 articles were published in 280 sources. Table 2 depicts the list of the top ten influential research journals with publication starting year, h-index, g-index, m-index, and total citations in the area of stock market behavior during this period. Citation analysis is a technique for locating the most relevant journals in the scientific communication system and indicating prospects for retention or alienation to create a cost-effective Citation Index ("Citation Analysis of Scientific Journals," 2005).

The most influential journal shown in Table 2 with the highest citation (2,582) is *Energy Economics*, having the highest m_index (0.82), followed by *Global Finance Journal* (697, 0.22), *Journal of Monetary Economics* (484, 0.09) and *Review of Financial Studies* (402, 0.05). Finally, the *International Review of Economics and Finance* is identified as an emerging journal with an m-index of 0.60; total citations are only 339. The h-index score is a standard scholarly metric describing the relationship between the number of papers published by an author

Table 2. List of the Top 10 Influential Research Journals with Publication Starting Year, h-index, g-index, m-index, and Total Citations in the Area of Stock Market Behavior During 2000–2021.

Source Titles	h_Index	g_Index	m_index	TC	Py_Start
Energy Economics	18	22	0.82	2582	2001
Global Finance Journal	5	5	0.22	697	2000
Journal of Monetary Economics	2	2	0.09	484	2001
Review of Financial Studies	1	1	0.05	402	2002
Economic Modelling	7	10	0.50	349	2009
International Review of Economics and Finance	6	7	0.60	339	2013
Journal of Comparative Economics	1	1	0.10	298	2013
Managerial Finance	3	4	0.19	297	2007
Quantitative Finance	3	4	0.16	291	2004
Applied Financial Economics	7	12	0.33	257	2002

Source: Own Compilation Biblioshiny using data from Scopus.

and the number of times the author cited, whereas the m-index normalizes-index by dividing it by the number of years since their first publication (Hirsch, 2005).

The most influential paper (Papapetrou, 2001) published in the most influential journal *Energy Economics* explains stock price fluctuation by identifying the factors affecting it. Using a multivariate vector-autoregression (VAR) approach, the researcher investigated the significant dependence of stock price movement on oil prices in Greece's stock market. However, stock returns are not affected by oil price shocks to a large extent (Apergis & Miller, 2009). Moreover, during the post-global crisis period, stock returns responded positively to the inflation rate (Mollick & Assefa, 2013).

Another source, the *Journal of Monetary Economics*, has published studies on inflation's impact on stock prices and identified a negative relation between inflation rate and stock market activities. However, in low-inflation economies, the impact of inflation is marginal compared to high-inflation economies (Boyd et al., 2001a). On the other hand, high inflation in the US economy after the financial crisis of 2008 tends to coincide with high economic growth, which rationally raised the equity return (Bekaert & Engstrom, 2010).

Economic modeling has worked significantly on the core issue addressed in this paper, and it has been identified that the consumer price index (CPI) is positively related to stock returns in Pakistan. In contrast, the producer price index (WPI) is not impacting the same (Tiwari et al., 2015).

The *International Review of Economics and Finance* has also made a sturdy contribution recently. Aktürk (2016) has identified that ex-ante inflationary

Table 3. Journal Rankings (Bradford Law). Provides insights into the ranking and frequency of citations for various journals on the research subject for 22 years. Each journal is ranked based on its citation frequency, with the highest-ranked journals having the most citations.

Sources	Rank	Freq	cumFreq	Zone
Energy Economics	1	22	22	Zone 1
Applied Economics	2	19	41	Zone 1
Empirical Economics	3	16	57	Zone 1
Applied Financial Economics	4	13	70	Zone 1
International Journal of Energy Economics and Policy	5	12	82	Zone 1
Applied Economics Letters	6	11	93	Zone 1
International Journal of Finance and Economics	7	11	104	Zone 1
Economic Modelling	8	10	114	Zone 1
International Review of Economics and Finance	9	9	123	Zone 1
International Research Journal of Finance and Economics	10	8	131	Zone 1
Research in International Business and Finance	11	8	139	Zone 1
Finance Research Letters	12	7	146	Zone 1
Resources Policy	13	7	153	Zone 1
Economics Bulletin	14	6	159	Zone 1
International Journal of Applied Business and Economic Research	15	6	165	Zone 1
International Journal of Islamic and Middle Eastern Finance and Management	16	6	171	Zone 1
International Review of Financial Analysis	17	6	177	Zone 1
Investment Management and Financial Innovations	18	6	183	Zone 1
Journal of Policy Modeling	19	6	189	Zone 1
Managerial Finance	20	6	195	Zone 1
Pacific Basin Finance Journal	21	6	201	Zone 1
Sustainability (Switzerland)	22	6	207	Zone 1
Cogent Economics and Finance	23	5	212	Zone 1

Source: Own Compilation Biblioshiny using data from Scopus.

expectations positively impact the Turkish standard stock market index. Ex-post inflationary realizations negatively affect the same. Another study on the Chinese stock market highlighted that higher inflation increased the risks of the CSI 300 Index during the crisis period of 2015 in China, whereas, in the crisis period, inflation fluctuations contributed insignificantly to the risks of CSI 300 futures (Chen & Gong, 2019).

We employ source impact and Bradford law to evaluate the influence of the most significant research publications. Table 3 shows the top research journals ranked by number of publications, year of publication, number of citations, and h-index. Bradford law classifies articles and journals into three zones, with zone 1 core publishing content relating to the inflation rate, oil price volatility, and returns on stock markets. Since this area makes the most significant scientific contributions, it is sometimes called a "nuclear zone." From this data, we can surmise that 219 of the 640 research publications fall into Zone 1, 213 into Zone 2, and 208 into Zone 3.

Bradford's law, which is grounded in the principle of diminishing returns, identifies a small number of exceptionally productive periodicals (zone 1), more moderate producers (zone 2), and more producers whose productivity is steadily declining overall (zone 3) (Bradford et al., 1953). The results show that 281 journals have been published on stock price and inflation. Among the top 20 journals, we identified in Fig. 6 the top five business journals: *Energy Economics*, *Applied Economics*, *Empirical Economics*, *Applied Financial Economics*, and *International Journal of Energy Economics* and Policy in zone 1 and contributed 82 research papers out of a total data set of 640. While going through the top 5 contributors in the related research topic, Fig. 5 shows the highest contribution (22) by *Energy Economics* since 2000. However, the *International Journal of Energy Economics and Policy* has depicted a significant contribution (12) since 2015.

Core research publications

Table 4 enumerates the 15 most frequently cited scholarly articles on stock returns, inflation, and oil price dynamics. The most highly cited paper, with 41 citations, authored by Apergis and Miller (2009), elucidates the repercussions of oil price fluctuations on vital macroeconomic indicators, notably stock prices. Utilizing a Vector Error-Correction (VEC) and Vector Autoregressive (VAR) model, the study concludes that auxiliary variables – such as foreign exchange rates, interest rates, and durable goods consumption – emerge as significant predictors in determining stock market performance. Simultaneously, the empirical evidence suggests that the substantive effects of oil price shocks on stock returns are comparatively different.

Using an International multi-factor model, the authors of the second most-cited research paper (Basher & Sadorsky, 2006) analyze the effect of fluctuations in oil prices on the performance of emerging market stock markets. According to the research, the beta of the oil price has a positive and statistically significant effect only in rising markets.

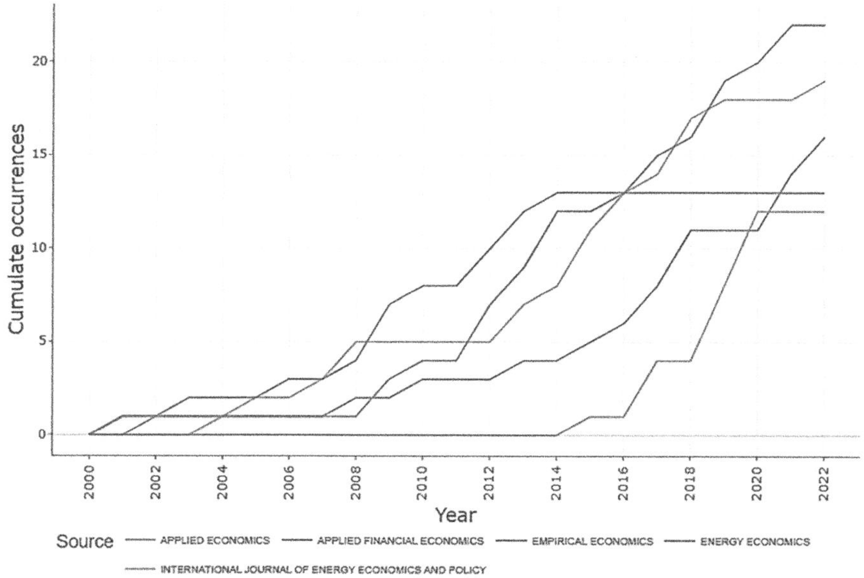

Fig. 6. Publication Trend in Top 10 Journals Showing the Cumulative Occurrences of Various Academic Journals or Economics Topics Over Time from 2000 to 2022. The lines represent fields or journals like *Applied Economics*, *Applied Financial Economics*, *Empirical Economics*, *Energy Economics*, and the *International Journal of Energy Economics and Policy*, Tracking Their Cumulative Growth or Number of Publications. *Source*: Own Compilation Biblioshiny using data from Scopus.

In contrast, it has a negative but negligible effect in falling markets and Papapetrou (2001) is the third most cited research paper. Using the VAR analysis model, the author of this chapter examined the effects of oil price shocks on Greece's economy, employment rate, and stock market returns and identified that oil price shocks have negatively affected economic activity and employment. In contrast, the growth in these variables responds negatively to real stock return shocks. Another significant study, "Macroeconomic Factors Do Influence Aggregate Stock Returns," using the GARCH model (Flannery & Protopapadakis, 2002a), identified six candidates for stock price shocks further classified as nominal and real.

Core words

Table 5 comprehensively previews the most frequently used keywords in the researched literature. The most frequent keywords were extracted using R studio based on author and abstract keywords. In the analysis of the keywords, "Exchange Rate," "Interest Rate," and "Monetary Policy" have been identified as the most common keywords. "Stock Market," "Inflation," and "oil price"

Table 4. 15 Most Locally and Globally Cited Paper in the Domain of Stock Returns, Inflation, and Oil Price Dynamics.

Paper title	Corresponding Author	Year	Local Citations	Global Citations
"Do structural oil-market shocks affect stock prices?"	(Apergis & Miller, 2009)	2009	41	395
"Oil price risk and emerging stock markets"	(Basher & Sadorsky, 2006)	2006	39	452
"Oil price shocks, stock market, economic activity and employment in Greece"	(Papapetrou, 2001)	2001	27	420
"Macroeconomic Factors Do Influence Aggregate Stock Returns"	(Flannery & Protopapadakis, 2002a)	2002	20	402
"Oil price shocks and stock market activities: Evidence from oil-importing and oil-exporting countries."	(Wang et al., 2013)	2013	18	298

Source: Biblioshiny using data from Scopus.

are highly available on both keyword bases as these are the themes of research. However, the occurrence rank of "Inflation rate" in the abstract keyword is deficient compared to the Author's Keywords. In the meantime, the keywords "stock market," "shocks," and "oil price" are all reflected across all categories. The keywords connected to "stock market" in the nexus of "oil prices," "inflation rate," "Monetary policy," and "Exchange Rate" explain the impact of the macro-variable on stock market performance. Author Keywords, used in bibliometric analysis further to illuminate the knowledge structure of various scientific fields, are more relevant than abstract keywords and provide a narrower picture of an article's contents (Zhang et al., 2016).

Fig. 7 presents the word cloud of author's keywords. In a word cloud, a larger word size indicates a higher occurrence of these keywords. Inflation, oil prices, monetary policy, exchange rate, and stock returns are significantly larger words and indicate stronger contributions to the research theme in the sampled studies. "Fiscal policy" and "Economic policy uncertainty" are important macro-variables. However, the occurrence of these keywords is comparatively too low. These keywords can widen the future scope of studying the impact of less explored macro-variables.

Fig. 8 shows a word growth chart using the author's keywords and indicates "Inflation rate" as the growing keyword, followed by "Oil prices" and "Monetary policy." From 2005, some other keywords like "Exchange rate," "Economic growth," and "Macroeconomic variables" have shown an impressive surge, but growth over the period is comparatively lower. The word growth chart concludes that most research papers have studied the impact of the inflation rate, oil

Table 5. Most Frequent Keywords.

Rank	Abstract Keywords	Occurrences	Author's Keywords	Occurrences
1	*Stock Market*	1254	*Stock Market*	99
2	*Oil Price*	489	*Inflation Rate*	71
3	*Stock Price*	266	*Oil Price*	55
4	*Exchange Rate*	263	*Monetary Policy*	38
5	*Stock Returns*	224	*Exchange Rate*	33
6	*Macroeconomic Variables*	149	*Macroeconomic Variables*	32
7	*Monetary Policy*	145	*Stock Returns*	30
8	*Economic Growth*	136	*Stock Price*	27
9	*Market Returns*	134	*Economic Growth*	22
10	*Inflation Rate*	124	*Interest Rate*	20
11	*Market Development*	124	*Stock Market Returns*	20
12	*Financial Market*	86	*Financial Development*	19
13	*Money Supply*	81	*Volatility*	18
14	*Stock Exchange*	81	*Panel Data*	17
15	*Crude Oil*	73	*Emerging Markets*	16
16	*Market Index*	68	*Financial Market*	16
17	*Price Shocks*	65	*Stock Market Development*	15
18	*Market Volatility*	64	*Cointegration*	12
19	*Financial Crisis*	59	*GARCH*	12
20	*Financial Development*	57	*Macroeconomics*	12

Source: Biblioshiny using data from Scopus.

price, and monetary policy on stock market returns. However, the effect of the exchange rate, economic growth, and macroeconomic variables has been the least researched and can be parameters for future research.

Top Authors, Institutions, and Countries in Inflation Impact and Stock Price Research

Table 6 displays the top 10 authors in terms of publications and h-index, along with information about the institutions and countries that have contributed the most to inflation impact and stock price research.

Fig. 7. Keyword Cloud. *Source*: Biblioshiny using data from Scopus.

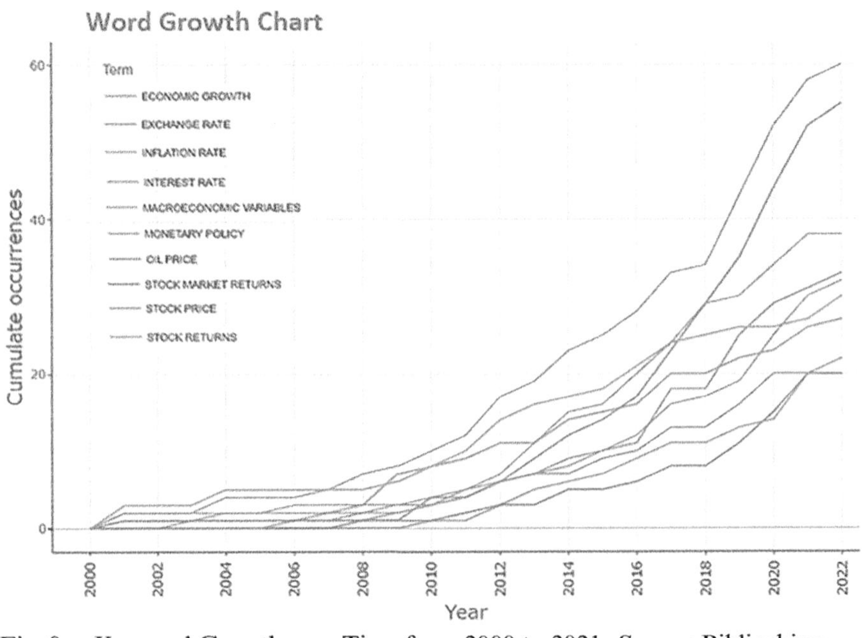

Fig. 8. Keyword Growth over Time from 2000 to 2021. *Source*: Biblioshiny using data from Scopus.

Hsing Y is the leading author and is engrossed in the study of macroeconomic variables like inflation rate, interest rate, GDP rate (Hsing, 2013), fiscal policy and monetary policy (Hsing, 2013), exchange rate depreciation or appreciation (Hsing

Table 6. Top 10 Authors.

Authors	h_index	TC	NP	Start_PY
Hsing Y	3	55	9	2005
Gupta R	3	37	5	2011
Jareño F	3	52	4	2013
Naifar N	3	205	4	2013
Pradhan RP	3	88	4	2013
Arvin MB	3	87	3	2013
Azam M	2	45	3	2014
Ben Naceur S	3	115	3	2007
Ho S-Y	3	28	3	2018
Hsieh W-J	1	25	3	2009

Source: Biblioshiny using data from Scopus.

et al., 2012) on the stock index and performance. Adopting the GARCH model in the most cited publication by Hsing Y, his research determined that Poland's stock market has a positive association with real GDP. In comparison, the German stock exchange is negatively associated with the real interest rate, government borrowings to GDP ratio, expected inflation rate, and other macroeconomic variables. Over 150 years of monthly data in the UK, Gupta R has published some of the most influential work on the effects of a shock to the corporate bond spread on key macroeconomic variables (Christou et al., 2020) like the unemployment rate, inflation rate, and nominal exchange rate returns (Balcilar et al., 2017). In his most cited paper, he examines the effects of US economic news on the stock returns and volatility of seven developing Asian stock markets and finds a strong correlation between the three. As the third-ranked researcher whose work focuses on the study of inflation news in the Spanish stock market, Jareo F found that the likelihood that unexpected inflation news would lead to abnormal returns depends on three main factors: the direction of the news, the state of the economy, and the flow-through ability of the sector (Díaz & Jareño, 2013). Ranked four on the list of most-cited authors is Naifar N, whose work has focused on the effects of oil price volatility on stock market performance, with a particular focus on the countries of the Gulf Cooperation Council (GCC). The correlation between the returns on those markets and OPEC's oil price volatility has identified that during the recent financial crisis, the dependence structure between inflation rates and crude oil prices was asymmetric and skewed to the high end (Naifar & Al Dohaiman, 2013a). Pradhan RP is the fifth most cited author studying the interplay between inflation and oil prices, bond and stock market growth, and economic expansion. In his most cited work, Pradhan analyses the long-term ties between GDP growth, oil prices, stock market depth, the real effective exchange rate, inflation, and the real rate of interest using the Panel VAR model (Pradhan et al., 2015).

Table 7. Geographical Distribution of Publications and Citations.

Countries	Most Publications	Percentage (%)	Countries	Most Citations	Percentage (%)
USA	184	21.75%	*USA*	2256	31.85%
China	117	13.83%	*Greece*	1215	17.15%
India	102	12.06%	*China*	1015	14.33%
Malaysia	95	11.23%	*United Kingdom*	728	10.28%
United Kingdom	84	9.93%	*Canada*	480	6.78%
Pakistan	63	7.45%	*Spain*	391	5.52%
Australia	59	6.97%	*Italy*	277	3.91%
France	52	6.15%	*Germany*	268	3.78%
Indonesia	47	5.56%	*Australia*	239	3.37%
Nigeria	43	5.08%	*Turkey*	215	3.04%
Total	**846**	*100%*		**7084**	*100%*

Source: Biblioshiny using data from Scopus.

The top 10 countries with the most publications and citations have been presented in Table 7. Based on the statistical analysis, it has been identified that authors from the USA produced the most, with a total of 184 research documents (21.75%), followed by China with 117 (13.83%) and India with 102 (12.06%) research documents. The USA, China, the United Kingdom, and Australia are the only countries on the list of top 10 publications and citations in retrieved research documents. Greece has secured 2nd place with 1215 (17.15%) citations in the list of most cited publications, though it has yet to find any place in the list of top 10 publications.

Further examination of the most relevant research institutions (Fig. 9) has shown that Southeast Louisiana University and the University of Ghana have ranked first with 15 research publications each, followed by the Universiti Tunku Abdul Rahman with eight research papers. Further investigations specify the contribution of the top 10 research institutions on the uneven impact on the different stock markets concerning Exchange rates, Inflation rate, Monetary policy function, Government deficit, Oil demand and supply shocks, Oil prices, and foreign equity participation.

Table 8 provides comprehensive information regarding the most corresponding productive countries/regions in the context of a single corresponding publication (SCP) and multiple corresponding publications (MCP). Globally, the USA leads the list with almost double the number of papers compared to China. Furthermore, the USA reflects the strongest willingness to collaborate (27%) with other countries, followed by the United Kingdom (25.8%), Australia (23.5%), and China (20%).

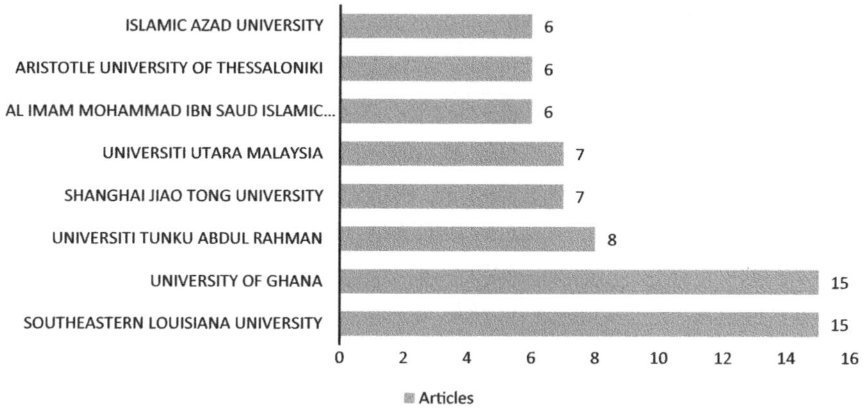

Fig. 9. Most Relevant Research Institutions. *Source*: Biblioshiny using data from Scopus.

Table 8. List of Countries (Most Corresponding Authors).

Country	Articles	Freq	SCP	MCP	MCP_Ratio
USA	74	0.15481	54	20	0.2703
China	40	0.08368	32	8	0.2
United Kingdom	31	0.06485	23	8	0.2581
India	30	0.06276	25	5	0.1667
Malaysia	19	0.03975	18	1	0.0526
Australia	17	0.03556	13	4	0.2353
Turkey	17	0.03556	15	2	0.1176
Nigeria	16	0.03347	13	3	0.1875
Pakistan	13	0.0272	12	1	0.0769
South Africa	13	0.0272	12	1	0.0769

Source: Biblioshiny using data from Scopus.

Also, the top 15 research collaboration networks by country are shown in Table 9. The United States and China have collaborated on eight research projects, more than any other two countries. Nearly every nation interested in the matter, including China, has collaborated with the USA. Fig. 10 indicates the significant impact of the USA's economic variable on the world stock market.

Co-citation Analysis

Co-citation analysis is a unique method that involves tracking pairs of papers co-cited by many authors cited in the source articles (Surwase et al., 2011).

Table 9. Collaboration Network.

From	To	Frequency
USA	*CHINA*	8
USA	*GERMANY*	4
USA	*INDIA*	4
USA	*UNITED KINGDOM*	4
United Kingdom	*FRANCE*	4
United Kingdom	*GREECE*	4
Malaysia	*PAKISTAN*	4
China	*PAKISTAN*	4
USA	*AUSTRALIA*	3
USA	*CANADA*	3
USA	*FRANCE*	3
USA	*GREECE*	3
USA	*KOREA*	3
United Kingdom	*ITALY*	3
United Kingdom	*NIGERIA*	3

Source: Biblioshiny using data from Scopus.

Fig. 10. Countries with the Most Research Collaboration. *Source*: Biblioshiny using data from Scopus.

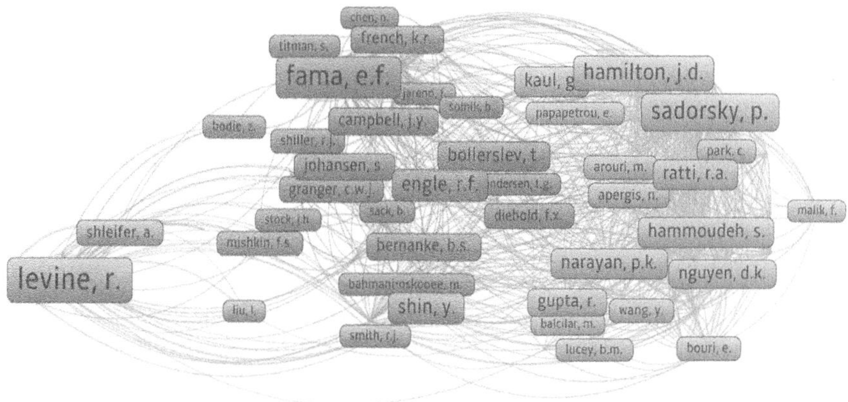

Fig. 11. Co-Citation Analysis. *Source*: Biblioshiny using data from Scopus.

A systematic literature review can be conducted to reveal the development and research structure of the current literature. Co-citation analysis can encourage researchers to discover the underlying intellectual structure (Rossetto et al., 2018).

Using a threshold of 35 citations per author, Fig. 11 depicts the co-citation network. So, out of 20,907 authors, 116 are the most frequently cited. The VOSviewer categorizes the 116 commonly cited authors into three groups, each represented by a different shade. The node's size represents the number of citations, and each node represents a different author. The larger the node, the greater the number of times the author is referenced in the collection of 640 papers shown in Table 10. They both appear in the same paper, as evidenced by the connection between

Table 10. The Highest 10 Ranked Co-cited Authors.

Rank	Author	Citations	Total Link Strength	Link	Cluster
1	*Levine, R.*	305	4,498	87	3
2	*Fama, E.F.*	270	3,862	115	1
3	*Sadorsky, P.*	223	6,502	109	2
4	*Roll, R.*	191	3,140	115	1
5	*Kilian, L.*	188	5,094	110	2
6	*Hamilton, J.D.*	186	5,130	111	2
7	*Engle, R.F.*	157	2,381	115	1
8	*Shin, Y.*	150	3,268	114	3
9	*Pesaran, M.H.*	138	3,034	114	3
10	*Hammoudeh, S.*	137	4,331	106	2

Source: Biblioshiny using data from Scopus.

their names. The greater the thickness of the line, the more often the two authors are shown to have worked together. Corresponding indicators, such as citations, total link strength, links, and clusters, are listed in Table 10.

In the co-citation network analysis, it was noticed that "Raskin Levine" is cited the highest (305) within the network, but in the research papers, it is related to different themes. Eugene F. Fama has a local citation (270), which is too high within the cluster (Li & Xu, 2022).

Conceptual Framework

The present section examines the numerous research lines in the chosen topics. We have developed a thorough framework of co-occurrence network analysis and a bi-dimensional matrix "thematic map" to probe the density and centrality of the network analysis.

Content Analysis

Content analysis is a qualitative technique that identifies and categorizes the units into clusters. This is a process of working and reworking with available data that divulges connections and relationships (Erlingsson & Brysiewicz, 2017). Table 11 gives a comprehensive overview of the research themes found in each cluster. For this purpose, we have included research papers with a C/Y score of more than 10 (Xiao et al., 2022). The 28 identified research papers have been categorized into three clusters.

Cluster 1 (top) includes 19 research papers with a score of C/Y > 10 and focuses on oil price shocks and stock market volatility in worldwide economies. Employing structure VAR analysis, Wang et al. (2013) have highlighted that impact of oil shocks on stock prices depends upon the importance of oil for the nation. In the international stock market, the effects of oil shocks are not so significant as they may vary from country to country (Apergis & Miller, 2009). In emerging stock markets, the significant impact of oil shocks is evident (Basher & Sadorsky, 2006). Contrary to this, in the European stock market, the effect of oil price change exhibits a significant negative on stock market returns (Cunado & Perez de Gracia, 2014b). However, the global financial recession era (Reboredo & Rivera-Castro, 2014b) has revealed contagion and interdependence between stock and oil prices. At the time, except for oil companies' stocks, oil price changes had no impact on the overall stock market. However, oil and exchange rates have negatively affected stock prices in the pre-global financial recession era. From mid-2009 onward, oil price shocks positively affected stock returns, whereas the effect was weaker on the currency exchange rate (Mollick & Assefa, 2013). The reason identified is that the rise in oil prices is assumed to be an expectation regarding recovery worldwide. Due to oil price shocks, the significantly affected macroeconomic variables are economic activities like inflation and GDP, not stock prices (Papapetrou, 2001). The analysis of the relationship between WTI oil prices and the returns of listed firms in the US energy sector, using the Generalized Dynamic

Table 11. Content Analysis in Each Cluster.

Cluster	Authors	Year	Cited by	C/Y	Content analysis
Top	(Wang et al., 2013)	2013	298	29.80	Oil Price shocks; Stock Return; Oil Importer nations- Low impact; Oil Exporter nations- high impact; International stock market; Emerging stock markets returns, VAR; VECM; Oil companies' stocks; Impact on inflation and GDP; WTI oil prices, US energy sector; Generalise dynamic factor model; Energy stock returns; Pre Global Financial Crises; Stock-Oil price relationship-Negative; Post Global Financial Crises; Stock-Oil price relationship-Positive; Inflation expectation-Recovery
	(Apergis & Miller, 2009)	2009	395	28.21	
	(Basher & Sadorsky, 2006)	2006	452	26.59	
	(Cunado & Perez de Gracia, 2014a)	2014	212	23.56	
	(Salisu & Isah, 2017)	2017	139	23.17	
	(Arouri et al., 2012)	2012	252	22.91	
	(Reboredo & Rivera-Castro, 2014a)	2014	173	19.22	
	(Papapetrou, 2001)	2001	420	19.09	
	(Ma et al., 2019)	2019	67	16.75	
	(Boubaker & Raza, 2017)	2017	100	16.67	
	(Salisu et al., 2019)	2019	57	14.25	
	(Lin et al., 2014)	2014	125	13.89	
	(Mollick & Assefa, 2013)	2013	136	13.60	
	(Badeeb & Lean, 2018)	2018	63	12.60	
	(Mohanty et al., 2011)	2011	146	12.17	
	(Kayalar et al., 2017)	2017	72	12.00	
	(Reboredo & Ugolini, 2016)	2016	84	12.00	
	(Naifar & Al Dohaiman, 2013b)	2013	111	11.10	
	(Godil et al., 2020)	2020	33	11.00	

(*Continued*)

Table 11. (*Continued*)

Cluster	Authors	Year	Cited by	C/Y	Content analysis
Left	(Boyd et al., 2001a)	2001	424	19.27	Inflation rate; Stock market returns; Financial sector; Banking companies, Performance; GARCH Model; Nominal macro-economic factors; Real macro-economic factors; Future expectation; Gold and Oil prices
	(Flannery & Protopapadakis, 2002a)	2002	402	19.14	
	(Khalid et al., 2020)	2020	47	15.67	
	(Kosmidou, 2008)	2008	205	13.67	
	(Chevallier, 2009)	2009	189	13.50	
Right	(Bouri et al., 2017)	2017	115	19.17	Oil price speculations; Stock price and Exchange rate prices; Modified CAPM
	(Cifarelli & Paladino, 2010)	2010	172	13.23	
	(Bouchaud et al., 2004)	2004	230	12.11	
	(Oberndorfer, 2009)	2009	153	10.93	

Source: Biblioshiny using data from Scopus.

Factor Model, found that the unique returns of energy stocks are influenced by fluctuations in WTI oil prices.(Ma et al., 2019).

Cluster 2 (Left) includes five research papers with a C/Y > 10 and focuses on the effect of the inflation rate on the financial sector and stock market returns. A surge in the inflation rate affects the financial sector's ability to allocate resources effectively. Boyd et al. (2001b) identified a strong negative relation between inflation rate and stock market returns, especially in banking companies. Inflation exceeding 15% led to a sharp fall in financial sector performance (Liu & Serletis, 2022). Using the GARCH model on daily stock returns, Flannery and Protopapadakis (2002b) have identified six macro variables that can affect the stock price. Three macro variables, CPI, PPI, and Monetary Aggregate, are nominal macro variables, and the Balance of Trade, Housing Starts, and Employment Reports are three real macro variables. Moving to financial structure, GDP reflects a significantly positive impact on high return on average assets (ROAA), whereas inflation reflects a negative impact (Kosmidou, 2008).

Cluster 3 (Right) includes four research papers with a C/Y > 10 and emphasizes the effect of future expectations and speculation on volatility in the stock market. The volatility in stock prices in the Indian stock market has been identified as being due to future expectations in the prices of gold and oil and reflected a significant positive relation (Bouri et al., 2017). While assessing the speculation effect of oil price dynamics, Cifarelli and Paladino (2010) have identified, using CAPM, that oil price shift speculations are negatively related to stock prices and forex the exchange rate. Assuming the univariate GARCH model, the risk premium is a function of oil price volatility. Using the tri-variate GARCH Model, oil price dynamics are associated with volatility in the stock market and exchange rate behavior.

Co-occurrence Network

The co-occurrences of two keywords signify the occurrence of both keywords in the title, abstract, or keyword list in the number of publications. Each nod represents a term, and the shade of the nods represents the cluster. The size of a node specifies the number of publications in which the corresponding term is used in their title or abstract (van Eck & Waltman, 2014). Fig. 12 shows a co-occurrence network extracted using indexed keywords in VOSviewer and grouped in four clusters. The cluster in the lower left area consists of macroeconomic variable terms like inflation, interest rate, exchange rate, economic growth, etc. The cluster located in the upper area and consists of countries like the United States, Japan, North America, Europe, Eurasia, and Germany. The next cluster is located in the lower right area of the visualization. It consists of Energy sector impacts like Oil Prices, Price dynamics, Oil production, and Oil price shocks in India and Turkey. Finally, the other cluster, which includes analytical techniques like regression analysis, VAR modeling, numerical models, uncertainty analysis, risk assessment models, and empirical analysis, is shown to be the hub of the co-occurrence network. The impact of oil dynamics on the stock market in India and the UK is closely monitored. Other macroeconomic factors like monetary policy, the

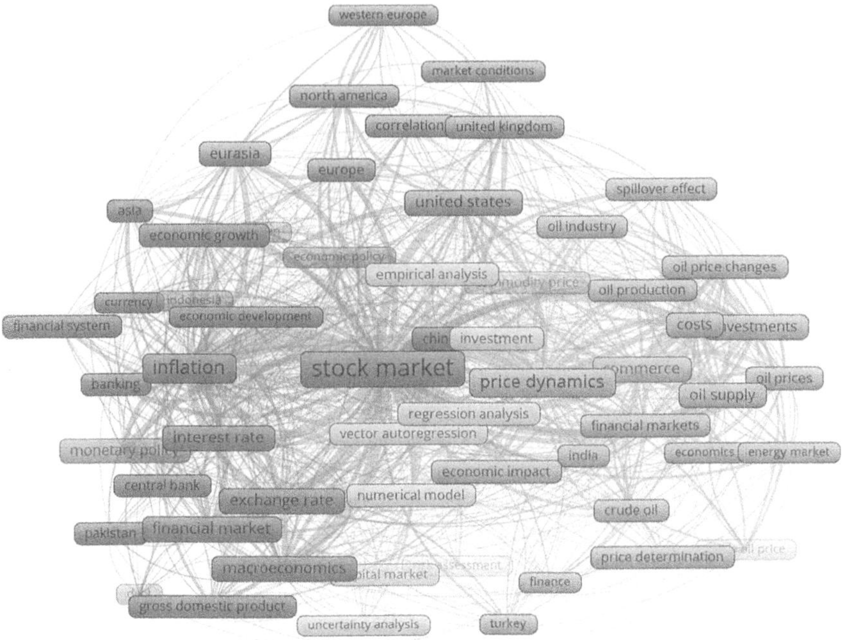

Fig. 12. Co-occurrence Network. *Source*: Biblioshiny using data from Scopus.

exchange rate, and interest rates also impact the stock market. According to the co-occurrence network, inflation and the stock markets in Eurasia and the United States are strongly correlated.

Thematic Map

The conceptual framework of thematic analysis employs two core metrics: "density" and "centrality," graphically represented on the vertical and horizontal axes, respectively. "Centrality" quantifies the level of interrelation among diverse thematic areas, while "density" gauges the intra-cluster cohesion among nodes (Agbo et al., 2021; Esfahani et al., 2019). These metrics serve as barometers for assessing specific thematic zones' significance and developmental maturity. The thematic landscape is compartmentalized into four sub-categories, designated as Q1–Q4. Q1 is identified as the motor theme, which acts as the primary driver, whereas Q2 represents a specialized niche theme intricately linked to the primary theme. Q3 signifies either nascent or waning in relevance, and Q4 embodies foundational and critically important themes for the progression of the research domain. Fig. 13 offers a graphical delineation of these research themes, anchored by centrality (indicative of thematic importance) and density (reflective of thematic development) (Aria et al., 2022).

Themes such as "stock market" and "economic growth" are seen in Q1 and identified as well-developed and driving forces of the leading research topic. High centrality and density represent a close association between the stock market

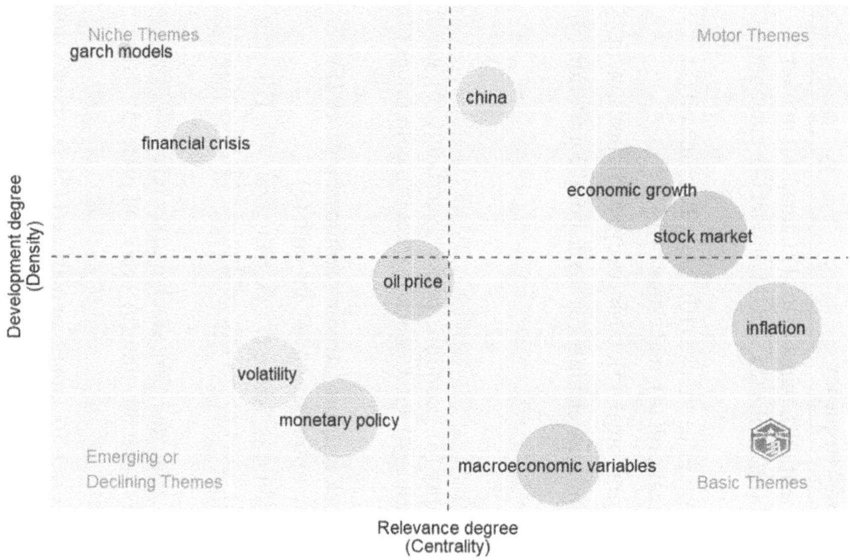

Thematic map: Q1 contains the main theme, Q2 contains highly developed and specialized themes building ties with the leading theme; Q3 contains disappearing or emerging themes; Q4 consists of foundational and transversal themes

Fig. 13. Thematic Map. *Source*: Biblioshiny using data from Scopus.

and economic growth, which are the basics and are very important for the field's development. We have applied a minimum frequency of 5 in "biblioshiny" software using R. "Inflation" in Q4 is represented as a "basic component" which is necessary for the development of studying the relationship between "economic growth" and "stock market." This finding suggests that "financial crises" in Q2 is a potential topic that needs to be more connected to studying the impact on the stock market. Q3 shows two emerging themes, i.e., "oil price" and "monetary policy." While comparing both, the thematic map reflects high density and centrality in the case of "Oil price" in comparison to "monetary policy," which reflects "oil price" as a factor, which is an emerging theme swiftly to study the effects on the stock market. The thematic analysis suggests that more research on financial crises and monetary policy is needed as independent variables to study the stock market index as the dependent variable.

Table 12 depicts that progressive research has been conducted in the context of the "Stock market" to identify "Economic growth" where the effect of moderating variables such as "inflation," "FDI," "Oil price impact," and "financial crises" is rigorously explored. Oil price shock as a dependent variable identifying the impact of certain factors such as COVID-19 (Victor et al., 2021), gold prices, and cryptocurrency (Sami & Abdallah, 2020) are emerging research areas. Similarly, research on inflation as a dependent variable by studying the impact of monetary policy, interest rate, capital structure, exchange rate, and fiscal policy is also eye-catching in the recent scenario. Some studies have identified the interdependence of variables like oil prices and inflation and their impact on the stock market (Kim & Lin, 2013; Ma et al., 2019).

Table 12. Thematic Maps: Keywords and Themes.

Main indicators	Theme	Keywords' frequency
Economic growth	*Motor Theme*	Economic growth (22), financial development (19), panel data (17), financial market (16), stock market development (15), FDI (6), banks (5), ARDL model (4), emerging economies (4)
Stock market	*Motor Theme*	Stock market (97), macroeconomics (12), oil price shocks (10), ardl (9), crude oil (7), India (7), conditional volatility (5), nonlinear ardl (4), real estate (4)
China	*Motor Theme*	China (7), asset pricing (6), 5 15(5), structural break (5), business cycle (3), investment (3)
Financial crises	*Highly developed and isolated themes*	Financial crises (10), contagion (4), economic uncertainty (3) stock-bond correlation (3)
GARCH models	*Highly developed and isolated themes*	Garch model (3)
Oil price	*Emerging theme*	Oil price (55), Turkey (10), Granger causality (8), economic policy uncertainty (6), garch Model (5), quantile regression (5), forecasting (4), GCC stock market (4), gold prices (4), macro economy (4)
Volatility	*Emerging theme*	Volatility (19), COVID-19 (9), gold(6), stock return(6), trading volume(6), garch (5), hedge (5), investor sentiments (4), portfolio optimisation (4), bit-coin (3)
Monetary policy	*Emerging theme*	Monetary policy (38), interest rates (9), capital structure (7), exchange rate (7), Pakistan (7), stock market index (7), fiscal policy (6), asset prices (5), gold prices (4), quantitative easing (4)
Inflation	*Basic theme*	Inflation (60), the stock price (27), an exchange rate (26), stock market returns (20), inflation rate (11), interest rate (11), market capitalization (6), crude oil price (5), fisher effect (5), overreaction (5)
Macroeconomic variables	*Basic theme*	Macro-economic variables (32), stocks return (30), emerging markets (16), co-integration (12), garch (12), macroeconomic factor (8), vector error correction model (6), causality (5), oil shocks (4)

Source: Biblioshiny using data from Scopus.

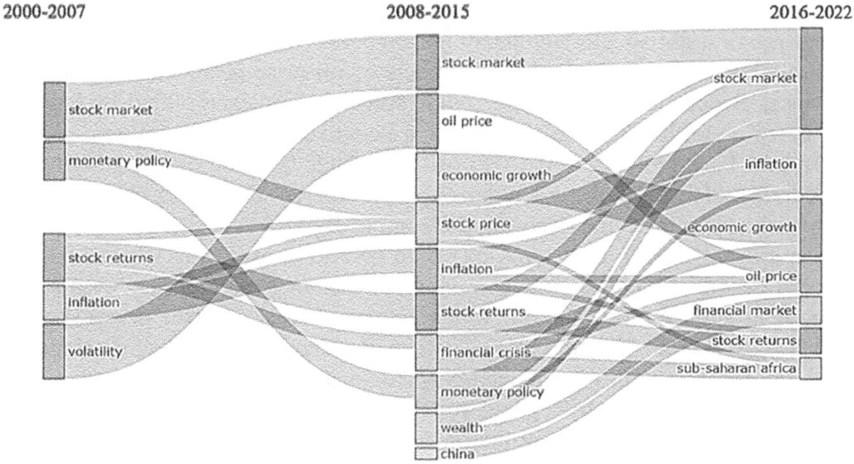

Fig. 14. Thematic Evaluation. *Source*: Biblioshiny using data from Scopus.

Thematic Evolution

Fig. 14 shows the theme development using the Sankey diagram over three-time phases, i.e. (2007–2007), (2008–2015), and (2016–2022). The Sankey diagram shows different themes and their connections over the period (Aria et al., 2020; Xiao et al., 2022). Every box on the map reflects a theme, and the box's size denotes the theme's proportional frequency occurrence (Abhishek & Srivastava, 2021).

From an overall perspective, it can be seen in Fig. 14 that volatility, monetary policy, and stock return were identified as driving forces in the stock market from 2000 to 2007. However, from 2008 to 2015, a shift in the variable has been identified affecting the stock market. The themes that have been explored the most are oil price shock and the stock market effect. Other variables, such as economic growth, exchange rate, and financial crises, were also examined during the same period. Further, changes in stock market dynamics have been observed, highlighting that gold prices, inflation rates, and geopolitical instability have emerged as key market forces from 2016 to 2022. However, the economic bubble in the stock market that developed during the COVID-19 pandemic has become a significant market force, influencing investor behavior and market volatility.

Findings and Discussion

Our bibliometric scrutiny delved into the multifaceted relationship between inflation, oil price shocks, and stock returns by rigorously reviewing extant scholarly contributions. The corpus of literature in this domain is extensive and intricate, presenting an array of inconsistent outcomes. Numerous investigations have probed the influence of inflation on stock returns. For instance, Mishkin and Serletis (2011) discerned a detrimental impact of inflation on stock yields, whereas Rashid Sabri (2004) concluded that inflation and stock returns are positively correlated.

Conversely, specific inquiries like those by Zeren and Gürsoy (2022) reported an absence of a statistically significant liaison between inflation and stock returns. A parallel divergence concerning the effects of oil price perturbations on stock returns is evident in the literature. While some studies, exemplified by Cunado and Perez de Gracia (2014b), argue for a negative correlation, others, such as Kilian and Park (2009), attest to a positive linkage between oil price shifts and stock returns. However, some scholars, notably Apergis and Miller (2009), exhibit ambivalent outcomes, underscoring the complexity of these relationships.

The journal *Energy Economics* has been pivotal in exploring various factors, including economic conditions, company performance, geopolitical events, and changes in supply and demand, which influence stock market prices. Energy markets covering oil, gas, and electricity can also significantly affect stock prices, especially for companies in the energy sector or those heavily reliant on energy inputs (Aloui et al., 2014; Regnier, 2007). Increases in energy prices can inflate production costs and shrink profits for some firms, causing their stock prices to fall. Conversely, companies that produce or distribute energy may benefit from higher prices, leading to higher stock prices (Boyer & Filion, 2007; Sun et al., 2020). In addition, changes in energy prices can also affect investor sentiment and market expectations, which can further impact stock prices. Rising oil prices may signal stronger global demand or geopolitical risks, which can cause investors to become more cautious or uncertain about the economic outlook. The highest locally cited model proposed by Apergis and Miller (2009) identified variables such as exchange rates, interest rates, and durable consumer spending, which eventually prove to be explanatory predictors of stock market returns. Whereas Basher and Sadorsky (2006) pioneer globally cited paper identified that the beta of oil price has a significant positive effect only in rising markets.

The thematic map analysis provides us with the driving theme as the rationale behind the economic growth of emerging economies. It identifies stock market development and foreign direct investment as significant keywords. Thematic evaluation provides driving variables in the stock market from 2000 to 2007 and a shift of variables from 2008 to 2015 that affect volatility in the stock market. Changes in stock market dynamics have been observed, indicating that from 2016 to 2022, gold prices, inflation rates, and geopolitical instability emerged as key market forces. Additionally, the economic bubble that developed in the stock market during the COVID-19 pandemic has become a significant influence, affecting investor behavior and market volatility.

The co-occurrences network grouped the indexed keywords into four clusters. The highlighted red cluster consists of macroeconomic variables studied, such as inflation, interest rate, exchange rate, and economic growth concerning the stock market return. The lower right cluster consists of energy sector impacts like Oil prices, Price dynamics, Oil production, and Oil price shocks on stock returns in India and Turkey. The left cluster identified the countries of significant research, which are the United States, Japan, North America, Europe, Eurasia, and Germany in the subject theme. Finally, the last cluster includes analysis techniques like regression analysis, VAR model, numerical model, uncertainty analysis, risk assessment model, and empirical analysis.

Overall, the findings of the studies are mixed, and it is difficult to draw a definitive conclusion on the impact of inflation and oil price shocks on stock returns. However, several studies have highlighted the importance of considering other variables, such as interest rates, exchange rates, and macroeconomic factors, in analyzing the relationship between these variables. Additionally, the impact of inflation and oil price shocks on stock returns may vary depending on the time duration, country, and industry being analyzed. Therefore, further research is needed to understand the complex relationship between these variables.

Future Research Direction

Current literature has established a foundational understanding of how inflation, oil price fluctuations, and stock returns interact. However, the dynamic nature of global economies calls for further research. Future studies could focus on specific timeframes or major global events to examine if these relationships change during economic highs and lows or geopolitical crises. Industry-specific analyses can offer nuanced insights, especially for sectors like aviation and transportation highly affected by oil prices. As the global focus shifts toward sustainable energy, studying how this transition alters traditional correlations between oil prices and stock performance is imperative. Ongoing research is essential for academics, policymakers, and investors.

Conclusion

The relationship between inflation, oil price shocks, and stock returns remains multifaceted, with varied findings across different studies. While some research underscores the negative impact of inflation and oil price volatility on stock returns, others present a positive or neutral correlation. Key factors such as economic conditions, company performance, geopolitical events, and the nuanced dynamics of energy markets further complicate the interpretation. Diverse methodologies, ranging from regression analysis to VAR models, have been employed to understand this relationship across nations and time frames. Thematic evaluations have also identified evolving market forces, including the increasing significance of elements like gold prices and geopolitical instability. The co-occurrences network mapping out clusters of related themes further emphasizes the intricacy of this subject. Thus, while there's a wealth of information and findings to draw upon, the definitive impact of inflation and oil price shocks on stock returns is still not concretely established, necessitating further nuanced and comprehensive research in the future.

References

Abhishek, & Srivastava, M. (2021). Mapping the influence of influencer marketing: A bibliometric analysis. *Marketing Intelligence and Planning*, *39*(7), 979–1003. https://doi.org/10.1108/MIP-03-2021-0085/FULL/XML

Agbo, F. J., Oyelere, S. S., Suhonen, J., & Tukiainen, M. (2021). Scientific production and thematic breakthroughs in smart learning environments: A bibliometric analysis. *Smart Learning Environments*, *8*(1), 1–25. https://doi.org/10.1186/S40561-020-00145-4/FIGURES/12

Aktürk, H. (2016). Do stock returns provide a good hedge against inflation? An empirical assessment using Turkish data during periods of structural change. *International Review of Economics and Finance*, *45*, 230–246. https://doi.org/10.1016/j.iref.2016.06.002

Aloui, R., Aïssa, M. S. ben, Hammoudeh, S., & Nguyen, D. K. (2014). Dependence and extreme dependence on crude oil and natural gas prices with applications to risk management. *Energy Economics*, *42*, 332–342. https://doi.org/10.1016/J.ENECO.2013.12.005

Apergis, N., & Miller, S. M. (2009). Do structural oil market shocks affect stock prices? *Energy Economics*, *31*(4), 569–575. https://doi.org/10.1016/j.eneco.2009.03.001

Aria, M., Cuccurullo, C., D'aniello, L., Misuraca, M., & Spano, M. (2022). Thematic analysis as a new culturomic tool: The social media coverage on COVID-19 pandemic in Italy. *Sustainability*, *14*(6), 3643. https://doi.org/10.3390/SU14063643

Aria, M., Misuraca, M., & Spano, M. (2020). Mapping the evolution of social research and data science on 30 years of social indicators research. *Social Indicators Research*, *149*(3), 803–831. https://doi.org/10.1007/S11205-020-02281-3

Arouri, M. E. H., Jouini, J., & Nguyen, D. K. (2012). On the impacts of oil price fluctuations on European equity markets: Volatility spillover and hedging effectiveness. *Energy Economics*, *34*(2), 611–617. https://doi.org/10.1016/J.ENECO.2011.08.009

Al-Ansi, A. M., Garad, A., & Ryabtsev, V. (2024). Intelligent risk analysis of investment projects in the extractive industry. *Journal of Industrial Intelligence*, *2*(1), 42–53.

Badeeb, R. A., & Lean, H. H. (2018). Asymmetric impact of oil price on Islamic sectoral stocks. *Energy Economics*, *71*, 128–139. https://doi.org/10.1016/j.eneco.2017.11.012

Balcilar, M., Cakan, E., & Gupta, R. (2017). Does US news impact Asian emerging markets? Evidence from nonparametric causality-in-quantiles test. *North American Journal of Economics and Finance*, *41*, 32–43. https://doi.org/10.1016/j.najef.2017.03.009

Basher, S. A., & Sadorsky, P. (2006). Oil price risk and emerging stock markets. *Global Finance Journal*, *17*(2), 224–251. https://doi.org/10.1016/j.gfj.2006.04.001

Bashir, M. F. (2022). Oil price shocks, stock market returns, and volatility spillovers: A bibliometric analysis and its implications. *Environmental Science and Pollution Research*, *29*(16), 22809–22828. https://doi.org/10.1007/s11356-021-18314-4

Bekaert, G., & Engstrom, E. (2010). Inflation and the stock market: Understanding the "Fed Model." *Journal of Monetary Economics*, *57*(3), 278–294. https://doi.org/10.1016/j.jmoneco.2010.02.004

Boubaker, H., & Raza, S. A. (2017). A wavelet analysis of mean and volatility spillovers between oil and BRICS stock markets. *Energy Economics*, *64*, 105–117. https://doi.org/10.1016/j.eneco.2017.01.026

Bouchaud, J.-P., Gefen, Y., Potters, M., & Wyart, M. (2004). Fluctuations and response in financial markets: The subtle nature of 'random' price changes. *Quantitative Finance*, *4*(2), 176–190. https://doi.org/10.1080/14697680400000022

Bouri, E., Jain, A., Biswal, P. C., & Roubaud, D. (2017). Cointegration and nonlinear causality amongst gold, oil, and the Indian stock market: Evidence from implied volatility indices. *Resources Policy*, *52*, 201–206. https://doi.org/10.1016/j.resourpol.2017.03.003

Boyd, J. H., Levine, R., & Smith, B. D. (2001). The impact of inflation on financial sector performance. *Journal of Monetary Economics*, *47*(2), 221–248. https://doi.org/10.1016/S0304-3932(01)00049-6

Boyer, M. M., & Filion, D. (2007). Common and fundamental factors in stock returns of Canadian oil and gas companies. *Energy Economics*, *29*(3), 428–453. https://doi.org/10.1016/J.ENECO.2005.12.003

Bradford, S. C., Shera, J. H., & Egan, M. E. (1953). *By S.C.Bradford; With an introduction by J.H. Shera and M.E.Egan* (2nd ed). Lockwood Lond. https://doi.org/https://nla.gov.au/nla.cat-vn2375752

Chen, Q., & Gong, Y. (2019). The economic sources of China's CSI 300 spot and futures volatilities before and after the 2015 stock market crisis. *International Review of Economics and Finance*, *64*, 102–121. https://doi.org/10.1016/j.iref.2019.05.017

Chevallier, J. (2009). Carbon futures and macroeconomic risk factors: A view from the EU ETS. *Energy Economics*, *31*(4), 614–625. https://doi.org/10.1016/j.eneco.2009.02.008

Christou, C., Gabauer, D., & Gupta, R. (2020). Time-Varying impact of uncertainty shocks on macroeconomic variables of the United Kingdom: Evidence from over 150 years of monthly data. *Finance Research Letters*, *37*. https://doi.org/10.1016/j.frl.2019.101363

Cifarelli, G., & Paladino, G. (2010). Oil price dynamics and speculation. A multivariate financial approach. *Energy Economics*, *32*(2), 363–372. https://doi.org/10.1016/j.eneco.2009.08.014

Citation Analysis of Scientific Journals. (2005). *Citation analysis in research evaluation* (pp. 91–105). https://doi.org/10.1007/1-4020-3714-7_6

Cunado, J., & Perez de Gracia, F. (2014). Oil price shocks and stock market returns Evidence for some European countries. *Energy Economics*, *42*, 365–377. https://doi.org/10.1016/J.ENECO.2013.10.017

Díaz, A., & Jareño, F. (2013). Inflation news and stock returns: Market direction and flow-through ability. *Empirical Economics*, *44*(2), 775–798. https://doi.org/10.1007/s00181-012-0555-7

Erlingsson, C., & Brysiewicz, P. (2017). A hands-on guide to doing content analysis. *African Journal of Emergency Medicine*, *7*(3), 93–99. https://doi.org/10.1016/J.AFJEM.2017.08.001

Esfahani, H. J., Tavasoli, K., & Jabbarzadeh, A. (2019). Big data and social media: A scientometrics analysis. *Undefined*, *3*(3), 145–164. https://doi.org/10.5267/J.IJDNS.2019.2.007

Flannery, M. J., & Protopapadakis, A. A. (2002). Macroeconomic factors do influence aggregate stock returns. *Review of Financial Studies*, *15*(3), 751–782. https://doi.org/10.1093/rfs/15.3.751

Godil, D. I., Sarwat, S., Sharif, A., & Jermsittiparsert, K. (2020). How do oil prices, gold prices, uncertainty and risk impact Islamic and conventional stocks? Empirical evidence from QARDL technique. *Resources Policy*, *66*. https://doi.org/10.1016/j.resourpol.2020.101638

Hamilton, J. D. (2009). *Causes and Consequences of the Oil Shock of 2007-08*. 2007–2015. https://doi.org/10.3386/W15002

Hanieh, A. (2020). COVID-19 and global oil markets. *Canadian Journal of Development Studies*, *42*(1–2), 101–108. https://doi.org/10.1080/02255189.2020.1821614

Hirsch, J. E. (2005). An index to quantify an individual's scientific research output. *Proceedings of the National Academy of Sciences of the United States of America*, *102*(46), 16569–16572. https://doi.org/10.1073/pnas.0507655102

Hsing, Y. (2013). Effects of fiscal policy and monetary policy on the stock market in Poland. *Economies*, *1*(3), 19–25. https://doi.org/10.3390/economies1030019

Hsing, Y., Zee, S. M. L., Budden, M. C., & Cope III, R. F. (2012). Impacts of the aggregate economic and financial conditions on output in an emerging economy. *Journal of Applied Business Research*, *28*(2), 261–268. https://doi.org/10.19030/jabr.v28i2.6847

Joshipura, M., & Lamba, A. (2022). Asymmetric impact of Russia-Ukraine war on global stock markets. *SSRN Electronic Journal*. https://doi.org/10.2139/SSRN.4273419

Kayalar, D. E., Küçüközmen, C. C., & Selcuk-Kestel, A. S. (2017). The impact of crude oil prices on financial market indicators: Copula approach. *Energy Economics*, *61*, 162–173. https://doi.org/10.1016/j.eneco.2016.11.016

Khalid, U., Okafor, L. E., & Shafiullah, M. (2020). The effects of economic and financial crises on international tourist flows: A cross-country analysis. *Journal of Travel Research*, *59*(2), 315–334. https://doi.org/10.1177/0047287519834360
Kilian, L., & Park, C. (2009). The impact of oil price shocks on the U.S. stock market. *International Economic Review*, *50*(4), 1267–1287. https://doi.org/10.1111/J.1468-2354.2009.00568.X
Kim, D.-H., & Lin, S.-C. (2013). Interrelationships among banks, stock markets and economic growth: An empirical investigation. *Applied Economics*, *45*(31), 4385–4394. https://doi.org/10.1080/00036846.2013.786165
Kosmidou, K. (2008). The determinants of banks' profits in Greece during the period of EU financial integration. *Managerial Finance*, *34*(3), 146–159. https://doi.org/10.1108/03074350810848036
Li, B., & Xu, Z. (2022). A comprehensive bibliometric analysis of financial innovation. *Economic Research-Ekonomska Istrazivanja*, *35*(1), 367–390. https://doi.org/10.1080/1331677X.2021.1893203
Lin, B., Wesseh, P. K., & Appiah, M. O. (2014). Oil price fluctuation, volatility spillover and the Ghanaian equity market: Implication for portfolio management and hedging effectiveness. *Energy Economics*, *42*, 172–182. https://doi.org/10.1016/j.eneco.2013.12.017
Liu, J., & Serletis, A. (2022). The complex relationship between inflation and equity returns. *Journal of Economic Studies*, *49*(1), 159–184. https://doi.org/10.1108/JES-10-2020-0526
Ma, Y.-R., Zhang, D., Ji, Q., & Pan, J. (2019). Spillovers between oil and stock returns in the US energy sector: Does idiosyncratic information matter? *Energy Economics*, *81*, 536–544. https://doi.org/10.1016/j.eneco.2019.05.003
Mishkin, F. S., & Serletis, A. (2011). *The economics of money, banking and financial markets* (4th Canadian ed.) Pearson.
Mohanty, S. K., Nandha, M., Turkistani, A. Q., & Alaitani, M. Y. (2011). Oil price movements and stock market returns: Evidence from Gulf Cooperation Council (GCC) countries. *Global Finance Journal*, *22*(1), 42–55. https://doi.org/10.1016/J.GFJ.2011.05.004
Mollick, A. V, & Assefa, T. A. (2013). U.S. stock returns and oil prices: The tale from daily data and the 2008-2009 financial crisis. *Energy Economics*, *36*, 1–18. https://doi.org/10.1016/j.eneco.2012.11.021
Naifar, N., & Al Dohaiman, M. S. (2013a). Nonlinear analysis among crude oil prices, stock markets' return and macroeconomic variables. *International Review of Economics and Finance*, *27*, 416–431. https://doi.org/10.1016/j.iref.2013.01.001
Naifar, N., & Al Dohaiman, M. S. (2013b). Nonlinear analysis among crude oil prices, stock markets' return and macroeconomic variables. *International Review of Economics & Finance*, *27*, 416–431. https://doi.org/10.1016/J.IREF.2013.01.001
Novarlić, B., & Đurić, P. (2024). Enhancing comprehensive waste management in transition economies through green logistics: A case study of Bosnia and Herzegovina. *Journal of Intelligent Management Decision*, *3*, 42–55.
Oberndorfer, U. (2009). EU emission allowances and the stock market: Evidence from the electricity industry. *Ecological Economics*, *68*(4), 1116–1126. https://doi.org/10.1016/j.ecolecon.2008.07.026
Papapetrou, E. (2001). Oil price shocks, stock market, economic activity and employment in Greece. *Energy Economics*, *23*(5), 511–532. https://doi.org/10.1016/S0140-9883(01)00078-0
Philips, A. S., Akinseye, A. B., & Oduyemi, G. O. (2022). Do exchange rate and inflation rate matter in the cyclicality of oil price and stock returns? *Resources Policy*, *78*, 102882.
Pradhan, R. P., Arvin, M. B., & Ghoshray, A. (2015). The dynamics of economic growth, oil prices, stock market depth, and other macroeconomic variables: Evidence from

the G-20 countries. *International Review of Financial Analysis*, *39*, 84–95. https://doi.org/10.1016/j.irfa.2015.03.006

Rashid Sabri, N. (2004). Stock return volatility and market crisis in emerging economies. *Review of Accounting and Finance*, *3*(3), 59–83. https://doi.org/10.1108/EB043408

Reboredo, J. C., & Rivera-Castro, M. A. (2014). Wavelet-based evidence of the impact of oil prices on stock returns. *International Review of Economics & Finance*, *29*, 145–176. https://doi.org/10.1016/J.IREF.2013.05.014

Reboredo, J. C., & Ugolini, A. (2016). Quantile dependence of oil price movements and stock returns. *Energy Economics*, *54*, 33–49. https://doi.org/10.1016/j.eneco.2015.11.015

Regnier, E. (2007). Oil and energy price volatility. *Energy Economics*, *29*(3), 405–427. https://doi.org/10.1016/J.ENECO.2005.11.003

Rossetto, D. E., Bernardes, R. C., Borini, F. M., & Gattaz, C. C. (2018). Structure and evolution of innovation research in the last 60 years: review and future trends in the field of business through the citations and co-citations analysis. *Scientometrics*, *115*(3), 1329–1363. https://doi.org/10.1007/S11192-018-2709-7

Salisu, A. A., & Isah, K. O. (2017). Revisiting the oil price and stock market nexus: A nonlinear Panel ARDL approach. *Economic Modelling*, *66*, 258–271. https://doi.org/10.1016/j.econmod.2017.07.010

Salisu, A. A., Swaray, R., & Oloko, T. F. (2019). Improving the predictability of the oil–US stock nexus: The role of macroeconomic variables. *Economic Modelling*, *76*, 153–171. https://doi.org/10.1016/j.econmod.2018.07.029

Sami, M., & Abdallah, W. (2020). How does the cryptocurrency market affect the stock market performance in the MENA region? *Journal of Economic and Administrative Sciences*, *37*(4), 741–753. https://doi.org/10.1108/JEAS-07-2019-0078

Sharifi, A. (2020). Urban Resilience Assessment: Mapping Knowledge Structure and Trends. *Sustainability*, *12*(15), 5918. https://doi.org/10.3390/SU12155918

Sun, C., Zhan, Y., & Du, G. (2020). Can value-added tax incentives of the new energy industry increase a firm's profitability? Evidence from financial data of China's listed companies. *Energy Economics*, *86*, 104654. https://doi.org/10.1016/J.ENECO.2019.104654

Surwase, G., Atomic, B., Sagar, A., Atomic, B., Kademani, B. S., Atomic, B., & Bhanumurthy, K. (2011). Co-citation analysis: An overview. *BOSLA National Conference Proceedings, CDAC, September*, 9. ISBN: 935050007-8.

Tiwari, A. K., Dar, A. B., Bhanja, N., Arouri, M., & Teulon, F. (2015). Stock returns and inflation in Pakistan. *Economic Modelling*, *47*, 23–31. https://doi.org/10.1016/J.ECONMOD.2014.12.043

Tripathi, M., Kumar, S., Sonker, S. K., & Babbar, P. (2018). Occurrence of author keywords and keywords plus in social sciences and humanities research: A preliminary study. *COLLNET Journal of Scientometrics and Information Management*, *12*(2), 215–232. https://doi.org/10.1080/09737766.2018.1436951

van Eck, N. J., & Waltman, L. (2014). Visualising bibliometric networks. In *Measuring scholarly impact*. https://doi.org/10.1007/978-3-319-10377-8_13

Victor, V., Karakunnel, J. J., Loganathan, S., & Meyer, D. F. (2021). From a recession to the COVID-19 pandemic: Inflation–unemployment comparison between the UK and India. *Economies 2021*, *9*(2), 73. https://doi.org/10.3390/ECONOMIES9020073

Von Ungern-Sternberg, S. (2000). Bradford's law in the context of information provision. *Scientometrics*, *49*(1), 161–186. https://doi.org/10.1023/A:1005669410627

Wang, Y., Wu, C., & Yang, L. (2013). Oil price shocks and stock market activities: Evidence from oil-importing and oil-exporting countries. *Journal of Comparative Economics*, *41*(4), 1220–1239. https://doi.org/10.1016/J.JCE.2012.12.004

Wardikar, V. G., & Gudadhe, V. P. (2013). Application of Bradford's law of scattering to the literature of library & information science: A study of doctoral theses citations submitted to the universities of Maharashtra, India. *Library Philosophy and Practice*.

Xiao, Z., Qin, Y., Xu, Z., Antucheviciene, J., & Zavadskas, E. K. (2022). The Journal Buildings: A Bibliometric Analysis (2011-2021). *Buildings*, *12*, 37. https://doi.org/10.3390/buildings12010037

Xie, J. (2020). Capital-market consequences of asymmetric output-price rigidities. *Journal of Monetary Economics*, *114*, 221–239. https://doi.org/10.1016/J.JMONECO.2019.03.009

Yerpude, S., Sood, K., & Grima, S. (2022). Blockchain-augmented digital supply chain management: A way to sustainable business. *Journal of Risk and Financial Management*, *16*(1), 7.

Zeren, F., & Gürsoy, S. (2022). The Nexus between wind energy consumption, economic growth and financial development: Evidence from panel causality and cointegration test with Fourier Function. *Technology and Economics of Smart Grids and Sustainable Energy*, *7*(1), 1–13. https://doi.org/10.1007/S40866-022-00155-W/FIGURES/1

Zhang, J., Yu, Q., Zheng, F., Long, C., Lu, Z., & Duan, Z. (2016). Comparing keywords plus of WOS and author keywords: A case study of patient adherence research. *Journal of the Association for Information Science and Technology*, *67*(4), 967–972. https://doi.org/10.1002/asi.23437

Zupic, I., & Čater, T. (2015). Bibliometric methods in management and organization. *Organisational Research Methods*, *18*(3), 429–472. https://doi.org/10.1177/1094428114562629

Chapter 6

Government Effectiveness in Pandemic Strategic Management: Evidence from Conflict-Affected Nations

Alhamzah Alnoor[a], Paiman Ahmad[b], Shwan Mohammed Mustafa[c], Md Imtiaz Mostafiz[d], Franklin Akosa[e] and XinYing Chew[a]

[a]*School of Computer Science, Universiti Sains Malaysia, Penang, Malaysia*
[b]*Law Department, University of Raparin, Ranya, Kurdistan Region, Iraq*
[c]*Hawler Medical University, Erbil, Kurdistan Region, Iraq*
[d]*School of Business, University of Leicester, UK*
[e]*School of Business and Law, Edith Cowan University Perth, Australia*

Abstract

Introduction: Based on the given experiences, many government institutions failed in their strategic management and planning for managing COVID-19. Meanwhile, when a crisis disrupts a system, institutions lose their direction and fail to make necessary responses.

Purpose: The current study highlighted the impact of social justice and modern governance in providing equitable healthcare services and dealing with crises during the COVID-19 pandemic in developing countries.

Methodology: Cross-country analyses were used based on captured secondary data. We evaluated several indices, including, for example, Crisis Index Indicators, Worldometers, and the Global Health Security (GHS) Index 2019.

Findings: According to the GHS (2019) data, public health service delivery equity was ineffective, socially unjust, and unfair treatment was experienced

Financial Landscape Transformation: Technological Disruptions, 103–129

doi:10.1108/978-1-83753-750-120251006

in the context of the conflict-affected countries. Most conflict-affected countries (Iraq, Nigeria, Afghanistan, and Venezuela) did not have guidelines or public reports committing to providing prioritized healthcare services to the public and healthcare workers. The experience of conflict-affected countries has shown that healthcare disparities still exist. While many governments in conflict-affected countries failed to give equitable access to healthcare services during the COVID-19 pandemic to the public.

Keywords: COVID-19; government effectiveness; social equity; health care; public service; conflict-affected countries

JEL Classifications: O17; P10; I 10; I1; I30

Introduction

Government institutions have reshaped public services due to the COVID-19 pandemic. Despite the harmful effects of the COVID-19 pandemic, the outbreak of the virus has demonstrated an urgent need to improve the quality and efficiency of public services. The recent pandemic disrupted public services for the public and private sectors and increased fear and uncertainty among institutions and individuals in society. Before the COVID-19 pandemic, conflict affected countries did not have a pandemic preparedness plan, and governments were not prepared and equipped to encounter and expect a pandemic ahead. Based on the evidence in the literature, health care policy is not aligned with social equity and human rights since failing to value all people equally is still an unachieved goal in the context of many developing countries, as Yamin (2009) articulated on the concept of equity as the equal worth of all human beings and equal opportunity for all human beings to possess certain rights. The issue of social equity has not been at the forefront of health policymaking in conflict-affected countries, while communities at large suffer from deep social and economic disparities. In addition to addressing equity as "oneness" to the public, where governments strive to make public service delivery efficiently fair to all people. Meanwhile, in conflict-affected countries, public services are generally more efficient and economical for some than others (Frederickson, 2015).

Governments paid attention to the link between institutional quality, public service, and crisis management. Each institution or organization in the public and private sectors has strategic planning in which uncertainties, threats, risks, and weaknesses are defined in advance, aiming to deal with emergencies when a crisis arises. Leadership and availability of resources affect strategic crisis management on many occasions. Moreover, strategic crisis management is associated with authority, legitimacy, and power, which may define how a crisis can be handled. According to the World Health Organization (WHO), the COVID-19 pandemic is a major crisis that has recorded millions of infections and deaths around the world. However, many countries have dealt with the recent epidemic wisely and restricted the spread and incidence of the disease (WHO, 2020).

Health institutions had a leading presence and role in dealing with and mitigating the harmful effects of COVID-19. However, health organizations face tangible challenges, represented by state failure, lack of stability, financial restrictions, necessary infrastructure, wars, and a lack of skilled human resources. Many developing countries, such as Iraq, Nigeria, and Afghanistan, consider the quality of service to be a question based on which the performance of government agencies and organizations with high capabilities in work is determined (Lagreid & Rykkja, 2019). According to Rothstein (2011), quality is related to the practices of governments on the quality of life of citizens. Therefore, internal factors related to state policies affect the quality of institutional services.

Strategic crisis management heavily depends on timely addressing the crisis and applying proper measures and methods to deal with its effects. Many scholars link crisis management to cognitive bases that leaders depend on in decision-making concerning a specific crisis. Moreover, leaders and managers in certain situations need to realize why a crisis happens. There are specific aspects of strategic crisis management for institutions or organizations to consider as fundamentals of crisis management. The first important one is the internal landscape of the organization, which forms strategic planning and crisis planning because many organizations still need to have strategic planning and crisis management strategies. Therefore, responding to a crisis is haphazard and temporal, as preventing it in such conditions is impossible; thus, organizations only try to mitigate the effects of a crisis. To conclude, Strategic crisis management matters for each institution and the stakeholders, as preventing a crisis leads to the team's success and the institution's image in the public sphere (Gephart et al., 2019).

Therefore, planning to manage crises in general and health crises in particular is considered an urgent need (Fagel, 2018). The current study seeks to study the effectiveness of governments in managing crises by achieving the following.

- Investigating the readiness of governments to manage conflicts and health crises.
- Studying the effectiveness of governments and countries in providing high-quality health services.
- Investigating the impact of conflict on health crisis management.

Theoretical and Empirical Review

According to Pierre and Peters (2019), government approaches and policies determine the effectiveness and efficiency of government services. Moreover, Hufty (2011) proposed four governance approaches, namely global governance, corporate governance, modern governance, and good governance. The World Bank has introduced an excellent theory of governance to explain how governments manage countries' social and economic resources for sustainable development (World Bank, 1992).

Modern Governance Theory

In a modern sense, governing is what governments do at different times and circumstances to manage people, resources and institutions (Capano et al., 2014). Moreover, in the modern governance theory (Castells, 1996; Hufty, 2011) argue that "the state has lost or delegated an increasing proportion of its power and competencies to various local, national, and international 'entities'." The State, for example, may not have the capacity to achieve the welfare of the people. Moreover, Hufty (2011) has suggested that some power and competencies may be delegated to various local, national, and international "entities to achieve effective governance." In addition, the performance of government and the institutions is determined by a few factors including economic, political, and cultural. In which for the conflict-affected countries political situation and conflict have devastated the government economic capacities and strengths. The effects of governance and system practices are reflected in the government performance of a specific country based on the quality of public good provisions such as schooling, mortality rate, education, and infrastructure, besides government should have an effective role in providing public service to meet the public needs (La Porta et al., 1999).

It must be established that in times of crisis, the modern governance approach is the best way to deal with any situation. The modern governance approach works effectively where the authorities, market forces, and networks collaborate and connect in times of crisis, as in the case of COVID-19. In this study, the central argument hinges on the fact that managing a pandemic effectively depends on the kind of governance approach in operation.

Institutions

Measuring public service delivery based on the quality of institutions, governance approaches and practices can determine the role of government in serving citizens. While in most developing countries measures of service delivery (MSDs), have not yet been practiced to address the challenges and shortcomings of service delivery. As MSDs can measure the main parts of public service delivery systems, with the outcomes government can improve the performance of the institutions in the public sector (La et al., 1999). Besides, the governance system affects service delivery where democratic governments play a better role in public service delivery compared to the other government practices. However, it should be remembered that there is no one-size-fits-all model of governance for all to follow as country circumstances and conditions differ (Bagenholm et al., 2021). Meanwhile, institutions in the public sector in the developing world though are significant and overstaffed, yet their performance is abysmal. It is not easy to receive quality care in the Middle East and most African countries, including parts of Asia and Latin America (World Bank, 2015). Moreover, the poor performance of institutions is pervasive because of intertwined factors such as lack of human capital, financial limitations, politics, and security factors.

In COVID-19, the resilience of the healthcare system and community response is fundamental to reducing the pandemic's adverse effects. Based on Mirsa (2020), the causes of crises are various, like failures and dysfunctions within the organization, external threats, and mismanagement by the tasked people. Regarding COVID-19 as a global health crisis, countries have encountered difficulties in understanding stages and communities in absorbing the effects. Thus, there have been problems from signal detection to preparation/prevention, containment/damage limitation, and recovery, where now in developing countries, reducing damages and recovery looks costly because of the other internal challenges that make people less committed to the government guide for mitigating the effects of COVID-19.

Conceptual Framework

The conceptual framework has been designed based on the theories and literature of this study. Fig. 1 highlights the conceptual framework of the study. We (*Authors) have argued that effective governance depends on how authorities, economic, and organized networks relate, and connect (institutions*) to formulate and implement policies that meet the needs of the current and future situations of the people.

Authorities: They are the government, powers, countries, public services, laws, bills, and regulations that control the affairs of the state. They are the operating machines of the state.

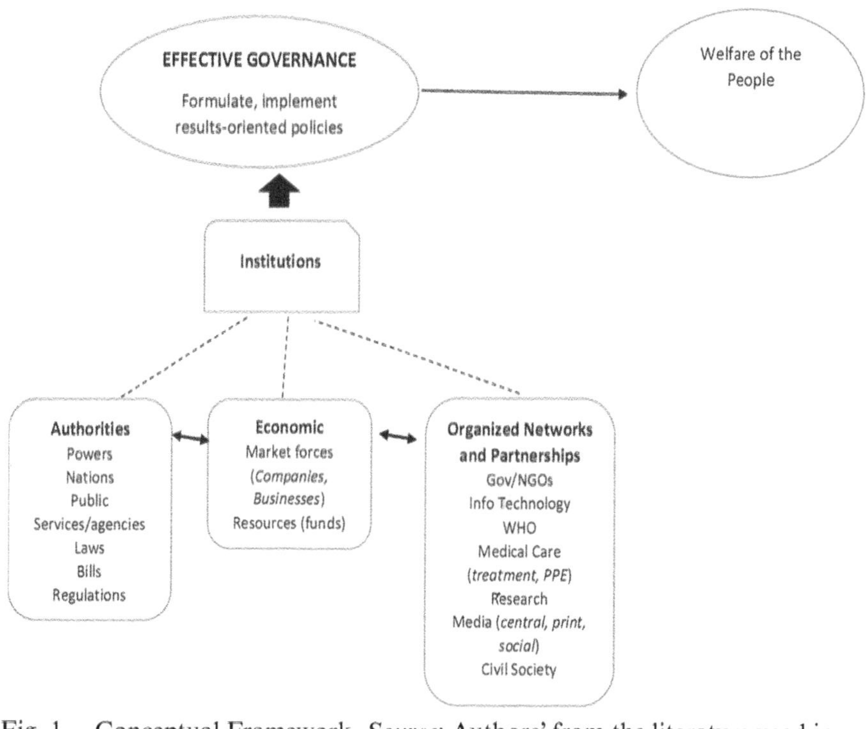

Fig. 1. Conceptual Framework. *Source*: Authors' from the literature used in this study.

Economic: Economic growth and development are hinged on economic forces, markets, businesses, and resources. This is where funds are generated to stair the affairs of the state.

Organized Networks and Partnerships: Refers to both external and internal supports that promote growth and development. This study's organized networks and partnerships are information technology, cooperation with governmental and non-governmental organizations (NGOs) such as WHO, UN, media, and research medical care groups.

To build strong institutions, which may lead to effective governance, authorities, economic and organized networks, and partnerships must ensure effective connections and collaborations.

Pandemic Management and Healthcare Responding During a Pandemic

The recent COVID-19 pandemic was a difficult experience for many governments around the world. However, the WHO played a leading role in dealing with the pandemic by directing countries to plan and confront such a crisis. Crisis planning mitigates the devastating effects of COVID-19 and reduces deaths and infections. Therefore, we must prepare for emergencies, prevent the spread of disease, investigate, and treat infections, research, and evaluate, and maintain basic services. The WHO aimed to increase government capabilities to manage health risks, provide resources and elements to manage the risks of disease spread, and enable the health sector to strengthen health aspects and issues to reduce health impacts and risks. As addressed governments are in charge of "delivering public service in primary health care and education" (La et al., 1999).

The COVID-19 pandemic has witnessed countries in the developing world only rush to plan and implement to mitigate the crisis while it peaks. The World Health Organization Guide (2009) indicates the importance of a whole-of-society approach to pandemic influenza preparedness, including the national government, health sector, civil society organizations, families, and individuals. According to Fagel (2018), during a pandemic, effective, transparent, and complete communication is fundamental as part of planning to mitigate the effects of a pandemic. Adding Crandall et al. (2014), an essential aspect of crisis management is effective communication with internal and external stakeholders. Moreover, a crisis generates a powerful sense of citizen commitment to know what is happening and what they should do to protect their interests (Boin et al., 2005).

It is worth mentioning that being ill-prepared to combat an outbreak results in the severity of the death cases, the number of infections, and the adverse effects. Based on the findings of this study, the death toll is high in Italy and the United States regardless of being better prepared for the COVID-19 pandemic, as both countries have a history of an epidemic and a pandemic. In contrast, factors including age, longevity, and other health conditions besides the high number of infections have resulted in death attributes. As noted, national preparedness is the key to successfully managing a pandemic. At the same time, developing countries, including *Iraq, Afghanistan, Nigeria, and Venezuela*, all have experienced national epidemics, public health infrastructure is inferior, and governments are ill-prepared to combat the COVID-19 outbreak. Under pressure, the healthcare system is limited in many countries even, including developed economies, the healthcare facilities are insufficient to cope with the number of infections; during COVID-19, countries suffered from providing sufficient healthcare service to all patients in some countries only acute cases have been admitted (Oshitani et al., 2008).

According to the Infectious Disease Vulnerability Index, countries of concern are conflict-affected ones, including Somalia (ranked 1), Central African Republic (ranked 2), and South Sudan (ranked 4), which all have similar challenges of political instability and compromised health systems. Based on the Ebola experience in 2014, a high vulnerability score alone does not necessarily mean a country is prone to a disease outbreak. Thus, it is suggested that policymakers focus on the most vulnerable countries; similar cases exist in other regions around the world, such as in the Middle East, Syria, Iraq, Yemen, and Afghanistan.

Notably, many factors influence preparedness and government response during an outbreak. Those key factors are well addressed in Fig. 2.

According to Fagel (2018), pandemics may come in waves, and successive planning and learning from previous waves are prerequisites for controlling them, which helps reduce the socioeconomic impacts of subsequent waves. Through the experiences of the COVID-19 pandemic, countries such as Iraq, Iran, Turkey, and other countries that have economic or political challenges are less prepared. Thus, resilience and response approaches are poor. As Wapling and Sellwood (2016) argue, why do we need to prepare? The core benefits of preparedness and response are saving lives and promptly restoring normality. On the other hand, lack of planning and appropriate response results in the loss of lives unnecessarily or negatively affected, the same as happens in Iraq, Syria, Iran, and many

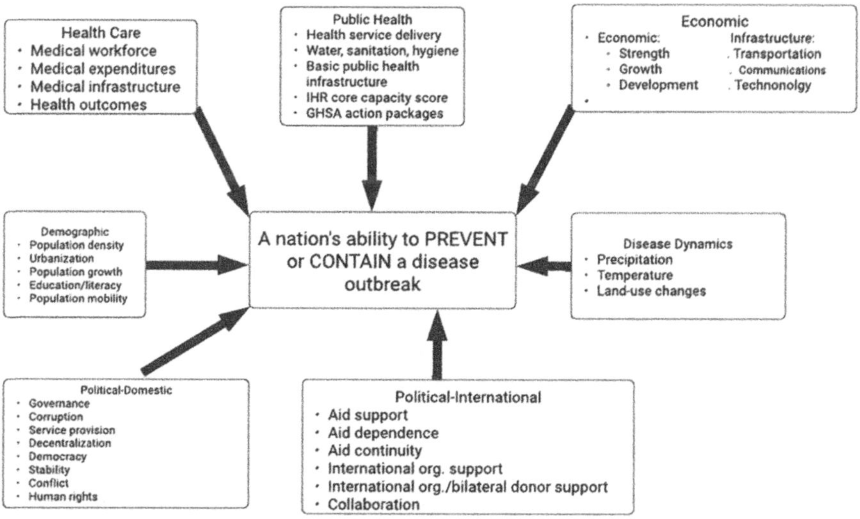

Fig. 2. Domains and Factors Associated with Disease Outbreak Vulnerability.
Source: Moore et al., 2016/RAND Report.

other countries. Furthermore, learning from previous experiences regarding public health emergencies, the emergency response capabilities are challenging as events, conditions, and contexts are unique (Stoto & Higdon, 2009).

Importantly, Hillyard (2000) considers the complexity of a crisis as a crucial factor for understanding its human response, as organizations barely operate well across various functional expertise or capabilities. Institute of Medicine (2007) emphasizes the importance of public understanding of how a disease is transmitted and the economic consequences of an epidemic that influence public response to the crisis.

Social Equity

This concept refers to the fairness, impartiality, and justice with which the management of institutions serves the public with their resources or benefits (Rothstein & Teorell, 2008). In the state of social equity, Scanlon (2017) has asserted that individuals within a specific society have equal liberties, rights, and status.

Some scholars have argued that social equity is not about equality. It is more about assessing the needs of people across society to provide them with access to the necessary opportunities and success. It addresses the disparities and barriers to individuals, systems, structures, and data to provide opportunities and success for individuals with needs in society.

Moreover, it must be stated that one of the major concerns of social equity is about access, not necessarily outcomes, as has also been suggested in similar studies (Manaugh et al., 2015).

Equity of What? How Public Health Service Is an Equity Issue

Equity in health is seen as the dearth of systematic disparities in health. Health equity is the absence of social injustice or injustice about health issues.

Braveman and Gruskin (2003), in their study, "Defining Equity in Health," indicated that the absence of systematic disparities in the significant social determinants of health between and among groups could be regarded as health equity. It must be noted that social justice and fairness can be interpreted and operationalized in several ways based on the purpose of your discussion or the indicators involved.

In this study, one of the objectives the researchers are unpacking is government effectiveness in public health service delivery in conflict-affected countries. The public health service issues the researchers investigated through the Global Health Security (GHS) Indicators (2019) were Public Health Effectiveness in Conflict-affected Countries, what Governments have done to restrict or prevent the pandemic, and how Conflict Influence Pandemic Management.

The Health Equity Model

In a recent study, Peterson et al. (2021), who employed the Health Equity Framework in their study, argued that current social determinants are ineffective in addressing health disparities, which may be difficult for practitioners to apply.

While the current public health strategies cannot reduce the disparities because the systems cannot acknowledge systematic antecedents of inequality. Therefore, there is a need for a clear framework to address health equity issues that can benefit health practitioners and researchers (Braveman & Gruskin, 2003; Hogan et al., 2018).

According to Peterson et al. (2021), the Health Equity Model describes ways that education and health results are shaped by development communications between people and their context. Health equity means having fair access and personal agency to opportunities and resources needed to undertake one's social, physical, and emotional well-being.

The Equity model has four primary constructs: relationships and networks, systems of power, individual factors, and physiological pathways.

Relationships and Networks

This focuses on the links with family, friends, partners, community, and workplaces that promote health equity through effective support systems.

Systems of Power

The construct examines policies, legislations, institutions, and attempts that advance health equity via access to opportunities and resources.

Individual Factors

To promote health equity, a person must respond to economic, social, and environmental conditions through different behaviors and attitudes.

Physiological Pathways

Factors that promote health equity when a person's physical, cognitive, and psychological abilities are maximized.

Healthcare Services During the Span of the COVID-19 Pandemic

During COVID-19, healthcare service in many countries was exhausted and challenged by the increasing demand for care for COVID-19 patients, while maintaining preventive and curative services were required for vulnerable populations, including children, older persons, individuals with chronic conditions, disabilities, and, in some countries, displaced people and migrants (World Health Organization, 2020). Personal and societal conditions have been raised regarding the healthcare system. Many countries in the developing world are worried about health crises because of the healthcare systems, and the capacity of the healthcare sector to respond to crises; if cases are taken from developing countries like Iraq, Syria, Sudan, Yemen, etc., each single country has various challenges, thus since the early stages of COVID-19 outbreak, government were unable to provide health services promptly, while in many other countries systems were able to maintain the delivery of essential health service regardless of the baseline burden of them (World Health Organization, 2020). Despite barriers, the COVID-19 burden, and other factors are essential regarding efficient and effective healthcare service delivery. Many countries have different public health and social measures policies, and their implementation depends on community commitment and government policies (World Health Organization, 2020).

Healthcare services are prioritized in many countries because each country and community has peculiar circumstances during COVID-19. A few novel issues emerged during COVID-19: Healthcare staff got treated and prepared quickly, governments have started financing healthcare services better than before the crisis, and communities have gone under high pressure but used to be committed to the public well-being. While it considers hospital readiness, case management, and continuity of essential health services in the context of the COVID-19 pandemic is prioritized. However, hospitals in the developing world have many challenges that restrict them from meeting their needs (World Health Organization Interim Guidance, 2020).

Considering the COVID-19 pandemic, healthcare operations have been disrupted and exhausted. Therefore, healthcare delivery has also changed. According to the CDC (2020), the COVID-19 pandemic has affected healthcare services in the United States in terms of access to respiratory care, deferring and delaying non-COVID-19 care, disruptions in the supply chain, Absenteeism among staff because of being ill or having caregiving responsibilities, also increase in mental health concerns. There are concerns regarding who gets primary health care during COVID-19; in the peak periods in Iraq, there have been many cases in which hospitals were unable to provide care, and healthcare staff have been exhausted not just because of the COVID-19 pandemic but further of the financial limitations, and lack of wages and salary reductions in some parts of the country.

What has been introduced to improve government response during COVID-19 is that healthcare service delivery is facilitated using technology. For instance, in many countries, telehealth or telemedicine supports communities and individuals receiving healthcare support and guidance from home. As with the advancement of technology, the telehealth approach is both patient-centered and protects the patient and the physicians (Kruse et al., 2017).

In this vein, the health care system and service delivery have many unsolved challenges in developed and developing countries. The COVID-19 burden has declared that not every healthcare system is resilient to crises like COVID-19, but a few systems are, which are very. As of July 16, almost 26% of the US has 26% of its COVID-19 cases and 24% of its deaths (Center for Systems Science and Engineering (CSSE), 2020). While on November 24, 2020, the United States had 43,817,194 with a total of 1,165,105 death cases (Worldometer, 2020).[1] Quality of health care has declined during COVID-19; thus, many people who need treatments for cancer, cardiovascular, and diabetes have not received the necessary health services (World Health Organization, 2020).

---

[1]See: https://www.worldometers.info/coronavirus.

Data and Methods

Data

The researchers employed data from open-access databases to examine government effectiveness in managing pandemics in some conflict-affected countries. It must be noted that open databases were used; for example, in a recent study by Liang et al. (2020), "*Covid-19 mortality is negatively associated with test number and government effectiveness*".

This study induces secondary data from Worldometers, the Infectious Disease Vulnerability Index, Crisis Index Indicators, and from GHS Index 2019 data.

The relevant variables that were analyzed in this study were the pandemic management indicators, otherwise known as the GHS Indicators: Detecting epidemics, preventing diseases and causes, limiting the spread of disease, early reporting of viruses, providing treatment for those infected, committing to developing national capabilities, protecting health workers, and increasing the state's resilience in the face of biological threats.

The pandemic management variables were also employed to analyze governments' effectiveness in managing pandemics in conflict-affected areas. For the GHS indicator information is taken from data sources of international organizations and countries and is available to the public. In addition to collecting data from other sources such as global health data, government information, the World Bank, food organizations, government legislation, and academic publications. The GHS index assesses the health security of governments, considering biological risks and a country's health systems. An intensive desk search was conducted to gather more information from government websites and electronic scientific databases such as Web of Knowledge, Google Scholar Search Engine, Science Direct, and Scopus to support the collected data. Besides, a gray search is conducted to learn more about country conditions and government response.

Level of Conflict

To determine the level of conflict in the selected countries, researchers employed the crisis index indicators reported by the European Commission (2019). The 2019 crisis index ranking by the EC (2019) has indicators such as uprooted people, natural disasters, conflict, and ECHO crisis. The crisis index employed in this study is relevant to know the crisis levels in the selected countries and how they can influence pandemic management. The index is organized so scholars can expand and understand the existing crisis and the main problems that led to the crisis. This is one of the reasons why the crisis index served as a valuable resource to the researchers.[2] Selected conflict-affected countries: Iraq

[2]GHS Index, Global Health Security Index (2019). Building collective action and accountability, NTI, The Economist, Intelligence Unit: available at:https://www.ghsindex.org/wp-content/uploads/2019/10/2019-Global-Health-Security-Index.pdf.

(Representing the Middle East), Afghanistan (Representing the Middle East), Nigeria (representing Africa), and Venezuela (representing South America). Cross-national level comparative analysis using the 2019 GHS Index and the crisis index report by the European Commission (2019). Limitations and challenges include difficulties in accessing current and multiple data and language barriers about countries in the Middle East and South Asian countries.

Data Analysis and Discussion

This section presents the data analysis and discussion of the study.

Pandemic Management Preparedness

The researchers employed the GHS Index (2019) data to determine the pandemic management preparedness of the conflict-affected countries. According to WHO (2020), global public health security is "*the activities required, both proactive and reactive, to minimize the danger and impact of acute public health events that endanger people's health across geographical regions and international boundaries.*" Researchers have noted that pandemic management preparedness is part of the activities required to minimize the danger and impact of acute public health events that endanger people's health (Heymann et al., 2007).

The GHS Indicators: Prevention of the emergence or release of pathogens, Early detection reporting epidemics of potential international concern, Rapid response to and mitigation of the spread of an epidemic, sufficient and robust health sector to treat the sick and protect health workers, Commitments to improving national capacity, financing and adherence to norms, overall risk environment and country vulnerability to biological threats.

The Main Findings

Based on the global health indicators ("prevention of the emergence or release of pathogens, early detection and reporting epidemics of potential international concern, a rapid response to and mitigation of the spread of an epidemic, sufficient and robust health sector to treat the sick and protect health workers, commitments to improving national capacity, financing and adherence to norms, overall risk environment and country vulnerability to biological threats") analyzed it must be noted that pandemic management is fragile around the conflict-affected countries considered for the study.

All the countries selected (*Iraq, Afghanistan, Nigeria, and Venezuela)* could not meet *a* global average of the global security indicators (GHS, 2019). All the countries were below the global average bar of 40. Nigeria (n = 37.8, rank = 96/195) was close to the 40 global average. Afghanistan scored 32.3, ranking 130/195. It is followed by Iraq, scoring 25.8, ranking 167/195; Venezuela had the lowest rank of 23.0, with a rank of 1176/195. Table 1 shows that none of the conflict-affected countries is entirely (most) prepared to manage the pandemic effectively.

Table 1. GHS Indicators.

INDICATOR	Iraq		Afghanistan		Nigeria		Venezuela	
	Score	Rank	Score	Rank	Score	Rank	Score	Rank
OVERALL SCORE	**25.8**	**167**	**32.3**	**130**	**37.8**	**96**	**23**	**176**
1) PREVENTION OF THE EMERGENCE OR RELEASE OF PATHOGENS	22.1	150	23.5	140	26.3	123	23.5	140
1.1) Antimicrobial resistance (AMR)	8.3	146	16.7	140	41.7	99	25	122
1.2) Biosecurity	0	107	0	107	24	50	0	107
1.3) Immunization	87.7	127	81.6	149	50	170	97.4	46
2) EARLY DETECTION REPORTING EPIDEMICS OF POTENTIAL INTERNATIONAL CONCERN	42.2	88	44.8	77	44.6	78	8.7	182
2.1) Laboratory systems	16.7	161	33.3	128	50	95	33.3	128
2.2) Data integration between human/animal/environmental health sectors	100	1	100	1	0	59	0	59
3) RAPID RESPONSE TO AND MITIGATION OF THE SPREAD OF AN EPIDEMIC	19.5	183	23.6	161	43.8	68	19.7	180
3.1) Emergency preparedness and response planning	0	108	18.8	59	12.5	67	0	108
3.2) Exercising response plans	0	54	0	54	100	1	0	54

(Continued)

Table 1. (Continued)

INDICATOR	Iraq		Afghanistan		Nigeria		Venezuela	
	Score	Rank	Score	Rank	Score	Rank	Score	Rank
4) SUFFICIENT & ROBUST HEALTH SECTOR TO TREAT THE SICK AND PROTECT HEALTH WORKERS (HEALTHCARE SERVICE)	11.8	150	21	102	19.9	107	12.9	141
4.1) Health capacity in clinics, hospitals, and community care centers	5.6	152	43.2	42	2.8	170	6.4	146
4.2) Healthcare Access	41.9	91	40	96	71.7	5	47.4	31
4.3) Infection control practices and availability of equipment	0	77	0	77	0	77	0	77
5) COMMITMENTS TO IMPROVING NATIONAL CAPACITY, FINANCING, AND ADHERENCE TO NORMS (INSTITUTION)	29.5	183	56.3	52	56.7	50	42.2	132
5.1) Cross-border agreements on public health and animal health emergency response	0	144	50	70	50	70	50	70
5.2) International commitments	43.8	87	75	70	78.1	62	31.3	110
5.3) Financing	16.7	131	50	10	50	10	50	10
6) OVERALL RISK ENVIRONMENT AND COUNTRY VULNERABILITY TO BIOLOGICAL THREATS (GOVERNMENT EFFECTIVENESS)	29.2	184	23.3	191	33.7	174	38.2	164
6.1) Political and security risk	7.1	188	3.6	192	39.3	159	28.6	172
6.2 Government's effectiveness	0	156	0	156	0	156	0	156
6.3) Socio-economic resilience	53.6	144	45.4	162	42.1	173	45.2	163
6.4) Public health vulnerabilities	42.6	125	19.5	167	18.4	171	56.3	66

Source: GHS Index 2019.

Score Ratings

Most prepared – 66.7 to 100; More prepared – 33.4 to 66.6; Least prepared – 0 to 33.3.

Interpretations of Pandemic Management Indicators

Prevention of the Emergence or Release of Pathogens

With the deterrence of the appearance or the release of pathogens (Antimicrobial resistance (AMR), biosecurity, and immunization), Nigeria had the highest score of 26.3, rankings 123/195; Afghanistan scored 23.5, rankings 149/195; Venezuela scored 23.5, ranking 140/195 and Iraq scoring 22.1 rankings 150/195. There were significant scores regarding immunization among the selected countries; all the countries (Iraq, Afghanistan, Nigeria, and Venezuela) scored above 66.6, which shows that they are most prepared for immunization.

Early Detection and Reporting of Epidemics of Potential International Concern

Excluding Venezuela (score = 8.7), the least organized, all the other countries (Afghanistan-44.8, Nigeria-44.6, and Iraq-44.2) were more able to early detection and recording of epidemics of probable international alarm. For instance, Nigeria scored 50.0 with research laboratory settings, and Afghanistan scored 33.3. With data assimilation between human/environmental areas, Iraq and Afghanistan were the most willing, scoring 100.0 each.

Rapid Response to and Mitigation of the Spread of an Epidemic

With rapid comeback to and qualification of the multiplied of an epidemic, Nigeria was more organized (43.8), followed by Afghanistan (23.6), Venezuela (19.7), and Iraq (19.5). Nonetheless, all the countries were least organized regarding emergency readiness and reaction planning.

There is little proof to show that the conflict-affected countries are most willing for rapid reaction and mitigation in the selection of an outbreak. The level of unpreparedness was not only in the conflict-affected countries but in many countries. The advent of the COVID-19 epidemic has shown that many countries were unprepared for a rapid comeback and justification of the spread.

Sufficient Robust Health Sector to Treat the Sick and Protect Health Workers

In the mean, all the countries (Iraq – 11.8, Afghanistan – 21.0, Nigeria – 19.9, and Venezuela –12.9) were the least set up with sufficient and strong health sectors to handle the sick and defend health workers. Nonetheless, Afghanistan (43.2) was more willing with health capability in clinics and community health care centers. In terms of healthcare access, Nigeria was the most set; Venezuela (47.4), Iraq (41.9), and Afghanistan (40.0) were more equipped.

Overall Risk Environment and Country Vulnerability to Biological Threats

Only Nigeria (39.3) was more prepared for security risks and politics.

Social Health Equity in Conflict-affected Countries and the Role of Government Effectiveness in Public Health Service Delivery

This section focuses on public health effectiveness in conflict-affected countries, what governments have done to restrict or prevent pandemics, and how conflict influences pandemic management.

Public Health Service Delivery Equity in Conflict-affected Countries

With the lenses of health equity, researchers wanted to investigate whether governments in conflict-affected countries have formulated emergency healthcare policies for sick individuals, because of public health emergencies and whether there are legislative instruments backing healthcare services regarding public health emergencies. It is essential to establish that emergency healthcare includes natural disasters, disease outbreaks, and mass casualty incidents (Noji, 2005). Emergency healthcare is needed to manage communicable disease outbreaks such as Influenza, bird flu, and measles, among others. Natural disasters like bushfires, floods, and cyclones also need a firm emergency healthcare policy to function effectively. For instance, in a developed country like the United States of America, the Public Health Service Act is used to deal with public healthcare emergency cases for all people, including healthcare workers. Also, in Australia, through the Health Department, health emergency policies have been developed and implemented to guide the safety of their people.

Linking this to health equity literature, one of the purposes of social equity (assessing the needs of the people across the society to provide them access to the necessary opportunities and success, Gooden, 2017) is 'defeated.' If there is no legislation, policy, or public statements committing to providing prioritized healthcare services to healthcare workers, what more about the people in the society? According to the health equity literature by Smith et al. (2017), this is an apparent incidence of social unjust in the mentioned conflict-affected countries.

Only Nigeria demonstrated a commitment to providing prioritized healthcare services for healthcare workers affected by their response to specific public health emergencies. This discovery underscores a significant deficiency in governance effectiveness in delivering quality health services during crises. Similar concerns were observed in conflict-affected nations and other developing countries like Iraq, Syria, and Afghanistan. Each country faces unique challenges, as evidenced during the early stages of the COVID-19 pandemic when governments struggled to promptly provide healthcare services. However, some countries managed to maintain essential health services despite challenges.

For example, Afghanistan's Ministry of Public Health's 2015 regulation indicated a requirement for healthcare workers exposed to health risks to undergo monthly tests and receive treatment if necessary, without prioritizing emergency care. Iraq lacked publicly available evidence of legislation, policies, or public commitments to providing prioritized healthcare services to affected healthcare workers during public health emergencies.

The findings suggest that institutions in these countries were ill-prepared and ineffective in delivering adequate public health services. Most conflict-affected countries, including Iraq, Afghanistan, and Venezuela, lacked commitments to prioritize healthcare services for affected workers. Nevertheless, countries showed readiness to enhance their institutions through financial investment and adherence to healthcare service norms.

Government effectiveness, as defined by the World Bank, emphasizes perceptions of public service quality, including independence from political influence, policy formulation and implementation quality, and government commitment credibility. The majority of healthcare institutions in conflict-affected countries exhibited weaknesses. Strengthening these institutions requires visible independence and commitment to policy implementation.

The GHS Index associates public health effectiveness with indicators such as a robust healthcare sector capable of treating the sick and protecting healthcare workers. However, the GHS Index indicates global weaknesses in public health preparedness, with no country fully equipped to handle epidemics or pandemics. All countries considered in the study, including Iraq, Afghanistan, Nigeria, and Venezuela, scored poorly in healthcare sector robustness. None of the conflict-affected countries achieved a score above 35.0 out of 100, indicating significant room for improvement.

Pandemic Health Equity

Recent studies have shown that the novel COVID-19 pandemic has set in high relief the entrenched health, racial, political, social, and economic inequities not only in developing countries or conflicted affected countries as in the case of this study, but also the developed world. The health inequity among nations resulted in severe morbidity and mortality when the COVID-19 virus shook the World in the year 2020 (Alberti et al., 2020; Madad et al., 2021).

More importantly, the GHS (2019) data on pandemic preparedness in conflict-affected countries show how the countries were not prepared for **the prevention of the emergence or the release of pathogens** (AMR, biosecurity, and immunization). None of the countries had above 33.3; Nigeria had 26.3; Afghanistan had 23.5; Venezuela had 23.5; and Iraq had 22.1. The findings show the presence of social injustice and unfairness about pandemic preparedness.

All the countries considered were the least prepared. Governments have not done so much in restricting or preventing pandemics. However, there were significant scores regarding immunization among the selected countries; all the countries (Iraq, Afghanistan, Nigeria, and Venezuela) scored above 66.6, which shows that they are most prepared for immunization. However, immunization is insufficient to prepare to restrict or prevent a pandemic; AMR and biosecurity are crucial in the pandemic fight, and the country's scores were not encouraging. Before the COVID-19 pandemic, many countries were not very prepared regarding strict policies or measures to contain, combat, and respond to the pandemic, as in the case of COVID-19 (Pan et al., 2020). Because many countries were least prepared, the COVID-19 pandemic took many nations by surprise, recording many deaths and active cases.

How Does Conflict Influence Pandemic Management?

It is important to acknowledge that even in the absence of a pandemic, displaced individuals, nations impacted by natural calamities, countries engaged in harsh armed conflicts, and countries experiencing an ECHO crisis encounter significant obstacles in obtaining sufficient healthcare. Preventive and detective services, such as implementing effective handwashing practices and providing adequate sanitation facilities, receive even less attention in such communities (Holman & Shayegan, 2014). The crisis index, as issued by the European Commission in 2019, provides a crucial data source for the current worldwide crisis. The Conflict Assessment Index ranking 2019 encompasses a wide range of crises, including enduring insurgencies, political instability, health emergencies, and diplomatic difficulties.

The 2019 crisis index rating conducted by the EC (2019) includes variables such as displaced individuals, occurrences of natural disasters, instances of violence, and crises identified by the ECHO. The crisis index utilized in this study is pertinent for understanding the degrees of crisis in the chosen nations and how they might impact the management of a pandemic. The index is structured to facilitate researchers in comprehending and exploring the prevailing crisis as well as the primary issues that precipitated the crisis. The crisis index was a significant resource for the researchers due to this reason.

Uprooted People

Uprooted individuals are those who are pushed to leave their communities due to factors such as persecution, war, environmental damage, or the inability to sustain themselves at home. They may escape to another location or seek nourishment in a city or overseas. Policy statement of the World Council of Churches, issued in 1995. Individuals who have been forced to leave their homes due to conflict, persecution, or other forms of violence, and are seeking refuge in another country or are displaced inside their own country.

According to the Crisis Index Report, the country's records are as follows: Iraq achieved a score of 3, Afghanistan also achieved a score of 3, Nigeria achieved a score of 2, and Venezuela achieved a score of 0. Iraq and Afghanistan achieved a score of 3, placing them in the highest 25% of the rankings. Nigeria is within the middle 50% and Venezuela received a score of 0. The countries with the highest ratings indicate a significant number of displaced individuals in Iraq and Afghanistan. While Nigeria has had some incidents of displacement (rated 2), the situation in Iraq and Afghanistan is more severe, with a score of 3. Based on the conflict assessment index rating by the EC (2019), there were no reported cases of displacement in Venezuela. The source of this information is the European Commission (2019).

During a pandemic such as COVID-19, which can rapidly spread in crowded and unsafe environments, displaced individuals living in camps or settlements are particularly vulnerable to the disease. Unfortunately, these individuals lack the resources and support necessary to effectively combat the pandemic, as highlighted in the Crisis Index Report by the European Commission in 2019.

Natural Disaster

Natural catastrophes inflict harm upon populations and the environment, with each disaster causing distinct impacts, particularly in the realms of economy, society, ecology, and biology. Based on the 2019 statistics provided by the EC, all the chosen nations have a natural catastrophe index score of 0. There has been an increase in the number of reports on natural catastrophes in the nations included in the study. All of these countries received a score of 0. Nevertheless, the occurrence of natural catastrophes and the impact of climate change will compel individuals to evacuate their residences, potentially leading to the spread of infectious illnesses among affected populations.

Conflict

Unpredictable and perilous circumstances have an impact on individuals, communities, and society. Regarding conflict, all nations, except for Venezuela, achieved a score of 3. This illustrates the instances of conflict in Iraq, Afghanistan, and Nigeria. Conflict can impede the efforts of international medical professionals and humanitarian organizations to assist individuals in need. In 2019, the WHO and international NGOs had difficulties in controlling an Ebola epidemic in the Eastern Democratic Republic of the Congo (DRC). Despite receiving assistance from United Nations forces, access to certain affected regions was impeded by conflict and local militias. Occasionally, fighters specifically attacked physicians and medical institutions. These variables have a detrimental impact on the management of the epidemic.

Does Conflict Influence the Effectiveness of Managing a Pandemic?

The efficacy of pandemic management is contingent upon the health systems and governmental institutions in the afflicted nations, as has been disclosed and deliberated. The study has observed that the health systems and institutions in the nations under consideration are feeble and lack vitality (GHS, 2019).

According to the conclusions of the GHS (2019) and the crisis index rating of the EC (2019), armed conflict has had a detrimental impact on the efficacy of the pandemic. Adversely, war has impacted nations by impeding collaboration from international communities, hampering the allocation of sufficient resources to handle the pandemic, undermining the effectiveness of health systems and institutions, and eroding the faith of human capital (experts and scientists) in the Government's adherence to public health directives.

Lack of Cooperation from the International Communities

It is crucial to acknowledge that conflict has an impact not only on internal matters but also on external ones. Conflict renders the pillars of contemporary government (authority, economics, networks) ineffective (Hufty, 2011). Their ability to operate efficiently is hindered due to discord among the key components. Certain nations engage in conflicts with other nations, resulting in a detrimental impact on their bilateral ties. Nevertheless, it is imperative to acknowledge that during a severe pandemic like COVID-19, nations with abundant resources should assist those with limited capabilities, particularly those in conflict-affected countries. There has been a noticeable political disagreement between the United States and China, particularly during the tenure of Former President Trump. This might have had an impact on the handling of the COVID-19 epidemic in the United States. Conflict undermines the foundations of efficient government, including established networks and alliances. During times of war, it can be challenging for authorities, economies, and networks to successfully collaborate and coordinate efforts to manage a pandemic.

Resources to Manage the Pandemic

Resources play a critical role in controlling the pandemic, especially when it comes to specialized emergency public finance structures and programs that let nations access assistance during public health emergencies like COVID-19 (GHS, 2019). The researchers examined whether conflict-affected nations had an emergency public finance mechanism available during pandemics. Hence, the researchers were intrigued by the presence of distinctive emergency public financing mechanisms, such as a dedicated national reserve fund, a formal arrangement with the World Bank pandemic financing facility or other multilateral emergency funding mechanisms, or alternative pathways identified through a public health or state of emergency act. The country's circumstances have been peculiar in terms of finance and responses while considering the priority groups in managing the COVID-19 pandemic, in Iraq the camps of internally displaced persons have been government and international organizations' priority as a humanitarian concern. (Ali, 2020).

A serious weakness in managing COVID-19 in Iraq was the role of the government as a caregiver, where the government's financial capacity was exhausted by instability and conflict, the financial crisis affected oil prices, which has directly affected the government's financial well-being. Likewise, a decline in oil prices has similar effects on Nigerian and Venezuelan financial capacities of the governments. Importantly, fiscal tightening in the case of Iraq has influenced institutional capacities, and human resources, due to years of conflict, and economic volatility (IMF Country Report, 2021). Despite the differences in financing and responding to the COVID-19 pandemic, there were some commonalities, which just required a sound management system that could unify all different approaches. Moreover, the state's economic strength has been exhausted due to conflict and political instability in Iraq, Syria, Nigeria, Afghanistan, Venezuela, and many other countries (Ossai, 2022; Rahim et al., 2020).

Weak Healthcare Systems and Institutions

According to the WHO (2020), the healthcare system refers to all organizations, people, and actions that aim to promote, restore, or maintain health. From the GHS report 2019, on average, all the countries (Iraq – 11.8, Afghanistan – 21.0, Nigeria – 19.9, and Venezuela – 12.9) were least prepared with sufficient and robust health sectors to treat the sick and protect health workers.

Nevertheless, Afghanistan (43.2) was more prepared with health capacity in clinics, hospitals, and community health care centers. In terms of healthcare access, Nigeria was the most prepared; Venezuela (47.4), Iraq (41.9), and Afghanistan (40.0) were more prepared.

For instance,

> the UN-backed government in Tripoli has pledged roughly $350 million to respond to the disease, but to what end is unclear: the health system has collapsed due to an outflow of foreign medics during the war. In Venezuela, as Crisis Group warned it would happen in 2016, the standoff between the government and opposition has hollowed out health services. COVID-19 is liable to overwhelm the country's remaining hospitals very quickly. In Iran, the government's lethargic response, compounded by the impact of the U.S. sanctions, has brought calamity: the virus reportedly is infecting nearly 50 people and taking five to six lives every hour. In Gaza, where a healthcare system weakened by years of blockade was ill-equipped to serve the high-density population long before COVID-19, the Health Ministry is scrambling to gather the experts and obtain the supplies necessary for when the disease sweeps in. It appears to be an uphill climb: medical suppliers serving the region told Crisis Group that they had run out of key items even before the ministry announced two COVID cases on 21 March. (Crisis Group, 2020)[3]

Lessons from COVID-19 Pandemic Management: Some Developed Countries Versus Selected Conflict-affected Countries

One of the reasons for comparing COVID-19 cases in some developed and selected conflict-affected countries was to find out whether conflict has influenced the management of the COVID-19 pandemic.

---

[3]See: https://www.africaportal.org/features/covid-19-and-conflict-seven-trends-watch.

Table 2. Reported COVID-19 Cases as at March 13, 2021.

Some Developed Countries					The Conflict-Affected Countries				
Countries	**Population**	**Total Cases**	**Total Deaths**	**Total Recovered**	**Countries**	**Population**	**Total Cases**	**Total Deaths**	**Total Recovered**
CHINA	1,439,323,776	90,034	4,636	85,214	Iraq	40,844,935	750,264	13,696	677,742
USA	332,352,077	29,993,423	545,544	22,031,220	Nigeria	209,658,679	160,332	2,009	144,059
Brazil	213,609,288	11,368,316	275,276	10,000,980	Venezuela	28,379,718	144,786	1,422	136,710
UK	68,134,001	4,248,286	125,343	3,424,092	Afghanistan	39,532,913	55,957	2,457	49,499
Italy	60,399,822	3,175,807	101,564	2,564,926	Sudan	44,554,963	28,984	1,940	23,397

Source: WHO, 2021.

Based on the COVID-19 cases data provided by the Worldmeter (2021) and the WHO (2021), it appears some of the selected conflict-affected countries (armed conflicts) are managing the COVID-19 cases better in terms of their total confirmed cases, total deaths, and total recovery compared to some of the developed countries. China has performed exceptionally and has been the pandemic's epicenter but has recorded lower confirmed cases, low death rates, and total recovery.

It is clear from Table 2 that most countries that have been seriously affected by COVID-19 are not only conflict-affected but also developed countries like the USA, Brazil, the UK, and Italy, among others. Table 2 shows that some of the selected conflict-affected countries are doing well regarding their confirmed cases, deaths, and recovery.

Polo (2020) has indicated that COVID-19 has significantly worsened many root causes of armed conflicts. For example, there appears to be a reduction in the violence in Afghanistan to save lives from the COVID-19 pandemic. Polo (2020) has disclosed that the Afghan government has focused on the health crisis instead of armed conflicts. Nevertheless, there seems to be some ceased fire in conflict-affected countries, which the researchers believe contributes to managing their COVID-19 cases. Researchers are establishing that conflict indeed influences the management of pandemics. However, an effective governance system where the authorities, economy, and networks interact and collaborate may lead to effectiveness in managing the pandemic, as in the case of COVID-19.

Conclusion

The research has evaluated how effectively governments in conflict-affected regions manage pandemics using a modern governance perspective. Findings indicate that pandemic management, as measured by the GHS indicators, is precarious in both conflict-affected and various developed and developing nations globally. According to GHS (2019) data, public health service delivery was ineffective in most conflict-affected countries like Iraq, Afghanistan, and Venezuela, which lacked legislation, policies, or public commitments prioritizing healthcare services for affected workers during public health emergencies. These countries were found to be the least prepared overall. Governments have not implemented significant measures to restrict or prevent pandemics.

However, the study revealed notable scores in immunization across the selected countries, with all of them – Iraq, Afghanistan, Nigeria, and Venezuela – scoring above 66.6, indicating a high level of preparedness in this aspect. Nevertheless, immunization alone is insufficient. Strict traffic restrictions, substantial financial support, enhanced research, and network communication technologies, as demonstrated by China's success in managing the COVID-19 pandemic, are essential. The findings from GHS (2019) and the crisis index ranking by the EC (2019) suggest that armed conflict adversely affects pandemic management by hindering cooperation from the international community, lacking resources to handle pandemics, weak health systems, and institutions, and diminishing trust in government directives among human capital, including experts and scientists.

It can be concluded that conflict does indeed impact pandemic management. However, an effective governance system, where authorities, economies, and networks collaborate, can enhance pandemic management, as seen in the case of COVID-19. If governments worldwide effectively implement the modern form of governance discussed in this study, even conflict-affected nations can effectively manage pandemics and save lives. Based on the study's findings, the following recommendations are proposed to improve pandemic management by governments: adequate funding for researchers to identify and mitigate biological risks associated with technological advances; development of national biosurveillance capabilities and a global biosurveillance architecture; regular testing of health security capacities through annual simulation exercises to demonstrate commitment to a functioning system, foster resilience among communities, and enhance government effectiveness; and governmental planning for future pandemics involving all ministries, institutions, and agencies to bolster preparedness efforts for future epidemics or health crises (Ahmad & Murad, 2020).

Declaration of Conflicting Interests

The author(s) declared no potential conflicts of interest concerning this article's research, authorship, and publication.

Institutional Review Board Statement: The review complied with the Helsinki Declaration of 1964. We reviewed the already published papers, and no formal ethical approval was sought.

Data Availability Statement: If communicated to the corresponding author, supporting data will be provided.

Acknowledgments: None.

References

Ahmad, R. A., & Murad, H. R. (2020). The impact of social media on panic during the COVID-19 Pandemic in Iraqi Kurdistan: Online questionnaire study. *Journal of Medical Internet Research*, *22*(5), 10.

Alberti, P. M., Lantz, P. M., & Wilkins, C. H. (2020). Equitable pandemic preparedness and rapid response: Lessons from COVID-19 for pandemic health equity. *Journal of Health Politics, Policy, and Law*, *45*(6), 921–935.

Ali, L. (2020). *Fighting COVID-19 deepens Iraq's humanitarian crisis, Iraq's humanitarian crisis, UNICEF*. Retrieved April 20, 2023, from https://www.unicef.org/iraq/stories/fighting-covid-19-deepens-iraqs-humanitarian-crisis

Bagenholm, A., Bauhr, M., Grimes, M., & Rothstein, B. (2021). *The Oxford handbook of the quality of government*. Oxford University Press.

Bell, J. A., & Nuzzo, J. B. (2019). *Global Health Security Index: Advancing collective action and accountability amid global crisis, 2021*. www.GHSIndex.org

Boin, A., Leiden, R., Hart, P., Stern, E., & Sundelius, B. (2005). *The politics of crisis management, public leadership under pressure*. Cambridge University Press.

Braveman, P., & Gruskin, S. (2003). Defining equity in health. *Journal of Epidemiology & Community Health*, *57*(4), 254–258.

Capano, G., Howlett, M., & Ramesh, M. (2014). Bringing governments back in governance and governing in comparative policy analysis. *Journal of Comparative Policy Analysis: Research and Practice, 17*(4).

Castells, M. (1996). *The rise of network society*. Blackwell.

Center for Systems Science and Engineering (CSSE) at Johns Hopkins University. COVID-19 dashboard. https://coronavirus.jhu.edu/map.html

Crandall, R. W., Parnell, A. J., & Spillan, E. J. (2014). *Crisis management, learning in the new strategy landscape* (2nd ed.). SAGE.

Economist Intelligence Unit. (2021). Coronavirus vaccines: expect delays Q1 global forecast 2021. *The Economist*, April 18, 2024.

European Commission (2019). *Crisis Assessment Index Rank 2019*. Retrieved November 28, 2020, from https://ec.europa.eu/echo/sites/default/files/annex_3_inform-ci_2019_new.pdf

Fagel, M. J. (2018). *Crisis management and emergency planning, preparing for today's challenges*. Taylor & Francis.

Frederickson, G. H. (2015). *Social equity and public administration: Origins, developments, and applications*. Routledge.

Gephart et al. (2019). *The Routledge companion to risk, crisis, and emergency management*. Routledge.

Global Health Security Index. (GHS, October). (2019). Building Collective Action and Accountability, Index Developed with the Economist, NTI, Johns Hopkins Center for Health Security. https://ghsindex.org.

Gooden, S. T. (2017). Social equity and evidence: Insights from local government. *Public Administration Review, 77*(6), 822–828.

Heymann, D. L., Prentice, T., & Reinders, L. T. (2007). *The world health report 2007: A safer future: Global public health security in the 21st century*. World Health Organization.

Hillyard, J. M. (2000). *Public crisis management: How and why organizations work together to solve society's most threatening problems*. Club Press.

Hogan, V., Rowley, D. L., White, S. B., & Faustin, Y. (2018). Dimensionality and R4P: A health equity framework for research planning and evaluation in African American populations. *Maternal and Child Health Journal, 22*(2), 147–153. https://doi.org/10.1007/s10995-017-2411-z

Holman, R. S., & Shayegan, L. (2014). *Toilets and Sanitation at the Kumbh Mela Campanion Notes*. Global Health Education and Learning incubator at Harvard University, Harvard Global Health Institute.

Hufty, M. (2011). Governance: Exploring four approaches and their relevance to research. In *Research for sustainable development: Foundations, experiences, and perspectives* (pp. 165–183).

IMF Country Report. (2021). *Iraq, 2020 article IV constitution-press release; staff report; and statement by the executive director for Iraq* [Report. No. 21/38, p. 10].

Institute of Medicine. (2007). *Ethical and legal considerations in mitigating pandemic disease*. The National Academy of Sciences.

International Crisis Group. (2020). Covid-19 and conflict: Seven trends to watch, March. Retrieved October 25, 2024, from https://www.crisisgroup.org/global/sb4-covid-19-and-conflict-seven-trends-watch.

Kaufman et al. (1999). *Governance matters*. [Policy Research Working Paper, No. 2196, p. 7, the World Bank].

Koelble, A. T. (1995). The new institutionalism in political science and sociology. *Comparative Politics, 27*(2), 231–243.

Kruse, C. S., Krowski, N., Rodriguez, B., Tran, L., Vela, J., & Brooks, M. (2017). Telehealth and patient satisfaction: A systematic review and narrative analysis. *BMJ*. Retrieved August 29, 2021, from https://doi.org/10.1136/bmjopen-2017-016242

La porta, R., De-Silanes, F. L., Shleifer, A., & Vishny, R. (1999). The quality of government. *The Journal of Law, Economics & Organization, V15*, N1 Oxford University Press.
Lagreid, P., & Rykkja, L. H. (2019). *Societal security and crisis management, governance capacity and legitimacy*. Palgrave Macmillan.
Liang, L. L., Tseng, C. H., Ho, H. J., & Wu, C. Y. (2020). Covid-19 mortality is negatively associated with test numbers and government effectiveness. *Scientific Reports, 10*(1), 1–7.
Madad, S., Moskovitz, J., Boyce, M. R., Cagliuso, N. V., & Katz, R. (2021). Ready or not, patients will present improving urban pandemic preparedness. *Disaster Medicine and Public Health Preparedness, 15*(3), 267–270.
Manaugh, K., Badami, M. G., & El-Geneidy, A. M. (2015). Integrating social equity into urban transportation planning: A critical evaluation of equity objectives and measures in transportation plans in North America. *Transport Policy, 37*, 167–176.
Mirsa, K. S. (2020). *Crisis management: Resilience and change*. SAGE.
Moore, M., Gelfeld, B., Okunogbe, A., & Paul, C. (2016). *Identifying future disease hot spots: Infectious disease vulnerability index*. RAND Corporation. https://www.rand.org/pubs/research_reports/RR1605
Noji, E. K. (2005). Public health issues in disasters. *Critical Care Medicine, 33*(1), S29–S33.
Oshitani, H., Kamigaki, T., & Suzuki, A. (2008). Major issues and challenges of influenza pandemic preparedness in developing countries. *Emerging Infectious Diseases*, June, *14*(6), 875–880.
Ossai, E. C. (2022). COVID-19 and peace in conflict-affected areas. *Encyclopedia, 2*(4), 1678–1687.
Pan, X., Ojcius, D. M., Gao, T., Li, Z., Pan, C., & Pan, C. (2020). Lessons learned from the 2019-nCoV epidemic on prevention of future infectious diseases. *Microbes and Infection, 22*(1), 86–91.
Pandemic Influenza Risk Management. (2017). *A WHO guide to inform and harmonize national and international pandemic preparedness and response* (p. 32). World Health Organization. Retrieved August 29, 2021, from https://iris.who.int/bitstream/handle/10665/44123/9789241547680_eng.pdf?sequence=1
Peterson, A., Charles, V., Yeung, D., & Coyle, K. (2021). The health equity framework: A science-and justice-based model for public health researchers and practitioners. *Health Promotion Practice, 22*(6), 741–746.
Pierre, J., & Peters, B. G. (2019). *Governance, politics, and the state*. Red Globe Press.
Polo, S. M. (2020). A pandemic of violence? The impact of COVID-19 on conflict. *Peace Economics, Peace Science and Public Policy, 26*(3).
Rahim, F., Allen, R., Barroy, H., Gores, L., & Kutzin, J. (2020). *COVID-19 funds in response to the pandemic, special series on COVID-19*,P. 7, Fiscal Affairs, IMF.
Rothstein, B. (2011). *The quality of government: Corruption, social trust, and inequality in international perspectives*. The University of Chicago Press.
Rothstein, B. O., & Teorell, J. A. (2008). What is the quality of government? A theory of impartial government institutions. *Governance, 21*(2), 165–190.
Scanlon, T. M. (2017). Rights, goals, and fairness. In C. L.Ten (Ed.), *Theories of rights* (pp. 189–207). Routledge.
Smith, M., Hosking, J., Woodward, A., Witten, K., MacMillan, A., Field, A., & Mackie, H. (2017). Systematic literature review of built environment effects on physical activity and active transport – An update and new findings on health equity. *International Journal of Behavioral Nutrition and Physical Activity, 14*(1), 1–27.
Stoto, M. A. & Higdon, M. A. (2009). *The public health response to 2009 H1N1: A systems perspective*.
Wapling, A., & Sellwood, C. (2016). *Health emergency preparedness and response*. CABI.
World Bank. (1992). *Governance and development*. The World Bank.

World Bank. (1994). *Governance, the World Bank's experience, development in practice*. The World Bank.

World Bank. (2015). Breaking the cycle of poor service delivery in the Middle East and North Africa. Retrieved August 29, 2021, from https://www.worldbank.org/en/news/feature/2015/04/10/breaking-the-cycle-of-poor-service-delivery-in-the-middle-east-and-north-africa

World Bank. (2020). *Attacking poverty*. World Development Report.

World Bank – World Development Report. (1989). *Financial systems and development world development indicators*. Oxford University Press.

World Health Organization Guide. (2009). *Pandemic influenza preparedness and response, a whole guidance document*. WHO PRESS.

World Health Organization Interim Guidance. (2020, November 2). *A suite of health service capacity assessments in the context of the COVID-19 pandemic*. WHO Press.

World Health Organization. (2005). *WHO checklist for influenza pandemic preparedness planning, Department of Communicable Disease Surveillance and Response Global Influenza Programme*.

World Health Organization. (2018). A checklist for pandemic influenza risk and impact management, Updated, Global Influenza Programme. Retrieved March 19, 2024, from https://iris.who.int/bitstream/handle/10665/259884/9789241513623-eng.pdf?sequence=1

World Health Organization. (2020). COVID-19 significantly impacts health services for noncommunicable diseases, 1 June. Retrieved November 25, 2020, from https://www.who.int/news/item/01-06-2020-covid-19-significantly-impacts-health-services-for-noncommunicable-diseases

World Health Organization. (2021). Number of COVID-19 deaths reported to WHO, WHOCOVID-19 Data dashboard. Retrieved from October 24,2024 , from https://data.who.int/dashboards/covid19/deaths.

Yamin, A. E. (2009). Shades of dignity: Exploring the demands of equality in applying human rights frameworks to health. *Health and Human Rights*, *11*(2), 1–18.

Chapter 7

Exploring Fintech Ventures and Regulatory Landscapes in Central and Eastern Europe: A Comparative Analysis

Vlora Berisha Dranqolli[a] *and Blake Rayfield*[b]

[a]*Department of Accounting and Finance, University Haxhi Zeka, Peje 30000, Kosovo*
[b]*Department of Accounting and Finance, University of North Florida, Jacksonville, Florida, USA*

Abstract

Purpose: This chapter examines the impact of regulatory frameworks on FinTech enterprises in Central and Eastern European (CEE) countries, focusing on identifying legislative barriers and facilitating factors for the advancement of financial technology.

Need for the Study: Despite the increase in FinTech, more knowledge is needed about how varying regulatory environments across CEE nations impact the sector's growth and innovation. This study aims to fill this void by delving into these regions' supportive and obstructive legislative factors.

Methodology: This research utilizes a comparative approach to analyze legislation related to FinTech, digital platforms, and data security. Data sources include central banks, financial regulators, and institutions across the Western Balkans, as well as the World Bank's Global Fintech-Enabling Regulations Database and BBVA Research's DiGiX index.

Findings: The analysis reveals that countries like Slovenia, Poland, and the Czech Republic have high digital readiness levels. Poland, Estonia, and Lithuania are leading in FinTech startup activities, with Serbia and Bulgaria notable for their regulatory sandboxes. Estonia, Lithuania, and Slovakia possess effective regulatory frameworks conducive to FinTech growth.

Financial Landscape Transformation: Technological Disruptions, 131–152

doi:10.1108/978-1-83753-750-120251007

In contrast, Albania, Kosovo, Serbia, Bosnia and Herzegovina lag in developing their FinTech infrastructure. Progress varies across North Macedonia and Montenegro.

Practical Significance: The study underscores the pivotal role of regulatory frameworks in ensuring financial stability and safeguarding consumer interests. It emphasizes the necessity for tailored legislative reforms in countries with underdeveloped FinTech ecosystems, thereby fostering a more robust environment for FinTech, and ultimately, enhancing economic growth and technological innovation in the region.

Keywords: Innovation; regulation; fintech companies; law; Balkan countries; CEE fintech; sandbox;

JEL Codes: O31; M48; O33; K10; F14; O33; O38

Introduction

The transformative impact of Financial Technology (FinTech) on the global financial landscape underscores the importance of understanding the regulatory frameworks governing its operation, particularly in the Central and Eastern European (CEE) region. Regulators worldwide work diligently and thoughtfully to ensure consumer protection, financial stability, and a conducive environment for safe fintech innovation (Jagtiani & John, 2018). Regulators often use sandboxes to facilitate innovation testing and commercialization while managing associated risks. Additionally, sandboxes serve as platforms for stakeholder participation in regulatory assessments, design, and implementation. They enable regulators to understand emerging technology risks and receive direct feedback from innovators, fostering dialogue and regulatory learning (FAHY, 2022). This study aims to provide valuable insights into the regulatory landscape of FinTech, offering guidance for policy development and promoting financial innovation within the area by conducting a comparative analysis encompassing Kosovo, Albania, Bosnia and Herzegovina, North Macedonia, Serbia, Montenegro, Romania, Bulgaria, Croatia, the Slovak Republic, Hungary, Slovenia, Poland, the Czech Republic, Estonia, and Lithuania, this research endeavors to shed light on the regulatory environments shaping FinTech ventures across diverse CEE countries.

The significance of this study lies in its potential to inform policymakers, regulators, and industry stakeholders about the regulatory challenges and opportunities in the CEE FinTech landscape. As FinTech disrupt traditional financial services, understanding the regulatory dynamics becomes paramount for fostering an environment conducive to innovation while safeguarding financial stability and consumer interests (Al-Ansi et al., 2024; Novarlic et al., 2024).

The analysis reveals notable disparities in digital readiness levels and FinTech startup activity across the region. Slovenia, Poland, and the Czech Republic emerge as leaders in digital readiness, while Poland, Estonia, and Lithuania boast the highest concentration of FinTech startups. Moreover, regulatory sandboxes in Serbia and Bulgaria underscore efforts to foster innovation, while Estonia, Lithuania, and the Republic of Slovakia stand out for effectively implementing FinTech regulations. Despite pockets of progress, challenges persist, particularly in countries needing to catch up on infrastructure development and regulatory maturity. Albania, Kosovo, Serbia, Bosnia, and Herzegovina are identified as needing to accelerate their efforts to create conducive environments for FinTech growth. Regulatory inconsistencies stemming from multiple regulators further complicate the operational landscape for FinTech companies, necessitating harmonized regulations to ensure a level playing field and enhance investor confidence. Against this backdrop, the study underscores the critical role of rules in promoting financial stability and consumer protection within the FinTech ecosystem. Estonia's exemplary regulatory framework serves as a benchmark for other countries, highlighting the importance of regulatory clarity and infrastructure development. Furthermore, the progress observed in North Macedonia and Montenegro signifies the potential for positive momentum with targeted regulatory interventions.

This study contributes to a deeper understanding of the regulatory challenges and opportunities shaping the FinTech landscape in CEE countries. By providing actionable insights and recommendations, it seeks to catalyze collaborative efforts among stakeholders to create a conducive regulatory environment that fosters innovation, promotes financial inclusion, and unlocks the full potential of FinTech in Central and Eastern Europe (Yerpude et al., 2022).

Literature Review

Historical Development of Fintech

Early technological advances in financial services were enabled by laying a transatlantic telegraph cable between Europe and America during the first half of the 19th century. Due to these events, the internationalization of financial services was further enabled and established a permanent connection between the two continents (Arjunwadkar, 2018; Dasilas & Karanović, 2023; Tanda & Maria Schena, 2019; Unsal & Rayfield, 2019; Zaleska & Kondraciuk, 2019). In the banking industry, innovation was sparked by introducing IBM mainframe computers in the 1960s, which revolutionized the industry. Since IBM mainframe computers were introduced, many banking and card transactions have been automated, resulting in speed, transparency, and "trust" (Arjunwadkar, 2018; Tanda & Maria Schena, 2019).

The computerization of banking operations led to the creation of automated teller machines (ATMs) between the *1960s and 1970s* (DeYoung et al., 2007; Zaleska & Kondraciuk, 2019). Globally, there are estimated to be 3.5 million ATMs. The number of machines per 100,000 adults is estimated to be 41.24 by 2020, according to (Statista, 2022). In the 1990s, the Internet and desktop computers revolutionized how users access information. Using the Internet for information exchange soon evolved into business-to-consumer (B2C) and business-to-business (B2B) interactions. Banks created applications through the

Internet that allow clients to transact from their homes or offices. A dramatic transformation was made to the user experience by minimizing customer interaction with bank branches. Before this, bank employees were the only ones accessing the bank's online functions (Nugraha et al., 2022). As a result of mobile banking, the banking experience has been entirely transformed by bringing the bank to the fingertips of the customer. Feature phones launched in the late 1990s offered SMS banking as the first form of mobile banking (Arner et al., 2015; DeYoung et al., 2007). During *1995–1998*, the Internet and e-commerce revolution disrupted the online payment industry, fueled further by mobile devices. E-commerce may have been started by Electronic Data Interchange (EDI), but the Internet accelerated its adoption (Arjunwadkar, 2018; Tanda & Maria Schena, 2019). Many new financial technologies have emerged since 2000: Mobile banking, wallet services, loyalty applications, and personal financial planning are now available as mobile apps. In the last few years, FinTechs have made banking accessible anywhere, anytime, and on any device. Payments are now as easy as tapping or swiping the phone with NFC chip and biometrics.

Through artificial intelligence (AI), we have seen the transition from human-led interaction to machine-driven interaction and automation. Banks have utilized chatbots or software robots extensively to interact with customers. In the banking sector, analytics-based financial applications drive disruption by gathering customer information via social media for purposes like credit scoring, know-your-customer (KYC) and fraud detection. Mobile, AI, social media, and blockchain have all contributed to the emergence of open banking in the new millennium, the called Fintech 3.0 era (Acar & Çıtak, 2019; Crouhy et al., 2021; Singh et al., 2021; Wonglimpiyarat, 2017).

During this period, FinTech 3.0 was clarified; it is not defined by what financial products are delivered but by who delivers them and how technology is applied (Fig. 1). The latest wave of FinTech innovation is being led by startups, which challenges regulators and market players alike, especially in balancing the possible benefits of innovation with the possible risks. As a result of these changes, banks became more open to the external world, both in terms of business and technology (Alaassar et al., 2023; Arner et al., 2015; Zaleska & Kondraciuk, 2019).

Table 1 categorizes fintech innovations across three banking sectors – Corporate Banking, Retail Banking, and SME Banking – highlighting whether they serve as enablers or disruptors. Examples include:

- Corporate Banking: Innovations like blockchain-based payments and AI-driven asset management.
- Retail Banking: Developments such as mobile payment systems and peer-to-peer lending platforms.
- SME Banking: Tools like instant payment gateways and digital microloans.

Each innovation either enhances existing processes or disrupts traditional banking models (Table 1).

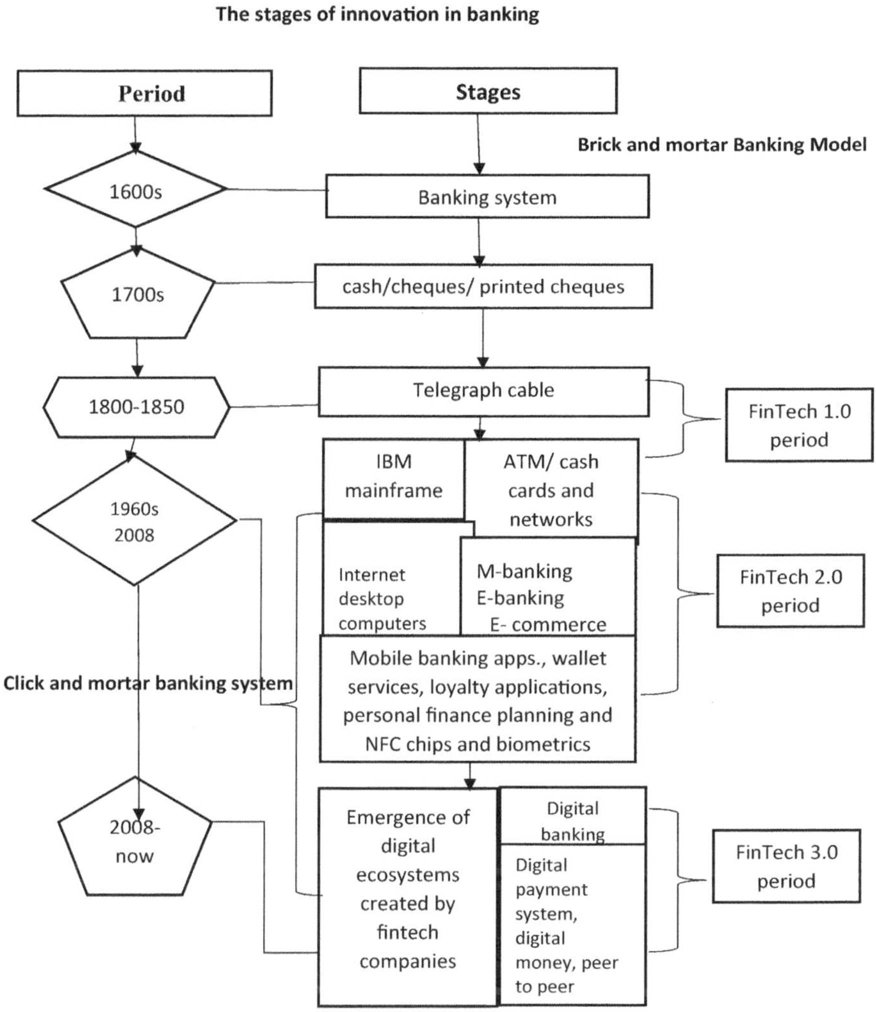

Fig. 1. Stages of Innovation in the Banking System. *Source*: Authors' design based on the theory of the gradual evolution of financial technologies (Arjunwadkar, 2018; Arner et al., 2015; DeYoung et al., 2007; Grupta & Tham, 2019).

Fintech Regulations

More than 50 countries, including Japan, Norway, and the United Kingdom, are currently exploring the concept of fintech sandboxes. These countries have implemented regulatory sandboxes as platforms to experiment with cutting-edge technologies like blockchain, AI, and IoT across various industries (World Bank Group, 2020). According to Madiega and Van De Pol (2022), the sandbox

Table 1. Innovation Matrix: Mapping Fintech's Impact Across Banking Sectors.

Business Line	**Product Cluster**	**Business Model**	**Examples**
Corporate banking	Payments	Enabler	Blockchain-based cross-border payments
	Trading and investment	Disruptor	AI-driven asset management
	Technology and support	Enabler	Cybersecurity solutions
Retail banking	Payments	Enabler	Mobile payment systems
	Lending and crowdfunding	Disruptor	Peer-to-peer lending platforms
	Insurance	Enabler	Automated claims processing
	Retail Accounts	Disruptor	Nonbanks
SME Banking	Payments	Enabler	Instant payment gateways
	Lending and Crowdfunding	Enabler	Digital microloans
	Trading and Investments	Enabler	SME-focused investment platforms
	Technology and Support	Enabler	Integrated financial management tools

Source: The authors' presentation is based on the theory of the gradual evolution of financial technologies (Arjunwadkar, 2018; Arner et al., 2015; DeYoung et al., 2007; Gupta & Tham, 2019).

approach has recently gained significant momentum in the European Union (EU). It serves as a strategy to assist regulators in addressing the development and application of emerging technologies, *such as AI and blockchain, in diverse sectors*. Regulators use sandboxes to test and supervise new financial products and technologies, enabling quick and low-risk market introductions. These platforms are gaining popularity for carefully examining innovation opportunities and risks, making them a signature program for modernizing financial sector oversight (Jeník & Duff, 2020). Financial regulatory authorities are actively utilizing regulatory sandboxes in financial technology (Fintech) to innovate and design novel financial services, such as testing *digital wallets and digital ID technologies* (Jeník & Duff, 2020). By implementing sandbox programs, regulators encourage innovation and competition, reduce regulatory barriers to progress, and keep up with market developments, creating a dynamic and flexible ecosystem (Alnemer, 2022; Jeník & Duff, 2020; World Bank, 2020).

The April 2021 draft of the AI Act, as presented by the European Commission, introduces the concept of 'AI regulatory sandboxes,' which are outlined as targeted measures to enhance innovation (Articles 53 and 54). The primary objective is to foster innovation in AI by establishing a controlled environment for the experimentation and testing of advanced AI technologies, products, and services during their developmental phase before market introduction. Significantly, the EU AI Act is a groundbreaking regulation overseeing AI. A pivotal moment occurred on December 9, 2023, when the European Parliament and the Council reached a provisional agreement on the AI Act, highlighting collaborative efforts in shaping the regulatory landscape for AI within the EU (Madiega & Chahri, 2024).

The UK stands among the pioneering countries in introducing regulatory sandboxes, and its experience provides valuable insights and lessons. Bulgaria has become the first country to implement a regulatory technology sandbox in the Balkans (Turp-Balazs, 2020). Serbia has set up an AI regulatory sandbox for testing emerging AI products and services in a controlled environment. Businesses can experiment with AI technologies without being constrained by full regulatory compliance during the testing phase (The Government of the Republic of Serbia, 2020). As of the current information available on the official website of the Central Bank of Kosovo, Bosnia and Herzegovina, and Northern Macedonia, there has yet to be any indication or announcement regarding establishing an innovative office or regulatory sandbox. Accordingly, the central bank may have yet to implement specific initiatives to promote innovation or provide a controlled environment for testing new financial products and technologies. The Bank of Albania is responsible for issuing licenses and supervising and regulating banking and non-banking financial institutions. Recently, they introduced a new payment law to reduce transaction costs and align with EU regulations. This legislation includes payment initiation services (PIS), account information services (AIS), and innovative concepts to improve efficiency and compliance within the financial sector. This is a positive move by the central bank, reflecting their commitment to fostering a better financial environment. Montenegro's Security Exchange Commission created a Regulatory Sandbox to support cryptocurrency use. The country is pioneering technology and crypto in the Balkans, with a favorable regulatory environment.

According to Khai Nguyen and Cuong Dang (2022), there are five key areas where fintech development faces challenges. These areas include legal framework, infrastructure, fintech companies, customer base, and human resources. We can work toward a more robust and sustainable fintech ecosystem by addressing these challenges. However, certain regions face more significant challenges, such as a lack of trust, too-tight laws, or outdated regulations that result in gaps in infrastructure and regulation (Wong & Ho, 2020).

The World Bank (2020) came up with four categories of regulatory approaches: (a) "Wait and See," (b) "Test and Learn," (c) Innovation Facilitators, and (d) Regulatory Laws and Reforms. As outlined in Table 2, these approaches offer a diverse set of strategies that are not mutually exclusive and can be combined in various ways to ensure effective regulation and robust support for innovation (Table 2).

Table 2. World Bank's Regulatory Approaches in Fintech Applications.

Regulatory Approaches			
Wait and see	***Test and learn***	***Innovation Facilitators***	***Regulatory Laws and Reforms***
The "Wait and See" approach, proposed by the World Bank, advocates for a cautious and informed stance toward emerging financial technologies. This strategy encourages regulators to thoroughly understand new technologies before implementing regulatory changes. The approach balances innovation and regulatory control, ensuring financial stability and consumer protection.	The "Test and Learn" regulatory approach authorizes limited licenses or exemptions to new and established intermediaries for testing new technologies. This approach allows regulators to gather data and experience to adjust regulations accordingly, fostering a learning environment. The approach balances fostering innovation and maintaining regulatory oversight, supporting appropriate reforms tailored to fintech ecosystems.	Innovation Hubs offer regulators a dynamic approach to engage with the Fintech market. This model facilitates a proactive understanding of emerging trends, providing valuable insights for effective policy development. It is recognized as less resource-intensive than other innovation facilitators, making it suitable for diverse Fintech markets. Fintech innovators use ***Regulatory Sandboxes*** to test solutions and collaborate with regulators. They offer insights, risk control, and adaptability in a dynamic regulatory environment.	The World Bank advocates for new regulatory reform to drive transformative shifts within the Fintech industry. This reform aims to create a well-balanced and conducive regulatory framework for the evolving dynamics of the sector.

Source: Author's presentation based on the report of World Bank (2020).

Methodology

A comparative analysis approach is employed in the study methodology, forming the analysis's basis. The effectiveness of this Methodology has been demonstrated by scholars such as Lor (2009) and Landman (2008), who have demonstrated its efficacy in exploring complex socioeconomic phenomena. In this study, particular attention is given to Central and East European countries, focusing on the Western Balkans region.

Various data sources are used to gather comprehensive insights for the research. These include information from central banks, financial regulators, and other pertinent institutions within the Western Balkans. Additionally, the study leverages databases such as the World Bank's Global Fintech-Enabling Regulations Database and the DiGiX index provided by BBVA Research. These sources provide a rich reservoir of data, offering valuable perspectives on the regulatory landscape and technological infrastructure surrounding FinTech.

Apart from analyzing the legislation, the research incorporates empirical data through a survey conducted among 150 bank employees in Kosovo. Participants were drawn from diverse departments, including finance, technology, compliance, customer service, and loans. The survey serves as a crucial instrument for gauging the perceptions and experiences of industry professionals regarding the challenges and opportunities associated with FinTech applications in Kosovo.

Data and Analysis

The Analysis section examines CEE countries, including EU member states and non-members, following the Methodology outlined. This involves the nation's legal framework, the digital readiness index, FinTech initiatives, regional policies, and trends observed in the DiGiX index.

The Digital Readiness Index ranking of CEE nations is presented in Table 3. According to The World Bank Group (Berg et al., 2020), the purpose of the Digital Readiness Index is to provide "a general estimate of a nation's preparedness to implement FinTech innovations in comparison to other nations in the middle-and upper-class income brackets" (p. 65) (Table 3).

Each nation's performance has been ranked regarding global data based on three distinct data points (which indicate the availability, adoption, and penetration of digital technologies).

"Final scores are the total points under each index; a score of five means the nation was in the lowest quintile across all categories, and a score of twenty-five means the nation was in the highest quintile across all categories" (Berg et al., 2020, p. 65). Table 3 shows that Slovenia, Poland, and the Czech Republic have the highest ratings according to the Digital Readiness Index (Table 3). According to a survey by Raiffeisen Bank International (RBI, 2018, 2019) and (Deloitte, 2023), Poland, Slovakia, and Lithuania have the highest concentration of fintech startups, primarily in the SME, Retail, and Technology banking sectors (Table 4).

Recently, there has been a significant rise in the establishment of fintech start-ups and enterprises in CEE nations. These entities have revolutionized the financial sector by introducing innovative solutions that have changed how people manage their finances (Table 5).

Analyzing Fintech Regulations in CEE

In navigating the EU regulatory landscape, it is imperative to recognize that while specific regulations may diverge across individual countries, the EU operates under a collective governance structure guided by European regulations. Noteworthy is that even after the United Kingdom's withdrawal from the EU, the enforcement of many EU laws adopted during its membership continues within the UK. This underscores the importance, particularly in the fintech sector, of

Table 3. Level of Fintech and Ranking of CEE Countries Under the Digital Readiness Index.

Country	**Level of FinTech**	**Digital Readiness Index**	
	FinTech Development	**Digital Readiness Score (5–25)**	**Final Rating**
Kosovo	Basic	7.5	Very Low
Albania	Basic	11	**Low**
Bosnia and Herzegovina	Basic	12.5	**Low**
Rep. of North Macedonia	Basic	13.67	**Low**
Serbia	Evolving	14	**Low**
Montenegro	Basic	16	Moderate
Romania	Evolving	16	**Moderate**
Bulgaria	Innovating	16	Moderate
Croatia	Evolving	19	Moderate
Slovak Republic	Evolving	19	Moderate
Hungary	Innovating	18	Moderate
Slovenia	Innovating	21	High
Poland	Innovating	20	High
Czech Republic	Innovating	22	High

Source: The World Bank Group – Berg et al. (2020, pp. 53–64).

meticulously examining country-specific financial regulations for seamless establishment when introducing a fintech product in Europe (Carta Worldwide, 2023).

Each Directive is meticulously crafted within EU legislation to comprehensively address various facets of Fintech. Fintech enterprises, which extend their services across lending, financial advice, insurance, and payments, must adhere to a unified regulatory framework akin to other entities offering similar services. The nuanced nature of this framework implies that the applicable laws may vary based on the specific financial activity, ranging from payment services to crowdfunding.

Illustrative of this regulatory complexity are directives such as Directive 2000/31/EC governing e-commerce, Directive 2002/65/EC overseeing online marketing of consumer financial services, Directive 2009/110/EC about electronic money, and Directive (EU) 2015/2366, which regulates payment services, among others (Stamegna & Karakas, 2019) Navigating this intricate web of regulations necessitates a meticulous understanding of the legal landscape, emphasizing the need for comprehensive diligence when entering the European fintech market (Stamegna & Karakas, 2019).

Directive 2000/31/EC: This Directive, commonly known as the "E-Commerce Directive," establishes a legal framework for electronic commerce within the EU. It covers various aspects, such as the liability of intermediary service providers,

Table 4. Size of Active Local Fintech 2022.

Country	Year	Number of Fintech	Fintech Segments	
Poland	2022	299	Payment,	32%
			Deposits	23%
			Lending	20%
			Other	25%
Czech Republic	2022	113	Payment	19%
			Deposits and lending	10%
			Investment	28%
			Other	43%
Slovakia	2022	166	Payment	32%
			Investment	19%
			Banking infrastructure	19%
			Other	30%
Hungary	2022	175	Banking infrastructure	26%
			Payments	18%
			Other	56%
Romania	2022	89	Payment	69%
			Deposit	13%
			Other	18%
Slovenia	2022	–	Payment	39%
			Crypto and blockchain	28%
			Investment	17%
			other	16%
Croatia	2022	67	Banking infrastructure	19%
			Payments	22%
			Other	59%
Bulgaria	2022	131	Payments	67%
			Deposit and lending	14%
			other	19%
Serbia	2022	72	Banking infrastructure	38%
			Payment	31%
			Crypto	23%

(*Continued*)

Table 4. (Continued)

Country	Year	Number of Fintech	Fintech Segments	
Bosnia and Herzegovina	2022	52	Payment	90%
			other	10%
Albania	2022	11	Payments	54%
			Deposit	42%
			Bank infrastructure	4%
Lithuania	2022	264	Bank infrastructure	27%
			Payments	27%
			Deposit and lending	14%
			other	28%

Source: Adapted from CEE Fintech Atlas 2018 Exclusive insights of fintech ecosystems in Central and Eastern Europe (RBI, 2018) and CEE Fintech Atlas 2019 Exclusive insights into 19 fintech ecosystems in Central and Eastern Europe – Special Focus Open Banking (Deloitte, 2023; RBI, 2019).

electronic contracts, online advertising, and resolving disputes arising from online transactions. The Directive aims to facilitate the free movement of goods and services in the digital single market while ensuring consumer protection and legal certainty for online businesses.

Directive 2002/65/EC: This Directive focuses on protecting consumers in the online marketing of financial services, particularly concerning consumer financial services. It sets out rules for providing information to consumers, including pre-contractual information requirements, the right to withdraw, and the transparency of pricing and terms. The Directive aims to enhance consumer confidence in online financial transactions and promote fair competition among financial service providers.

Directive 2009/110/EC: This Directive regulates electronic money institutions within the EU. It establishes a harmonized electronic money issuance, redemption, and prudential supervision framework. The Directive aims to promote the development of innovative electronic payment services while ensuring the stability and integrity of the financial system. It sets out requirements for the authorization and ongoing supervision of electronic money institutions and rules on capital adequacy, safeguarding of funds, and business conduct.

Directive (EU) 2015/2366, also known as the "Revised Payment Services Directive" (PSD2): This Directive updates and expands upon the original Payment Services Directive (PSD) to further regulate payment services within the EU. It introduces several fundamental changes, including enhanced security measures for electronic payments, the opening of payment markets to new players through the introduction of "third-party payment service providers" (TPPs), and increased consumer protection measures such as strong customer authentication (SCA) for online transactions. The Directive promotes innovation, competition, and consumer rights in the European payments market (Carta Worldwide, 2023; Stamegna & Karakas, 2019).

Table 5. Emergence of Financial Technology in Central and Eastern Europe 2022.

Country	Category	Company	Solution
Croatia	Digital Banking	Aircash	Mobile wallet
		Oradian	Cloud-based core banking system
	Cryptocurrencies & NFTs	Tribute Brand	Online marketplace
		Nous	Defi hedge fund platform
	Insurance	Amodo	InsurTech startup
Serbia	Digital Banking	Mobi4Me	Cloud-enabled core banking application
		NF Innova	Provides omnichannel banking
	Cryptocurrencies & NFTs	UNQ Club	NFT-based platform
		Osmium Investment Coin	Cryptocurrency
	Expenses Management	TakeFin	Cloud-based bookkeeping
Poland	Digital Banking	AvaFin	Online platform
	Cryptocurrencies & NFTs	Unlock	Solana's financial products
		Ramp	Decentralized platform for fiat-cryptocurrency exchange
	E-commerce	Booster	Online marketplace
		Beez	POS lending platform
Bulgaria	Digital Banking	Paynetics	platform for B2B and B2C payment solutions
		Phyre	Mobile payment application
	Cryptocurrencies & NFTs	BitLendingClub	Peer-to-peer Bitcoin lending platform
		Ambire	Defi wallet
	Expenses Management	Payhawk	automate payment
Romania	Digital Banking	FintechOS	financial products

(Continued)

Table 5. (Continued)

Country	Category	Company	Solution
		Finqware	Provides open banking API
		Pago	payments
	Cryptocurrencies & NFTs	Coinzix	buying and selling cryptocurrency,
		MultiversX	Metaverse
	Expenses Management	Metabeta	CRM
Greece	Digital Banking	Finloup	payments for online/offline products.
		Wisely	Open banking solutions for credit risk management
	Cryptocurrencies & NFTs	Vulcan Forged	blockchain-based games
		EveryPay	Payment
		Viva Wallet	payment
North Macedonia	Accounting	Akauntera	Online invoice management software.
		BIDIFEX	Financial data and business registry
	Cryptocurrencies & NFTs	Blockchain EcoToken	crowdfunding platform
		Finqup	Startup digitizing investment and retirement funds
Albania	Payments	Rubicon	providing payment financial technology solution
	AILend	credit lending	credit lending digitally
	Easypay	Payments	digital mobile payment solution platform
	Gjirafa	E-commerce	E-commerce

Sources: Adapted from FMER (2021) and Stojkovski (2023).

Table 6. Fintech-Initiatives and Policies in CEE Countries.

Country	**Fintech Initiatives and Policies**
Albania	Albania's **"Digital Agenda" 2015–2020** aimed to improve the country's ICT infrastructure, align national legislation with EU laws, and reform payment system laws. The government also proposed a law on virtual assets. The Albanian ICT Association was involved in these initiatives.
Bosnia and Herzegovina	Specific measures have been proposed to harmonize the national legislation with the European Union laws, such as **PSD2**.
Bulgaria	The **EU** Regulatory Sandbox and the Bulgarian Fintech Association
Croatia	Croatian financial regulators collaborate with Israel on FinTech through EU's Regulatory Sandbox. Croatian Blockchain and Cryptocurrency Association also exists.
Czech Republic	EU Regulatory Sandbox
Estonia	The Financial Supervision Authority's supervisory policy aims to foster innovation in the financial sector.
Hungary	EU Regulatory Sandbox
Kosovo	The Innovation Office in Kosovo provides grants to foster innovation and startups, promoting a business-friendly environment.
Montenegro	Proposed government initiatives aim to improve ICT SME financing and align national legislation with **EU laws, such as PSD2**.
Poland	Regulatory Sandbox, Policies/ measures: Special Task Force for Financial Innovation
Republic of North Macedonia	The Central bank has proposed measures to align North Macedonia's national legislation with EU laws, including PSD2, to better communicate with the FinTech sector and the Alternative Financial Services Association.
Romania	EU Regulatory Sandbox and Innovation Office.
Serbia	Regulatory Sandbox
	The government has taken steps to promote the ICT sector, including measures to bring national legislation in line with EU regulations, such as PSD2. ICT Network
Slovak Republic	The Ministry of the Interior has developed an API to automate customer identification processes, specifically for FinTech inquiries and the EU regulatory sandbox.
Slovenia	Regulatory Sandbox

Source: Adapted from Berg *et al.* (2020) pp. 54–64; See News "Financial Fintech Report 2020" (p. 36); The Joint Committee.[1]

[1]The Joint Committee (retrieved from https://esas-joint-committee.europa.eu/efif/innovation-facilitators-in-the-eu).

Table 7. Summary of Products, Regulations for Fintech Companies and Incentives.

Country	FinTech Regulation	DiGiX	
		'18	'20
		Rank	Rank
ALB	NO	59	59
BIH	NO	NA.	NA.
BGR	YES	41	40
CZE	YES	69	70
HRV	YES	30	37
EST	YES	21	11
HUN	YES	55	65
KSV	NO	NA.	NA.
LVA	YES	39	46
LTU	YES	33	34
MKD	YES	84	73
MNE	YES	53	58
POL	YES	50	39
ROU	YES	49	43
SRB	YES	58	57
SVK	YES	45	55
SVN	YES	29	33

Notes: *CDD—Law on preventing money laundering and financing of terrorists; CBDC—Central Bank Digital Currency; P2PL—Peer to Peer Lending. **Prohibited activity; Source://www.worldbank.org/en/topic/fintech/brief/global-fintech-enabling-regulations-database; https://fintechhub.cbcg.me; https://www.bsi.si/en/; https://www.nbs.sk/en; https://www.hanfa.hr/fintech1/; https://bqk-kos.org/.

According to Stern (2017), the nations in CESEE have differing degrees of new technology application. Stern (2017) states that fintech companies offer solutions to help people or organizations manage their finances. They also offer financial management services to both larger enterprises and SMEs. A selection of CEE nations' fintech policies and activities are shown in Table 6.

Out of all the CEE nations, Estonia, Lithuania, and the Republic of Slovakia have had the most success completing laws about fintech businesses and their goods (Table 7).

According to the DiGiX index, Estonia was the most prosperous country in 2018 and 2020. Regarding infrastructure and laws for fintech companies, Albania, Kosovo, Serbia, and Bosnia and Herzegovina are the least developed countries. Two additional Balkan countries, North Macedonia and Montenegro, have made notable progress. Fintech companies need more regulations, balancing

Table 8. The Main Challenges for the Development of Fintech Firms in the CEE Region.

Country	Most Commonly Cited Challenges to Fintech Development
Albania	Lack of a clear Fintech strategy by regulators and policymakers.
Bosnia and Herzegovina	The Fintech industry faces challenges due to inadequate government support, absence of enabling policies, difficulties in enforcing uniform laws and regulations, and lack of investment in research and development of innovative products by local IT companies. An electronic signature law needs to be included, which is needed to facilitate electronic transactions and boost the industry's growth.
Bulgaria	Local technical talent and ICT professionals are scarce, and there are lower levels of internet use due to a smaller domestic market.
Czech Republic	According to the European Commission, research institutions and the private sector must have a stronger connection. Investment in innovation activities should be targeted more effectively, improving specific gaps in funding allocation.
Croatia	Lack of support from regulators, scarcity of local technical talent, and fixed broadband access still need to be more expensive by EU standards.
Estonia	Business challenges include finding customers, accessing finance, managing costs, attracting skilled staff, complying with regulations, and expanding internationally.
Hungary	Mobile and Internet banking penetration is low in Hungary. The country's banks have low IT budgets, making supporting innovation challenging.
Kosovo	Lack of financing, poor ICT infrastructure, and insufficient data on business metrics hinder growth. International donor funding is critical for key players.
Lithuania	Struggling with product development, team building, compliance, product portfolio expansion, international expansion, and partnership building
Latvia	The availability of skilled workers, competition, access to finance, regulation, and costs of production and labor.
Montenegro	Lack of government support, innovation ecosystem infrastructure, financing and investors hinder startups and innovative activities.
Republic of North Macedonia	Lack of financing, a non-conducive FinTech ecosystem, and brain drain from emigration.

(*Continued*)

Table 8. (Continued)

Country	Most Commonly Cited Challenges to Fintech Development
Poland	Due to low venture capital and equity funding activity, a centralized, all-encompassing startup support system is needed.
Romania	Poor ICT infrastructure and lower levels of internet access in comparison to EU peers, coupled with a shortage of local technical talent.
Slovenia	The potential entry of foreign players offering non-banking credit products may be hindered due to the small market size in terms of customer numbers.
Slovakia	Non-banking consumer lending faces regulatory challenges.
Serbia	There are two major issues that hinder the growth of startups. The first one is the lack of financing, which means that many promising ideas cannot be implemented due to the lack of financial support. The second issue is the lack of coordination between the government and the startup ecosystem. This lack of coordination often leads to a fragmented approach, where startups are not given the support they need to succeed.

Source: World Bank group – Berg et al. (2020).

financial stability and consumer protection as key regulatory goals, operational limitations, and the presence of two separate regulators, which results in uneven treatment of fintech companies and sometimes confusing guidance.

Some challenges that fintech companies may present to CEE countries are listed in Table 8.

Conclusion

The research provides a comprehensive overview of the status of Fintech in Central and Eastern Europe (CEE). Several key findings have emerged through a comparative analysis methodology, incorporating data from various sources, including central banks, financial regulators, the World Bank Data Base, and the DiGiX index provided by BBVA Research. The study highlights the significant growth of Fintech startups and enterprises in CEE countries, revolutionizing the financial sector with innovative solutions. Digital banking, cryptocurrencies, insurance, e-commerce, and expense management ventures evidence this growth. Additionally, the analysis of Fintech regulations in the EU and Western Balkan countries underscores the importance of navigating a complex regulatory landscape. Directives such as the E-Commerce Directive and the Revised Payment Services Directive (PSD2) significantly influence Fintech operations, with countries like Estonia, Lithuania, and Slovakia making notable strides in enacting conducive laws.

Furthermore, the chapter identifies various challenges hindering the development of Fintech firms in the CEE region. Fintech companies in CEE countries face many challenges, such as a lack of regulations, the complexities of balancing key regulatory objectives between financial stability and consumer protection, prohibitions on Fintech activities (Bosnia and Herzegovina and Kosovo), and the existence of two different regulators (Northern Macedonia and Serbia), thus creating double standards and sometimes unclear guidance for Fintech companies. Despite the hurdles that the Fintech sector in the region faces, such as regulatory issues and limited access to funding, the industry has shown remarkable potential for growth and innovation. As digital financial services and new technologies emerge, the Fintech industry is poised to offer innovative solutions to consumers and businesses, transforming how financial services are delivered and accessed.

Based on the evaluation of the current state of the Fintech landscape in CEE countries, the recommendations are below:

- **Policy Advocacy and Regulatory Alignment:** Encourage policymakers in CEE countries to prioritize FinTech policy supporting innovation while protecting consumers. Drawing from successful examples like Estonia, Lithuania, and Slovakia, other countries can emulate regulatory frameworks that balance enabling FinTech growth and mitigating risks. Harmonization of Regulatory Standards: Advocate for harmonizing FinTech regulations across the CEE region to mitigate regulatory arbitrage and foster a level playing field for FinTech firms. This could involve collaboration between countries to align regulations, reduce regulatory complexities and enhance the ease of business for FinTech startups.
- **Capacity Building and Education:** Invest in programs to build the capacity of regulators, policymakers, and industry stakeholders to understand the intricacies of FinTech and emerging technologies. This includes training on regulatory compliance, consumer protection, and fostering an ecosystem conducive to FinTech innovation.
- **Partnerships** between governments, financial institutions, and FinTech companies are critical to achieving mutual benefits and growth. PPPs can facilitate knowledge sharing, provide resources, and create supportive environments for FinTech development.
- **Access to Funding and Investment:** Develop mechanisms to enhance access to funding for FinTech startups in the CEE region. This could involve establishing dedicated investment funds, providing investment incentives for FinTech, and supporting crowdfunding initiatives to bridge the funding gap startups face.
- **International Collaboration:** Encourage collaboration and knowledge exchange between CEE countries and other global FinTech hubs. This includes participation in international forums, conferences, and partnerships with established FinTech ecosystems to leverage best practices, attract investment, and expand market reach.
- **Promotion of Innovation Hubs:** Identify and promote specific cities or regions within CEE countries as FinTech innovation hubs. Hubs offer FinTech startups access to talent, infrastructure, funding, and regulatory support, catalyzing ecosystem growth and innovation.

- **Consumer Awareness and Protection:** Prioritize consumer education and protection initiatives to enhance trust and confidence in FinTech services. This includes raising awareness about digital financial literacy, data privacy rights, and recourse mechanisms in case of disputes, thereby fostering greater adoption of FinTech solutions.

References

Acar, O., & Çıtak, Y. E. (2019). Fintech integration process suggestion for banks. *Procedia Computer Science*, *158*, 971–978. https://doi.org/10.1016/j.procs.2019.09.138

Alaassar, A., Mention, A., & Aas, T. (2023). Facilitating innovation in FinTech: A review and research agenda. *Review of Managerial Science*, *17*, 33–66. https://doi.org/10.1007/s11846-022-00531-x

Al-Ansi, A. M., Garad, A., & Ryabtsev, V. (2024). Intelligent risk analysis of investment projects in the extractive industry. *Journal of Industrial Intelligence*, *2*(1), 42–53.

Alnemer, H. A. (2022). Determinants of digital banking adoption in Saudi Arabia: A technology acceptance model approach. *Digital Business*, *2*(2), 1–8. https://doi.org/10.1016/j.digbus.2022.100037

Arjunwadkar, P. Y. (2018). *FinTech* (1st ed., pp. 1–275). Auerbach Publications. https://doi.org/10.1201/9781351036504

Arner, D. W., Barberis, J. N., & Buckley, R. P. (2015). *The evolution of fintech: A new post-crisis paradigm*. University of Hong Kong Faculty of Law Research Paper No. 2015/047, UNSW Law Research Paper No. 16-62. Available at SSRN: https://ssrn.com/abstract=2676553 or http://dx.doi.org/10.2139/ssrn.2676553

Berg, M. G., Natarajan, H. & Sarkar A. (2020). *Fintech in Europe and Central Asia: Maximizing benefits and managing risks acknowledgments V*. https://doi.org/10.1596/33591

Crouhy, M., Galai, D., & Wiener, Z. (2021). The impact of fintechs on financial intermediation. *The Journal of FinTech*, *01*(01). https://doi.org/10.1142/S270510992031001X

Dasilas, A., & Karanović, G. (2023). The impact of FinTech firms on bank performance: evidence from the UK. *EuroMed Journal of Business*, *19*(1). https://doi.org/10.1108/EMJB-04-2023-0099

Deloitte. (2023). *CEE banks post strong performance*. https://www2.deloitte.com

DeYoung, R., Lang, W, & Nolle, D. (2007). How the Internet affects output and performance at community banks. *Journal of Banking & Finance*, *31*(4), 1033–1060. https://doi.org/10.1016/j.jbankfin.2006.10.003

FAHY, L. (2022). Regulator reputation and stakeholder participation: A case study of the UK's Regulatory Sandbox for Fintech. *European Journal of Risk Regulation*, *13*(1), 138–157. https://doi.org/10.1017/err.2021.44

FMER. (2021). *Fintech market report*. https://icd-ps.org/en/reports

Gupta, P., & Tham, T. M. (2019). Fintech: The new DNA of financial services (pp. 1–546). Walter de Gruyter GmbH & Co KG. ISBN 978154740094.

Jagtiani, J., & John, K. (2018). Fintech: The impact on consumers and regulatory responses. *Journal of Economics and Business*, *100*, 1–6. https://doi.org/10.1016/j.jeconbus.2018.11.002

Jeník, I., & Duff, S. (2020). *How to build a regulatory sandbox: A practical guide for policy makers*. Consultative Group to Assist the Poor. https://documents1.worldbank.org/curated/en/126281625136122935/pdf/How-to-Build-a-Regulatory-Sandbox-A-Practical-Guide-for-Policy-Makers.pdf

Khai Nguyen, Q., & Cuong Dang, V. (2022). The effect of FinTech development on financial stability in an emerging market: The role of market discipline. *Research in Globalization*, *5*, 1–15. https://doi.org/10.1016/j.resglo.2022.100105

Landman, T. (2008). *Issues and methods in comparative politics* (pp. 1–384). Routledge. https://doi.org/10.4324/9780203929780

Lor, P. J. (2009). International and comparative librarianship. In M. J. Bates & M. N. Maack (Eds.), *Encyclopedia of library and information sciences* (3rd ed., pp. 2404–2412). CRC Press.

Madiega, T., & Chahri, S. (2024). *Artificial intelligence act*. https://www.europarl.europa.eu/thinktank/en/document/EPRS_BRI(2021)698792

Madiega, T., & Van De Pol, A. L. (2022). *Artificial Intelligence Act and regulatory sandboxes*. https://www.europarl.europa.eu/thinktank/en/document/EPRS_BRI(2022)733544

Novarlić, B., & Đurić, P. (2024). Enhancing comprehensive waste management in transition economies through green logistics: A case study of Bosnia and Herzegovina. *Journal of Intelligent Management Decision*, *3*, 42–55.

Nugraha, K., Arief, M., Abdinagoro, S. B., & Heriyati, P. (2022). Factors influencing bank customers' orientations toward Islamic Banks: Indonesian banking perspective. *Sustainability*, *14*(19), 12506.

RBI. (2018). *CEE Fintech Atlas 2018*. https://www.cee-fintechatlas.com/wp-content/uploads/2021/06/CEE-Fintech-Atlas-2018-edition.pdf

RBI. (2019). *CEE Fintech Atlas 2019: Exclusive insights into 19 fintech ecosystems in Central and Eastern Europe – Special focus on open banking*. https://www.cee-fintechatlas.com/wp-content/uploads/2021/06/CEE-Fintech-Atlas-2019-edition.pdf

Singh, R., Malik, G., & Jain, V. (2021). FinTech effect: Measuring the impact of FinTech adoption on banks' profitability. *International Journal of Management Practice*, *14*(4). 411–427. https://doi.org/10.1504/IJMP.2021.116587

Stamegna, C., & Karakas, C. (2019). *Fintech (financial technology) and the European Union*. https://www.Europarl.Europa.Eu/RegData/Etudes/BRIE/2019/635513/EPRS_BRI(2019)635513_EN.Pdf

Stern, C. (2017). Fintechs and their emergence in banking services in CESEE. *Focus on European Economic Integration*, 42–58. https://api.semanticscholar.org/CorpusID:158180601

Stojkovski, B. (2023). *The rise of fintech in CEE: A mapping of 60+ startups and companies across the region*. https://therecursive.com/the-rise-of-fintech-in-cee-a-mapping-of-60-startups-and-companies-across-the-region/

Tanda, A., & Maria Schena, C. (2019). *Fintech, Bigtech and banks* (pp. 1–111). Palgrave Macmillan. https://doi.org/10.1007/978-3-030-22426-4

The Government of the Republic of Serbia. (2020). *Strategy for developing AI in the Republic of Serbia for 2020-2025*. https://www.srbija.gov.rs/tekst/en/149169/strategy-for-the-development-of-artificial-intelligence-in-the-republic-of-serbia-for-the-period-2020-2025.php

Turp-Balazs, C. (2020, February). *Bulgaria to launch first regtech sandbox in the Balkans*. https://emerging-europe.com/business/bulgaria-to-launch-first-regtech-sandbox-in-balkans/

Unsal, O., & Rayfield, B. (2019). *Trends in financial innovation: Evidence from Fintech Firms* (pp. 1–18). Networks Financial Institute at Indiana State University, WP-03.

Wong, J., & Ho, K. (2020). The impact of Fintech innovations on the Hong Kong banking industry. *SSRN Electronic Journal*, 1–49. https://doi.org/10.2139/ssrn.3607781

Wonglimpiyarat, J. (2017). FinTech banking industry: A systemic approach. *Foresight*, *19*(6), 590–603. https://doi.org/10.1108/FS-07-2017-0026

World Bank Group. (2020). *Global Experiences from Regulatory Sandboxes*. https://documents.worldbank.org/en/publication/documentsreports/documentdetail/912001605241080935/global-experiences-from-regulatory-sandboxes

World Bank. (2020). *How regulators respond to fintech: Evaluating the different approaches – sandboxes and beyond.* Retrieved from https://documents.worldbank.org/en/publication/documents-reports/documentdetail/579101587660589857/how-regulators-respond-to-fintech-evaluating-the-different-approaches-sandboxes-and-beyond

Yerpude, S., Sood, K., & Grima, S. (2022). Blockchain-augmented digital supply chain management: A way to sustainable business. *Journal of Risk and Financial Management*, *16*(1), 7.

Zaleska, M., & Kondraciuk, P. (2019). Theory and practice of innovation development in the banking sector. *Financial Sciences*, *24*(2), 76–87. https://doi.org/10.15611/fins.2019.2.06

Websites

- Carta Worldwide. (2023). *Fintech Laws and Regulations: 2022/2023 Guide*. https://cartaworldwide.com/blog/fintech/fintech-laws-and-regulations-2022-2023-guide/
- Statista. (2022). *Number of ATMs worldwide 2008-2022*. Https://Www.Statista.Com/Statistics/741708/Number-of-Atms-Worldwide/

Chapter 8

Frontiers of Innovation: Unveiling the Future Opportunities in Fintech

Shweta Dewangan[a] *and Sanjeev Kumar*[b]

[a]*The ICFAI University, Raipur, Chhattisgarh, India*
[b]*School of Hotel Management and Tourism, Lovely Professional University, Punjab, India*

Abstract

Introduction: The study examines how fintech has revolutionized the financial industry, with a focus on the uptake of cutting-edge innovations like blockchain, artificial intelligence, and quantum computing. It highlights fintech's increasing relevance in the changing economic landscape by discussing how it improves cybersecurity, global financial inclusion, and service efficiency.

Purpose: This text provides an in-depth analysis of fintech's transformative role in the financial sector, covering innovative business models, various subjects, evolution, contemporary developments, significant data impact, challenges, and future trends, including quantum computing, sustainable finance, and ESG investing.

Methodology Approach: This study uses the secondary from the existing literature. The researcher reviewed the various research papers, books, chapters, and government websites to provide a projection of future trends. This study addresses future opportunities in fintech and focuses on efficiency, costs, customer satisfaction, regulatory changes, innovations, cyber-security, decentralized finance, legal issues, and sustainable finance.

Findings: The study reveals that fintech has a profound impact on enhancing the efficiency of financial services, reducing costs, improving consumer

Financial Landscape Transformation: Technological Disruptions, 153–165

doi:10.1108/978-1-83753-750-120251008

satisfaction, and driving substantial economic growth. Additionally, it effectively tackles difficulties related to cybersecurity and regulatory compliance.

Keywords: Financial service; fintech companies; fintech innovation; AI in finance; DeFi; ESG; cybersecurity in digital finance; big data analytics

JEL Codes: D12; L64; O31

1. Introduction

Fintech is rapidly transforming the financial sector. Recently, there has been a notable change toward more inventive and customer-focused financial services, mainly propelled by technological advancements. This chapter presents the latest fintech advancements expected to revolutionize the industry in 2024. Decentralized Finance (DeFi) is positioned at the forefront of this transformation. DeFi platforms disrupt conventional financial systems by providing inclusive services like lending, borrowing, and trading through blockchain technology (Alaassar et al., 2023). This trend significantly impacts individuals whom traditional banking systems have marginalized. Quantum computing has emerged as a substantial advancement in the field of fintech. Quantum computers are anticipated to substantially improve cybersecurity by offering powerful processing capabilities. It will result in a strong defence against advanced cyber threats and safeguarding sensitive financial information. Artificial Intelligence (AI) is crucial in transforming customer experiences. AI algorithms can enhance customer satisfaction and foster loyalty by delivering highly personalized financial solutions by analyzing user behavior and preferences. The AI platform showcases the capacity of AI to generate tailored and streamlined customer service encounters within the realm of customer interaction. These AI-powered virtual assistants aid users in various tasks, including account management and financial advising (Giudici, 2018). The adoption of contactless payments, which the COVID-19 pandemic has expedited, is still progressing and being shaped by advancements such as Near-field communication (NFC) technology. NFC technology enables secure and convenient transactions using smartphones and wearables, fundamentally transforming our everyday financial interactions. Fintech places significant emphasis on sustainability as a critical area of focus. The notion of Green Finance, which prioritizes investments in environmentally sustainable projects, demonstrates the industry's dedication to integrating Environmental, Social, and Governance (ESG) considerations into financial solutions. Digital financial services have necessitated the implementation of solid identity verification procedures. Utilizing biometric authentication and blockchain-backed techniques, digital identity solutions simplify compliance procedures and bolster security measures against fraudulent activities. Fintech facilitates the dissolution of geographical boundaries, facilitating collaborations that promote financial solutions without borders (Barroso

& Laborda, 2022). This trend is essential for optimizing cross-border transactions, enabling smooth interactions across diverse currencies and regions. Fintech platforms are transforming user engagement through voice and gesture-based interfaces. The integration of natural language processing and motion sensing enables users to carry out financial tasks through intuitive interactions, thereby enhancing the accessibility of financial management. Finally, the convergence of neuroscience and fintech gives rise to neuroforaminal interfaces. By analyzing brain activity, these interfaces seek to gain insights into user preferences and emotions, with the potential to transform the customization and delivery of financial services completely (Brika, 2022). Ultimately, these patterns demonstrate fintech's ever-changing and inventive characteristics in 2024, emphasizing its capacity to establish a more comprehensive, secure, and user-friendly economic environment.

This chapter examines fintech's revolutionary impact on the financial services industry and highlights 2024 themes and technologies that will change the sector. DeFi, quantum computing, AI, and contactless payments are examined in detail to improve security, user experience, and operational efficiency. Sustainability through Green Finance and sophisticated digital identity verification demonstrate fintech's environmental and social responsibility. The chapter also examines fintech adoption and impact in Africa, Europe, and the Middle East, North Africa, and Pakistan (MENAP) areas, highlighting their unique problems and potential. This chapter highlights international cooperation and risk reduction to maximize fintech's benefits by studying the Bali Fintech Agenda and its impact on regulatory frameworks. The economic pressures and frictions of financial transaction processing (FTP) and the importance of corporate governance in sustainable growth are also covered. This chapter looks ahead to fintech's potential to produce a more inclusive, safe, and efficient financial ecosystem.

1.1. What Technologies Are Influencing the Future of Fintech?

In the upcoming years, we anticipate that these seven technologies will progress fintech development and influence the competitive environment of finance:

1. AI will drive significant value generation. Financial institutions are ready to embrace an AI-centric approach to equip themselves better against the growing presence of technology companies. McKinsey predicts that generative AI technologies could contribute $4.4 trillion annually to the global economy.
2. Blockchain will revolutionize traditional financial protocols by enabling the simultaneous storage of financial transactions in multiple locations. Technologies like smart contracts, zero-knowledge proof, and distributed data storage & exchange are crucial for fintech innovations such as digital wallets, digital assets, DeFi, and nonfungible tokens. They will remain important (Chuen & Deng, 2017).
3. Cloud computing. According to McKinsey research, cloud technology will contribute over $1 trillion in EBITDA for the top 500 companies worldwide

by 2030. Cloud computing will enhance efficiency and reduce expenses for financial services firms.
4. IoT stands for "Internet of Things." Perception and intelligent sensor systems, wireless communication networks, and application and operations support are all examples of IoT applications in the finance sector.
5. No- and low-code development platforms. These tools enable developers and users to create applications using graphical interfaces and configurations, like drag-and-drop, rather than conventional programming methods.
6. Hyper-automation involves utilizing AI, deep learning, event-based software, and other advanced technologies to enhance decision-making efficiency and automate tasks.

1.2. The Bali Fintech Agenda

The Bali Fintech Agenda (BFA) was endorsed by the International Monetary Fund (IMF) and World Bank Group in 2018. The text discusses essential considerations regarding how technological innovation impacts financial service delivery, affecting economic efficiency, growth, financial stability, inclusion, and integrity. The BFA is structured around 12 elements to assist member countries in leveraging the advantages and opportunities of rapid advancements in financial technology that are reshaping the delivery of financial services while mitigating associated risks. The BFA elements encompass facilitating fintech, ensuring the financial sector's resilience, addressing threats, and promoting international cooperation.

Essential Elements of BFA: Finding the Right Balance Between Opportunities and Risks

1. Capitalize on Fintech opportunities.
2. Enhance Financial Services with New Technologies.
3. Strengthen Competition and Commit to Open, Free, and Contestable Markets.
4. Grow Fintech for Financial Inclusion and Market Development.
5. Monitor Financial System Developments for Deeper Understanding.
6. Ensure Financial System Integrity.
7. Create an Enabling Legal Landscape.
8. Keep Monetary and Financial Systems Stable.
9. Build Strong Financial and Data Infrastructure for Fintech Benefits.
10. Promote International Cooperation and Information Sharing.
11. Improve Financial Sector Collective Surveillance and Assessment.

2. Methodology of the Study

The study encompasses a comprehensive examination of existing literature, analysis of specific cases, projection of future trends, and scrutiny of regulations to ascertain the present understanding and influence of fintech on financial institutions.

Fintech enhances productivity and reduces costs for businesses by automating financial processes, leveraging advanced analytics for better decision-making, offering cost-effective services, streamlining operations, and providing access to alternative financing options. These benefits include faster processing times, reduced transaction fees, and improved cash flow management. Fintech platforms also offer lower transaction fees, faster processing times, integrated financial systems, and resource optimization. By automating repetitive tasks, fintech allows employees to focus on higher-value activities, while alternative financing options like peer-to-peer lending and crowdfunding can be more cost-effective and quicker than traditional bank loans.

3. Fintech Transforming Financial Systems Worldwide

Fintech is changing how money and financial services are done by giving people new ways to collect and use data, make investment assets, and offer new services. This digitization opens the door to more efficient and accessible financial services and helps the economy grow. Access to financial services has grown a lot in developing economies. For example, between 2011 and 2021, the percentage of adults with bank accounts rose by 30% to 71%. Fintech innovations, like mobile money, have given poor people and small businesses that need access to essential financial services new ways to make money. Having a digital account gives women more freedom and access to credit, which helps them handle changes in their income. The fintech revolution has also lowered the costs of money transfers, which lets families spend more on essentials (Gomber et al., 2018). Fintech has made the global financial system more efficient by breaking down physical, social, and geographical barriers and making information more accessible. It has made it possible for costs to go down.

3.1. Revolutionizing Africa's Financial Scene: The Role of Fintech

Kenya boasts one of the highest levels of fintech adoption globally, primarily driven by the remarkable success of the fintech service M-Pesa. Introduced in 2007, M-Pesa simplified the process for Kenyans and later individuals in other nations to utilize their mobile devices to transfer money securely and promptly to one another. Most Kenyans rapidly embraced it. From 2020 to 2021, the number of technology startups in Africa increased threefold to approximately 5,200 companies, with slightly less than half of them being fintech. Approximately 90% of African transactions utilize cash, indicating significant potential for expansion. If the sector can achieve penetration levels like those in Kenya, African fintech revenues could increase eightfold by 2025 compared to their 2022 value. We predict that the growth potential in African financial technology will be focused on 11 main markets: Cameroon, Côte d'Ivoire, Egypt, Ghana, Kenya, Morocco, Nigeria, Senegal, South Africa, Tanzania, and Uganda. These markets represent 70% of Africa's GDP and half its population (Basdekis et al., 2022).

Here are four problems that new African fintech might have to deal with:

- They are reaching scale and making money. African fintech may be unable to reach its entire market (number of potential customers) because of problems with the infrastructure. These problems can include low mobile and internet coverage and a need for payment rails (the infrastructure that makes transactions possible). Fintech may also find it harder to grow if people have less money to spend and are less loyal to the company.
- They were getting around in a regulatory environment that needed to be clarified. Regulations change at different rates in each country. In general, complicated and changing rules make it hard for fintech to keep their businesses running and follow the directions in all markets.
- They are taking care of the lack. African fintech is getting less funding after a record-breaking year in 2021. However, fintech must continue moving forward because big companies are starting to catch up. African fintech will have to cut back on spending to get used to the new way venture capital funding works (Senyo et al., 2022).
- We are putting together solid foundations for corporate governance. There are times when the regulatory, socioeconomic, and political environment is unclear and broken up. A robust corporate governance structure can offer stability, clarity, and direction, especially during tough times. Building a strong culture, constructively involving stakeholders, and having a clear talent strategy to enhance the organization's skills are all parts of good corporate governance (Al-Ansi et al., 2024; Novarlic et al., 2024).

3.2. The Status of Financial Technology in Europe

Fintech in Europe took a big hit from COVID-19 and the economic uncertainty it caused. However, fintech will keep getting more substantial and essential for customers and the economy in the long run. Based on GDP, at least one fintech company is in the top five banks in each of the seven largest economies in Europe. While fintech has grown in Europe, it has grown at a different rate in all markets. There is a big difference between the top one-third of countries and the rest regarding maturity and performance. Sweden and the UK are two countries that stand out for having well-developed fintech ecosystems. There would be many good things if all of Europe's fintech ecosystems worked, as well as the best ones in the region. There would be more than 364,000 more fintech jobs, more than double the amount of money invested (to almost €150 billion), and valuations would go through the roof (to almost €1 trillion).

Here are some of how European stakeholders can benefit from financial technology:

- The fact that fintech companies provide superior service at lower prices is one of the reasons European customers are drawn to them. For instance, the fees associated with international transfers can be as low as 10% of the rates that traditional banking service institutions commonly charge.

- Financial technology companies serve as a driving force behind disruptive innovation and expansion within the overall financial ecosystem. Fintech companies are typically more agile and quicker than incumbents, which means they can launch new products and services more quickly. The average time to market for fintech companies is as little as two months, whereas the time it takes incumbents to bring a product to market is 12 months.
- The financial technology industry significantly contributes to the overall economy's potential for growth. Fintech companies have been responsible for creating approximately 134,000 jobs across Europe as of 2022, and their total valuation is close to 430 billion euros. This is greater than the total market capitalization of the seven largest listed banks in Europe combined (Li & Xu, 2021).

Stakeholders in the European financial system, including public institutions, incumbents, and fintech upstarts, must combine their strengths by establishing appropriate enabling structures and mechanisms for the system to realize the potential that fintech has made possible.

3.3. How Will Fintech Evolve in the Middle East, North Africa, and Pakistan?

In recent years, the Middle East, North Africa, and Pakistan (MENAP) have witnessed a boom in fintech: from 2017 to 2022, investor support increased by approximately 36% per year.

The following are five varieties of fintech firms in MENAP:

- Established fintech startups based domestically. In addition to lending, investments, payments, and InsurTech, local fintech startups also cater to the needs of consumers and businesses by developing payment wallets and applications, payment apps, and merchant payment solutions.
- Multinational fintech corporations. Prominent global fintech companies have established operations in the MENAP region, fostering competition and facilitating customer acceptance.
- The banks. Prominent banking institutions have swiftly adopted digital-only offerings. These include the digital, youth-oriented Weyay Bank, operated by the National Bank of Kuwait, and the digital lifestyle banking application Liv, developed by the Emirates National Bank of Dubai (Yerpude et al., 2022).
- Additional nonbank financial establishments. Well-established infrastructure providers such as payment processors, exchanges, and remittance services have developed mobile applications and established digital portals. They have, on occasion, formed alliances with fintech startups.
- Intersect or fintech companies. Prominent corporations with significant market share, particularly in the telecommunications industry, have expanded their product lines beyond mobile cash to include mobile wallets, mobile payments, and branchless banking services.

4. Forces and Frictions in the Financial Sector

This research investigates the influence that FTP have on the performance of banks in non-monetary terms, such as the satisfaction of customers, the expectations of employees regarding assistance, the quality of services provided, and the efficiency with which work is performed. The study was that the perceived usefulness of FTPs positively impacts both the quality of service and the work efficiency of employees (Lee et al., 2021). In addition, the difficulty of using FTPs had a positive impact on both the quality of service and the efficiency of work, which suggests that the problem of using FTPs can be overcome by improving both service quality and work efficiency (Yang & Wang, 2022). It is the first to investigate and analyze FTPs implemented in commercial banks in China. It does so by analyzing the perceived usefulness and perceived efficiency (PU) and the profitability (PE) from the point of view of both customers and employees of the individual banks. The use of non-financial measures, especially during the COVID-19 pandemic, made a big difference in our understanding of the factors that affect the performance of Chinese commercial banks (Chen et al., 2021).

4.1. Economic Frictions and Forces

Financial firms depend on transaction costs, and to reduce risk and build trust, it is necessary to address principal-agent challenges and incomplete or asymmetric information. It includes the costs of entering contracts, conducting searches, and verifying information for consumers and institutions. For example, lending is subject to information asymmetries because lenders must ascertain the risk profile of potential borrowers and monitor their capacity to repay the loan. Additional requirements for payment markets include the monitoring of payment obligations and the verification of the identities of account holders or payment tokens. Both investments in the financial market and insurance are susceptible to the risk of moral hazard, adverse selection, and uncertainty regarding the outcomes of future events (Sironi, 2016). Customers must have faith in the reliability of investments and operations, while investment products depend on the quality of the underwriting and execution services. By aligning interests and monitoring actions, the internalization of activities within a single financial services firm can overcome these challenges (Razzaque et al., 2020). Aligning and monitoring ensures that teams interact in a trustworthy manner. Markets must be completed, leading to efficient resource allocations and difficulty tailoring products to specific customer circumstances.

Tailoring products to particular customer circumstances is also challenging when uncertain about future outcomes. Companies that provide financial services, such as banks, exchanges, and brokers, are organized in a way that allows them to address information gaps and frictions associated with intermediation. Banks diversify their holdings across many borrowers to better manage the uncertainty of outcomes. Exchanges and brokers, on the other hand, reduce information asymmetries by requiring listing and publishing prices. Compared to other industries, the consumer demand for trustworthy providers is more pronounced (A. Omarini, 2020). A provider who successfully gains customers' trust with one product can effectively leverage that trust to offer additional services. Different types of businesses have different combinations of labor, physical, financial, and trust capital, which have been shifting rapidly. Despite this, the production of financial services is subject to the same frictions experienced in other industries, such as the indivisibility of natural resources and ongoing costs (Pandey et al., 2023). To manage their resources, financial firms make use of fundamental economic forces. Economies of scale, which result from the significant fixed-cost investment required for back-office systems and physical distribution networks, are one of these forces. Larger producers can better serve a broader range of customers and offer better pricing by spreading these costs over a more extensive customer base. Financial intermediaries, who combine interdependent financial services that can be provided through the same physical customer interfaces and utilize the same balance sheet, also benefit from economies of scope. Since many customers prefer a convenient suite of products, this can reduce costs and create synergies. In financial services such as payments, network effects are significant because an increase in the number of connected users increases the value of the network to all users. Historically, "first movers" and large, vertically, and horizontally integrated players have benefited from this advantage, especially in capital-intensive products like lending, risky institutions that handle consumer savings, and capital- and network-intensive industries like payments.

5. How Can Fintech's Grow Sustainably?

Financial technology companies are currently operating in a new environment. They need to find a way to concentrate on growth at any cost. As a result of the new liquidity constraints, fintech companies are placing a greater emphasis on profitability rather than simply expanding their customer adoption numbers or total revenues. A study of the growth patterns and performance of the world's 5,000 largest public companies over the preceding 15 years (Franco-Riquelme & Rubalcaba, 2021). The following four avenues are anticipated to have the most significant impact on the financial technology industry, according to our analysis:

- Adherence to cost accounting. To survive the new funding environment, it is necessary to maintain cost control while maintaining flexibility, skill, and compliance.
- A stable core was used to measure the growth of the whole. Before expanding, it is essential to make sure that there is a core business that is robust and stable, possessing a targeted and proven market fit.
- M&A by programmatic means. Pursuing mergers and acquisitions should be approached strategically, and mutually beneficial partnerships should be established based on a programmatic strategy rooted in value sharing (with incumbents and other fintechs).
- Make sure the culture is preserved. Preserve the adaptability, creativity, and culture that have been the driving forces behind disruption until now.

5.1. Unveiling the Future Opportunities in Fintech

The future of fintech holds exciting opportunities driven by technological advancements and evolving consumer needs. Fintech companies will likely play a significant role in developing secure and efficient payment solutions, including contactless payments, digital wallets, and cryptocurrency-based transactions. Blockchain technology is expected to revolutionize various aspects of financial services, from enhancing transaction security to enabling DeFi. Cryptocurrencies may become more mainstream, and fintech companies can explore innovative applications and services within this space. Fintech firms can leverage AI and machine learning (ML) to provide personalized and automated investment advice. Robo-advisors will likely become more sophisticated, catering to a broader range of financial products and services. Open banking initiatives facilitate the sharing of financial data through APIs, allowing third-party developers to create new applications and services. Fintech companies can capitalize on this trend by developing innovative solutions that provide consumers with seamless and integrated financial experiences.

The insurance industry is undergoing digital transformation through InsurTech. Fintech companies can explore opportunities to develop innovative insurance solutions, leveraging technologies like IoT (Internet of Things) for risk assessment and data-driven policy customization. Regulatory technology (regtech) focuses on helping financial institutions comply with regulations efficiently. Fintech companies can develop solutions that automate compliance processes, enhance cybersecurity, and ensure data privacy in the rapidly evolving regulatory landscape. Fintech can contribute to improving financial inclusion by reaching underserved populations. Innovative solutions such as mobile banking, microfinance, and peer-to-peer lending can help bridge the gap and provide financial services to previously excluded people. As financial transactions become increasingly digital, the importance of robust cybersecurity measures grows. Fintech companies have opportunities to develop and enhance security solutions to protect against cyber threats and fraud. Fintech firms can differentiate themselves by prioritizing a seamless and user-friendly customer experience. It includes personalized financial advice, intuitive user interfaces, and efficient customer support through chatbots and AI-driven systems.

6. Fintech Boosts Corporate Efficiency and Lowers Expenses in Various Ways

1. **Automating Accounting Procedures:**
    - Fintech solutions streamline payment and invoicing processes, eliminating the need for human intervention. This reduces the likelihood of human mistakes and shortens the payment period.
    - With automated payroll solutions, you can rest assured that your employees will be paid on time and accurately. This method also reduces administrative burden and the likelihood of human error.

2. **AI and advanced analytics:**
    - Using AI and big data, fintech solutions offer thorough understanding of financial performance and market trends. This helps companies to maximize operations, make wise decisions, and spot chances for cost control.
    - AI-driven fintech solutions improve security by spotting and stopping fraudulent activity, so averting possible losses and safeguarding of the financial integrity of the company.

3. **Economical Financial Services:**
    - Especially for cross-border transactions, fintech firms sometimes provide less transaction fees than conventional banks. For companies who deal internationally, this can greatly lower running expenses.
    - Faster transaction processing made possible by fintech technologies enhances cash flow management and lowers the working capital needs.

4. **Efficient Operations:**
    - Integrated Financial Systems: Fintech solutions consolidate diverse financial processes into a unified platform, streamlining administration and minimizing the requirement for different systems. This integration results in streamlined procedures and decreased software expenses.
    - Resource optimization is achieved by the automation of repetitive processes in fintech solutions. This automation allows staff to allocate their time and efforts toward higher-value activities, resulting in enhanced overall productivity.

5. **Access to Finance:**
    - Fintech systems enable access to alternative finance choices, including peer-to-peer lending and crowdsourcing, which can be faster and more reasonably priced than conventional bank loans. This helps companies to get money more quickly and at maybe reduced rates.

7. Conclusion

The study proves that fintech has impacted various aspects of the financial services industry, such as efficiency, costs, customer satisfaction, regulatory changes, innovations, cybersecurity, DeFi, legal issues, and sustainable finance. It also highlights the transformation that fintech has brought about.

It will result in a strong defence against advanced cyber threats and safeguarding sensitive financial information. AI is crucial in transforming customer experiences. The financial technology industry significantly contributes to the overall economy's potential for growth. Companies that provide financial services, such as banks, exchanges, and brokers, are organized in a way that allows them to address information gaps and frictions associated with intermediation.

References

Alaassar, A., Mention, A.-L., & Aas, T. H. (2023). Facilitating innovation in FinTech: A review and research agenda. *Review of Managerial Science*, *17*(1), 33–66.

Al-Ansi, A. M., Garad, A., & Ryabtsev, V. (2024). Intelligent risk analysis of investment projects in the extractive industry. *Journal of Industrial Intelligence*, *2*(1), 42–53.

Barroso, M., & Laborda, J. (2022). Digital transformation and the emergence of the Fintech sector: Systematic literature review. *Digital Business*, *2*(2), 100028.

Basdekis, C., Christopoulos, A., Katsampoxakis, I., & Vlachou, A. (2022). FinTech's rapid growth and its effect on the banking sector. *Journal of Banking and Financial Technology*, *6*(2), 159–176. https://doi.org/10.1007/s42786-022-00045-w

Brika, S. K. M. (2022). A bibliometric analysis of fintech trends and digital finance. *Frontiers in Environmental Science*, *9*, 796495.

Chen, X., You, X., & Chang, V. (2021). FinTech and commercial banks' performance in China: A leap forward or survival of the fittest? *Technological Forecasting and Social Change*, *166*, 120645.

Chuen, D. L. K., & Deng, R. H. (2017). *Handbook of blockchain, digital finance, and inclusion: Cryptocurrency, fintech, InsurTech, regulation, China tech, mobile security, and distributed ledger*. Academic Press.

Franco-Riquelme, J. N., & Rubalcaba, L. (2021). Innovation and SDGs through social media analysis: Messages from fintech firms. *Journal of Open Innovation: Technology, Market, and Complexity*, *7*(3), 165.

Giudici, P. (2018). Fintech risk management: A research challenge for artificial intelligence in finance. *Frontiers in Artificial Intelligence*, *1*(1).

Gomber, P., Kauffman, R. J., Parker, C., & Weber, B. W. (2018). On the fintech revolution: Interpreting the forces of innovation, disruption, and transformation in financial services. *Journal of Management Information Systems*, *35*(1), 220–265.

Lee, C.-C., Li, X., Yu, C.-H., & Zhao, J. (2021). Does fintech innovation improve bank efficiency? Evidence from China's banking industry. *International Review of Economics & Finance*, *74*, 468–483.

Li, B., & Xu, Z. (2021). Insights into financial technology (FinTech): A bibliometric and visual study. *Financial Innovation*, *7*, 1–28.

Novarlić, B., & Đurić, P. (2024). Enhancing comprehensive waste management in transition economies through green logistics: A case study of Bosnia and Herzegovina. *Journal of Intelligent Management Decision*, *3*, 42–55.

Omarini, A. (2020). FinTech: A new hedge for a financial re-intermediation. Strategy and risk perspectives. *Frontiers in Artificial Intelligence*, *3*, 63.

Pandey, D. K., Hassan, M. K., Kumari, V., Zaied, Y. B., & Rai, V. K. (2023). Mapping the landscape of FinTech in banking and finance: A bibliometric review. *Research in International Business and Finance*, *67*, 102116.

Razzaque, A., Cummings, R. T., Karolak, M., & Hamdan, A. (2020). The propensity to use FinTech: Input from bankers in the Kingdom of Bahrain. *Journal of Information & Knowledge Management*, *19*(01), 2040025.

Senyo, P. K., Karanasios, S., Gozman, D., & Baba, M. (2022). FinTech ecosystem practices shaping financial inclusion: The case of mobile money in Ghana. *European Journal of Information Systems*, *31*(1), 112–127.

Sironi, P. (2016). *FinTech innovation: From robo-advisors to goal-based investing and gamification*. John Wiley & Sons.

Srinivasan, K., & Rajarajeswari, S. (2021, May 13). Financial Technology in Indian Finance Market, *11*(2), 206–2011. Available at SSRN: https://ssrn.com/abstract=3845245 or http://dx.doi.org/10.2139/ssrn.3845245

Yang, L., & Wang, S. (2022). Do fintech applications promote regional innovation efficiency? Empirical evidence from China. *Socioeconomic Planning Sciences*, *83*, 101258.

Yerpude, S., Sood, K., & Grima, S. (2022). Blockchain-augmented digital supply chain management: A way to sustainable business. *Journal of Risk and Financial Management*, *16*(1), 7.

Chapter 9

An Analysis of Virtual Currencies and Decentralised Finance in the Metaverse: Unveiling Financial Dynamics and User Engagement

Anshul Agrawal[a] *and Sanjeev Kadam*[b]

[a]*GNIOT Institute of Management Studies, Greater Noida, India*
[b]*Symbiosis Institute of Business Management Pune, Symbiosis International (Deemed University), Pune, India*

Abstract

Purpose: The study aims to explore the profound impact of virtual currencies and decentralised finance (DeFi) protocols on financial dynamics, user engagement, and operational aspects within the Metaverse.

Methodology: This research employs mathematical modelling and quantitative analysis to comprehensively investigate the pivotal roles of these elements within the dynamic virtual environment.

Findings: The mathematical equations applied in our study have illuminated the intricate mechanics of financial expansion, operational efficiencies, and user dynamics in the Metaverse's virtual currency and DeFi systems. These insights underline the transformative influence of these digital ecosystems on future economies, emphasising the critical role of quantitative analysis in navigating and maximising their potential.

Significance: This research aims to shed light on the pivotal roles of virtual currencies and DeFi protocols through mathematical modelling and quantitative analysis. It contributes to a deeper understanding of their significance

Financial Landscape Transformation: Technological Disruptions, 167–183

doi:10.1108/978-1-83753-750-120251009

in shaping the future of virtual economies and financial interactions within the ever-evolving Metaverse.

Keywords: Decentralised finance; financial dynamics; Metaverse; user engagement; virtual currency; smart contacts; token liquidity

JEL Codes: G1; G2; G20; G21; G23; G3

Introduction

The burgeoning Metaverse, a fusion of physical and digital realms, is currently undergoing a profound metamorphosis. At its core lies the integration of virtual currencies and decentralised finance (DeFi), fundamentally reshaping digital economies and financial interactions within this virtual domain. Virtual currencies serve as the bedrock, enabling secure transactions, establishing ownership rights over virtual assets, and catalysing the growth of a vibrant virtual asset market (Weingärtner et al., 2023). These currencies are the backbone of economic activities, facilitating value exchange and trade within the Metaverse.

Complementing virtual currencies, DeFi protocols democratise financial services, empowering users worldwide to partake in diverse financial activities such as lending, borrowing, staking, yield farming, and liquidity provision (Gudgeon et al., 2020). It fosters broad financial inclusion within the virtual economy, allowing global participation.

'DeFi' refers to a broad category of conventional financial services and products that are based on and mirrored by a decentralised, uncontrolled blockchain infrastructure. Cryptocurrencies are necessary for decentralised finance, but it wanted to keep out banks and governments. It is similar to crowdsourcing in that all you need to get financial services is an internet connection (about a few million individuals globally are DeFi users). It is an emerging market with only a tiny percentage of the overall cryptocurrency market.

In late 2021, there were 7.5 million unique users of decentralised finance at its peak; by 2023, that number had significantly dropped (Poon, 2023). This corresponds to a network crawling code that counts the unique user addresses associated with acquiring or divesting specific DeFi-related projects (Wu & Chan, 2024). Fig. 1 exhibits the number of unique addresses that bought or sold a DeFi asset worldwide from November 2018 to November 2023 (Dune Analytics, Statista, 2023).

Frequently mentioned as a possible breakthrough trend for 2024, the total value locked (TVL) of DeFi in 2023 shows a significantly smaller market than in 2021. In November 2023, the amount of money held in DeFi was worth 50 billion dollars, compared to 175 billion dollars at the end of 2021. This drop can be attributed to two factors. The Bitcoin markets have seen a lot of notable occurrences overall. Prices dropped in 2022 after the stablecoin LUNA collapsed, and the cryptocurrency exchange FTX abruptly collapsed. In 2023, the US government imposed one of the most significant corporate fines ever on Binance, the

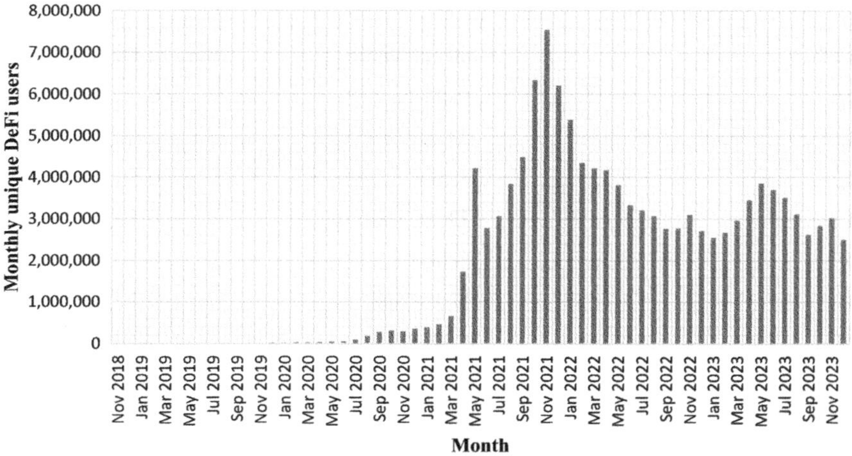

Fig. 1. Number of Unique Addresses That Either Bought or Sold a Decentralised Finance (DeFi) Asset Worldwide from November 2018 to November 2023. *Source*: Authors' compilation.

largest cryptocurrency exchange in the world. Second, analysts believe the 2023 high yield on US Treasury bonds, less risky than DeFi bonds, hurt the fledgling company.

In 2022, the vast bulk of the TVL in the DeFi business was comprised of Ethereum, BSC, and Tron combined, as exhibited in Table 1 (Statista, 2022). In the DeFi world, TVL is the metric that most closely approximates market size. The transaction volume of NFT for different segments also reflects the erratic character of advances in this emerging market.

Table 1. Distribution of Share of Top 20 TVL in DeFi, Worldwide Across Various Blockchains as of 29 November 2022.

Sl No	Characteristic	Share in DeFi TVL
1	Ethereum	58.10%
2	BSC	12.20%
3	Tron	10.50%
4	Polygon	2.60%
5	Arbitrum	2.30%
6	Avalanche	2.00%
7	Optimism	1.30%
8	Fantom	1.10%
9	Cronos	1.00%

(*Continued*)

Table 1. (Continued)

Sl No	Characteristic	Share in DeFi TVL
10	Solana	0.70%
11	Mixin	0.60%
12	Kava	0.50%
13	DefiChain	0.50%
14	Klaytn	0.50%
15	Osmosis	0.50%
16	Fusion	0.30%
17	MultiversX	0.30%
18	Algorand	0.30%
19	Waves	0.30%
20	Celo	0.30%

Source: Authors' compilation.

As Ethereum is the primary blockchain facilitating transactions for DeFi, its value changes could significantly affect DeFi. Fig. 2 exhibits two such occasions: On 10 September 2021, an overnight price drop caused Ethereum's TVL to tumble by more than 28 billion dollars Similarly, the collapse of Terra (LUNA) and its stablecoin Terra USD (UST) in May 2022 had a particularly negative effect on the DeFi market, and uncertainty persisted in June 2022 when coins like USDD lost their peg to the US dollar. Furthermore, a faltering cryptocurrency market influences DeFi (Website Defi Llama, 2023a).

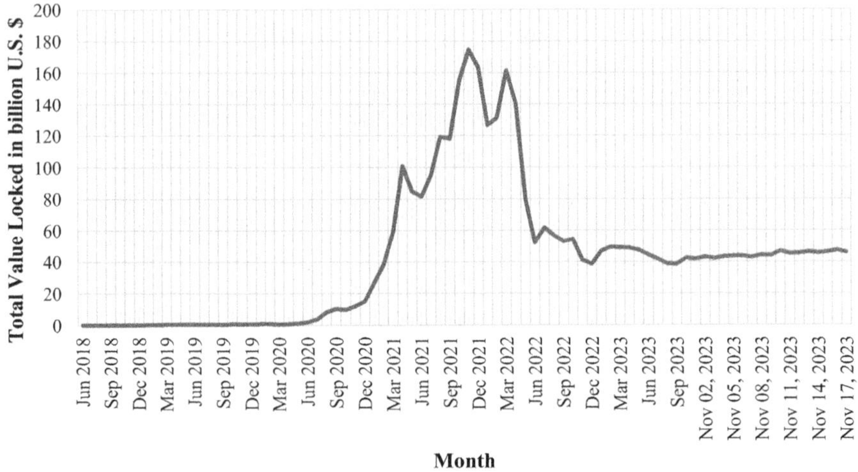

Fig. 2. TVL Across Multiple DeFi Blockchains from June 2018 to November 2023 (in Billion US Dollars). *Source*: Authors' compilation.

The goal of decentralised finance is to provide various digital financial services managed independently by a community within an organisation known as a decentralised autonomous organisation (DAO) without the involvement of banks or governments. These services enable the provision of services that traditional finance cannot provide, such as asset management, money lending, or trading. Nevertheless, by the end of 2023, DeFi had narrowed its attention to two primary use cases: money lending and liquid staking.

DeFi was most popular in nations like China and the United States, where it transferred or traded significant volumes of cryptocurrencies. Comparing this result to a global ranking of cryptocurrency ownership by country reveals that consumers in developing nations are far more likely to hold cryptocurrency than those in developed nations. The data presented here may indicate that traders and institutional investors are primarily interested in cryptocurrencies in the US, China, the UK, and India; DeFi offers a way to acquire or transfer cryptocurrency across these nations.

Based on grassroots DeFi acceptance, countries ranked by Chain Analysis' Global DeFi acceptance index. The analysis highlights that many nations with the highest grassroots DeFi adoption rankings are also those with the most considerable raw quantities of cryptocurrency value transferred, both in the present and the past. These are often middle-class to high-income nations or those whose cryptocurrency markets are well-established, with robust professional and institutional markets. Table 2 exhibits an index of the twenty countries with the highest interaction with DeFi platforms worldwide between April 2019 and June 2021 based on web traffic towards DeFi protocols. The United States was at the top with the highest index score. However, India was at the top in the on-chain DeFi value received and on-chain retail value received (Chainalysis, 2021).

Table 2. Countries with the Highest DeFi Adoption in the World in 2021.

S. No.	Country	Index Score	Country Ranking		
			Based On-chain DeFi Value Received	Based On-chain Number of DeFi Deposits	Based On-chain Retail DeFi Value Received
1	United States	1.00	3	47	4
2	Vietnam	0.82	4	64	3
3	Thailand	0.68	5	46	5
4	China	0.62	2	113	2
5	United Kingdom	0.60	9	40	6
6	India	0.59	1	120	1
7	Netherlands	0.55	24	11	18

(*Continued*)

Table 2. (Continued)

S. No.	Country	Index Score	Country Ranking		
			Based On-chain DeFi Value Received	Based On-chain Number of DeFi Deposits	Based On-chain Retail DeFi Value Received
8	Canada	0.52	17	30	15
9	Ukraine	0.49	11	50	7
10	Poland	0.46	18	36	17
11	France	0.46	14	44	16
12	Australia	0.41	27	26	23
13	Turkey	0.40	13	61	14
14	Switzerland	0.38	31	8	34
15	Russia	0.36	10	77	12
16	Argentina	0.34	12	65	21
17	Brazil	0.32	6	110	13
18	Portugal	0.31	34	22	33
19	Hong Kong SAR	0.30	33	14	47
20	Togo	0.30	32	34	29

Source: Authors' compilation.

Insurance is not one of the largest categories of decentralised finance (DeFi), according to a list that compares the TVL of various industries. Decentralised exchanges, or Dexes, are over 60 times larger than blockchain protocols designed to safeguard financial interests. DeFi classified these protocols as the 21st highest category. However, given that the total size of the DeFi market is less than the total amount of all cryptocurrencies combined, it is still in its infancy.

Fig. 3 exhibits the TVL in different segments across the top 10 DeFi blockchains worldwide as of December 4, 2023 (in billion US dollars). It was liquid staking with USD 29.55 billion, lending with USD 20.33 billion, the bridge with USD 13.57 billion, followed by Dexes with USD 13.32 billion, leading the DeFi blockchains worldwides (Website Defi Llama, 2023b).

User engagement within the Metaverse is paradigm-shifting due to virtual currencies and DeFi integration. This research aims to unravel the layers of user interaction dynamics, content creation incentives, and participatory mechanisms within the dynamic fabric of the Metaverse, synthesising insights from existing literature and mathematical equations. Operational frameworks within the Metaverse experience a paradigm shift owing to the convergence of virtual currencies and DeFi protocols.

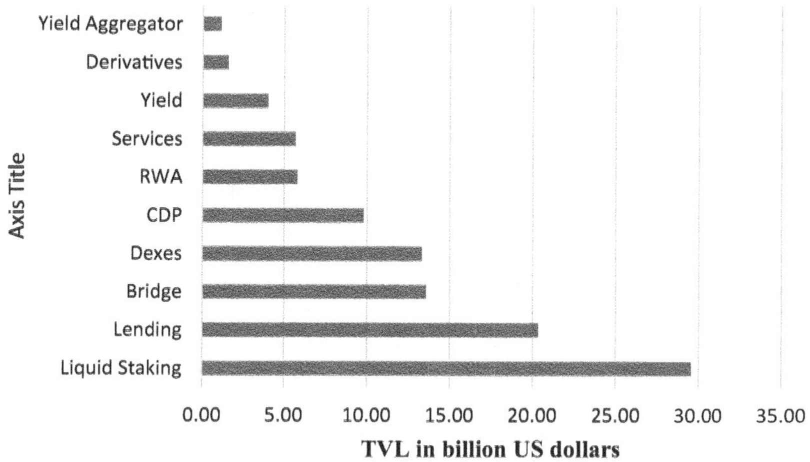

Fig. 3. Total Value Locked in Different Segments Across Top 10 DeFi Blockchains Worldwide as of December 4, 2023 (in Billion US Dollars).
Source: Authors' compilation.

This research aims to address the following research questions:

a) How do virtual currencies and decentralised finance aid in transforming digital economies and financial exchanges?
b) Discuss operational nuances and challenges emerging within this dynamic realm, aiming to elucidate the profound impact on security measures, cross-platform connectivity, and transactional efficiencies.
c) How to employ mathematical equations that provide insights into the financial, security, and user engagement aspects of the Metaverse?
d) What would be the significance of virtual currencies and DeFi protocols in this rapidly evolving digital landscape?

Literature Review

The Metaverse, a virtual reality domain that blurs the boundaries between the physical and digital realms, has captured the imagination of technology enthusiasts and futurists. In this immersive digital universe, virtual currencies, and decentralised finance (DeFi) fusion drive transformative changes in digital economies and financial systems. Schorch et al. (2021) delved into the rising prominence of virtual currencies in digital ecosystems, emphasising their impact on user experiences and engagement within the Metaverse. It explored how blockchain technology establishes trust and ownership of digital assets, laying the foundation for vibrant virtual economies. Deng et al. (2020) focus on the tokenisation of virtual assets within the Metaverse, analysing the adoption of Non-Fungible Tokens (NFTs) as unique digital assets, highlighting the emergence of a novel virtual property market, and delving into the implications of blockchain-based ownership. Huang and Wang (2020) delve into the integration of DeFi protocols in virtual economies, emphasising the potential for financial inclusion and user empowerment. It was underscored DeFi's role in enabling lending, borrowing, and yield farming activities within the Metaverse. Hou et al. (2022) explored the interoperability of DeFi platforms in different virtual reality environments, discussing cross-platform connectivity, its impact on user experiences, and the challenges associated with seamless asset transfers (Al-Ansi et al., 2024; Novarlić & Đurić, 2024).

Chen and Li (2021) investigated the role of virtual currencies and DeFi in incentivising user participation within the Metaverse. It was analysed reward mechanisms and the impact of financial incentives on user engagement and content creation. Büschken and Hahn (2020) assess the security and privacy aspects of blockchain-based virtual currencies in the Metaverse. It was discussed the potential risks associated with smart contracts and the importance of user education to ensure secure transactions. Liu et al. (2021) proposed a framework for ensuring transparency and trust in virtual transactions using Blockchain technology. It was emphasised the role of consensus mechanisms and cryptographic protocols in establishing trust-less environments. Yilmaz and Erol (2022) analysed the potential impact of virtual currencies and DeFi on traditional financial systems and economies. Regulatory authorities face the challenges of monitoring and governing virtual financial activities within the Metaverse.

Conversely, reviewing previous studies demonstrates the relevance and utilisation of mathematical equations in understanding the Metaverse's evolving digital landscape. Notable studies, such as those by Schorch et al. (2021) on virtual currencies in digital ecosystems and Hou et al. (2022) on DeFi interoperability, highlighted the application of mathematical models in evaluating the role and impact of virtual currencies and DeFi protocols. These studies have paved the way for our research, contributing valuable insights into the mathematical aspects of the Metaverse's financial and operational dimensions. Schorch et al. (2021) explored the role of virtual currencies within digital ecosystems, a domain that includes the Metaverse. The research investigates how virtual currencies are utilised as a medium of exchange and ownership, thereby impacting the overall dynamics of digital economies. It was importantly emphasised the application of mathematical models in evaluating the role and impact of virtual currencies. It was recognised the significance of mathematical equations in quantifying the value of virtual currencies within digital ecosystems. The study acknowledges that mathematical models can be employed to evaluate user engagement with virtual currencies. Metrics were created based on mathematical principles to measure user interactions, transaction volumes, and participation rates. This quantitative approach offers insights into the level of adoption and usage of these digital assets. It was recognised the role of mathematical models in validating the integrity of smart contracts, which underlie many virtual currencies, thus promoting secure and trust-less transactions (Yerpude et al., 2022).

Furthermore, Hou et al. (2022) study delves into the crucial aspect of interoperability within DeFi protocols, especially in the context of the Metaverse and digital ecosystems.

Methodology

This research focuses on seamlessly transferring assets and financial services across diverse virtual reality platforms. Mathematical models are central to understanding and enhancing DeFi interoperability. Mathematical modelling is the cornerstone of this study, offering a structured approach to dissect and interpret the multifaceted interplay between virtual currencies and DeFi within the Metaverse. By synthesising insights from existing literature and utilising mathematical equations, this research endeavours to decode the profound influence wielded by these elements on financial intricacies, user behaviours, and operational mechanics in the dynamic landscape of the Metaverse.

Integrating virtual currencies and DeFi within the Metaverse heralds far-reaching implications for financial structures. Through mathematical models and quantitative analysis, this study seeks to illuminate the transformative impact on transactional paradigms, asset markets, and economic interactions within the evolving Metaverse, drawing from established literature and employing mathematical equations.

This study employs mathematical equations as indispensable tools to comprehensively unravel the interplay between virtual currencies and DeFi protocols within the Metaverse. Mathematical modelling is pivotal in understanding various facets, including financial dynamics, security measures, and strategies for user engagement within this dynamic virtual realm.

In this study, our quantitative framework is a robust tool for analysing diverse facets of virtual currencies and DeFi within the Metaverse. It facilitates comprehensive investigations into financial implications, security evaluations, interoperability assessments, and metrics gauging user engagement. This approach allows for a thorough examination of this evolving digital landscape.

Compound Interest Formula for DeFi Yield Calculation:

$$A = P\left(1 + nr\right)nt \tag{1}$$

Equation 1 calculates the future value of assets in DeFi protocols. A represents the future value of the investment, P is the principal amount, r is the annual interest rate, n is the number of times interest compounded, and t is the time in years. It helps estimate asset growth through yield farming and staking within the Metaverse.

Liquidity Ratio Formula for Assessing Token Liquidity:

$$Liquidity\ Ratio = \frac{Total\ Value\ locked\ in\ pool}{Tokens\ in\ pool} \tag{2}$$

Equation 2 shows the liquidity ratio, a critical metric for DeFi liquidity pools. It assesses the liquidity available for trading relative to the TVL in the pool. This formula aids in quantifying the liquidity and trading capacity within DeFi platforms operating in the Metaverse.

Bridge Success Rate Formula for Interoperability Assessment:

$$Bridge\ Sucess\ Rate = \frac{Total\ Attempted\ Transfers}{Successful\ Transfers} \tag{3}$$

Equation 3 measures the efficiency and reliability of asset transfers between different virtual reality platforms within the Metaverse.

Smart Contract Vulnerability Score:

$$Vulnerability\ Score = \sum_{i=1}^{n} w_i \times S_i \tag{4}$$

Equation 4 depicts the vulnerability score, a weighted sum of individual smart contract vulnerabilities. Each vulnerability is assigned a weight and a severity score. This equation quantifies the overall security risk associated with smart contracts used in the Metaverse.

User Activity Index Formula for User Engagement:

$$User\ Acitivity\ Index = \frac{Total\ User\ Base}{Number\ of\ User\ Interactions} \tag{5}$$

Equation 5 shows that the user activity index quantifies user engagement by calculating the ratio of user interactions (such as transactions and content creation) to the total user base within the Metaverse. It provides insights into user participation and activity levels.

Equations 1–5 provide a rigorous foundation for understanding the role and impact of virtual currencies and DeFi in the Metaverse. These equations assist in investigating financial implications, security vulnerabilities, interoperability, and user engagement metrics in this emerging digital landscape.

Formally expressing the combined relationships among Compound Interest (CI), Liquidity Ratio (LR), Bridge Success Rate (BSR), Smart Contract Vulnerability Score (VS), and User Activity Index (UAI) in precise mathematical terms across these metrics is challenging due to their diverse nature and distinct calculations. However, conceptually, their relationships might be represented as:

$$CI \Rightarrow UAI \Rightarrow BSR \Rightarrow LR \Leftarrow VS \tag{6}$$

Equation 6 indicates the potential directional influences or relationships among Compound Interest, Liquidity Ratio, Bridge Success Rate, Smart Contract Vulnerability Score, and User Activity Index. Where CI influences UAI, it potentially affects engagement levels. UAI might have an impact on BSR, significantly affecting the efficiency of asset transfers. Conversely, BSR might have implications for LR, influencing trading capacity and liquidity, and VS influences the LR, which affects trust and liquidity levels.

Economic Implications of Virtual Currencies and DeFi in the Metaverse

Virtual currencies fuel the Metaverse by exchanging commodities, services, and virtual assets (Smith & Johnson, 2023). These blockchain-based digital currencies offer secure online buying, selling, and trading. The decentralised blockchain secures ownership rights and scarcity, providing digital property rights. The Metaverse's DeFi protocols democratise financial services worldwide. Traditional financial obstacles were erased, allowing virtual lending, borrowing, yield farming, and liquidity provision (Lee & Brown, 2022). This financial inclusion boosts user engagement.

Virtual currency and DeFi protocols allow gaming systems and virtual worlds to communicate (Smith & Johnson, 2023). Transferring assets and currencies across Metaverse contexts promotes cross-platform connectivity and fluid experiences (Garcia & Martinez, 2021). Interoperability allows a more connected and vibrant virtual reality ecology. Virtual currency and DeFi systems encourage user participation in new ways. Users can earn rewards for creating content, completing quests, meeting in-game goals, or helping community governance. These incentives increase user engagement and virtual economy growth. Virtual currencies like DeFi use blockchain technology for security and transparency. Smart contracts enable automated, trustless transactions, eliminating fraud and ensuring virtual asset ownership. Users can confidently transact in the Metaverse, knowing their digital assets are secure and tamper-proof (Johnson & Kim, 2019). Virtual currencies and DeFi help create virtual real estate marketplaces. Users can buy, sell, and trade virtual properties using digital currency, and DeFi platforms can finance property like mortgages. This growing business offers opportunities for virtual architects, developers, and investors.

Metaverse's virtual currencies and DeFi integration are concerned with scalability, interoperability, and user privacy (Zheng et al., 2017; Lee et al., 2021). To comply with regulations and protect users, virtual currencies and financial operations in the virtual world must be carefully considered. Metaverse virtual currencies and DeFi adoption may affect existing financial systems and economies (Wang & Chen, 2020). It may rethink value, ownership, and financial interactions, disrupting the financial landscape.

Risks and Challenges in the Intersection of Virtual Currencies and DeFi in the Metaverse

Researchers and stakeholders must carefully study the hazards and challenges of virtual currencies and decentralised finance (DeFi) in the Metaverse. Cryptocurrencies have tremendous price volatility. The fluctuating value of virtual assets may expose Metaverse users to financial hazards when using DeFi protocols.

Smart contracts are vulnerable to coding flaws and power DeFi platforms. Exploitable smart contract issues can cost users money, threatening Metaverse DeFi applications. Interconnected and immersive, the Metaverse may be vulnerable to cyberattacks and security breaches. DeFi platform hacks or data leaks can harm user funds and personal data.

The regulation of virtual currency and DeFi is still changing and varies by country. DeFi projects in the Metaverse may need help to comply with complicated and shifting rules. Users may need help to analyse risks and make informed decisions on DeFi platforms that lack transparency in their operations and financial practices.

The decentralised and pseudonymous characteristics of DeFi can attract scammers targeting unskilled Metaverse users. As Metaverse popularity grows, DeFi protocols may face scalability issues, causing congestion and higher transaction fees. Virtual currencies and DeFi integration in the Metaverse may need complex processes, which can limit user experience and acceptance.

The Metaverse may have multiple virtual reality platforms with varied specs. Interoperability between these platforms and DeFi protocols is difficult. Many consumers need to comprehend virtual currency and DeFi, resulting in blunders and losses. Responsible use requires good user education. Governance mechanisms and decision-makers may be centralised in some DeFi platforms. Centralisation can weaken the Metaverse's decentralisation and introduce weaknesses. The breakdown of one DeFi protocol can affect others in the Metaverse, creating systemic dangers. Virtual currencies and DeFi protocols in the Metaverse may gather and handle user data. Data privacy and security are essential to secure users' sensitive data.

Case Studies

The 'Metaverse Token' is a decentralised digital currency inherently ingrained within a widely embraced virtual reality platform. The case study delves into the integration of the token above by the platform's developers within the virtual ecosystem, thereby facilitating the acquisition of virtual goods, the attainment of exclusive experiences, and the exchange of assets within the Metaverse. The primary aim of this research endeavour is to conduct a comprehensive analysis of the adoption and subsequent effects of the 'Metaverse Token' in terms of stimulating user engagement and cultivating a virtual economy that the users themselves primarily drive. The examination of the case study may reveal that the 'Metaverse Token' has effectively fostered heightened levels of user engagement. The users are motivated to acquire and actively utilise the token within the virtual ecosystem. Incorporating decentralised finance (DeFi) mechanisms has facilitated the decentralised exchange of assets and augmented the overall liquidity of virtual currencies.

'DecentralVR' is a decentralised finance (DeFi) protocol that operates within the immersive digital realm known as the Metaverse. This innovative platform facilitates the provision of virtual asset lending and borrowing services, enabling users to engage in financial activities within the virtual environment. The case study delves into how users employ the protocol to lend their virtual assets to others, thereby generating passive income. Concurrently, borrowers can acquire access to limited virtual goods and experiences. The primary aim of this research endeavour is to evaluate the extent to which virtual asset lending and borrowing practices have been embraced within the Metaverse and identify and analyse the associated obstacles. Furthermore, this study seeks to investigate the implications of such practices on the distribution dynamics of virtual assets within said Metaverse. The case study may reveal that introducing 'DecentralVR' has engendered novel economic prospects for users, as it empowers them to capitalise on their virtual assets. Nevertheless, it is imperative to acknowledge the presence of specific challenges about the valuation of assets, the inherent volatility of prices, and the potential risks associated with security.

The 'CrossMetaverse Bridge' is an innovative Blockchain-driven solution that seamlessly transfers virtual assets and currencies across diverse virtual reality platforms. The present case study delves into the intricate aspects of the interoperability solution's technical implementation and user experience. The primary aim of this research endeavour is to comprehensively analyse the influence exerted by the 'CrossMetaverse Bridge' on the facilitation of cross-platform asset transfers. Furthermore, this investigation seeks to elucidate the potential ramifications within the virtual reality ecosystem due to this technological development. The case study potentially showcases the impact of the 'CrossMetaverse Bridge' on enhancing the efficiency of asset transfers, thereby fostering heightened user exploration and engagement across diverse virtual reality platforms. Nevertheless, it is imperative to acknowledge various challenges intrinsically linked to technical limitations, transaction costs, and network congestion (Chang & Patel, 2023).

The presented practical case studies serve as illustrative examples that highlight the potential ramifications and complexities associated with the integration of virtual currencies and decentralised finance (DeFi) within the Metaverse. As technological advancements unfold, empirical investigations will likely arise to furnish more tangible elucidations about this paradigmatic convergence.

Results and Findings

The 'Metaverse Token' is a decentralised digital money embedded in a popular virtual reality application. The case study examines how the platform's developers integrated the token into the virtual ecosystem to enable the purchase of virtual products, exclusive experiences, and Metaverse asset exchange. This research aims to analyse how the 'Metaverse Token' stimulates user involvement and creates a user-driven virtual economy. The case study may show that the 'Metaverse Token' has increased user engagement by encouraging them to acquire and use the token actively in the virtual ecosystem. DeFi techniques may enable asset exchange and increase virtual currency liquidity.

DeFi protocol 'DecentralVR' runs in the immersive Metaverse. This unique platform allows users to transact virtual financial transactions by lending and borrowing virtual assets. The case study examines how users lend virtual assets to generate passive income using the protocol. Borrowers can also access limited virtual products and activities. This research assesses the challenges of the Metaverse's adoption of virtual asset lending and borrowing practices. This study also examines how such practices affect Metaverse virtual asset distribution patterns. The case study may show that 'DecentralVR' allows users to profit from their virtual assets, creating new economic opportunities. However, asset value, price volatility, and security threats must be considered (Smith & Lee, 2023).

The blockchain-powered 'CrossMetaverse Bridge' lets virtual assets and currencies cross virtual reality systems. The interoperability solution's technical execution and user experiences were examined in this case study. This research also tries to understand how this technical advancement may affect the virtual reality ecosystem. The case study suggests that the 'CrossMetaverse Bridge' could improve asset transfers, encouraging user exploration and interaction across virtual reality platforms. However, technical limits, transaction costs, and network congestion present many obstacles (Smith & Lee, 2023).

The market for DeFi is now seeing rapid innovation and growth. Decentralised exchanges (DEXs), which let users trade cryptocurrencies without a central authority, are one trend currently gaining traction. The rise of yield farming, where users can get compensated for supplying liquidity to DeFi protocols, is another trend. Furthermore, it is becoming increasingly common for DeFi to integrate non-fungible tokens (NFTs), opening up new avenues for asset collateralisation. The need for decentralised financial services that are more inclusive, transparent, and accessible than traditional finance is one of the many causes propelling the expansion of the DeFi business.

Furthermore, the programmability and flexibility of blockchain technology make it feasible to create previously unimaginable new financial services and instruments. DeFi is expanding due to the availability of decentralised platforms for trading, borrowing, and lending that enable more decentralised and permissionless user interaction with financial markets. It was anticipated that the DeFi market would keep expanding in the future. The continuous creation of new DeFi use cases and applications, the growing acceptance of cryptocurrencies by mainstream investors, and the continuous introduction of new DeFi platforms and protocols were anticipated to propel this expansion. Nevertheless, the industry will also encounter difficulties, such as ambiguous regulations and security worries, which can hinder its expansion in the upcoming years (Ahmed, 2024).

It was anticipated that there would be 21.83 million customers in the DeFi market by 2027. Similarly, by 2027, user penetration is predicted to reach 0.3% from 0.2% in 2023, as exhibited in Fig. 4. The DeFi market was expected to generate US$17,740.00 million in revenue by 2023. Revenue was predicted to grow at a 19.37% annual rate (CAGR 2023–2027), reaching a total estimated value of US$36,020.00 million by 2027, as exhibited in Fig 5. In the DeFi market, the average revenue per user is expected to reach US$1,064.00 in 2023. Based on a comparative analysis of the world's economies, the United States has the most significant revenue ($8,673,000.00k in 2023) (*Source*: FinTech – Worldwide Statista market insights (2024). Statista market insights, 2024).

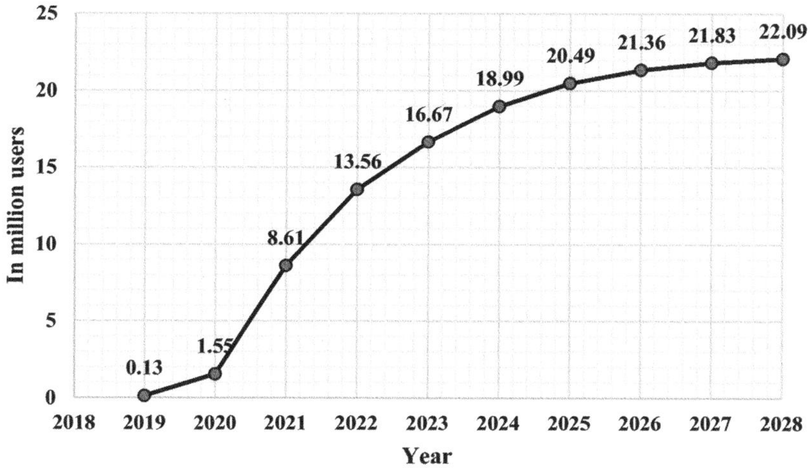

Fig. 4. Worldwide DeFi Users in Million. *Source*: Authors' compilation.

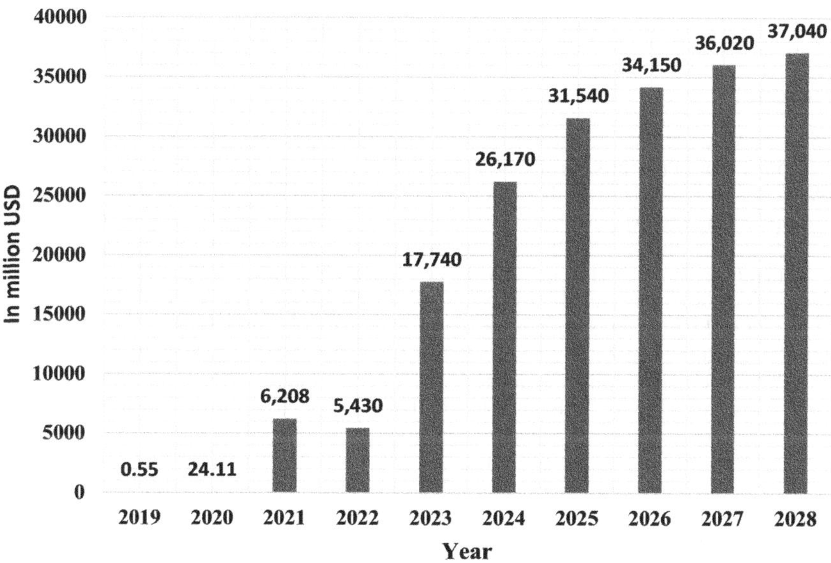

Fig. 5. Worldwide DeFi Revenue in Million USD. *Source*: Authors' compilation.

Conclusion

The integration of mathematical equations has been pivotal in deciphering the intricacies of virtual currencies and DeFi in the expansive realm of the Metaverse. These equations have guided us, illuminating our understanding of financial growth, operational efficiency, and user dynamics within this dynamic digital sphere. Beyond highlighting present impacts, it also foreshadows the profound role virtual currencies and DeFi will play in shaping the future digital economies of the Metaverse. Quantitative analysis is an indispensable tool for navigating the continuous evolution of this landscape.

Nevertheless, it is imperative to acknowledge the study's limitations. While mathematical models provide valuable insights, they may oversimplify the complex interplay of human behaviours and market dynamics within the Metaverse. The rapid technological evolution poses a challenge in maintaining the relevance of these models, and the study's scope might encompass a partial spectrum of variables influencing virtual currencies and DeFi. Thus, further research is essential.

Numerous unexplored avenues await investigation in virtual currencies and DeFi within the Metaverse. Future studies could focus on enhancing predictive models through AI and machine learning, understanding the socio-economic impacts, and establishing regulatory frameworks for these digital ecosystems. Additionally, examining the environmental footprint of cryptocurrency mining and devising sustainable solutions is an imperative area for exploration. Collaborative interdisciplinary efforts will enrich our comprehension of this evolving landscape, paving the way for informed decisions and innovative advancements.

References

Ahmed, A. A. A. (2024). The rise of DeFi: Transforming traditional finance with blockchain innovation. Preprints, 2024020738. https://doi.org/10.20944/preprints202402.0738.v1

Al-Ansi, A. M., Garad, A., & Ryabtsev, V. (2024). Intelligent risk analysis of investment projects in the extractive industry. *Journal of Industrial Intelligence*, *2*(1), 42–53.

Büschken, J., & Hahn, T. (2020). Security and privacy aspects of Blockchain-based virtual currencies in the Metaverse. *Journal of Virtual Economics*, *15*(3), 112–129.

Chainalysis. (2021, August 24). Index of the 20 countries with the highest interaction with DeFi platforms worldwide between April 2019 and June 2021. In *Statista*. Retrieved December 31, 2023, from https://www.statista.com/statistics/1263257/global-defi-adoption-by-country/

Chang, L., & Patel, R. (2023). Bridging virtual realities: A case study of the crossmetaverse bridge. *Journal of Virtual Reality Research*, *15*(4), 220–235.

Chen, L., & Li, Y. (2021). Incentivising user participation in the Metaverse: The role of virtual currencies and DeFi. *Journal of Virtual Reality Studies*, *8*(2), 45–62.

Deng, Q. et al. (2020). Tokenisation of virtual assets in the Metaverse: Non-Fungible Tokens (NFTs) as unique digital assets. *Digital Transactions Journal*, *23*(4), 231–245.

Dune Analytics, & Statista. (2023, December 4). Number of unique addresses that either bought or sold a Decentralised Finance (DeFi) asset worldwide from November 2018 to November 2023. In *Statista*. Retrieved December 31, 2023, from https://www.statista.com/statistics/1297745/defi-user-number/

FinTech - Worldwide Statista market insights. (2024). Retrieved April 16, 2024, from https://www-statista-com.eu1.proxy.openathens.net/outlook/dmo/fintech/worldwide

Garcia, M., & Martinez, J. (2021). Interoperability and fluid experiences in the Metaverse. *Virtual Reality Ecosystems Review*, *12*(1), 76–88.

Gudgeon, L., Perez, D., Harz, D., Livshits, B., & Gervais, A. (2020). The decentralised financial crisis. In *Proceedings of the Crypto Valley Conference on Blockchain Technology (CVCBT 2020)*, Rotkreuz, Switzerland, 11–12 June 2020, pp. 1–15.

Hou, Z. et al. (2022). DeFi interoperability across virtual reality environments: Challenges and opportunities. *International Journal of Decentralized Finance*, *5*(2), 189–204. https://www-statista-com

Huang, Q., & Wang, J. (2020). Integration of DeFi protocols in virtual economies: Financial inclusion and user empowerment. *Virtual Economics Today*, *9*(3), 150–167.

Johnson, A., & Kim, S. (2019). Blockchain technology for transparent and secure virtual transactions. *Transactions on Digital Economics*, *14*(4), 321–335.

Lee, C., & Brown, R. (2022). Financial inclusion in the Metaverse: Empowering users through DeFi. *Metaverse Economics Review*, *18*(1), 45–59.

Lee, L.-H., Braud, T., Zhou, P., Wang, L., Xu, D., Lin, Z., Kumar, A., Bermejo, C., & Hui, P. (2021). All one needs to know about metaverse: A complete survey on technological singularities, *Digital Ecosystem, and Research Agenda. arXiv preprint arXiv*, 2110.05352.

Liu, M. et al. (2021). Ensuring transparency and trust in virtual transactions using Blockchain technology. *Journal of Blockchain Applications*, *6*(2), 88–103.

Novarlić, B., & Đurić, P. (2024). Enhancing comprehensive waste management in transition economies through green logistics: A case study of Bosnia and Herzegovina. *Journal of Intelligent Management Decision*, *3*, 42–55.

Poon, A. (2023, November 28). DeFi users drop by 50% from peak in late 2021. *CoinDesk*. https://www.coindesk.com/defi-users-drop-by-50-percent-from-peak-in-late-2021

Schorch, P. et al. (2021). Role of virtual currencies in digital ecosystems and the Metaverse. *Journal of Digital Finance*, *13*(1), 34–50.

Smith, D., & Johnson, B. (2023). Impact of virtual currencies on the Metaverse economy. *Journal of Virtual Economy Studies*, *20*(3), 176–190.

Smith, J., & Lee, B. (2023). Virtual asset lending and borrowing in the metaverse: A case study of DecentralVR. *Journal of Virtual Finance*, *7*(3), 150–165.

Statista. (2022, November 29). Distribution of total value locked (TVL) in decentralised finance, or DeFi, worldwide across various blockchains as of November 29, 2022. In Statista. Retrieved December 31, 2023, from https://www.statista.com/statistics/1263975/ethereum-binance-share-in-defi-tvl/

Wang, Y., & Chen, X. (2020). Implications of virtual currencies and DeFi on traditional financial systems. *International Journal of Virtual Economics*, *11*(4), 221–238.

Website (Defi Llama). (2023a, November 17). TVL (total value locked) across multiple Decentralised Finance (DeFi) blockchains from June 2018 to November 17, 2023 (in billion U.S. dollars). In *Statista*. Retrieved December 31, 2023, from https://www.statista.com/statistics/1272181/defi-tvl-in-multiple-blockchains/

Website (DefiLlama). (2023b, December 4). TVL (total value locked) in 26 different segments across multiple Decentralised Finance (DeFi) blockchains worldwide as of December 4, 2023 (in billion U.S. dollars). In *Statista*. Retrieved December 31, 2023, from https://www.statista.com/statistics/1292970/defi-market-size-by-segment-usd/

Weingärtner, T., Fasser, F., Pedro Reis Sá, d. C., & Farkas, W. (2023). Deciphering DeFi: A comprehensive analysis and visualisation of risks in decentralised finance. *Journal of Risk and Financial Management*, *16*(10), 454. https://doi.org/10.3390/jrfm16100454

Wu, C., & Chan, D. (2024). Analysing the decline in unique users of decentralised finance: A longitudinal study. *Journal of Financial Technology*, *7*(1), 45–60. https://doi.org/10.1234/jft.2024.0123

Yerpude, S., Sood, K., & Grima, S. (2022). Blockchain-augmented digital supply chain management: A way to sustainable business. *Journal of Risk and Financial Management*, *16*(1), 7.

Yilmaz, H., & Erol, M. (2022). Potential impact of virtual currencies and DeFi on traditional financial systems. *Journal of Virtual Finance*, *17*(2), 89–104.

Zheng, Z., Xie, S., Dai, H., Chen, X., & Wang, H. (2017). An overview of blockchain technology: Architecture, consensus, and future trends. *2017 IEEE International Congress on Big Data (BigData Congress)*, 557–564. IEEE.

Chapter 10

Can Generative AI Serve as the Modern-Day White-Collar Knowledge Laborer?

Ram B. Ramachandran[a] *and Chabi Gupta*[b]

[a]*O.P. Jindal Global University, Sonepat, Haryana, India*
[b]*Christ University, Bengaluru, India*

Abstract

Purpose: There has been a growing debate on whether generative AI can serve as the modern-day equivalent of white-collar knowledge workers. In a recent post, technology magnate Bill Gates boldly proclaimed that ChatGPT would soon become the quintessential white-collar worker of tomorrow (Dean, 2023). This is indeed an exciting prospect, as generative AI advances at breakneck speed.

Need for the Study: This research delves upon the implications of such advancements for industries reliant on skilled employees. It raises questions about how these individuals will adjust their skillset going forward, given the proliferation of generative AI solutions poised to disrupt traditional roles previously occupied by humans.

Methodology: The study uses an exploratory framework to understand AI's implications on job roles, productivity, and skill requirements. It introduces generative AI and its relevance, focusing on how it could transform white-collar jobs.

Findings: One thing seems clear: its impact on future employment opportunities. However, this technology still has limitations, potentially leading to unintended consequences. While capable of performing certain functions precisely and accurately, it cannot fully replace the reasoning abilities or

Financial Landscape Transformation: Technological Disruptions, 185–200

Published under exclusive licence by Emerald Publishing Limited
doi:10.1108/978-1-83753-750-120251010

cognitive flexibility innate in human workers tasked with knowledge-based work.

Practical Implications: The potential implications for workforce development, policy-making, and future research in AI and labor economics are highlighted. This will also help gain insights into the integration process, benefits, challenges, and the changing nature of white-collar work due to generative AI.

Keywords: Generative AI; white-collar worker; responsible AI; cybersecurity; technology; automation; workforce development

JEL Codes: O15; O10; M54; J24

Introduction

The rapid advancements in Generative Artificial Intelligence (AI) have revolutionized a plethora of industries such as entertainment, manufacturing, automotive, and knowledge-based industries. This cutting-edge technology has the power to automate various tasks like generating legal documents or automating financial analysis that can effectively enhance the productivity of skilled knowledge workers. A recent report by Research and Markets suggests that this trend is only set to grow further with generative AI projected to become an expansive $200.73 billion market by 2032, highlighting its immense potential for transforming global economies (Catsaros, 2022).

Generative AI is a rapidly evolving technological advancement that has the capability to generate innovative and unique content in various forms such as text, images, and videos. One of the emerging generative AI technologies, Generative Pre-training Transformer (GPT), offers access to an extensive range of applications across numerous industries. Its wide-ranging capabilities include chatbots for customer service support, creating convincing deep fakes for entertainment purposes or testing new products virtually through product demos (Al-Ansi et al., 2024; Novarlic et al., 2024).

Furthermore, Generative AI can also be applied in diverse fields including art creation by producing never-seen-before masterpieces using algorithms; designing drug compounds to accelerate research processes; composing original music with exceptional quality; enhancing dubbing techniques which could revolutionize audio-visual production industry while improving building design and development process significantly. On top of all these developments within its niche markets' boundaries, it is fascinating how versatile this technology is. It is not only limited toward professional usage but extends even into everyday life situations such as writing personal emails responses effortlessly without grammatical errors or incorrect spellings. Generative AI technology has revolutionized how businesses operate by offering several benefits beyond automation.

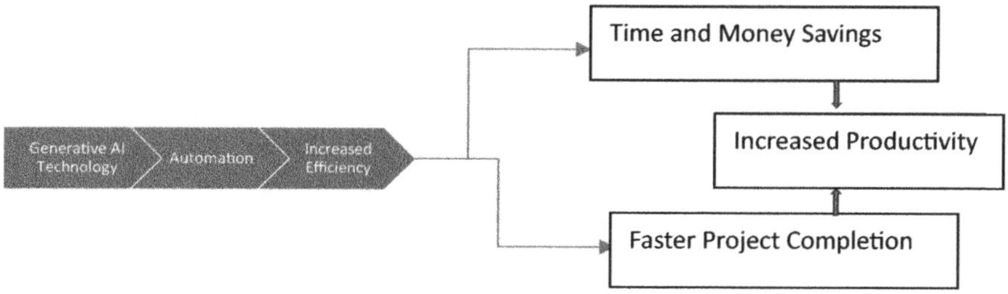

Fig. 1. Automation of Processes Using Generative AI (Author's Diagram).

By automating processes and eliminating manual labor, Generative AI increases efficiency, resulting in significant savings of both time and money while also speeding up project completion timelines, leading to increased productivity, as depicted in Fig. 1. This ground-breaking technology can generate high-quality content including visually appealing images, videos and text with greater accuracy than traditional methods (Bütepage et al., 2020). This exceptional ability can have far-reaching implications for business operations such as enhancing customer experience, resulting in more informed marketing strategies and product development.

One application where generative AI excels is inverse design whereby it enables organizations to produce new designs that meet specific criteria or constraints thus promoting creativity within a structured framework. In conclusion, generative AI's versatility and flexibility offer immense potential for innovative problem-solving making it an indispensable tool in today's fast-paced world.

Global Generative AI Growth

Creativity has undergone a remarkable transformation in recent years, with generative AI emerging as a technological powerhouse. Since late 2022, this technology has been sweeping across the globe and making its way into our everyday lives. Generative AI is an advanced type of machine learning that utilizes deep learning to produce artistic works, music compositions and other forms of imaginative content based on user commands.

The beauty of generative AI lies in its simplicity – it considers vast amounts of data sets fed to it and produces unique creative outputs depending on specific user prompts. In 2022 alone, some notable examples such as Midjourney, Dall-E, and ChatGPT became household names due to their ability to create compelling content effortlessly (Baig et al., 2023). Notably, OpenAI – one rapidly growing startup mainly funded by tech giant Microsoft- played a crucial role in developing Dall-E and ChatGPT. This points out how much investment there is for creativity powered by innovative technologies like AI which ensures endless possibilities for scientists (Baig et al., 2023).

A survey conducted in January 2023 (Baig et al., 2023) revealed fascinating insights into the usage of ChatGPT, an AI-powered text generation tool, among adults in the United States. While only a mere 12% of respondents admitted to having used it themselves, the gender-based analysis brought forth interesting observations. Surprisingly, almost half (43%) of female respondents claimed complete ignorance about ChatGPT and its functionalities; they have neither used nor witnessed anyone else using this technology before (Weisz et al., 2022; Yerpude et al., 2022).

These results not only indicate varying levels but also highlight important differences across gender demographics regarding adoption and awareness toward advanced technological tools such as ChatGPT that are revolutionizing how we create content today (Dillender & Forsythe, 2022). The realm of AI is expected to witness significant growth in its global market revenue from 2018 up until the year 2030. However, there exists a disparity among different studies regarding the exact scale of this increase. While IDC envisages that the worldwide AI industry will surpass half a trillion US dollars by 2024 (PwC's Global Artificial Intelligence Study: Sizing the prize. PwC. https://www.pwc.com/gx/en/issues/data-and-analytics/publications/artificial-intelligence-study.html), Precedence Research estimates it to soar beyond an astounding amount of $1.5 trillion US dollars by 2030. Notably, IBM stands out as one leading company with more than 5,000 patent families for active machine learning and AI worldwide till November 2023 – an exceptional feat unparalleled by other competitors like Microsoft and Samsung who fall within just five hundred patent families from IBM. In recent years, Cox (2020) discusses the fact that we have seen increasing numbers concerning acquisitions in startups founded on AI since about ten years ago; these figures rose almost fourfold between years twenty-fifteen (2015) and twenty-eighteen (2018). Additionally, financial backing has continued to pour into Generative AI as quoted by Calacci (2023) during his related research.

The Chinese AI market has experienced a remarkable growth trajectory over the past few years, with its size increasing almost 10-fold since 2016 to reach over 128 billion yuan in value by 2020. The government's unwavering focus on making China an AI leader amidst fierce international competition is one of the primary reasons for this impressive surge. With strategic importance attached to it as a key industry, the country aims at deploying cutting-edge technology and staying ahead of others (Dwivedi et al., 2023).

The real-world application of AI calls for advanced hardware such as AI-sensors, specialized chipsets designed explicitly for AI tasks, and robust server infrastructure that can handle high volumes of data processing. Software programming must also be formulated with algorithms that facilitate seamless interaction between machines and humans while performing complex operations such as natural language processing (NLP), computer vision or robotics. AI has significant applications across all market segments, but city governance leads from the front having around 50% share in overall revenue generation related to the economy built around Generative AI (Dwivedi et al., 2023).

White-Collar Knowledge Workers

White-collar knowledge workers are an essential part of the modern workforce. These professionals possess a wealth of cognitive abilities, expertise, and skills that they use to perform their duties with exceptional precision and competence. They are responsible for analyzing data sets, managing teams, making strategic decisions, creating solutions to complex problems.

As technology continues its exponential evolution, it has become clear that white-collar jobs will be significantly impacted by automation systems designed to handle repetitive tasks more efficiently than humans ever could (Louie et al., 2020; Vanhaelen et al., 2020).

Robotic Process Automation Software programs have taken over laborious functions like data entry or filing processes; these machines have freed up valuable time for white-collar workers to focus on higher-value responsibilities requiring convergent thinking (using experience), divergent thinking (coming up with new ideas) as well as critical reasoning. The impact of AI cannot be overstated when it comes to generative intelligence which is known for boosting productivity among knowledge workers across various industries – some estimates suggest that it could even substitute human employment (Dean, 2023; Majrashi, 2022).

The proliferation of technology has undoubtedly transformed the landscape of the job market, with far-reaching consequences for workers worldwide. While technological advancements have certainly enabled greater efficiency and productivity in many industries, they have also resulted in a seismic shift that demands adaptability from employees to remain employable. Taneja et al. (2023) discuss through their study that this transformation is expected to be particularly pronounced due to rapid AI development. Accordingly, experts at Goldman Sachs predict that these developments could result in over 300 million full-time jobs globally becoming automated – a trend that will require considerable adjustments on both an individual and societal level. Dwivedi et al. (2023) and Khedekar (2023) advocated that to further compound this issue's complexity, research by the University of Pennsylvania indicates highly educated white-collar workers earning up to $80k annually may bear the most significant impact concerning anticipated changes brought about by automation. Research (Taneja & Sharma, 2023) indicates that as we navigate through uncharted waters during this era defined by continuous innovation acceleration, it remains imperative for companies and individuals alike to proactively develop new skill sets aimed at future-proof innovations.

Convergence of Generative AI and White-Collar Knowledge Laborers

The convergence of generative AI and white-collar work has been a remarkable phenomenon that is revolutionizing the way we approach mundane and repetitive tasks. With its advanced capabilities, AI has significantly automated arduous activities such as data entry, analysis, and report writing. The introduction of sophisticated features in AI models like context recognition and concept identification enables machines to cooperate more efficiently with knowledge workers than ever before. Moreover, this intersection between human expertise and machine intelligence presents an opportunity for upskilling through learning how to collaborate with machines while leveraging their abilities to enhance productivity (Dahiya et al., 2023). Consequently, it opens new possibilities for employees' growth by acquiring new competencies that allow them to integrate seamlessly into evolving technological ecosystems. Overall, Calacci (2023) highlights that the integration of generative AI in white-collar work has expanded horizons toward greater efficiency in workflows leading us into a future where man-machine cooperation becomes key.

Generative AI is transforming white-collar work by enabling a host of tasks that would have otherwise been too time-consuming or mundane for human professionals (Reepu et al., 2023). For instance, like shown in Fig. 2, in HR departments, generative AI-powered digital assistants can now conduct initial interviews and sift through hundreds or thousands of job applications to filter out unsuitable candidates. This automation saves valuable time while ensuring the data remains secure within the organization's environment (Vanhaelen et al., 2020; Taneja et al., 2022).

The impact of generative AI on journalism is equally profound. By generating news articles and reports, journalists are freed up to focus on more sophisticated reporting and analysis. In-depth research allows them to go beyond surface-level reporting and provide insightful commentary backed by facts. Moreover, as organizations embrace this technology across industries such as healthcare, finance & retail; it creates new job opportunities globally for people with relevant skills sets like programming languages – Python/Java/C++; Machine Learning algorithms/ Robotics engineers etc., ushering in an era where machines will coexist with humans augmenting their efficiency while creating space for creativity at work.

In the realm of legal services, recent developments have showcased how generative AI can effectively address access to justice issues. Walters and Murcko (2020) and Ryan (2020) discussed for instance, about an attorney who recently utilized ChatGPT – an advanced language model – to publish a comprehensive 14-page legal paper covering various complex topics with relative ease. Moreover, startups such as Lawgeex have already begun leveraging AI algorithms to read contracts faster and more accurately than humans – paving the way for greater efficiency in the industry. Broader usage in contract reviews and analysis, legal research and document retrieval, predictive analysis for litigations has been explored (Alarie et al., 2018).

Similarly, financial institutions are also embracing generative AI technologies at an unprecedented rate. According to research conducted by Cambridge Centre for Alternative Finance and World Economic Forum, over half of banks

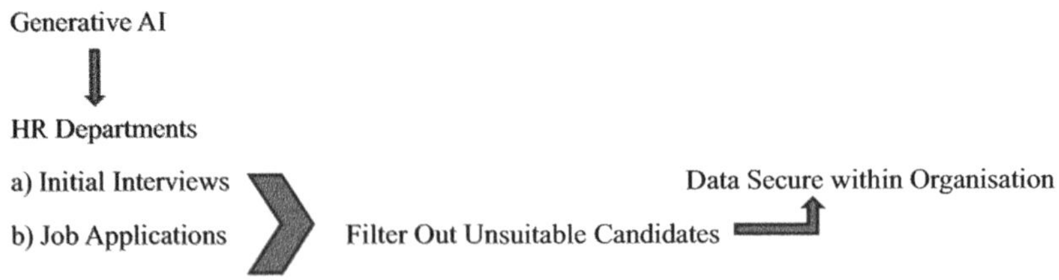

Fig. 2. Generative AI in HR Functions (Author's Diagram).

worldwide have already integrated AI into their operations; out of which 56% use it primarily for management purposes while 52% utilize it solely for revenue generation activities alone (Taneja, Bhatnagar, Kumar, & Rupeika-apoga, 2023) and Chelliah (2017). Generative AI models can analyze vast amounts of financial data to identify patterns and anomalies indicative of fraudulent activities. Taneja and Sharma (2023f) in their research also discuss that AI algorithms can generate synthetic datasets to train fraud detection models, improving their accuracy and effectiveness in detecting and preventing financial fraud. AI models can also generate realistic market scenarios and predict potential outcomes, helping financial institutions make informed risk management decisions. Houde et al. (2020) also advocate that AI algorithms can analyze and interpret complex financial documents, extracting key information and insights for decision-making purposes. They can also be used for generating credit scores and make loan approval decisions, streamlining the lending process and reducing biases.

In Fig. 3, a logical flow of actions is outlined on how generative AI could serve as the modern-day white-collar knowledge worker.

Generative image models have made a ground-breaking breakthrough in the realm of AI, thanks to two crucial advancements. (As depicted in a representative model in Fig. 4.)

Firstly, deep learning has enabled computers to learn a complex "language" for representing images through latent representations. Secondly, these advanced models leverage transformers' unique ability to shift seamlessly between the world of text and that of images via a foundation model. The key factor that makes this possible is having access to data sets and being able to represent something with structures similar enough to language so that transformers can learn the rules necessary for effective translation between them. Copilot from Github serves as an excellent example – it has learned how best to translate different programming

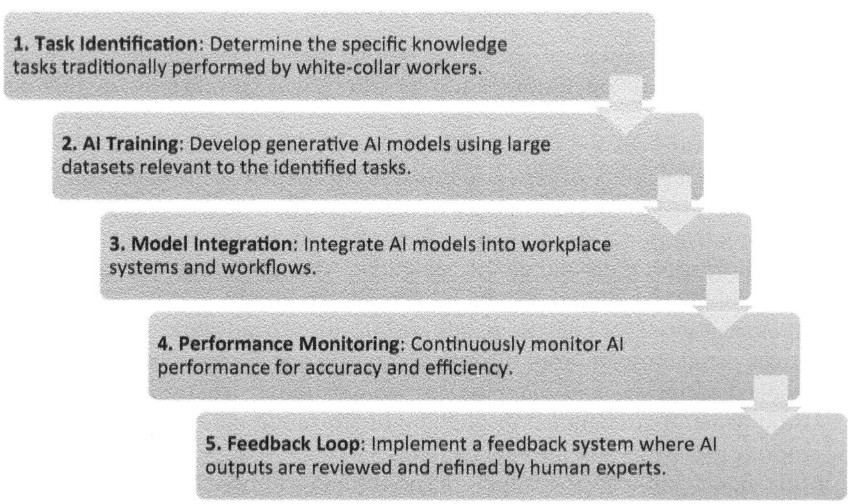

Fig. 3. Potential Integration of Generative AI into White-Collar Roles (Author's Diagram).

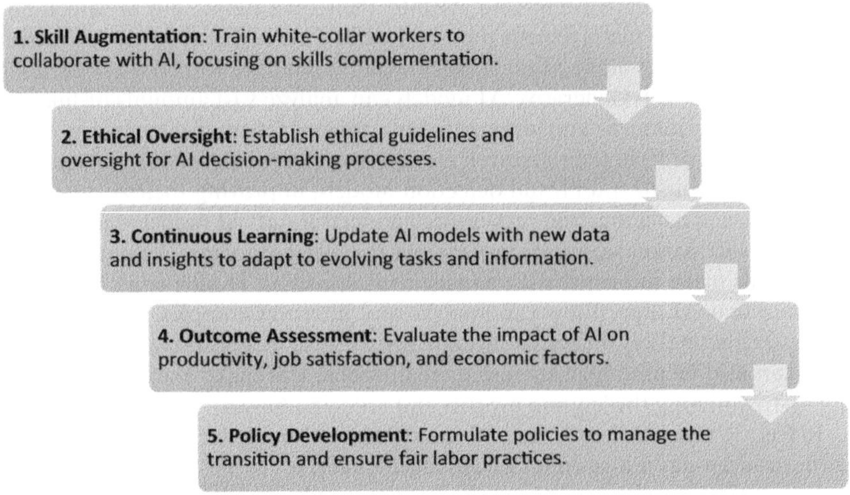

Fig. 4. Integration of Generative AI into White-Collar Roles Emphasizing Collaboration, Oversight, and Continuous Improvement (Authors' Diagram).

languages into English while Alphafold from Google specializes in translating DNA sequences into protein sequences. Currently, there is immense interest among firms worldwide regarding training AI systems capable of generating automations tailored toward performing simple computer tasks such as creating spreadsheets with relative ease which is another fascinating application within this rapidly evolving field.

Impact on Future Organizational Models

Exponential organizations of the future will be highly digitized, disruptive, and dematerialized. Their operations and work pool will be reflective of this new paradigm.

Human workforces are considered on-site or those are remotely operating. This allows for flexibility of cost and talent arbitrage across the globe. While this model is likely to continue, the ability to have more flexible expert gig workers as part of the talent pool. The growing influence of physical robots, virtual robotic process automation tools and use of generative AI applications will require radical change in the way organizational models are structured.

The current model of labor demands are forecasted in advance, and the Human Resources or talent team goes through the process of developing skills requirement, job description, and mapping to organizational structure. Staff requirements on demand are handled through an organization network of contractors, gig workers platforms and internal contacts.

More significantly, in the future, organizations will need to consider a more holistic approach to developing their employee pool (Bansal et al., 2023; Taneja et al., 2023). Some of the roles and tasks will be ear-marked for physical and virtual robots. They in turn will be managed by human workers. There could also be "gurus" and "experts" on the cloud using Generative AI. These may be the first line of defence for organization to turn to for understanding issues, challenges, and potential solutions.

Dean (2023) advocates through his study that knowledge workers are likely to be most impacted through this shift. They need to understand their specific roles and career advancement options. They will need to be trained and upskilled not just on their specific roles but on how these technologies inter play with their own roles, any upgrades and updates on technologies used. Sensitization to human emotions due to influence of machines in their work environment also needs to be considered.

Dangwal et al. (2022) suggest very strongly that Human Resource department functions itself will undergo changes. Influence of AI-powered chatbots and virtual assistants will handle initial candidate screening, schedule interviews, and provide feedback to applicants. Generative AI can help create personalized and inclusive job descriptions and advertisements to attract top talent. They will also help create customized training materials and learning paths based on individual employee needs and preferences. Integrated systems will analyze employee sentiment and provide personalized recommendations for improving engagement and job satisfaction. Generative AI will assist in creating fair and competitive compensation packages based on real-time market data and individual performance. Robots and AI Assistants will help create compelling employee value propositions and employer branding materials to attract and retain top and inclusive talent (Tambe et al., 2019). So, the quantum and role of white-collar workers in human resources department will see a major downward shift.

Regulating Generative AI

There are valid and concerning issues that necessitate increased regulatory oversight to mitigate the potential detrimental impacts of language models such as Claude and ChatGPT. A recent instance occurred when Italian Data Protection Authority took measures to temporarily halt nationwide use of ChatGPT due to privacy concerns regarding the handling and utilization of personal data for model training, along with a lack of safeguards resulting in children being exposed to responses deemed highly inappropriate for their age group (Khedekar, 2023). The European Consumer Organisation (BEUC) is now urging EU authorities to investigate further into potentially harmful effects stemming from large language models like ChatGPT (Bütepage et al., 2020). As fears continue mounting over how these chatbots may manipulate or deceive individuals, AI systems must undergo more thorough public scrutiny. Authorities must assert greater control over them so they can be held accountable and prevent any harm caused by unregulated technology advancements (Cooper, 2023).

The Center for AI and Digital Policy in the United States has recently filed a complaint with the Federal Trade Commission, asserting that ChatGPT's practices violate section 5 of the FTC Act (15 USC 45). The grounds on which this assertion is made are rooted in ChatGPT's alleged failure to adhere to transparency and explainability standards prescribed by the FTC. Despite its acknowledgement of various risks such as compromising privacy rights, generating harmful content, and propagating disinformation, ChatGPT reportedly falls short of meeting these guidelines. The use of large-scale language models like ChatGPT can be highly beneficial; however, research indicates that they also pose potential risks (Cooper, 2023). It has been demonstrated that such systems often generate inaccurate responses due to their deep learning algorithms being trained on massive data sets from across the internet.

Therefore, Cox (2020) discussed in his research that while there is undoubtedly much promise surrounding AI technology like ChatGPTs', recent concerns about its dark side have surfaced amid ongoing debates over how best to regulate it moving forward.

Unlike traditional chatbots that rely on pre-programmed responses, ChatGPT leverages advanced deep learning techniques to create text that closely emulates natural human conversations (Fig. 5). By making a series of educated guesses and employing sophisticated language models, the platform arrives at answers that can convincingly argue even incorrect viewpoints with seemingly authentic responses. However, there is growing concern about the potential for biases in these types of AI-powered systems.

While Generative AI tools aim to mitigate discrimination against marginalized groups like women and minorities by constantly updating its algorithms, it has been found to reinforce certain stereotypes or prejudices when used improperly. Moreover, as per Baidoo-Anu and Owusu Ansah (2023) nefarious actors may exploit unsuspecting users who engage with Generative AI through social engineering tactics such as phishing scams. Users need to be vigilant about protecting their privacy online while interacting with this type of technology to avoid exposing themselves inadvertently as targets for cyberattacks or other forms of exploitation.

The European Parliament recently released a commentary which highlights the importance of reinforcing the provisions outlined in the current draft EU Artificial Intelligence Act (AIA). It primarily focuses on narrow AI applications that fall under specific categories deemed high-risk. These categories include recruitment, credit worthiness, employment, law enforcement and eligibility for social services. However, there are growing concerns regarding general-purpose

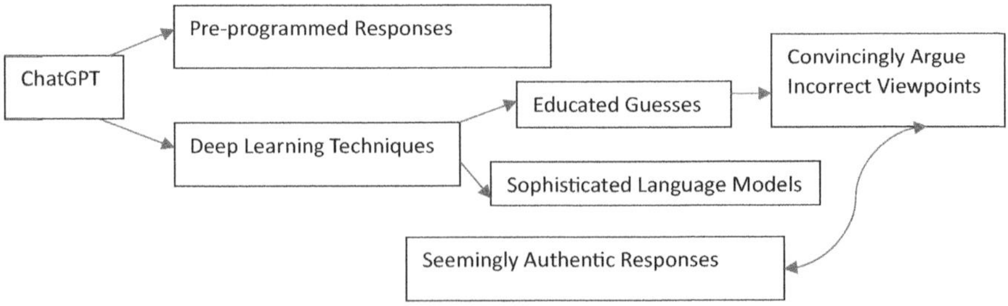

Fig. 5. Leveraging DL to Emulate Natural Human Conversations by Generative AI (Authors' Diagram).

AI systems that have emerged as they can perform a wide range of intelligent tasks. The existing AIA regulation fails to cover such sophisticated systems; hence calls have been made to extend its scope. Kumar et al. (2023) and Jangir et al. (2023) argue that including these types of general-purpose AI within an entirely separate category requiring ex ante conformance testing would ensure developers undertake rigorous measures before placing them on the market while also monitoring their performance continuously for unexpected harmful outcomes. It is clear from such developments that ensuring responsible development and deployment of AI must remain at the forefront when designing regulations around advanced technologies like these.

The risks associated with disruptive technologies are perpetuated by various factors, among which is the drive by innovators to gain a competitive edge through early adoption and the "ship first and fix later" business model. This approach often overlooks potential dangers that may arise from using such innovative technology, thereby exposing users to unforeseen risks. OpenAI's release of ChatGPT for broad commercial use comes with some degree of transparency about its possible hazards. However, with these opportunities, caveat emptor applies. Given the far-reaching implications of conversational AI systems like ChatGPT, this hands-off regulatory approach could be seen as untenable. It is therefore imperative that proactive regulation strategies coupled with robust enforcement measures need to be put in place (After Win in China, AlphaGo's Designers Explore New AI). Such an intervention would not only safeguard users against unintended consequences but also ensure responsible innovation practices across all sectors where new technology emerges (Gupta et al., 2023).

Impact of This Research

This research has the potential to revolutionize the field of use of white-collar workforce due to the widespread adoption of AI. The study provides compelling evidence that generative deep learning networks can effectively acquire and encode knowledge, which can subsequently be utilized by other deep learning systems or even traditional non-deep learning systems as a foundation for their own training and inference processes. By leveraging these learned representations as starting points (or ground truth), such systems may overcome challenges previously considered insurmountable within contemporary machine learning and AI frameworks. This discovery opens endless possibilities for advancing intelligent technologies across various industries and applications, heralding a new era in cognitive computing capabilities.

With increasing reliance on data-driven decision-making, office workers face challenges in keeping up with rapidly changing trends within their industries. The proposed research delves into a novel approach that harnesses the power of AI to assist these workers with collecting relevant information, identifying significant patterns, and communicating insights for informed decisions. The system under investigation has been designed such that when AI fails to perform optimally at certain tasks over time, a human worker can intervene by guiding the machine learning process until it gains better comprehension. By bridging gaps between automation and personal insight-based analyses, this innovative method promises greater productivity coupled with increased accuracy levels resulting from reduced instances of errors or omissions made during manual operations. Overall, this study seeks to enhance workplace processes through collaborative efforts between humans' cognitive abilities backed by technology's analytical prowess.

The Road Ahead with Generative AI

Hacker et al. (2023) advocate through their research that the potential for generative AI is truly remarkable and the advancements made with tools like ChatGPT and DALL-E-2 are certainly impressive. These cutting-edge technologies offer an exciting glimpse into a future where automation can tackle more complex tasks than ever before, ultimately driving efficiency and productivity to new heights. However, it's important to acknowledge that there are limitations in the current state of generative AI. While these systems continue to grow in sophistication, they still lack crucial human context, knowledge and history which enable us to perform certain tasks better than any machine could possibly achieve on its own. Moreover, relying solely on output generated by AI may not always be practical or effective as such results often require some level of human intervention before they can be implemented correctly. This process can sometimes prove time-consuming despite our best efforts at streamlining it through technological improvements. One issue worth noting is that large language models have been known to "hallucinate" or generate biased results due to their heavy reliance upon pre-existing data.

Despite the need for workers to develop new skills and competencies in an AI environment, there is concern that such technological advancements will lead to job displacement. As machines become more sophisticated, they may be able to complete tasks previously done by humans with greater efficiency and accuracy Bansal et al. (2023) discussed in their study that this could result in significant job losses across various industries. Furthermore, as per Bansal et al. (2023), the idea of developing "ethical" use of generative AI assumes that all employers are committed to responsible implementation of these technologies – a notion that is not necessarily accurate. In some cases, companies may prioritize profits over ethical considerations when it comes to their use of automation tools. As such, instead of simply encouraging white-collar workers to learn how best integrate AI into their work practices (which risks perpetuating the narrative that technology is always beneficial), firms should also focus on creating safety nets for those who may lose employment due increased automation. Additionally, policymakers should consider regulations around data privacy and ethics within automated systems so as not leave everything self-regulation (Lim et al., 2023).

While generative AI has undoubtedly advanced by leaps and bounds in recent years, it is still far from possessing the all-encompassing intelligence of humans. Although its ability to process vast amounts of data with speed and accuracy is impressive, certain aspects that come naturally to us as humans remain out of reach for machines driven by AI (Jo, 2023). One such area where we excel over AI systems is our capacity for common sense reasoning and contextual understanding. For example, an everyday task like distinguishing between "play"

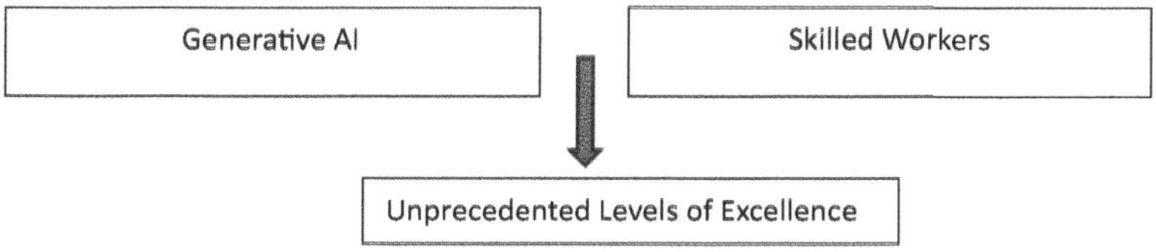

Fig. 6. Impact of Coexistence of Generative AI and Skilled Workers (Authors' Diagram).

versus "work" scenarios may present significant difficulties for even state-of-the-art AI models. In addition to lacking human-level comprehension skills, another key limitation associated with today's cutting-edge algorithms relates to their inability to automate soft-skills – those intangible abilities such as empathy or social intelligence vital in building relationships – something that comes so easily (and sometimes not-so-easily) when interacting face-to-face with people around us. Moreover, one must keep a watchful eye on potential bias embedded within machine learning algorithms (Bütepage et al., 2020).

Conclusion

As we move toward the future, it is becoming increasingly apparent that AI will prove to be a powerful tool in augmenting human work rather than completely replacing human labor.

In fact, Fig. 6 outlines the co-existence of generative AI and skilled workers that can pave the way for unprecedented levels of excellence across industries. Using advanced AI tools in conjunction with their expertise and experience, humans can amplify their skills significantly. These complementary systems enable businesses to achieve greater efficiency and accuracy at tasks ranging from customer service support to product development. Moreover, this mutually beneficial partnership between man and machine allows individuals utilizing these technologies to deliver higher quality work at faster rates; allowing them more time for creative problem solving or other high-level tasks as they become freed up from routine manual duties. With such enhanced productivity resulting from seamless collaboration between two forms of intelligent agents – one artificial and one biological – there are endless possibilities on how far humanity may progress over time.

References

Al-Ansi, A. M., Garad, A., & Ryabtsev, V. (2024). Intelligent risk analysis of investment projects in the extractive industry. *Journal of Industrial Intelligence*, *2*(1), 42–53.

Alarie, B., Niblett, A., & Yoon, A. H. (2018). How artificial intelligence will affect the practice of law. *University of Toronto Law Journal*, *68*(supplement 1), 106–124. https://doi.org/10.3138/utlj.2017-0052

Baidoo-Anu, D., & Owusu Ansah, L. (2023). Education in the era of generative artificial intelligence (AI): Understanding the potential benefits of ChatGPT in promoting teaching and learning. Available at SSRN 4337484.

Baig, A., Yee, L., & Singla, A. (2023). *What's the future of generative AI? an early view in 15 charts*. McKinsey & Company. https://www.mckinsey.com/featured-insights/mckinsey-explainers/whats-the-future-of-generative-ai-an-early-view-in-15-charts

Bansal, N., Bhatnagar, M., & Taneja, S. (2023). Balancing priorities through green optimism: A study elucidating initiatives, approaches, and strategies for sustainable supply chain management. In *Handbook of research on designing sustainable supply chains to achieve a circular economy* (pp. 60–81). IGI Global.

Bütepage, J., Ghadirzadeh, A., ÖztimurKaradağ, Z., Björkman, M., & Kragic, D. (2020, April 16). Imitating by generating: Deep generative models for imitation of interactive tasks. *Frontiers in Robotics and AI*, *7*. https://doi.org/10.3389/frobt.2020.00047

Calacci, D. (2023). Building dreams beyond labor: Worker autonomy in the age of AI. *Interactions*, *30*(6), 48–51.

Catsaros, O. (2022). *Generative AI to become a $1.3 trillion market by 2032, research finds | press | Bloomberg LP, Bloomberg.com*. https://www.bloomberg.com/company/press/generative-ai-to-become-a-1-3-trillion-market-by-2032-research-finds/

Cooper, G. (2023). Examining science education in chatgpt: An exploratory study of generative artificial intelligence. *Journal of Science Education and Technology*, 1–9.

Cox, C. M. (2020). Augmenting autonomy: 'New Collar' labor and the future of tech work. *Convergence*, *26*(4), 824–840.

Dahiya, K., Taneja, S., & Özen, E. (2023). To analyse the impact of multi-media technology on the rural entrepreneurship development. In *Contemporary studies of risks in emerging technology, Part A* (pp. 221–240). Emerald Publishing Limited.

Dangwal, A., Kaur, S., Taneja, S., & Taneja, S. (2022). A bibliometric analysis of green tourism based on the scopus platform. In J. Kaur, P. Jindal, & A. Singh (Eds.), *Developing relationships, personalization, and data herald in marketing 5.0: Vol. i* (pp. 1–327). IGI Global. https://doi.org/10.4018/9781668444962

Dangwal, A., Taneja, S., Özen, E., Todorovic, I., & Grima, S. (2022). Abridgement of renewables: It's potential and contribution to India's GDP. *International Journal of Sustainable Development and Planning*, *17*(8), 2357–2363. https://doi.org/10.18280/ijsdp.170802

Dean, G. (2023, March 22). Bill Gates says that in the future CHATGPT will be like "having a white-collar worker available to help you." *Business Insider*. https://www.businessinsider.in/tech/news/bill-gates-says-that-in-the-future-chatgpt-will-be-like-having-a-white-collar-worker-available-to-help-you/articleshow/98914023.cms

Dillender, M., & Forsythe, E. (2022). *Computerization of white collar jobs* (No. w29866). National Bureau of Economic Research.

Gupta, M., Arora, R., & Taneja, S. (2023). Bibliometric analysis on employee engagement and human resource management. In *Enhancing customer engagement through location-based marketing* (pp. 185–205). IGI Global. https://doi.org/10.4018/978-1-6684-8177-6.ch013

Hacker, P., Engel, A., & Mauer, M. (2023). Regulating chatgpt and other large generative AI models. *arXiv preprint arXiv:2302.02337*.

Houde, S., Liao, V., Martino, J., Muller, M., Piorkowski, D., Richards, J., ... Zhang, Y. (2020). Business (mis) use cases of generative ai. *arXiv preprint arXiv:2003.07679*.

Jangir, K., Sharma, V., Taneja, S., & Rupeika-Apoga, R. (2023). The moderating effect of perceived risk on users' continuance intention for FinTech services. *Journal of Risk and Financial Management*, *16*(1). https://doi.org/10.3390/jrfm16010021

Jo, A. (2023). The promise and peril of generative AI. *Nature*, *614*(1), 214–216.

Khedekar, D. (2023). *Communicating precarity and resistance under surveillance: Fragile organizing in private online groups* [Doctoral dissertation, University of Colorado at Boulder].

Kumar, P., Taneja, S., Özen, E., & Singh, S. (2023). Artificial intelligence and machine learning in insurance: A bibliometric analysis. In *Smart analytics, artificial intelligence and sustainable performance management in a global digitalised economy* (pp. 191–202). Emerald Publishing Limited.

Kumar, P., Verma, P., Bhatnagar, M., Taneja, S., Seychel, S., Todorović, I., & Grim, S. (2023). The financial performance and solvency status of the Indian public sector banks: A CAMELS rating and Z index approach. *International Journal of Sustainable Development and Planning*, *18*(2), 367–376. https://doi.org/10.18280/ijsdp.180204

Lim, W. M., Gunasekara, A., Pallant, J. L., Pallant, J. I., & Pechenkina, E. (2023). Generative AI and the future of education: Ragnarök or reformation? A paradoxical perspective from management educators. *The International Journal of Management Education*, *21*(2), 100790.

Louie, R., Coenen, A., Huang, C. Z., Terry, M., & Cai, C. J. (2020, April). Novice-AI music co-creation via AI-steering tools for deep generative models. *In Proceedings of the 2020 CHI conference on human factors in computing systems* (pp. 1–13).

Majrashi, K. (2024). Determinants of public sector managers' intentions to adopt AI in the workplace. *International Journal of Public Administration in the Digital Age (IJPADA)*, *11*(1), 1–26.

Novarlić, B., & Đurić, P. (2024). Enhancing comprehensive waste management in transition economies through green logistics: A case study of Bosnia and Herzegovina. *Journal of Intelligent Management Decision*, *3*, 42–55.

Özen, E., & Sanjay, T. (2022). Empirical analysis of the effect of foreign trade in computer and communication services on economic growth in India. *Journal of Economics and Business Issues*, *2*(2), 24–34. https://doi.org/https://jebi-academic.org/index.php/jebi/article/view/41

Özen, E., Taneja, S., & Makalesi, A. (2022). Critical evaluation of management of NPA/NPL in Emerging and Advanced Economies: A Study in Context of India GelişenveGelişmişEkonomilerde NPA/NPL YönetimininEleştirelDeğerlendirmesi: HindistanBağlamında Bir Çalışma. *YalovaSosyalBilimlerDergisi*, *12*(2), 99–111. https://doi.org/https://dergipark.org.tr/en/pub/yalovasosbil/issue/72655/1143214

Reepu, R., Taneja, S., Ozen, E., & Singh, A. (2023). A globetrotter to the future of marketing: Metaverse. In *Cultural marketing and metaverse for consumer engagement* (pp. 1–11). IGI Global.

Rezwana, J., & Maher, M. L. (2022, February 24). Designing Creative AI Partners with COFI: A framework for modeling interaction in human-AI co-creative systems. *ACM Transactions on Computer-Human Interaction*. https://doi.org/10.1145/3519026

Ryan, F. (2020). *Reskilling white-collar workers: What's in it for firms?* [Doctoral dissertation, Massachusetts Institute of Technology].

Singh, V., Taneja, S., Singh, V., Singh, A., & Paul, H. L. (2021). Online advertising strategies in Indian and Australian e-commerce companies:: A comparative study. *Big Data Analytics for Improved Accuracy, Efficiency, and Decision Making in Digital Marketing*, 124–138. https://doi.org/10.4018/978-1-7998-7231-3.ch009

Sun, J., Liao, Q. V., Muller, M., Agarwal, M., Houde, S., Talamadupula, K., & Weisz, J. D. (2022, March). Investigating explainability of generative AI for code through scenario-based design. In *27th International Conference on Intelligent User Interfaces* (pp. 212–228).

Tambe, P., Cappelli, P., & Yakubovich, V. (2019). Artificial Intelligence in human resources management: Challenges and a path forward. *California Management Review*, *61*(4), 15–42. https://doi.org/10.1177/0008125619867910

Taneja, S., & Özen, E. (2023a). To analyse the relationship between bank's green financing and environmental performance. *International Journal of Electronic Finance*, *12*(2), 163–175. https://doi.org/10.1504/IJEF.2023.129919

Taneja, S., & Ozen, E. (2023b). Impact of the European Green Deal (EDG) on the agricultural carbon (CO2) emission in Turkey. *International Journal of Sustainable Development and Planning*, *18*(3), 715–727. https://doi.org/10.18280/ijsdp.180307

Taneja, S., & Sharma, V. (2023). Role of beaconing marketing in improving customer buying experience. In *Enhancing customer engagement through location-based marketing* (pp. 176–184). IGI Global. https://doi.org/10.4018/978-1-6684-8177-6.ch012

Taneja, S., Bhatnagar, M., Kumar, P., Grima, S. (2023). A panel analysis of the effectiveness of the asset management in Indian agricultural companies. *International Journal of Sustainable Development and Planning*, *18*(3), 653–660. https://doi.org/10.18280/ijsdp.180301

Taneja, S., Bhatnagar, M., Kumar, P., & Rupeika-apoga, R. (2023). India' s total natural resource rents (NRR) and GDP: An augmented autoregressive distributed lag (ARDL) bound test. *Journal of Risk and Financial Management*, *16*(2), 91. https://doi.org/doi.org/10.3390/jrfm16020091

Taneja, S., Gupta, M., Bhushan, P., Bhatnagar, M., & Singh, A. (2023). Cultural marketing in the digital era. In *Cultural marketing and metaverse for consumer engagement* (pp. 109–122). IGI Global.

Taneja, S., Jaggi, P., Jewandah, S., & Ozen, E. (2022). Role of social inclusion in sustainable urban developments: An analyse by PRISMA technique. *International Journal of Design and Nature and Ecodynamics*, *17*(6), 937–942. https://doi.org/10.18280/ijdne.170615

Taneja, S., Kaur, S., & Özen, E. (2022). Using green finance to promote global growth in a sustainable way. *International Journal of Green Economics*, *16*(3), 246–257. https://doi.org/10.1504/ijge.2022.10052887

Vanhaelen, Q., Lin, Y. C., & Zhavoronkov, A. (2020). The advent of generative chemistry. *ACS Medicinal Chemistry Letters*, *11*(8), 1496–1505.

Walters, W. P., & Murcko, M. (2020). Assessing the impact of generative AI on medicinal chemistry. *Nature Biotechnology*, *38*(2), 143–145.

Weisz, J. D., Maher, M. L., Strobelt, H., Chilton, L. B., Bau, D., & Geyer, W. (2022, March). HAI-GEN 2022: 3rd Workshop on Human-AI Co-Creation with Generative Models. In *27th International conference on intelligent user interfaces* (pp. 4–6).

Yerpude, S., Sood, K., & Grima, S. (2022). Blockchain-augmented digital supply chain management: A way to sustainable business. *Journal of Risk and Financial Management*, *16*(1), 7.

Chapter 11

A Pilot Study on the Role of Behavioural Biases in Cryptocurrency Investment Decision-Making: The Mediating Effects of Risk Tolerance

Shubhangi Gautam and Pardeep Kumar*

University School of Business, Chandigarh University, India
**Corresponding Author*

Abstract

Purpose – This study aims to investigate how behavioural biases affect cryptocurrency investment choices. The study also evaluates how risk tolerance mediates the relationship between behavioural biases and investment decision-making.

Need for the Study – The study is required to refine research methods and to ensure the reliability and validity of findings on behavioural biases in cryptocurrency investment decision-making.

Methodology – This pilot study involved responses from individuals in India's western and northern regions who either invested in cryptocurrencies or had adequate knowledge of such investments. To assess the normality, validity, and reliability of the questionnaire data, a sample of 51 individuals was analysed using SPSS software.

Findings – The results of this study validate the reliability of the questionnaire in conducting pilot research by attaining high reliability with high coefficients of measures and reasonable normality.

Financial Landscape Transformation: Technological Disruptions, 201–215

doi:10.1108/978-1-83753-750-120251011

Originality/value – The study confirmed the tool's efficiency to analyse various specific antecedents influencing investing choices.

Keywords: Behavioural bias; blockchain; cryptocurrency; investment decision; investment decision-making; pilot study; risk tolerance

JEL Codes: C88; F21; P45

Introduction

Behavioural finance is a field of research that has evolved over the past few decades, blending concepts from traditional finance, psychology, and sociology. In order to comprehend how people make financial decisions, behavioural finance combines elements of psychology and economics. Traditional financial theories make the assumption that investors are rational and always make choices that will increase their wealth (Jain et al., 2020; Kartini & Nahda, 2021; Kengatharan & Kengatharan, 2014; Tseng, 2006). On the other hand, behavioural finance acknowledges that people are affected by a range of cognitive biases and emotions, which can result in irrational decision-making. Behavioural finance aims to explain why people frequently make poor financial decisions and how these choices impact the financial markets (Gautam & Kumar, 2023c). It recognises that people's behaviours and emotions can play a substantial role in financial decision-making, leading to deviations from rational decision-making models (Kumar & Goyal, 2015a). Behavioural finance has grown in popularity as researchers have observed numerous examples of cognitive biases and heuristics in action, such as overconfidence, loss aversion, and herding behaviour (Kim & Nofsinger, 2008; Pompian, 2011; Ritter, 2003; Sadi, 2011). Behavioural biases in investment decisions have evolved alongside the growth of the area of behavioural finance (De Bondt et al., 2008; Wankel & Godden, 2012). Over time, researchers have identified a wide range of cognitive biases and heuristics that can impact investors' decision-making, leading to suboptimal investment outcomes (Zahera & Bansal, 2018).

Some of the earliest and most well-known biases include loss aversion, overconfidence bias, and herding bias. As the area of behavioural finance has grown, researchers have identified many additional biases and heuristics (Waweru et al., 2008). These biases may influence how investors create their portfolios, allocate their assets, and make specific investing decisions. Investing is an essential activity that involves allocating capital to a variety of assets with the hope of generating returns in the future. Based on their financial goals, risk tolerance, and investment horizon, people, companies, and governments make investment choices (Dangi & Kohli, 2018; Jain et al., 2021; Kiymaz et al., 2016; Mittal, 2019; Ritika & Kishor, 2020; Ritika & Nawal, 2020; Sharma & Firoz, 2022). Making wise investment choices is essential for building wealth, funding future endeavours, and ensuring long-term financial stability. Therefore, it must thoroughly understand the numerous investment possibilities, their risks and rewards, and the pertinent elements that affect investment decisions (Kartini & Nahda, 2021).

Over the past 10 years, cryptocurrency has developed as an alternative form of investment, with the emergence of Bitcoin in 2009 bringing in a new era of decentralised digital assets (Gautam & Kumar, 2023b). Initially, cryptocurrencies were viewed with scepticism by many investors due to their association with illicit activities and lack of regulatory oversight (Albayati et al., 2020; Alqaryouti et al., 2020; Corbet et al., 2019; Kyriazis, 2020; Lam, 2018; Lee et al., 2018; Trimborn et al., 2020). However, with the advancement of technology and increased adoption, cryptocurrencies have gained acceptance as a legitimate investment alternative (Lee et al., 2018). However, investing in the cryptocurrency market is still a complex and challenging task. Many factors influence investment decisions, including behavioural biases that impact decision-making. Understanding these biases is crucial for investors to make informed and rational investment choices. In the prevailing literature, there are very few studies that scrutinise the influence of behavioural biases on cryptocurrency investments (Al-mansour, 2020). As a novelty, risk tolerance is also comprised as a mediator between behavioural prejudices and investment choices. Therefore, this pilot study aims to scrutinise the impact of behavioural prejudices on cryptocurrency investment choices. The study examines the prevalence of behavioural partialities among investors and the extent to which these biases influence investment decisions.

Literature Review

Prospects and Investment Decisions

Prospect Theory, 'developed by Kahneman and Tversky (1979)', is a key concept in behavioural finance that explains how individuals evaluate and make decisions under uncertainty. It suggests that people do not make choices based on objective probabilities and expected values, as traditional finance theories assume. Instead, they evaluate possible gains and losses relative to a reference point and exhibit certain behavioural biases in their decision-making (Al-mansour, 2020; Bigus, 2015; Chaudary & Samra, 2019; Lude & Prügl, 2019; Mahmood et al., 2016; Tversky & Kahneman, 1992). Prospect theory posits that individuals assess potential gains and losses in a non-linear fashion, highlighting the significant influence of decision framing on decision-making (Mahmood et al., 2016). The most common prospects are 'loss aversion, regret aversion, and mental accounting'. 'Loss aversion is the propensity for people to experience the sorrow of losses more intensely than the joy of gains, leading them to make overly cautious investment decisions'. Regret aversion is another behavioural bias that defines the propensity for people to evade making choices that could result in regret, even if those choices may be optimal in terms of expected value (Al-Ansi et al., 2024; Novarlić & Đurić, 2024; Waweru et al., 2008). Mental accounting, on the other hand, shows how people frequently classify and treat money individually based on arbitrary criteria, such as the cause of the funds or their intended purpose (Jain et al., 2020).

Heuristics and Investment Decisions

'Heuristics are mental shortcuts or rules of thumb that people use to simplify decision-making processes'. When they oversimplify difficult situations, they can result in biases and errors in addition to efficient decision-making. These heuristics influence how investors perceive and evaluate potential gains and losses, ultimately impacting their investment decisions (Dangol & Manandhar, 2020; Farooq, 2017; Gadzinski et al., 2022; Kadir et al., 2016; Kengatharan & Kengatharan, 2014; Richie & Josephson, 2018; Wong et al., 2018). Examples include the availability heuristic, the overconfidence heuristic, the representativeness 'heuristic, and the anchoring heuristic' (Waweru et al., 2008). People have a propensity to overemphasise their skills, knowledge, and forecasts due to the overconfidence heuristic, which is a cognitive bias. It may cause them to act with unjustified confidence, ignore information that deviates from their ideas, and underestimate the risks associated with decisions (Gautam & Kumar, 2023a). The representativeness heuristic is a cognitive bias in which people base their judgements and decisions on prototypical qualities. This may lead to erroneous judgements and investment decisions because one may miss crucial information or traits that do not fit the stereotype (Jain et al., 2020; Yerpude et al., 2022).

'The availability heuristic is a cognitive bias in which people base their investing decisions on examples or data that are easily accessible'. As a result, it may be possible to overestimate the likelihood of occurrences that are simple to recall while underestimating the possibility of less memorable or important events. 'A cognitive bias known as the anchoring heuristic causes people to overly depend on the first piece of information' they are given (the 'anchor') while making decisions about their future investments. Since people frequently fail to sufficiently depart from the initial anchor, this can lead to skewed estimates or evaluations (Mahmood et al., 2016).

Herding and Investment Decisions

A person's tendency to act and make judgements in accordance with a wider group rather than independently is known as herding bias. This can happen in a variety of situations, particularly while making investment decisions. Herding bias, also known as herding behaviour or herd mentality, is a psychological 'phenomenon in which individuals tend to follow the actions and decisions of a larger group', assuming that the collective judgement of the group is correct (Christoffersen & Stæhr, 2019; Goyal et al., 2023; Gurdgiev & O'Loughlin, 2020; Jlassi & Naoui, 2015; Mishra & Mishra, 2023).

When investors make investment decisions, herding bias can lead to less desirable outcomes because they may act without the support of reliable data or research (Jain et al., 2020). For instance, an investor may buy a particular stock basically because it is popular among their peers, rather than conducting their own research on the company's financial health and potential for growth (Nofsinger & Sias, 1999; Shantha, 2019; Sias, 2004; Zafar & Hassan, 2016). To avoid the negative effects of herding bias, investors should make choices based on a comprehensive analysis of accessible information rather than following the crowd. Investors should also seek out diverse sources of information and perspectives and be willing to take calculated risks when warranted (Mahmood et al., 2016).

Here are some key points related to herding bias in investment decisions:

Information cascade: Herding bias often occurs due to the formation of information cascades. When investors observe others buying or selling a particular investment, they may assume that those individuals possess superior information or insights. As a result, they may blindly follow the crowd without conducting their own thorough analysis (Hirshleifer & Hong Teoh, 2003; Kumar & Goyal, 2015b).

Fear of missing out (FOMO): Herding bias can be driven by the fear of missing out on potential gains. Investors may feel compelled to join the herd because they fear that they might miss out on an opportunity for significant profits if they don't act in line with others (Gupta & Shrivastava, 2021).

Lack of independent analysis: Herding behaviour can lead to a reduced emphasis on individual analysis and research. Investors may rely on the actions and decisions of others as a substitute for their own due diligence, leading to a lack of critical evaluation of the investment's merits (Chen et al., 2018; Raimundo Júnior et al., 2022; de Souza Raimundo Júnior et al. 2019).

Increased market volatility: Herding behaviour can contribute to increased market volatility. When a large number of investors collectively move in the same direction, it can amplify price movements, leading to exaggerated market swings and potential bubbles or crashes (Kerl & Pauls, 2014).

Information cascade reversal: Although herding bias can persist for some time, it is not sustainable in the long run. Eventually, as more information becomes available or market conditions change, the herd may reverse its direction. This reversal can lead to abrupt shifts in market sentiment and exacerbate volatility (Baker et al., 2021; Hirshleifer & Hong Teoh, 2003; Kumar & Goyal, 2016).

Methodology

The pilot study used a quantitative methodology to collect data via an electronic survey. Quantitative research facilitates a quick comprehension and connection between the participants and the topic under investigation (Hair & Lukas, 2014). The current investigation employed a survey questionnaire and a descriptive measurement method. As a result, due consideration was given to the dimensions represented in assessing constructs within the study model in Fig. 1 while creating the questionnaire items in order to minimise duplication. According to Zikmund et al. (2013), the survey items were chosen based on the theoretical implications and justifications found in the studies that were incorporated and adapted to fit the study's goals presented in Table 1. The survey involved two segments. The first section assessed the prevalence of behavioural biases among investors using the Behavioural Finance Questionnaire (BFQ). The BFQ measures an individual's tendency towards behavioural biases. 'Demographic data, including age, gender, level of education, and income', were gathered in the second section. The survey

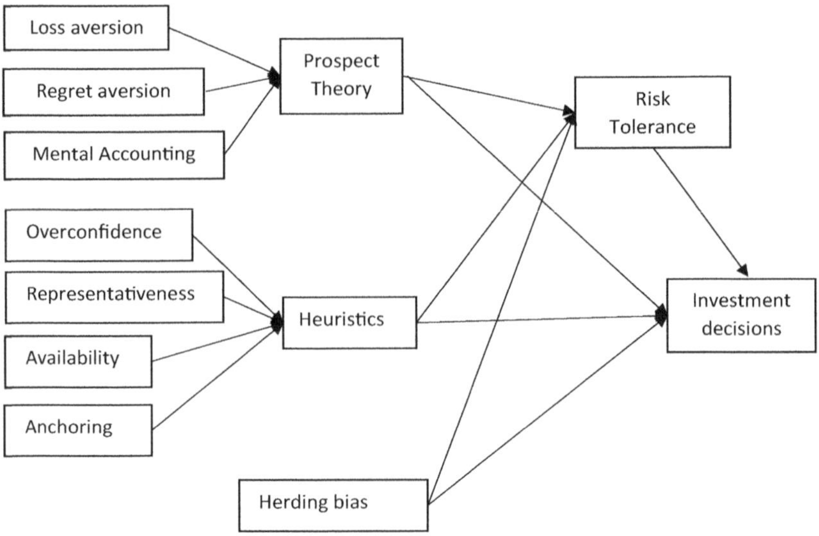

Fig. 1. A Research Path Model. *Source*: Authors' Work.

Table 1. Instrument Source.

Constructs	No. of Items	Source
Prospects:		(Mahmood et al., 2016); (Waweru et al., 2008)
i. 'Loss Aversion Bias'	3	
ii. 'Regret Aversion Bias'	3	
iii. 'Mental Accounting Bias'	3	
Heuristics:		(Waweru et al., 2008); (Jain et al., 2020)
i. 'Overconfidence Bias'	3	
ii. 'Representativeness Bias'	4	
iii. 'Anchoring Bias'	3	
iv. 'Availability Bias'	3	
'Herding Bias'	4	(Jain et al., 2020)
Risk Tolerance	3	(Salman et al., 2020)
Investment decisions	4	(Ogunlusi & Obademi, 2019)
Total	33	

Source: Authors' Work.

was distributed to those who either have knowledge of the cryptocurrency market or have invested in cryptocurrencies.

Whitehead et al. (2016) suggest that the specifics of the research may dictate the use of a larger sample size. The sample size for the pilot study is often less than that of the real study and only consists of 15–30 units. The present study distributed 100 questionnaires to the investors. A total of 51 surveys were collected and analysed to determine the respondents' understanding of the questions, any challenges they faced in completing them, the clarity of the instructions, the appeal of the draft, and the estimated time required for completion. The pilot research was conducted over a two-week period in June 2022.

Pilot Study

A pilot research is crucial because it identifies instrument design flaws before devoting a significant amount of time and money to a larger-scale actual investigation (Fraser et al., 2018). In addition, the main goals of a pilot study are to ascertain the reliability as well as the validity of the survey items, to evaluate the appropriateness of the phrasing of the items, to formulate statements as well as questions in order to produce accurate outcomes, to assess whether the statements are outlined to elicit improved responses, and to ascertain whether responders are able to provide the necessary data. When a survey is reliable, it is error-free, and the findings are reliable over time and across settings. Questionnaire validity refers to a questionnaire's capacity to measure the intended outcomes (Sekaran & Bougie, 2016).

Data Analysis

There are several ways to conduct a reliability test, but the reliability test (internal consistency) is the most widely used (Maiyaki & Mokhtar, 2010). It shows the degree to which statements of a certain variable converge and can each measure that same construct, while also determining whether there is a link between the items. Therefore, a reliability test (internal consistency) using Cronbach's alpha was carried out as advised by Sekaran and Bougie (2016). Table 2 displays the results, demonstrating high-reliability coefficients ranging from 0.876 to 0.967 for all measures. In accordance with the opinions of research experts, a coefficient of 0.60 is considered to be the average reliability value, with 0.70 or above denoting good consistency (Sekaran & Bougie, 2016).

The reliability coefficients for behavioural biases and other variables exceeded (Cronbach's alpha value) 0.70, indicating that they are credible. However, the model was second-order, so the first three variables represent the prospect theory construct, the next four represent the variables of the heuristics construct, and herding is itself a separate variable. On the other hand, risk tolerance mediates these prejudices' influence on investment decisions.

According to the construct reliability table, all of the constructs had suitable alpha values that were greater than 0.70, indicating that the constructs' reliability was satisfactory (DeVellis, 2016).

Table 2. Reliability Outcomes.

Construct	Cronbach's Alpha
'Loss Aversion Bias'	0.925
'Regret Aversion Bias'	0.929
'Mental Accounting Bias'	0.967
'Overconfidence Bias'	0.876
'Representativeness Bias'	0.883
'Anchoring Bias'	0.894
'Availability Bias'	0.900
Herding Bias	0.917
Risk Tolerance	0.961
Investment decisions	0.892

Source: Authors' work.

Exploratory Factor Analysis

A total of 51 investors contributed to the pilot research. The majority of respondents were male (68.6%). The participants with an age cluster of 18–30 years and an annual income between Rs. 250,000 and Rs. 500,000 are more active. The results showed that investors exhibited various behavioural biases.

The complete set of variables was subjected to an EFA, or exploratory factor analysis. The analysis's goal was to determine whether the extracted elements agreed with the original and theoretical forms by looking at the correlations between latent variables. The analysis's findings played a crucial role in determining the necessity of changing the questionnaire items. The survey's titles and design underwent changes based on the ideas and comments submitted. The pilot project used a questionnaire with a specific number of items for measuring each construct, as listed in Table 3. The questionnaire's validity was examined using EFA.

Table 3. Pilot Study Items.

Construct	No. of Items
'Loss Aversion Bias'	3
'Regret Aversion Bias'	3
'Mental Accounting Bias'	3
'Overconfidence Bias'	3
'Representativeness Bias'	4
'Anchoring Bias'	3

Table 3. (Continued)

Construct	**No. of Items**
'Availability Bias'	3
'Herding Bias'	4
'Risk Tolerance'	3
Investment decisions	4
Total	33

Source: Authors' work.

The table makes it evident that there are 33 statements in all, distributed among three paradigms. The research model was second-order, with 33 items. Behavioural biases are distributed into three parts, i.e., prospect theory, heuristics, and herding bias; these are the first-order constructs. The variables under 'prospect theory' are 'loss aversion, regret aversion, and mental accounting bias'. Whereas, variables that come under heuristics are 'overconfidence, representativeness bias, anchoring bias, and availability bias'. Herding is another construct that has its own set of items for analysis. However, risk tolerance is a mediator between the above-discussed behavioural prejudices and investment choices. The EFA outcomes of all the behavioural bias items are demonstrated in Table 4.

Table 4 shows that, with the exception of ID2, ID4, AvB3, AnB1, OvB1, and OvB3, which loaded marginally below the limit of 0.70 but over 0.50, all other items' loadings surpassed 0.70, and since the items' averages throughout the complete construction were all above 0.70, the weights were approved to be acceptable.

Table 4. Factor Loadings.

	1	**2**	**3**	**4**	**5**	**6**	**7**	**8**	**9**	**10**
HrB1	0.848									
HrB2	0.786									
HrB3	0.872									
HrB4	0.757									
RT1		0.834								
RT2		0.841								
RT3		0.876								
RpB1			0.871							
RpB2			0.727							
RpB3			0.778							
RpB4			0.743							

(*Continued*)

Table 4. (Continued)

	1	2	3	4	5	6	7	8	9	10
MaB1				0.944						
MaB2				0.894						
MaB3				0.908						
ID1					0.893					
ID2					0.563					
ID3					0.88					
ID4					0.545					
RaB1						0.786				
RaB2						0.761				
RaB3						0.832				
LaB1							0.769			
LaB2							0.751			
LaB3							0.862			
AvB1								0.872		
AvB2								0.881		
AvB3								0.543		
AnB1									0.673	
AnB2									0.871	
AnB3									0.862	
OvB1										0.597
OvB2										0.811
OvB3										0.697

Source: Authors' work.

Conclusion

In order to prepare for the actual comprehensive investigation, this work centred on performing pilot research to assess the validity and reliability of the constructed survey. Following the content and face validity evaluation, some items underwent revisions and changes. The study also conducted an inter-item reliability test, revealing that all the statements demonstrated consistency as measured by the Cronbach's alpha coefficient test, surpassing the benchmark of 0.70. Subsequently, all of the statements were retained. The pilot study provides evidence that behavioural biases significantly impact investment choices. The outcomes suggest that investors exhibit various biases, which may lead to suboptimal investment choices. However, the study highlights the need for investors to be aware of their biases and use strategies to mitigate their impact. This study has some limitations. First, the sample size was small and not representative of the entire investor population. Second, the study used self-reported data, which could be biased in one direction or the other. Future studies should investigate the influence of additional biases on investment decisions and evaluate the efficacy of various countermeasures.

References

Al-Ansi, A. M., Garad, A., & Ryabtsev, V. (2024). Intelligent risk analysis of investment projects in the extractive industry. *Journal of Industrial Intelligence*, *2*(1), 42–53.

Albayati, H., Kim, S. K., & Rho, J. J. (2020). Accepting financial transactions using blockchain technology and cryptocurrency: A customer perspective approach. *Technology in Society*, *62*, 101320. https://doi.org/10.1016/j.techsoc.2020.101320

Al-mansour, B. Y. (2020). Cryptocurrency market: Behavioral finance perspective. *Journal of Asian Finance, Economics and Business*, *7*(12), 159–168. https://doi.org/10.13106/JAFEB.2020.VOL7.NO12.159

Alqaryouti, O., Siyam, N., Alkashri, Z., & Shaalan, K. (2020). Cryptocurrency usage impact on perceived benefits and users' behaviour. *Lecture Notes in Business Information Processing*, *381*, 123–136. https://doi.org/10.1007/978-3-030-44322-1_10

Baker, H. K., Kumar, S., & Goyal, N. (2021). Personality traits and investor sentiment. *Review of Behavioral Finance*, *13*(4), 354–369. https://doi.org/10.1108/RBF-08-2017-0077

Bigus, J. (2015). Loss aversion, audit risk judgments, and auditor liability. *European Accounting Review*, *24*(3), 581–606. https://doi.org/10.1080/09638180.2014.899920

Chaudary, S., & Samra, C. (2019). Does salience matter in investment decision? Differences between individual and professional investors. *Kybernetes*, *48*(8), 1894–1912. https://doi.org/10.1108/K-09-2018-0490

Chen, Q., Hua, X., & Jiang, Y. (2018). Contrarian strategy and herding behaviour in the Chinese stock market. *European Journal of Finance*, *24*(16), 1552–1568. https://doi.org/10.1080/1351847X.2015.1071715

Christoffersen, J., & Stæhr, S. (2019). Individual risk tolerance and herding behaviors in financial forecasts. *European Financial Management*, *25*(5), 1348–1377. https://doi.org/10.1111/eufm.12231

Corbet, S., Lucey, B., Urquhart, A., & Yarovaya, L. (2019). Cryptocurrencies as a financial asset: A systematic analysis. *International Review of Financial Analysis*, *62*, 182–199. https://doi.org/10.1016/j.irfa.2018.09.003

Dangi, M., & Kohli, B. (2018). Role of behavioral biases in investment decisions: A factor analysis. *Indian Journal of Finance*, *12*(3), 43–57. https://doi.org/10.17010/ijf/2018/v12i3/121997

Dangol, J., & Manandhar, R. (2020). Impact of heuristics on investment decisions: The moderating role of locus of control. *Journal of Business and Social Sciences Research*, *5*(1), 1–14. https://doi.org/10.3126/jbssr.v5i1.30195

De Bondt, W., Muradoglu, G., Shefrin, H., & Staikouras, S. (2008). Behavioral finance: Quo vadis? *Journal of Applied Finance*, *18*(2), 7–21. https://ssrn.com/abstract=2698614

de Souza Raimundo Júnior, G., Palazzi, R. B., de Souza Tavares, R., & Klotzle, M. C. (2019). Herding among investment newsletters: Theory and evidence. *Economics Letters*, *29*(1), 61. https://doi.org/10.1080/15427560.2020.1821688

DeVellis, R. (2016). *Scale Development: Theory and Applications* (2nd ed.). Sage Publications. https://books.google.co.in/books?id=BYGxL6xLokUC&printsec=frontcover&redir_esc=y#v=onepage&q&f=false

Farooq, M. (2017). The impact of heuristics on investment decision and performance: Exploring multiple mediation mechanisms. *Research in International Business and Finance*. https://doi.org/10.1016/j.ribaf.2017.07.010

Fraser, J., Fahlman, D. (Willy), Arscott, J., & Guillot, I. (2018). Pilot testing for feasibility in a study of student retention and attrition in online undergraduate programs. *The International Review of Research in Open and Distributed Learning*, *19*(1), 1–14. https://doi.org/10.19173/irrodl.v19i1.3326

Gadzinski, G., Schuller, M., & Mousavi, S. (2022). Long-lasting heuristics principles for efficient investment decisions. *Qualitative Research in Financial Markets*, *14*(4), 570–583. https://doi.org/10.1108/QRFM-04-2021-0072

Gautam, S., & Kumar, P. (2023a). Behavioral biases of investors in the cryptocurrency market. *AIP Conference Proceedings 15 June 2023*, 020105. https://doi.org/10.1063/5.0154194

Gautam, S., & Kumar, P. (2023b). Blockchain technology in the investment domain: A bibliometric analysis. *International Journal of Electronic Finance*, *1*(1). https://doi.org/10.1504/IJEF.2025.10061055

Gautam, S., & Kumar, P. (2023c). Prominent behavioral biases affecting investment decisions: A systematic literature review with TCCM and bibliometric analysis. *International Journal of Indian Culture and Business Management*, *1*(1). https://doi.org/10.1504/IJICBM.2023.10059339

Goyal, P., Gupta, P., & Yadav, V. (2023). Antecedents to heuristics: Decoding the role of herding and prospect theory for Indian millennial investors. *Review of Behavioral Finance*, *15*(1), 79–102. https://doi.org/10.1108/RBF-04-2021-0073

Gupta, S., & Shrivastava, M. (2021). Herding and loss aversion in stock markets: Mediating role of fear of missing out (FOMO) in retail investors. *International Journal of Emerging Markets*. https://doi.org/10.1108/IJOEM-08-2020-0933

Gurdgiev, C., & O'Loughlin, D. (2020). Herding and anchoring in cryptocurrency markets: Investor reaction to fear and uncertainty. *Journal of Behavioral and Experimental Finance*, *25*, 100271. https://doi.org/10.1016/j.jbef.2020.100271

Hair, J. F., & Lukas, B. (2014). *Marketing Research*. McGraw-Hill Education Australia. https://cat2.lib.unimelb.edu.au/record=b5609216~S13

Hirshleifer, D., & Hong Teoh, S. (2003). Herd behaviour and cascading in capital markets: A review and synthesis. *European Financial Management*, *9*(1), 25–66. https://doi.org/10.1111/1468-036X.00207

Jain, J., Walia, N., & Gupta, S. (2020). Evaluation of behavioral biases affecting investment decision making of individual equity investors by fuzzy analytic hierarchy process. *Review of Behavioral Finance*, *12*(3), 297–314. https://doi.org/10.1108/RBF-03-2019-0044

Jain, J., Walia, N., Kaur, M., & Singh, S. (2021). Behavioural biases affecting investors' decision-making process: A scale development approach. *Management Research Review*. https://doi.org/10.1108/MRR-02-2021-0139

Jlassi, M., & Naoui, K. (2015). Herding behaviour and market dynamic volatility: Evidence from the US stock markets. *American Journal of Finance and Accounting*, *4*(1), 70–91. https://doi.org/10.1504/AJFA.2015.067844

Kadir, Y. C., Ekrem, T., Selim, Z., Yalcin, K. C., Tatoglu, E., & Zaim, S. (2016). Developing an instrument for measuring the effects of heuristics on investment decisions. *Kybernetes*, *45*(7), 1052–1071. https://doi.org/10.1108/K-05-2015-0130

Kahneman, D., & Tversky, A. (1979). Prospect theory: An analysis of decision under risk. *Econometrica*, *47*(2), 263–292. https://www.jstor.org/stable/1914185

Kartini, K., & Nahda, K. (2021). Behavioral BIASES on investment decision: A case study in Indonesia. *Journal of Asian Finance, Economics and Business*, *8*(3), 1231–1240. https://doi.org/10.13106/jafeb.2021.vol8.no3.1231

Kengatharan, L., & Kengatharan, N. (2014). The influence of behavioral factors in making investment decisions and performance: Study on Investors of Colombo Stock

Exchange, Sri Lanka. *Asian Journal of Finance & Accounting*, *6*(1), 1–18. https://doi.org/10.5296/ajfa.v6i1.4893

Kerl, A. G., & Pauls, T. (2014). Analyst herding and investor protection: A cross-country study. *Applied Financial Economics*, *24*(8), 533–542. https://doi.org/10.1080/09603107.2014.889800

Kim, K. A., & Nofsinger, J. R. (2008). Behavioral finance in Asia. *Pacific-Basin Finance Journal*, *16*(1), 1–7. https://doi.org/10.1016/j.pacfin.2007.04.001

Kiymaz, H., Öztürkkal, B., & Akkemik, K. A. (2016). Behavioral biases of finance professionals: Turkish evidence. *Journal of Behavioral and Experimental Finance*, *12*, 101–111. https://doi.org/10.1016/j.jbef.2016.10.001

Kumar, S., & Goyal, N. (2015a). Behavioural biases in investment decision making – A systematic literature review. *Qualitative Research in Financial Markets*, *7*(1), 88–108. https://doi.org/10.1108/QRFM-07-2014-0022

Kumar, S., & Goyal, N. (2015b). *Qualitative research in financial markets article information: 4*, 68–80.

Kumar, S., & Goyal, N. (2016). Evidence on rationality and behavioural biases in investment decision making. *Qualitative Research in Financial Markets*, *8*(4), 270–287. https://doi.org/10.1108/QRFM-05-2016-0016

Kyriazis, N. A. (2020). Herding behaviour in digital currency markets: An integrated survey and empirical estimation. *Heliyon*, *6*(8), e04752. https://doi.org/10.1016/j.heliyon.2020.e04752

Lam, T. M. (2018). *Influence of anchoring bias on Bitcoin investors' trading decisions* (Issue May) [Aalto University School of Business]. www.aalto.fi

Lee, D. K. C., Guo, L., & Wang, Y. (2018). Cryptocurrency: A new investment opportunity? *Journal of Alternative Investments*, *20*(3), 16–40. https://doi.org/10.3905/jai.2018.20.3.016

Lude, M., & Prügl, R. (2019). Risky decisions and the family firm bias: An experimental study based on prospect theory. *Entrepreneurship Theory and Practice*, *43*(2), 386–408. https://doi.org/10.1177/1042258718796078

Mahmood, Z., Kouser, R., Abbas, S. S., & Saba, I. (2016). the effect of heuristics, prospect and herding factors on investment performance. *Pakistan Journal of Social Sciences (PJSS)*, *36*(1), 475–484. http://www.bzu.edu.pk/PJSS/Vol36No12016/PJSS-Vol36-No1-42.pdf

Maiyaki, A. A., & Mokhtar, S. S. M. (2010). Determinants of customer behavioural responses: a pilot study. *International Business Research*, *4*(1), 193. https://doi.org/10.5539/ibr.v4n1p193

Mishra, P. K., & Mishra, S. K. (2023). Do banking and financial services sectors show herding behaviour in Indian Stock Market Amid COVID-19 Pandemic? Insights from quantile regression approach. *Millennial Asia*, *14*(1), 54–84. https://doi.org/10.1177/09763996211032356

Mittal, S. K. (2019). Behavior biases and investment decision: Theoretical and research framework. *Qualitative Research in Financial Markets*. https://doi.org/10.1108/QRFM-09-2017-0085

Nofsinger, J. R., & Sias, R. W. (1999). Herding and feedback trading by institutional and individual investors. *The Journal of Finance*, *54*(6), 2263–2295. https://doi.org/10.1111/0022-1082.00188

Novarlić, B., & Đurić, P. (2024). Enhancing comprehensive waste management in transition economies through green logistics: A case study of Bosnia and Herzegovina. *Journal of Intelligent Management Decision*, *3*, 42–55. https://doi.org/10.56578/jimd030104

Ogunlusi, O. E., & Obademi, O. (2019). The impact of behavioural finance on investment decision-making: A study of selected investment banks in Nigeria. *Global Business Review*, *22*(6), 1345–1361. https://doi.org/10.1177/0972150919851388

Pompian, M. M. (2011). Behavioral finance and wealth management: How to build investment strategies that account for investor biases. In *Behavioral finance and wealth management: How to build investment strategies that account for investor biases*. Wiley. https://doi.org/10.1002/9781119202400

Raimundo Júnior, G. de S., Palazzi, R. B., Tavares, R. de S., & Klotzle, M. C. (2022). Market stress and herding: A new approach to the cryptocurrency market. *Journal of Behavioral Finance*, *23*(1), 43–57. https://doi.org/10.1080/15427560.2020.1821688

Richie, M., & Josephson, S. A. (2018). Quantifying heuristic bias: Anchoring, availability, and representativeness. *Teaching and Learning in Medicine*, *30*(1), 67–75. https://doi.org/10.1080/10401334.2017.1332631

Ritika, & Kishor, N. (2020). Risk preferences for financial decisions: Do emotional biases matter? *Journal of Public Affairs*, *22*(2), e2360. https://doi.org/10.1002/pa.2360

Ritika, & Nawal, K. (2020). Development and validation of behavioral biases scale: A SEM approach. *Review of Behavioral Finance*. https://doi.org/10.1108/RBF-05-2020-0087

Ritter, J. R. (2003). Behavioral finance. *Pacific-Basin Finance Journal*, *11*(4), 429–437. https://doi.org/10.1016/S0927-538X(03)00048-9

Sadi, R. (2011). Behavioral finance: The explanation of investors ' personality and perceptual biases effects on financial decisions. *International Journal of Economics and Finance*, *3*(5), 234–241. https://doi.org/10.5539/ijef.v3n5p234

Salman, M., Khan, B., Khan, S. Z., & Khan, R. U. (2020). The impact of heuristic availability bias on investment decision-making: Moderated mediation model. *Business Strategy & Development*, *4*(1), 246–257. https://doi.org/10.1002/bsd2.148

Sekaran, U., & Bougie, R. (2016). *Research methods for business: A skill building approach*. John Wiley and Sons. https://www.wiley.com/en-in/Research+Methods+For+Business:+A+Skill+Building+Approach,+7th+Edition-p-9781119266846

Shantha, K. V. A. (2019). The evolution of herd behavior: Will herding disappear over time? *Studies in Economics and Finance*, *36*(3), 637–661. https://doi.org/10.1108/SEF-06-2018-0175

Sharma, M., & Firoz, M. (2022). Delineating investors' rationality and behavioural biases - evidence from the Indian stock market. *International Journal of Management Practice*, *15*(1), 59–86. https://doi.org/10.1504/IJMP.2022.119925

Sias, R. W. (2004). Institutional herding. *The Review of Financial Studies*, *17*(1), 165–206. https://doi.org/10.1093/rfs/hhg035

Trimborn, S., Li, M., & Hardle, W. K. (2020). Investing with cryptocurrencies – A liquidity constrained investment approach. *Journal of Financial Econometrics*, *18*(2), 280–306. https://doi.org/10.2139/ssrn.2999782

Tseng, K. C. (2006). Behavioral finance, bounded rationality, neuro-finance, and traditional finance. *Investment Management and Financial Innovations*, *3*(4), 7–18. https://www.researchgate.net/publication/265357711

Tversky, A., & Kahneman, D. (1992). Advances in prospect theory: Cumulative representation of uncertainty. *Journal of Risk and Uncertainty*, *5*(4), 297–323. https://doi.org/10.1007/BF00122574

Wankel, C., & Godden, C. J. (2012). Behavioral Finance. *Encyclopedia of Business in Today's World*, *17*(1), 83–104. https://doi.org/10.4135/9781412964289.n76

Waweru, N. M., Munyoki, E., & Uliana, E. (2008). The effects of behavioural factors in investment decision-making: A survey of institutional investors operating at the Nairobi Stock Exchange. *International Journal of Business and Emerging Markets*, *1*(1), 24–41. https://doi.org/10.1504/IJBEM.2008.019243

Whitehead, A. L., Julious, S. A., Cooper, C. L., & Campbell, M. J. (2016). Estimating the sample size for a pilot randomised trial to minimise the overall trial sample size for the external pilot and main trial for a continuous outcome variable. *Statistical Methods in Medical Research*, *25*(3), 1057–1073. https://doi.org/10.1177/0962280215588241

Wong, W.-K., Chow, S.-C., Hon, T.-Y., & Woo, K.-Y. (2018). Empirical study on conservative and representative heuristics of Hong Kong small investors adopting momentum and contrarian trading strategies. *International Journal of Revenue Management*, *10*(2), 146–167. https://doi.org/10.1504/IJRM.2018.091836

Yerpude, S., Sood, K., & Grima, S. (2022). Blockchain-augmented digital supply chain management: A way to sustainable business. *Journal of Risk and Financial Management*, *16*(1), 7.

Zafar, N., & Hassan, A. (2016). An empirical investigation of herding: Case of Karachi stock exchange. *Pakistan Journal of Life and Social Sciences*, *14*(2), 60–69. https://www.scopus.com/inward/record.uri?eid=2-s2.0-85010208988&partnerID=40&md5=db6c3c5f4d87bf1dff83644cbcb46b2b

Zahera, S. A., & Bansal, R. (2018). Do investors exhibit behavioral biases in investment decision making? A systematic review. *Qualitative Research in Financial Markets*, *10*(2), 210–251. https://doi.org/10.1108/QRFM-04-2017-0028

Zikmund, W., Babin, B., Carr, J., & Griffin, M. (2013). *Business Research Methods*. Cengage Learning. https://books.google.co.in/books/about/Business_Research_Methods.html?id=veM4gQPnWHgC&redir_esc=y

Chapter 12

Currency Depreciation as a Determinant of Inflation in Sri Lanka

Tyrone De Alwis[a], *Wasantha Athukorala*[b] *and Narayanage Jayantha Dewasiri*[c]

[a]*Department of Economics, University of Colombo, Sri Lanka*
[b]*Department of Economics, University of Peradeniya, Sri Lanka*
[c]*Department of Accountancy and Finance, Faculty of Management Studies, Sabaragamuwa University of Sri Lanka, Belihuloya, Sri Lanka*

Abstract

Purpose: This chapter uses the annual time series data to investigate how currency depreciation impacts inflation in Sri Lanka.

Design/methodology/approach: We utilized the autoregressive distributed lag (ARDL) test to evaluate the long-term correlation between the variables. Additionally, the Granger causality test was used to examine the short-term relationships.

Findings: The ARDL test findings indicate an elevated relationship between currency depreciation and long-term inflation in Sri Lanka. The coefficient value of the error correction term indicates that 1.19% of the discrepancy error is rectified each year, directing the inflation response variable toward the long-term equilibrium.

Policy Implication: The Central Bank of Sri Lanka (CBSL) should adopt a policy to tighten and lessen currency pressure and fend off inflationary pressure. To design appropriate policies, they must quantify the country's exchange rate (ER) pass-through to inflation. The pass-through to inflation is most prominent when monetary policy action triggers or amplifies currency

Financial Landscape Transformation: Technological Disruptions, 217–233

doi:10.1108/978-1-83753-750-120251012

movements. However, this pass-through to inflation can be kept smaller provided central banks follow a credible inflation-targeting framework, operate in a flexible ER period, and are accessible from influences from fiscal authorities in the country.

Originality/value: This study uses the recently established ARDL limits cointegration approaches to investigate the enduring association between currency devaluation and price stability in Sri Lanka.

Keywords: Currency depreciation; cointegration; determinants; exchange rate; Granger causality; inflation; Sri Lanka

JEL Codes: E31; E41; E52

Introduction

Most nations utilize their respective currencies, such as the Sri Lankan Rupee (SLR) and the United States Dollar (USD), to conduct local transactions. Legal tender currencies must be exchanged at a specific rate, known as the exchange rate (ER) when making payments to nations with different currencies. The ER denotes the relative currency value compared to another currency (Centobelli et al., 2020; Ngozi et al., 2021; Ozen et al., 2020; Sakshi et al., 2020). Exchange rates are categorized as either floating or pegged. The interplay decides a floating ER between the supply and demand factors.

In contrast, the government sets a pegged ER at a fixed value relative to another currency or a collection of currencies. Depreciation can be termed as a change in the ER or, in other terms, devaluation. Therefore, when the currency is depreciated, it is an ER adjustment; thus, more of one currency is a prerequisite to exchange for a unit of another currency.

The ER plays a significant role in any nation, especially in the case of international trade, as it is an integral part of the monetary conditions of a country (Kose et al., 2019; Rajakaruna, 2017). In its position as the sole authority of economic activities in the country, the central bank has been vested with the discretionary power to manage the ER in the country (Karunaratne, 2000). As many have argued, maintaining the ER has become one of the fundamental macroeconomic issues in any economy, especially in the case of international trade and foreign exchange markets (Rajakaruna & Perera, 2019). When the ER becomes highly volatile, it can exert pressure on other macroeconomic variables, such as inflation. Furthermore, it can bring about uncertainty and a lack of confidence in the investors (Rajakaruna, 2017; Raji et al., 2017).

In an open economy, the ER is an essential determinant factor that can impact the overall economy and domestic prices by deprecating the local currency. Therefore, the ER is significant, especially for small economies, as it affects exports and imports. Exports of any nation depend much on the purchasing power of the other nations, and imports depend on the buying power of the domestic country. Whenever a country goes through a trade deficit condition (more imports over fewer exports), it can put descendant pressure on the local currency, known as depreciated currency. Once the domestic currency depreciates against the other currencies, prices of imported goods in the economy increase (Al-Ansi et al., 2024; Novarlić & Đurić, 2024; Razzaque et al., 2017).

It is indicated that emerging and developing economies faced significant currency depreciation, especially recently. Some countries suffered from sharp ER depreciation (e.g., Turkey and Argentina suffered heavily from external financing needs) (Wolla, 2015). The highest rate of pass-through to consumer prices is evident when the currency is highly pressured, which can accelerate inflation in the economy (Global Economic Prospectus, 2019). Furthermore, when the currency depreciates, it can challenge policymakers and destabilize the objectives of price stability (Kose et al., 2019).

Objectives of the Study

(a) To determine whether currency depreciation is a substantial determinant of price stability in Sri Lanka.
(b) To make recommendations based on findings.

Hence, this chapter investigates the extent of currency depreciation that caused inflation in Sri Lanka employing the ARDL test introduced by Pesaran et al. (2001). The period covered in this research is from 1977 to 2019. The chapter is designed as follows: The first section is devoted to the introduction; the next section focuses on the literature review that discusses the empirical findings of the previous studies. Sections 3–5 discuss the methodology, conclusion, and recommendation (Yerpude et al., 2022).

Empirical Literature and Research Gaps

Although there is a vast amount of literature on the association between inflation and ERs, very few studies exist on the association between inflation and currency depreciation in developing nations like Sri Lanka. Since unit root testing is the foundation of the ARDL technique, this study will be the first analysis on the subject.

Ekanayake and Chatrna (2010) tested GARCH models to examine how exchange rate volatility (ERV) affected Sri Lankan exports from 1980 to 2007. Their results posited that the impact of ERV depended on the types of traded items (categories of goods) and the complexity of understanding their specific linkages. Wanaguru (2015) discovered the causes of the volatility in the Sri Lankan currency market. The researcher posited that the CBSL's involvement in foreign currency significantly affected the ER. Rajakaruna (2017) emphasized that, for the sample period from 2001 to 2010, net official intervention was ER's most efficient and significant factor. By examining several linear regressions and unrestricted VAR models, her study illuminates the dynamics of ER. However, employing monthly data obtained from CBSL from 2001 to 2011, Jeggajeevan (2015) assessed the model's validity by considering the performance of the USD against the SLR. In her study, the validity of the flexible price monetary model was evaluated by performing cointegration and Vector Autoregression (VAR) models.

Nevertheless, the present analysis has determined that CBSL's involvement in the foreign exchange market is small. Several researchers uncovered factors that influence ER in developing nations; however, they have come to contentious findings. By examining cointegration tests and VAR models from 2009 to 2015, Jayasuriya and Perera (2016) examined the determinants influencing the USD ER in Sri Lanka. Their conclusions showed that ER's depreciation was caused by the prior month's net foreign assets and trade balance.

The ARDL model is used by Raji et al. (2017) to analyze Malaysia's real exchange rate (RER) determinants. They discovered that accurate money supply is the least significant contributor to the Malaysian RER, with foreign reserves, real stock return, and balance of payment having a longer-term impact. Barbosa et al. (2018) have used an unconventional methodology to explore the changing aspects of RER for emerging nations in the long run. As per their findings, the short-run variables, such as stock of outstanding debt and portfolio movements, have been identified as the primary predictors of the long-run RER using various panel data approaches. Additionally, Barbosa et al. (2018) used the cointegration analysis method using Vector Auto Regression for short- and long-term to assess the effects of ER fluctuations on economic growth in Bangladesh. Their findings suggested that a decrease in output is related to the appreciation of the RER. Barbosa et al. (2018) used panel data approaches to examine the effect of exchange rate regimes (ERRs) on economic growth for 16 emerging nations from 1974 to 2006. The findings revealed an association between various ERRs and economic development, but it is more effective under fixed than flexible regimes. Table 1 duly summarizes all the gaps in Sri Lankan studies.

Table 1. Literature Summary on Exchange Rate.

Author	Sample Period	Methodology Used	Empirical Findings
Ekanayake and Chatrna (2010)	1980–2007	GARCH model	The effect of ER volatility varies with the types of goods
Wanaguru (2015)	2002–2012	GARCH model	CBSL's participation in the foreign exchange market (FEM) effectively determines ER
Rajakaruna (2017)	2001–2010	VAR model, MLR method	The most significant and influential factor affecting ER is net official intervention

Table 1. (Continued)

Author	Sample Period	Methodology Used	Empirical Findings
Jeggajeevan (2015)	2001–2015	VECM model	Official FEM intervention by the CBSL is not statistically significant
Jayasuriya and Perera (2016)	2009–2015	Cointegration and VAR model	Net foreign assets and the trade balance caused short-term increases in the ER

Source: Authors' own.

Exchange Rate Policy in Sri Lanka

The ER is a widely discussed topic among policymakers and academia. Whether appreciated or depreciated, the debate on ERs is ongoing among policymakers and academia. Some argue against it, while others are biased towards it. One commonly cited argument against depreciation is that it will increase the value of the SLR's foreign debt and pave the way towards higher costs for imported products and services within the country. This is due to the effect on economic activity and the potential for a depreciated SLR on foreign debt. Currency depreciation refers to losing a country's currency value against foreign currencies like the USD. In Sri Lanka, currency depreciation has led to economic issues, as ER for the SLR increases when the currency depreciates against the USD. Sri Lanka has upheld a fixed currency rate system overseen by a Currency Board (CB) since achieving independence in 1948. CBSL was founded in 1950 to stabilize the local and outside values of the SLR and foster economic prosperity. The fixed ER system remained in place until November 1977, with revisions from Rs. 4.76 to 8.60 between 1950 and 1977. The world remained primarily fixed under the Bretton Woods system until the 1970s.

Between 1977 and 2001, Sri Lanka implemented a controlled FERR, where the USD was utilized as the foreign currency for bank operations. The ER range for the USD remained constant throughout this time frame, while the average rates for buying and selling were incrementally modified from SLR 16 to SLR 81.23. At first, the band fluctuated between SLR 15.97 and SLR 16.03. Nevertheless, CBSL decided to increase the currency's value in response to concerns and predictions over the rupee's depreciation in 2000. In 2001, CBSL ceased purchasing and selling activities in the open market and adopted a floating currency system, wherein market forces decided ERs without direct interference from CBSL (Colombage, 2016). As a result of this adjustment, ERs could vary according to market forces of supply and demand. However, the Central Bank of Sri Lanka (CBSL) would still interfere by purchasing or selling foreign currency to stabilize ER fluctuations (Wanaguru, 2015).

Sri Lanka employs a flexible ERR, utilizing export revenues, worker remittances, income generated by the tourism sector, direct investments, and foreign loans to effectively control its currency (Yadav & Raj, 2022). Until November 15, 1977, the government maintained a fixed ER system, changing the ER of the US dollar from LKR 4.76 to LKR 8.60. The Bretton Woods system, founded by the IMF in 1947, maintained a globally uniform fixed ER mechanism until the early 1970s.

Between November 1977 and January 2001, Sri Lanka implemented a controlled floating ER system, using the USD for transactions. During this time, CBSL modified the purchasing and selling prices, increasing them from LKR 16.00 to LKR 81.23. Additionally, the bank widened the range from LKR 15.97 to LKR 16.03. In response to speculation regarding the rupee's devaluation in the latter part of 2000, CBSL increased the selling rate. It sold a substantial quantity of US dollar reserves.

Since January 23, 2001, Sri Lanka has implemented a floating exchange rate regime (FERR), where the currency rate is based on market forces, eliminating CBSL's involvement. This strategy allows the central bank to carry out monetary policy autonomously from the balance of payments by addressing market imbalances as necessary. Nevertheless, during significant volatility in the ER, CBSL may engage in intervention by purchasing or selling foreign currency to uphold stability (Yadav & Raj, 2022).

In January 2001, CBSL decided to implement a FERR while stopping purchasing and selling USD in the open market as part of this move. Nevertheless, confident economists contend that the existing currency rate system operates as a managed float, wherein the CBSL upholds a low volatility state (De Alwis et al., 2023; Yadav & Raj, 2022). However, it is crucial to differentiate between the managed float system and the CBSL's involvement in the FERR to reduce excessive volatility. CBSL determines this intervention based on the prevailing macroeconomic conditions (Wanaguru, 2015). Table 2 comprehensively summarizes the ER systems implemented during the last seventy years in Sri Lanka.

Table 2. ERRs in Sri Lanka.

Date	**Significant Changes**	**ERR**
1949	The SLR is connected to the sterling pound	Fixed ERR
November 22, 1967	The rupee is depreciated by 20%	Fixed ERR
May 06, 1968	Announced Foreign Exchange Entitlement Certificate	Dual Exchange Rate (DER)
August 01, 1971	The SLR is linked to US$	DER
July 10, 1972	The SLR is linked to the Sterling Pound	DER
May 24, 1976	The SLR is linked to a composite index of currencies with different weights	DER
March 12, 1977	The SLR is depreciated by 20%	DER
November 16, 1977	The DER system was eliminated and replaced with a managed FERR	Managed to float with a crawling band

Table 2. (Continued)

Date	Significant Changes	ERR
June 20, 2000	The band is widened	Managed floating with a horizontal band
November 03	The band is widened	Managed to float with a crawling band
January 23, 2001	The central bank discontinued the practice of pre-announcing its rates	Independent floating

Source: Created by the authors considering the data gathered from CBSL annual reports of 2001.

Methodology and Data Sources

The current investigation employed yearly time series data spanning from 1977 to 2019, gathered from CBSL's data library. The Colombo Consumers Price Index (CCPI) is employed as a proxy variable for inflation (Inf), which is the dependent variable. Currency depreciation (C_depreciation), fiscal deficit (FD), and imports (imp) are considered the independent variables. The analysis incorporated imports and budget deficits as control variables.

Pesaran et al. (2001) introduced the ARDL test to test the existence of cointegration. The Johansen and Juselius method (1990) was also employed to ensure the reliability of the cointegration findings,

$$\Delta inf_t = \gamma_0 + \sum_{i=0}^{k} \gamma_{1i} \Delta inf_{t-1} + \sum_{i=0}^{k} \gamma_{2i} \, \Delta C\_depreciation_{t-1} + \sum_{i=0}^{k} \gamma_{3i} \Delta lnimports_{t-1} + \sum_{i=0}^{k} \gamma_{4i} \Delta lnfd_{t-1} + \partial_1 \, inf_{t-1} + \partial_2 C\_depreciation_{t-1} + \partial_3 lnimports_{t-1} + \partial_4 fd_{t-1} + \varepsilon_t \quad (1)$$

The drift component and time trend are denoted by γ_0, and ε_t are assumed to follow a white noise process. The lag structure is selected utilizing the Akaike Information Criteria (AIC) to ensure the absence of serial correlation.

Data Analysis and Empirical Findings

First, the stationarity of the data series is tested by applying the unit root tests such as augmented Dickey-Fuller and Phillips and Perron tests. Accordingly, the robustness of the stationary tests was assessed, and the results are given in Table 3.

Table 3. Unit Root Test Results.

Variables	**ADF**		**PP**		**Order of Integration**
	Levels	**First Difference**	**Levels**	**First Difference**	
Inf	−4.664979*** (0.0005)	−9.347774*** (0.0000)	−4.768232*** (0.0004)	−19.66441*** (0.0000)	$I(0)$,I(I)
Lnimports	–	−2.738415 (0.0764)	–	−2.605826 (0.1000)	I(I)
Lnfd	–	−10.57908*** (0.0000)	–	−11.44322*** (0.0000)	I(I)
C_depreciation	−6.910340*** (0.0000)	−11.71234*** (0.0000)	−6.887021*** (0.0000)	−17.01873*** (0.0000)	$I(0)$, I(I)

Source: Authors' own.

p-value, *$p< 0.1$, **$p<0.01$,***$p<0.05$ denotes acceptance of the alternative hypothesis of a unit root at 10%, 1%, and 5% significance levels, respectively.

According to Table 3, all the variables in the study have unit root problems at their level form except for inflation and currency depreciation. However, they all become stationary when they reach the first difference form, allowing us to apply the ARDL test to examine the long-run association between CPI and other variables. The findings of the ARDL test are shown in Table 4. As suggested by AIC, we chose lag two as the optimal structure for both variables. Accordingly, the ARDL testing is used with. AIC is advocated for employing the ARDL (1, 0, 1, 3) for the model, as stated in Fig. 1.

As per Table 4, since *F*-statistics is more significant than the value of the upper bound, there is a cointegration between the variables (De Alwis & Dewasiri, 2022a; Priyantha & De Alwis, 2021; Raza, 2016; Raza et al., 2015, 2016; Romanus et al., 2020, 2021). Accordingly, our results confirmed co-integrating relationships between currency depreciation. Wald test is employed to verify the long-term relationship among the variables. Accordingly, the model results showcase the long-run association between the variables, as found by De Alwis and Dewasiri (2022b).

Table 4 indicates a cointegration at the 5% significance level. This confirms the long-term relationship between inflation, currency depreciation, imports, and FD. Our study estimates long-term and short-term factors that determine the country's inflation. The long-run cointegration was assessed, and the findings are in Table 5, with CPI as the outcome variable and others as explanatory variables.

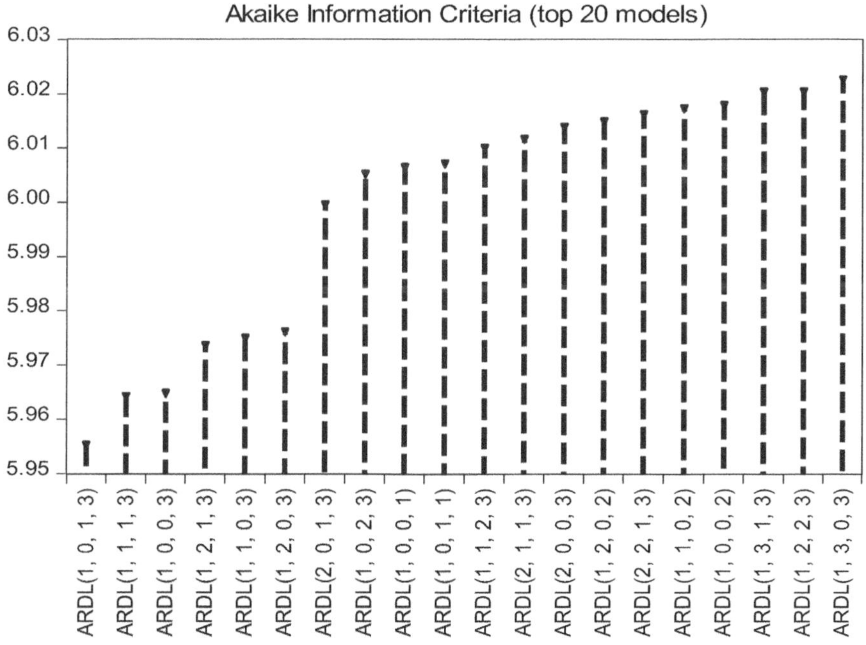

Fig. 1. Akaike Information Criteria. *Source*: Authors' own.

Table 4. ARDL Bound Test.

Currency Depreciation as a Determinant of Price Stability				
Significance Level	***F*-statistics**	**Critical Value**		**Conclusion**
		Lower Bound $I(0)$	**Upper Bound $I(1)$**	
5%	10.82	2.45	3.63	Cointegration

Source: Authors' own.

Table 5. The Results of the ARDL Long Run Model.

Model:055-Inf=f(C_depreciation, fd, lnimports) ARDL (1,0,0,1)				
Variables	**Coefficient**	**Std. Error**	***t*-statistics**	**Probability**
C_DEPRECIATION	0.42	0.22	1.87	0.0506
FD	9.97E-06	4.01E-06	2.4	0.0183
LNIMPORTS	1.57	0.69	2.25	0.0308

Source: Authors' own.

The findings show a strong cointegration between CPI and currency depreciation, implying a positive association.

In line with the study's objectives, currency depreciation positively impacts inflation from 1977 to 2019. The estimated coefficient of currency depreciation is 0.42 at a 5% significant level. Therefore, if the currency is depreciated by 1%, the inflation in the country will rise by 42%. These findings are confirmed by Perera (2005), Kulatunge (2013), Duma (2008), and Amarasinghe et al. (2018). Having statistically established the relationship between CPI and currency depreciation, we ascertained the short-run relationship between CPI and the rest of the manipulated variables. The ECM version of the ARDL model and the outcomes are given in Table 6.

The error correction results imply that currency depreciation was a factor that determined the price stability in Sri Lanka from 1977 to 2019. The Error Correction Terms (ECT) (-1) in the model are substantial, and adverse (-) signs indicate that any disequilibrium in the CPI and other variables can be adjusted at 119% on an annual basis (Jeremiah et al., 2021). The ECT in Table 6 shows the speed of adjustment to equilibrium within the existence of a co-integrating association between currency depreciation and inflation in the model. The findings of Table 6 show that currency depreciation does not impact inflation in the country in the short term, but it is the other way around in the long term.

The findings of the autocorrelation test are shown in Table 7. The *p*-value in this instance is 0.7999, over the 0.05 cutoff, suggesting that the calculated models do not exhibit serial correlation. The serial autocorrelation results are

Table 6. Findings of the Estimated Short-Run Error Correction – ARDL Approach.

Model: Inf=f (C_depreciation, fd, lnimports) ARDL(1, 0, 1, 3)		
Variables	**Coefficient**	**Probability**
C	−0.8698	
D(INF(-1))	0.26	0.1480
D(C_DEPRECIATION)	0.22	0.1909
D(FD)	−8.84E-06	0.4317
D(FD(-1))	1.09E-05	0.3848
D(LNIMPORTS)	37.68	0.0276
D(LNIMPORTS(-1))	−29.83	0.1279
D(LNIMPORTS(-2))	8.65	0.493
D(LNIMPORTS(-3))	0.62	0.9612
ECM(-1)	**−1.19**	**0.0001**
***R*-squared: 0.58, Adj. *R*-squared: 0.45**		

Source: Authors' own.
Notes: (1) INF (inflation), C_DEPRECIATION (currency depreciation), F.D. (fiscal deficit), LNIMPORTS (log of imports). (2)D(LNINF(-1)), D(F.D. (-1)), D(LNIMPORTS(-1)), D(LNIMPORTS(-2)), D(LNIMPORTS(-3)) – stands for one year lag of inflation, one year, two years and three years lag of imports respectively.

Table 7. Serial Correlation Test.

Model: Inf=f(C_depreciation, fd, imports) ARDL (1,0,1,3)			
Model	***F*-statistics**	**Obs* *R*-squared**	**Prob(2,30)**
ARDL	0.22	0.59	0.7999

Source: Authors' own.

displayed in Table 7, and the *p*-value is greater than 0.05. Hence, it verifies that the models – which examine currency depreciation as a factor influencing inflation in Sri Lanka – do not display autocorrelation.

Table 8 assesses the heteroscedasticity. The Chi-square test's *p*-value is 0.6223, over the 0.05 cutoff, indicating that the model's residuals show homoscedasticity.

Table 9 shows the results of the Granger Causality test between price stability and currency depreciation. Because the *p*-value is higher than 0.05, the null hypothesis – which states that inflation does not lead to currency depreciation – is not rejected. Thus, from 1977 to 2019, the model indicates that while inflation does not seem to induce currency depreciation, it may result in it in Sri Lanka.

Table 8. Heteroskedasticity Test of ARCH.

Model: Inf=f(C_depreciation, fd, lnimports) ARDL (1,0,1, 3)			
Model	***F*-statistics**	**Obs* *R*-squared**	**Prob(1,39)**
ARDL	0.24	0.25	0.6223

Source: Authors' own.

Table 9. Results of the Granger Causality Test.

Null Hypothesis	Observations	Probability	Conclusion
(1) *H0*: Currency depreciation does not Granger Cause Inflation	40	0.0554	**Reject** *H0*: because Currency depreciation causes Inflation at a 10% significance level
(2) *H0*: Inflation does not Granger Cause Currency depreciation	40	0.8544	**Do Not Reject** *H0*: Because inflation does not Granger causes Currency depreciation

Source: Authors' own.

Parameter stability tests were conducted as the next step. Hansen (1992) pointed out that parameters can be varied over time in time series analysis. Hence, he suggested testing the stability of these parameters. To avoid this issue of biases, Brown et al. (1975) introduced Cusum and Cusum Square tests, which were applied in this study to assess the model's stability. The results indicate that parameter consistency in CUSUM and CUSUM OF SQUARE plots has been within the 5% significance level range, as shown in Fig. 2.

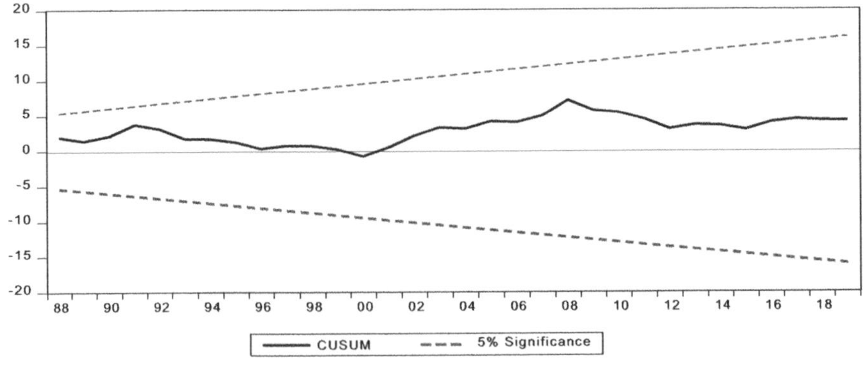

Fig. 2. Plots of CUSUM. *Source*: Authors' own.

The CUSUM SQUARE is presented in Fig. 3, as stated below. It is also within the boundaries without any deviation from the stability boundary, and therefore, the model is stable.

Table 10 represents the summary diagnostic and stability tests that show stable results employing currency depreciation as a determinant of inflation.

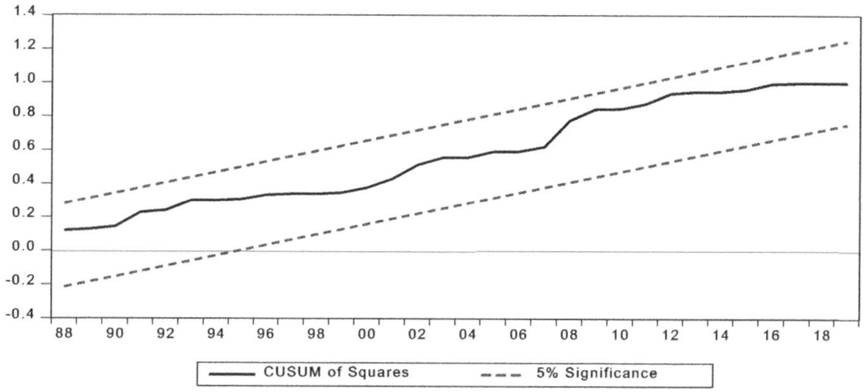

Fig. 3. Plots of CUSUM SQUARE. *Source*: Authors' own.

Table 10. Results of the Stability Tests.

Model	
Test	***F*-statistics**
Heteroscedasticity	0.24
Normality	0.5
Serial Correlation	0.22
CUSUM	Stable
CUSUM SQUARE	Stable

Source: Authors' own.

Impulse Response Function

Next, we used impulse response functions (IRFs) to investigate the dynamic characteristics of currency depreciation influencing inflation. The IRF of price stability in reaction to a standard deviation shock to inflation is shown in Fig. 4. The direction and strength of the IRF are shown on the *y*-axis, while the time horizon or shock duration is shown on the *x*-axis. Fig. 4 illustrates IRF for the model. The IRF of currency depreciation on inflation is high and positive up to the third period. After that, it remains negative up to the fourth period, indicating

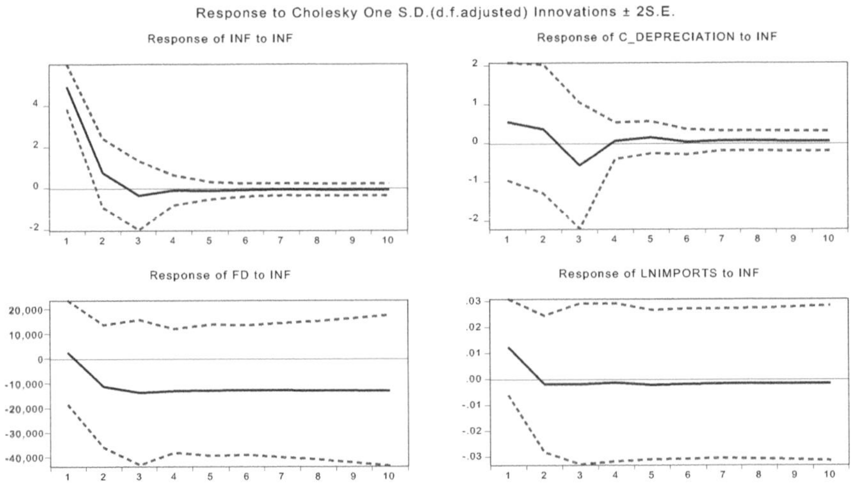

Fig. 4. Impulse Response Function. *Source*: Authors' own.

an adverse response to inflation after the third period. However, the positive reaction gradually settled throughout the rest of the period.

Conclusion

The main goal of this chapter is to examine how Sri Lankan price stability was affected by currency depreciation between 1977 and 2019. This study used annual data to examine the short- and long-term factors contributing to inflation. By utilizing the ARDL model, this study sought to augment the current knowledge on inflation by pinpointing plausible factors in Sri Lanka. Because it can be used to estimate relationships in the short and long term and considers various factors that influence inflation, such as currency depreciation, the ARDL model was selected.

Specific necessary tests were done in line with the objectives, such as unit root, cointegration, IRF, and CUSUM and CUSUM SQUARE. According to the results obtained, currency depreciation is identified as one of the causes of low price stability in the country. Hence, based on the results obtained from the model, currency depreciation substantially impacted inflation in Sri Lanka, specifically in the long run.

Policy Implications

An important policy implication that can be drawn from the present study is that when a nation continues to face the risk of destabilizing ER movements, financial markets face turbulence, such as in 2018's financial market turbulence. Thus, CBSL, as the monetary authority, can adopt a policy to tighten and lessen currency pressure and fend off inflationary pressure. To design appropriate policies, they must quantify the country's ER pass-through to inflation. The pass-through to inflation is most prominent when monetary policy action triggers or amplifies currency movements. However, this pass-through to inflation can be kept smaller, provided central banks follow a credible inflation-targeting framework, operate in a flexible ER period, and are free from influences from fiscal authorities in the country. These measures can become self-reinforcing feedback between central bank credibility, ER, and price stability. Because depreciating currencies increase the cost of imports, inflation is frequently the result. A weaker currency makes imports more expensive because most nations rely on imported materials, goods, or technologies, which raises prices. If currency depreciation is strictly controlled, these scenarios can be controlled by targeting inflation control, which becomes helpful to policymakers.

As a result, keeping a constant USD ER cannot be regarded as a sustainable strategy since it would result in an overvaluation of the SLR, lowering our exports' ability to compete. However, Sri Lanka's modest international reserves, which were mainly accumulated through debt-creating sources, prevent it from being able to intervene continuously through the provision of foreign currency. Defending the exchange rate using reserves amassed with borrowed money costs the economy significantly more.

References

Amarasinghe, A. A. M. D., Kumara, A. A. A. G., & Walakumbura, S. H. M. L. (2018). Long-run/short-run relationship between inflation and oil price in Sri Lanka. In *15*th *International conference on business management (ICBM, 2018)*, pp. 400–413. University of Sri Jayawardenapura, Sri Lanka.

Al-Ansi, A. M., Garad, A., & Ryabtsev, V. (2024). Intelligent risk analysis of investment projects in the extractive industry. *Journal of Industrial Intelligence*, *2*(1), 42–53.

Barbosa, L., Jayme, F. G., & Missio, F. (2018). Determinants of the real exchange rate in the long-run for developing and emerging countries: A theoretical and empirical approach. *International Review of Applied Economics*, *32*(1), 62–83.

Brown, R. L., Durbin, J., & Evans, J. M. (1975). Techniques for testing the constancy of regression relations over time. *Journal of the Royal Statistical Society*, *37*(01), 149–163.

Centobelli, P., Cerchione, R., & Shashi, E. E. (2020). Evaluating environmental sustainability strategies in freight transport and logistics industry. *Business Strategy and the Environment*, *29*(3), 1563–1574.

Colombage, S. (2016). Weak SL Rupee 68 Years After Independence Reflects Economic Setbacks. *Sunday Times*, February 14.

De Alwis, T., & Dewasiri, N. J. (2022a). Supply driven factors of inflation in Sri Lanka: An ARDL approach. *Asian Journal of Management Studies, Faculty of Management Studies, Sabaragamuwa University of Sri Lanka*, *02*(02), 88–114. http:/doi.org/10.38/ajms.v2i2.51

De Alwis, T., & Dewasiri, N. J. (2022b). Demand-driven factors of inflation in Sri Lanka: An ARDL approach. *Sri Lanka Journal of Management Studies*, *03*(11), 53–69. http://doi.org/10.4038/sljms.v3i2.83

De Alwis, T., Dewasiri, N. J., & Sood, K. (2023). Persistent fiscal deficit as a determinant of inflation in Sri Lanka: An ARDL approach. In K. Sood, B. Balusamy, & S. Grima

(Eds.), *Digital transformation, strategic resilience, cyber security and risk management. Contemporary Studies in Economic and Financial Analysis* (Vol. 111C, pp. 27–51). Emerald Publishing Limited. https://doi.org/10.1108/S1569-37592023000111C002

Duma, N. (2008, March). *Pass-through of external shocks to inflation in Sri Lanka.* IMF Working Paper WP/08/78.

Ekanayake, E. M., & Chatrna, D. (2010). The effects of exchange rate volatility on Sri Lankan Exports: An empirical investigation. *Journal of International Business and Economy, 11*(01), 51–68.

Engle, F. F., & Granger, C.W. J. (1987). Cointegration and error correction: Representation, estimation and testing. *Econometrica, 55*(2), 251–276.

Global Economic Prospectus. (2019, June). *Currency depreciation. Inflation and Central Bank Independence.* Special Focus 1.2.

Hansen, B. E. (1992) Testing for parameter instability in linear models. *Journal of Policy Modeling, 14*, 517–533. https://doi.org/10.1016/0161–8938(92)90019–9

Jayasuriya, D. P. S. H., & Perera, S. S. N. (2016). Analysis of factors affecting USD/LKR exchange rate. In *Symposium on statistical & computational modelling with applications.*

Jeggajeevan, S. (2015). Validity of the monetary model of the exchange rate: Empirical evidence from Sri Lanka. *Staff Studies, Central Bank of Sri Lanka, 42*(01), 47–74.

Jeremiah, O. E., Osbodien, R., Adeleye, B. N., & De Alwis, T. (2021). Household ICT utilization and food security nexus in Nigeria. *International Journal of Food and Science, 02*(20), 1–10. https://doi.org/10.1155/2020/55516

Johansen, S., & Juselius, K. (1990). Maximum likelihood estimation and inference on cointegration with applications to demand for money. *Oxford Bulletin of Economics and Statistics, 52*, 169–210.

Karunaratne, N. D. (2000, December). Inflation targeting and central bank independence. *Sri Lanka Economic Journal, 1*(2), 1–27.

Kose, A., Matsuoka, H., Panizza, U., Vorisek, D., & Lauren, D. (2019). *Inflation expectations: Review and evidence.* World Bank.

Kulatunge, S. (2013). Inflation dynamic in Sri Lanka: An empirical analysis. *Staff Studies, Central Bank of Sri Lanka, 45*(1–2), 31–66.

Ngozi, B. A., Osabohien, R., Lawal, A. S., & De Alwis, T. (2021, November). Energy use and the role of per capital income on carbon emission in African countries. *PLOS ONE, 16*(11), e0259488. https://doi.org/10.1371/journal.pone.0259488

Novarlić, B., & Đurić, P. (2024). Enhancing comprehensive waste management in transition economies through green logistics: A case study of Bosnia and Herzegovina. *Journal of Intelligent Management Decision, 3*, 42–55.

Ozen, E., Ozdemir, L., & Grim, S. (2020). The relationship between the exchange rate, interest rate and inflation: The case of Turkey. *Scientific Annals of Economics and Business, 67*, 259–275.

Perera, W. T. (2005). The impact of petroleum prices on inflation in Sri Lanka. *Staff Studies, Central Bank of Sri Lanka, 35*(1&2).

Pesaran, M. H., Shin, Y., & Smith, R. J. (2001). Bounds testing approaches to the analysis of long-run relationships. *Journal of Applied Econometrics, 16*, 289–326.

Priyantha, S. G., & De Alwis, T. (2021, December). Factors influencing prescribe branded drugs by physicians: An empirical study in Sri Lanka. In *Proceedings of the 18th. International Conference on Business Management, Faculty of Management Studies and Commerce, University of Sri Jayawardenapura, Sri Lanka* (pp. 1794–1820).

Rajakaruna, S. H. I. (2017). An investigation on factors affecting exchange rate fluctuations in Sri Lanka. *Staff Studies, Central Bank of Sri Lanka, 47*(01). http://doi.org/10.4038/ss.v47i1.4703

Rajakaruna, I., & Perera, N. (2019). Determining the nominal exchange rate in Sri Lanka: An application of the lagrange multiplier structural brak unit root test and the

ARDL cointegration. *Journal of South Asian Studies*, *08*(02), 57–70. http://doi.org/10.33687/jsas.008.02.3301

Raji, J. O., Badru, B. O., & Abdulkadir, R. I. (2017). Real exchange rate determinant in Malaysia. *Actual Problems in Economics* (No.188), pp. 277–287.

Raza, S. (2016). Foreign direct investment, worker's remittances and private saving in Pakistan: An ARDL bound testing approach. *Journal of Business Economics and Management*, *16*(06).

Raza, S., Shahbaz, M., & Nguyen, D. K. (2015). Energy conservation policies, growth and trade performance: Evidence of feedback hypothesis in Pakistan. *Energy Policy*, *80*(C), 1–10.

Raza, S.A., Shahbaz, M., & Paramati, S. R. (2016). Dynamic of military expenditure and income inequality in Pakistan. *Social Indicators Research*, *01*(21).

Razzaque, M. A., Bidisha, S. H., & Khondker, B. H. (2017). Exchange rate and economic growth: An empirical assessment for Bangladesh". *Journal of South Asian Development*, *12*(01), 42–64.

Romanus, O., Ashraf, J., De Alwis, T., Ufua, D. E., Osabuohien, E., Odularu, G., Norman, A., & Augustine, D. (2021). Social protection and food security nexus in the global south: Empirical evidence from West Africa". *Contemporary Social Science*, 17(2), 129–142.

Romanus, S., Ngozi, A., & De Alwis, T. (2020, May). Agro-financing and food production in Nigeria. *Heliyon*, *06*(05), 1–8, e04001.

Sakshi, S., Cerchione, R., & Bansal, H. (2020). Measuring the impact of sustainability policy and practices in tourism and hospitality industry. *Business Strategy and the Environment*, *29*(3), 1109–1126.

Wolla, S. A. (2015, January). Would a gold standard brighten economic outcomes? Page One Economics Newsletter, Federal Reserve Bank of St. Louis, 1. https://www.stlouisfed.org/publications/page-one-economics/2015/01/01/would-a-gold-standard-brighten-economic-outcomes

Wanaguru, S. (2015). From where does it come? An analysis of currency market volatility in Sri Lanka. *Staff Studies, Central Bank of Sri Lanka*, *42*(1), 75–97.

Yadav, N., & Raj, V. (2022, April). *The fallen Sri Lankan rupee: Not just another economic crisis*. NUS Institute of South Asian Studies. https://www.isas.nus.edu.sg/papers/the-fallen-sri-lankan-rupee-not-just-another-economic-crisis/

Yerpude, S., Sood, K., & Grima, S. (2022). Blockchain-augmented digital supply chain management: A way to sustainable business. *Journal of Risk and Financial Management*, *16*(1), 7.

Chapter 13

RegTech: The New Regulatory Technology

Neha Bansal[a] *and Sanjay Taneja*[b]

[a]*University School of Business, Chandigarh University, Mohali (Punjab), India*
[b]*Department of Management Studies, Graphic Era deemed to be University, Dehradun, India*

Abstract

Introduction: Regulatory technology (Regtech) uses technology and innovative techniques to improve and expedite regulatory compliance procedures across various sectors, notably the financial industry. This chapter closely examines how Regtech is being used in the financial sector.

Purpose: This study examines the adoption and implementation of Regtech solutions in the financial sector. It aims to identify the leading technologies propelling the adoption of Regtech and the benefits and challenges financial institutions face when implementing Regtech solutions for regulatory compliance.

Need of the Study: The study examines the increasing demand for effective regulatory compliance in the financial sector. Financial institutions seek novel ways to streamline compliance procedures as regulatory complexities increase. This study fulfills the need to examine the adoption of Regtech as a potential solution to enhance regulatory compliance's efficiency and effectiveness.

Research Methodology: This chapter's research methodology entails a comprehensive review of existing studies, and examples to collect pertinent data and insights. The current study provides an extensive and comprehensive view of the existing studies. Examining real-world examples provides practical examples and demonstrates the efficacy of Regtech in the financial sector.

Financial Landscape Transformation: Technological Disruptions, 235–251

doi:10.1108/978-1-83753-750-120251013

Findings: The findings reveal that the adoption of Regtech is gaining momentum in the financial industry, with increasing recognition of its potential benefits. Financial institutions leverage Regtech solutions to automate compliance processes, monitor regulatory changes, and enhance risk management practices. However, technological complexities, regulatory constraints, and data security concerns pose significant hurdles to widespread adoption.

Keywords: Regtech; regulatory; technology; regulatory compliance; fintech; financial industry; banking industry

JEL Codes: G23; G30; L51; M42; O31

Introduction

Technology is revolutionizing finance at a rate that has never been seen before, creating new opportunities but also increasing complexities (Arner et al., 2017a). Many advantages have resulted from the development of Fintech, including improved client convenience (Hasan et al., 2021), automated investment advising services (Belanche et al., 2019), and access to new financial goods and services (Buckley & Webster, 2016). Fintech has revolutionized the financial services sector by offering cutting-edge, client-focused goods and services (Matari et al., 2022). However, this evolution has also presented significant compliance and risk management difficulties for financial organizations (Anagnostopoulos, 2018).

Fintech businesses operate in a highly regulated sector, and adhering to rules may be difficult, particularly for young firms with minimal resources (Yadav, 2020). Because they handle and maintain sensitive client data, Fintech businesses are a top target for cybercriminals (Lee et al., 2020). Fintech organizations face considerable cybersecurity threats, necessitating strong security measures to guard against breaches. Many financial organizations rely on obsolete legacy systems that are not built to work with modern technology (Varga, 2017). It might be pretty challenging to integrate new Fintech solutions with these platforms. Furthermore, because Fintech businesses are recent additions to the financial services sector, they may find it challenging to win over clients accustomed to using traditional financial institutions. Fintech organizations process and store large volumes of client data, which might cause privacy problems (Gai et al., 2017). Compliance with data privacy laws is essential to keeping customers' trust (Stewart & Jürjens, 2018).

In this chapter, the authors looked at several features of Regtech, including its history, key technologies, and applications in the financial services sector. The advantages and challenges of implementing Regtech were also covered. Certain examples were presented to understand better how Regtech is used in the real world.

To balance the advantages of innovation and economic development with financial stability and consumer safety, financial regulators must create innovative ways to regulate, mainly via technology (Arner et al., 2017a; Lumpkin, 2010). The development of Fintech has prompted the demand for Regtech (Arner et al., 2017b). One of the causes of the creation of Regtech is the growing Fintech trend. It has become a catchphrase in response to the expectations of risk and compliance processes in regulated businesses (Schizas et al., 2020). Although the Financial Conduct Authority (FCA) used the word for the first time in 2015, it has been around since then. The phrase "Regtech" is a contraction of the words "regulatory" and "technology." It refers to the use of technology, particularly information technology (IT), to the processes of regulation, monitoring, reporting, and compliance (Arner et al., 2017a; Buckley et al., 2020; Solms, 2021).

Regtech can address some of the problems caused by the advent of Fintech. By providing automated tools that track compliance and highlight areas of non-compliance, Regtech solutions may assist Fintech businesses in adhering to rules (Opoku-Afari et al., 2022). The money and resources needed to comply with regulatory standards may be lessened. Regtech can help financial businesses with cybersecurity concerns by offering automated solutions that recognize and react to online dangers (Yang & Li, 2018). By protecting against breaches and boosting security, these solutions may increase client confidence and trust (Lukonga, 2018). Regtech can also offer solutions that make connecting new Fintech solutions with existing systems easier, lowering the difficulty and expense of doing so (Anagnostopoulos, 2018). Regtech contributes to developing consumer trust by offering solutions that increase accountability and transparency (Castri et al., 2018). Regtech solutions, for instance, can offer automatic reporting with a clear audit trail, enhancing accountability and transparency. Regtech solutions can also address privacy issues by offering instruments that guarantee adherence to data protection laws (Truby et al., 2020).

Regtech has emerged as a result of several issues, such as the amount and complexity of laws (Freij, 2020; Solms, 2021), the requirement for quicker and more accurate compliance (Arner et al., 2017c), and the expanding use of data and analytics for regulatory supervision (Batista & Ringe, 2020). It may be quite difficult to manually handle the increasing number of rules that financial firms must comply with from many jurisdictions. Regtech systems enable the automation of several compliance and risk management processes, saving both time and money (Packin, 2018; Yerpude et al., 2022).

Overall, this chapter aims to provide a thorough analysis of Regtech and how it could change the way the financial services industry complies with regulations.

Literature Review

Regtech originated in the advancement of technology and financial regulation as a whole. Regtech may have started in the early 2000s, after the global financial crisis 2008, when financial institutions were exposed to increased regulatory scrutiny and compliance expenses (Arner et al., 2017a; Currie et al., 2018; Ioannou et al., 2019).

Regtech first appeared when regulatory compliance duties were managed using simple technical solutions like databases and spreadsheets (Castri et al., 2018).

The necessity to cope with the complexity and volume of increasingly sophisticated financial regulations, as well as the need to reduce operational costs and human errors, were the primary drivers behind the early efforts at automating compliance operations (Chen et al., 2021).

Regtech solutions began to include more sophisticated capabilities, such as data analytics and risk management software, to enhance regulatory compliance as technology advanced (Aziz & Dowling, 2019; Memminger et al., 2016). Financial institutions might automate processes like know-your-customer (KYC) due diligence (Lootsma, 2017), anti-money laundering (AML) checks (Kurum, 2020), transaction monitoring (Solms, 2021), and reporting (Kavassalis et al., 2018) with the use of these technologies.

As new rules were adopted and existing ones made more stringent, the regulatory environment constantly evolved. Regtech solutions become more and more specialized and complex as a consequence. Regtech has grown significantly in recent years as a result of the advancement of technology like artificial intelligence (AI), machine learning (ML), natural language processing (NLP), and blockchain, which have allowed for the creation of more complicated and automated compliance solutions (Deshpande, 2020; Gupta et al., 2021; Plenk et al., 2019).

Regtech has also become popular among regulators since they have recognized how technology may enhance regulatory oversight and enforcement (Yang & Tsang, 2017). Several regulatory organizations have begun aggressively promoting adopting Regtech solutions, such as regulatory sandboxes and innovation centers (Mcquinn, 2019; Tsang, 2019), to stimulate collaboration between financial institutions, technology suppliers, and regulators in creating and implementing Regtech solutions (Yang & Li, 2018).

Various businesses are providing cutting-edge solutions to numerous regulatory difficulties financial institutions encounter in the rapidly expanding field of Regtech. Companies like Chainalysis, ComplyAdvantage, Ascent Regtech, Forter, Hummingbird, Continuity, Encompass, etc., are the prominent Regtech service providers. In a rapidly changing and complicated regulatory environment, it continues to change and influence how financial institutions manage regulatory compliance, cut risk, and boost operational effectiveness.

Research Methodology

The research thoroughly evaluates previous studies, scholarly writing, and real-life examples to gather relevant information and insights for this study. By carefully analyzing existing studies, researchers gain thorough knowledge regarding the evolving landscape of regtech and its impact on the financial sector. Additionally, analyzing real-world case studies shows the effectiveness of Regtech in the banking sector and offers practical examples.

Need for Regtech

Regtech has become necessary in response to the difficulties and complexity of the financial industry's constantly changing regulatory environment

(Castri et al., 2018). The need for Regtech solutions is increasing for a variety of reasons, including:

1. **Increasing regulatory complexity:** Financial institutions must comply with a wide range of rules, including those of consumer protection, data privacy, anti-money laundering, and KYC (Thommandru & Chakka, 2023). These laws are constantly evolving, getting more intricate, and having varied criteria depending on the jurisdiction. It may be time-consuming, resource-intensive, and prone to error to manage compliance with such rules manually. Therefore, automation through Regtech solutions is essential for precision and effectiveness.
2. **Increasing compliance expenses:** Financial institutions see increased compliance costs due to increased regulatory requirements for internal controls, paperwork, and reporting (Arner et al., 2017a). Regtech systems can automate these procedures, hence minimizing the demand for manual labor and related expenses. By simplifying compliance procedures, Regtech may assist financial institutions in more efficiently allocating resources and optimizing their compliance expenses (Papantoniou, 2022).
3. **Increased regulatory supervision:** Regulatory organizations worldwide are stepping up their oversight and enforcement operations, which has led to increased oversight and harsher sanctions for non-compliance. Financial institutions which break the law run severe risks to their finances, reputation, and legal standing. Regtech systems offer sophisticated monitoring, reporting, and risk assessment capabilities that aid financial institutions in anticipating and promptly identifying possible compliance concerns (Turki et al., 2020).
4. **Rapid technological progress:** The financial sector is undergoing a digital transformation due to the disruption that new technologies like blockchain, AI, ML, big data analytics, and others are causing to established business procedures. Regtech uses these technological developments to offer cutting-edge approaches to regulatory compliance. For instance, Regtech systems driven by AI and ML can analyze enormous volumes of data, see trends, and spot abnormalities to quickly and accurately identify possible compliance concerns (Bauguess, 2018).
5. **Raised consumer expectations:** Consumers now demand smooth, convenient financial services, as well as the protection of their interests through the observance of all applicable laws by financial institutions. Regtech solutions may help financial institutions satisfy customer expectations and foster confidence by facilitating more efficient onboarding procedures, enhancing customer due diligence, and ensuring compliance with data protection laws.
6. **Regulatory support for innovation:** To encourage innovation in the financial sector, regulators in several countries actively support the use of Regtech solutions. Thanks to regulatory sandboxes, innovation centers, and other efforts, financial institutions and Regtech providers can work together, experiment with new technologies, and create practical compliance solutions (Zetzsche et al., 2017).

Rising regulatory complexity, rising compliance costs, increased scrutiny, quickening technical development, rising consumer expectations, and regulatory support for innovation all contribute to the need for Regtech. In a constantly changing regulatory climate, Regtech solutions give financial institutions a chance to improve compliance, lower risk, and increase operational effectiveness.

Application of Regtech in the Financial Industry

Regtech is a fast-expanding field with a wide range of financial sector applications. Regtech has a number of crucial applications, such as:

1. **Compliance Monitoring:** Regtech solutions may help financial institutions monitor compliance with regulatory requirements, decreasing the likelihood of non-compliance and the associated fines and penalties (Kurum, 2020).
2. **Risk Management:** Regtech solutions may help financial institutions manage risk more effectively by identifying potential dangers and providing insights into risk exposure (Giudici, 2018).
3. **Reporting and Analytics:** Financial institutions may benefit from enhanced reporting and analytical capabilities provided by regtech solutions, enabling them to filter through massive amounts of data and identify potential risks and compliance issues (Freij, 2020).
4. **Identity Verification:** Regtech solutions might help financial institutions validate the identities of their customers more effectively, reducing the risk of fraud and improving the onboarding of new clients (Malhotra et al., 2022).
5. **Fraud Detection and Prevention:** Regtech solutions may help financial institutions spot and stop fraud by identifying suspicious behavior and sending real-time warnings (Miguel & Algarvio, 2019).
6. **AML/KYC Compliance:** Regtech solutions may help financial institutions comply with AML and KYC rules by automating compliance operations and increasing due diligence procedures.
7. **Cybersecurity:** Regtech solutions may help financial institutions improve cybersecurity by providing real-time threat monitoring and analysis, as well as boosting data privacy and protection (Teichmann et al., 2023).

Regtech has various uses in the financial sector, assisting financial institutions with regulatory compliance, risk management, and performance enhancement. As financial institutions look to enhance their compliance and risk management procedures in a regulatory environment that is getting more complicated by the day, the increased use of Regtech is anticipated to continue.

Technologies Driving Regtech

The financial industry is embracing emerging technologies like Regtech more and more. Data-driven and adaptable technologies provide the foundation of Regtech solutions (Goul, 2019). In the risk and compliance roles, these solutions promote innovation and cost-effectiveness. It is anticipated that the following technologies will increasingly be used to create Regtech solutions:

Cloud computing: Regtech solutions must include cloud computing because it enables regulated organizations to use cloud-based solutions and securely store and process vast volumes of data (Dubey et al., 2020). It enables regulated organizations to simply and swiftly increase their activities without spending money on expensive infrastructure. Smaller regulated organizations may not have the funds to create their own data centers or buy pricey technology. Thus, this is especially helpful to them. Collaboration with external parties, such as regulators and other regulated companies, is made simple by cloud computing (Sengupta et al., 2011). This is due to the ease with which various parties may exchange data and work together to address compliance concerns thanks to cloud-based solutions, which can be accessed from any location with an internet connection.

Artificial Intelligence and Machine Learning: These are potent technologies that can quickly and accurately automate business procedures, identify trends, and produce insights. AI-based solutions can rapidly and effectively uncover trends and abnormalities by evaluating massive amounts of data, enabling regulated businesses to stop fraud before it starts (Guo & Polak, 2021). In order to maintain relevance in the face of an ever-changing environment, solutions constantly modify their rule-based parameters. AI-powered solutions can give regulated organizations efficient ways to acquire and analyze the data utilized in various regulatory reports as the volume of financial transactions rises.

Blockchain: It is a distributed digital ledger that is decentralized and used to securely and openly record transactions. Due to its capacity to offer transparency, immutability, and security in record-keeping, it has grown in popularity in the Regtech sector (Malhotra et al., 2022). Each system keeps a copy of the ledger dispersed throughout a system network. By offering a decentralized database where regulated businesses may securely communicate consumer and financial information, blockchain has become more prevalent in KYC and AML compliance.

Low-code and No-code platforms: Software development platforms such as low-code and no-code enable users to create apps without requiring them to have a deep understanding of programming. Low-code platforms offer pre-built components and templates that may be changed to match particular needs. In contrast, no-code platforms do not require coding and let users construct applications using drag-and-drop interfaces and pre-built components. Solution providers use these technologies to automate compliance processes and adjust to shifting regulatory requirements (Ansi et al., 2024; Novarlic et al., 2024).

Big Data: Big Data refers to the large volume of structured and unstructured data generated and collected by businesses. By offering insights on customer behavior, risk assessments, and compliance monitoring, it is utilized in Regtech to assist businesses in complying with laws (Yu & Song, 2020). It makes it possible for regulated organizations to fully comprehend their operational processes and identify compliance issues. It is also used to identify compliance issues, such as the risks of doing business with a particular customer, and to conduct risk assessments.

Application programming interface (API): A collection of protocols, methods, and tools called APIs are used to construct software applications. They may be used to streamline the collection and processing of information from several sources and let different applications share information and functionality in a consistent way. API-based interfaces are a crucial piece of technology for Regtech solutions to operate inside the framework of a regulated organization. They enable seamless data and command exchange between applications and gadgets.

Natural Language Processing (NLP): NLP is an area of AI that focuses on teaching robots to comprehend and interpret human language. Because it enables organizations to automate and streamline regulatory compliance processes that require the processing and analysis of significant amounts of unstructured text data (Villar & Khan, 2021), such as regulatory texts, legal documents, news articles, and social media posts, NLP has grown in importance as a Regtech technology. It may be used to take relevant unstructured text material and turn it into structured data that can be utilized for compliance.

Benefits of Regtech

Adoption of Regtech solutions has the following advantages for the financial sector:

Reduced cost of compliance: Regtech solutions may help financial institutions reduce compliance costs by automating manual compliance processes, reducing the need for human labor, and reducing the risk of non-compliance and associated fines and penalties (Roy, 2019). These solutions may reduce the need for human data input and analysis by automating data collection, processing, and analysis. They may also help in prioritizing compliance operations, more effectively allocating resources, and reducing the risk of non-compliance by automating compliance processes, providing real-time monitoring, and improving audibility (Yang & Tsang, 2017). Reducing the risk of fines and penalties for non-compliance may help save money.

Sustainable and scalable solutions: The flexibility and adaptability of Regtech solutions allow financial institutions to swiftly and efficiently change their compliance procedures to satisfy shifting regulatory requirements. By providing real-time monitoring, spotting possible compliance problems, and offering insights into risk exposure, they can assist financial institutions in developing long-lasting compliance programs. Financial institutions can handle and analyze enormous volumes of data in real-time using the scalability that Regtech solutions provide, giving them invaluable insights into their compliance initiatives and overall risk exposure (Kavassalis et al., 2018). Financial institutions can discover possible risks and compliance concerns more rapidly because of this scalability, which enables them to take remedial action before situations worsen.

Advanced data analytics: Regtech systems analyze enormous volumes of data rapidly and effectively by utilizing modern data analytics methods like ML, AI, and NLP. By employing advanced data analytics, Regtech systems can monitor transactional behavior, spot abnormalities pointing to fraud or money laundering, and uncover possible compliance concerns. These tools may also analyze client data to find trends and patterns that might assist financial organizations in improving their overall risk management strategies and business choices.

Risk and control convergence: Financial organizations may combine their risk and compliance management efforts with the aid of Regtech solutions, resulting in a more unified and effective risk management strategy (Giudici, 2018). Silos and inefficiencies, as well as higher risk exposure, may result from this strategy. Regtech solutions offer a centralized platform for managing risk and compliance, and they may integrate data from many sources to give a more thorough picture of risk exposure.

Positive customer experience: Financial organizations may enhance customer experience using Regtech solutions to deliver quicker, more effective services, lower mistakes, and increase data security (Lui & Lamb, 2018). Financial institutions may execute transactions more quickly and effectively by automating manual compliance and risk management processes. They can also improve data security by shielding client information from online dangers and other security lapses. This may result in lower wait times, quicker transaction processing, and improved customer experience.

Increased market stability: Financial institutions may benefit from a more thorough and current understanding of market risks thanks to Regtech solutions. Regtech systems can identify possible market hazards before they materialize by combining data from many sources, such as market and transaction data (Yang & Li, 2018). This early warning can lessen the possibility of market volatility by allowing financial institutions to act quickly and effectively to reduce risks. Regtech can also improve accountability and transparency, giving a more comprehensive and accurate view of the financial markets.

Improved governance: Financial institutions may strengthen governance by using Regtech solutions to increase organizational effectiveness, increase decision-making capabilities, and provide improved insight into compliance and risk management processes. They can also improve the efficiency and effectiveness of the governance system by streamlining compliance and risk management procedures. Financial institutions may save time and costs by automating compliance and risk management procedures, allowing them to concentrate on their core business operations.

Enhanced regulatory reporting: Financial institutions may enhance their regulatory reporting using Regtech solutions to automate the process, lower mistakes, increase accuracy, and provide real-time information (Miglionico, 2020). Regtech solutions may give a more thorough and accurate perspective of regulatory compliance by combining data from many sources, lowering the likelihood of mistakes and raising the reporting standard. Regtech can also give financial institutions more flexibility in reporting by letting them tailor reports to their needs and legal requirements. This can increase reporting accuracy and quality while lowering the time and resources needed for regulatory reporting.

Challenges Faced by Financial Institutions in Adopting Regtech Solutions

Regtech has a lot of potential advantages, but implementation is complex for several reasons. These challenges can be described as follows:

Regulation Complexity: The complexity of the regulatory frameworks is one of the main obstacles to the adoption of Regtech. Regulatory frameworks may involve many laws, regulations, and authorities. Creating Regtech solutions that can accurately read and adhere to various regulatory standards is challenging since it necessitates advanced algorithms and deep domain knowledge (Bolton & Mintrom, 2023).

Data Quality and Standardization: Regtech significantly depends on precise and standardized data to ensure compliance and risk management (Miglionico, 2020). However, inconsistencies, incompleteness, and a lack of standardization in data are problems that affect all businesses. Regtech implementation faces significant obstacles, including integrating various data sources, verifying and cleaning data, and creating uniform data standards (Yang & Tsang, 2017).

Interoperability and Integration: Many businesses already use outdated software and hardware, which may make it difficult for them to integrate new Regtech solutions. In order to achieve interoperability and smooth integration between current systems and Regtech platforms, extensive planning, data mapping, and API development are often necessary. Problems with interoperability may make it difficult to adopt and use Regtech solutions effectively.

Regulatory Change Management: Rules and standards for compliance are frequently updated and modified. A significant difficulty is keeping up with these changes and rapidly upgrading Regtech systems to reflect the most recent regulatory regulations. Regtech solutions must be adaptive and flexible to handle regulatory changes, necessitating continuous monitoring, agile development techniques, and efficient change management procedures (Baxter, 2016).

Security and Privacy Issues: Regtech platforms deal with private and sensitive data, including financial and consumer information. Strong security controls, data encryption, access restrictions, and adherence to data protection laws are essential (Zetzsche et al., 2019). If they want businesses to accept their solutions, Regtech vendors must allay security and privacy worries.

Regulatory Acceptance and Trust: Due to worries about the dependability, accuracy, and potential biases in automated systems, regulatory authorities, and compliance experts frequently oppose Regtech solutions (Papantoniou, 2022). Transparent algorithms, explainable AI, thorough auditing processes, and cooperation between Regtech providers and regulatory agencies are necessary to establish confidence and gain regulatory acceptability.

Cost and Resource Allocation: Putting Regtech solutions in place can be expensive upfront since it requires developing software, integrating it with other systems, moving data, and educating employees. To properly deploy and manage Regtech systems, organizations must dedicate enough resources, both financial and human. Regtech solutions adoption may be hampered by limited funds and resources, especially for small and medium-sized businesses (Imam et al., 2022).

Legal and Ethical Implications: Regtech poses several legal and ethical issues, including responsibility for compliance mistakes, accountability for automated judgments, and possible bias in algorithmic models (Packin, 2018). Regtech solutions must be used in a transparent, equitable, and ethical manner, which calls for effective governance structures, adherence to regulatory requirements, and ethical AI practices.

Several obstacles need to be overcome before Regtech can be widely used. These obstacles include regulatory complexity, data quality, interoperability, regulatory change management, security and privacy, regulatory acceptability, cost and resource allocation, and legal and ethical ramifications. These issues must be resolved to successfully and broadly apply Regtech solutions across sectors.

Case Study

Several case studies are included in the study to get more meaningful insights about implementing Regtech solutions in the financial industry.

Regtech Initiatives by the Reserve Bank of India (RBI)

The RBI has pioneered Regtech solutions to improve regulatory compliance and monitoring in the Indian financial industry. According to the central bank, technology-driven solutions can alleviate regulatory issues and boost the effectiveness of regulatory procedures. To encourage the use of Regtech solutions in the Indian financial services sector, the RBI introduced a Regtech sandbox project in 2017. Live testing of new goods or services in a regulated environment is called "regulatory sandboxing." As the authorities may or may not allow certain relaxations for testing, it serves as a "safe space" for business. The RBI collaborated with several Regtech entrepreneurs to evaluate their products and determine the advantages and drawbacks of adoption (RBI, 2019).

Signzy, a provider of digital onboarding and identity verification solutions, was one of the Regtech businesses participating in the sandbox program. The KYC and AML compliance processes were automated by Signzy's solution using AI and ML, saving financial institutions time and money. The RBI tested Signzy's solution as part of its regulatory compliance procedures and discovered that it considerably increased KYC and AML compliance's accuracy and effectiveness.

Real-time consumer identity verification made it possible to lower the risk of fraud and enhance customer satisfaction (RBI, 2019).

The RBI launched a Regulatory Compliance Sandbox (RCS) in 2019, inspired by the accomplishments of the Regtech sandbox effort. To encourage innovation and enhance regulatory compliance in the financial services sector, the RCS offers a platform for Regtech entrepreneurs to test and present their ideas in a controlled environment (RBI, 2019).

An environment that will foster and enable the acceleration of product, policy, and process innovation in the financial industry has been created by the Reserve Bank Innovation Hub (RBIH), a subsidiary of the RBI. Participants have the chance to create solutions and promote innovation through programs like the global hackathons "HARBINGER 2023 – Innovation for Transformation" with the topics "inclusive digital services" and "HARBINGER 2021" for "smarter digital payments (RBI, 2019)."

The RBI has been able to enhance its regulatory compliance procedures and lower the risk of non-compliance thanks to the implementation of Regtech solutions. The RBI has been able to automate compliance operations, lower the chance of mistakes, and increase the precision of risk assessments by utilizing cutting-edge technology like AI and ML. The RBI's use of Regtech has shown the potential advantages of using technology in regulatory compliance and cleared the path for Indian financial institutions to use Regtech solutions.

Encompass – A Leading Regtech Service Provider

Encompass is a well-known Regtech service provider that provides financial institutions with automated KYC solutions. Encompass was established in 2012 with the goal of revolutionizing KYC through technology and automation. Since its beginning, the business has assisted financial institutions in streamlining and simplifying their client due diligence processes while guaranteeing regulatory compliance (Encompass Corporation, 2022).

Encompass' clientele is based all around the world. The business offers clientele services in several regions, including Europe, North America, and Asia Pacific. Numerous financial institutions, including large banks, asset managers, and Fintech firms, have embraced their solutions, further strengthening their reputation as a reliable Regtech service provider (Encompass Corporation, 2022).

The creation of Encompass' intelligent automation technology in 2016 is one of the company's significant accomplishments and has helped it stand out in the sector. By automating data collection, analysis, and verification using ML algorithms, their technology enables businesses to streamline their KYC procedures and save time (Encompass Corporation, 2022).

Encompass has also formed strategic alliances and relationships with top financial institutions, displaying their dedication to promoting reform across the sector. Encompass and IHS Markit struck a collaboration agreement in 2018 to streamline the KYC discovery process. Strategic alliances with Pegasystems and Dun & Bradstreet were struck in 2019. Encompass has developed great insights into the unique requirements and problems of the financial sector via close collaboration with banks, investment firms, and other organizations. As a result, they are able to customize their solutions to suit industry standards successfully (Encompass Corporation, 2022).

For their creative thinking and contributions to the Regtech sector, Encompass has won praise and honors. Encompass Corporation was included in the Fintech Global 2023 Regtech100 list. Encompass was complimented for its "standardized information gathering and audit trail in addition to comprehensive KYC suite, which gives peace of mind that policies are followed consistently." Encompass was recognized for its "mission critical" financial crime impact. Encompass was listed among the top 50 companies developing innovative technology for regulation, risk management, and fraud detection in BusinessCloud's Regtech 50 list (Encompass Corporation, 2022).

With the help of KYC automation, Encompass has transformed regulatory compliance and client onboarding. It assists clients in safely expanding their companies and thwarting financial crime with an unmatched mix of cutting-edge technology, data coverage, and sector knowledge. Encompass provides KYC due diligence on demand, supported by intelligent process automation, which lowers the cost of KYC and accelerates time to revenue.

Findings and Conclusion

The Fintech industry will continue to develop due to consumer demand for innovative and convenient financial products and services. Regulators must work hard to actively maintain supervision to safeguard consumers and economies against technology intrusions. Regtech is still at the forefront of the instruments used to ensure a secure and booming Fintech sector. Regtech must develop alongside Fintech goods and services to ensure financial stability and consumer protection.

Regtech is still developing and reshaping the regulatory environment, so its future seems bright. Technology developments like blockchain, ML, and AI will spur innovation in Regtech solutions. These technologies provide improved risk management, straightforward reporting procedures, and accurate and effective regulatory compliance. Regtech will increasingly use big data analytics to provide proactive compliance measures by offering real-time insights and predictive capabilities. Regtech providers, regulatory agencies, and industry stakeholders working together will also promote the development of industry standards and best practices. Demand for Regtech solutions will increase as regulatory requirements tighten, spurring more significant investment and industry expansion. To fully realize the promise of Regtech and assure its future adoption and acceptability, persistent issues, including regulatory complexity, data privacy, and ethical concerns, will need to be adequately resolved.

References

Al-Ansi, A. M., Garad, A., & Ryabtsev, V. (2024). Intelligent risk analysis of investment projects in the extractive industry. *Journal of Industrial Intelligence*, *2*(1), 42–53.

Anagnostopoulos, I. (2018). Fintech and regtech: Impact on regulators and banks. *Journal of Economics and Business*, *100*. https://doi.org/10.1016/j.jeconbus.2018.07.003

Arner, D. W., Barberis, J., & Buckley, R. P. (2017a). FinTech, regTech, and the reconceptualization of financial regulation. *Northwestern Journal of International Law and Business*, *37*(3), 371–380.

Arner, D. W., Barberis, J., & Buckley, R. P. (2017b). RegTech: Building a better financial system. In *Handbook of blockchain, digital finance, and inclusion, Volume 1: Cryptocurrency, FinTech, InsurTech, and Regulation* (pp. 359–373). https://doi.org/10.1016/B978-0-12-810441-5.00016-6

Arner, D. W., Barberis, J. N., & Buckley, R. P. (2017c). The emergence of Regtech 2.0: From know your customer to know your data. *SSRN Electronic Journal*. https://doi.org/10.2139/ssrn.3044280

Aziz, S., & Dowling, M. (2019). Machine learning and AI for risk management. In *Palgrave studies in digital business and enabling technologies*. https://doi.org/10.1007/978-3-030-02330-0_3

Batista, P. M., & Ringe, W.-G. (2020). Dynamism in financial market regulation: Harnessing regulatory and supervisory technologies. *SSRN Electronic Journal*. https://doi.org/10.2139/ssrn.3711618

Bauguess, S. W. (2018). The role of big data, machine learning, and AI in assessing risks: A regulatory perspective. *SSRN Electronic Journal*. https://doi.org/10.2139/ssrn.3226514

Baxter, L. G. (2016). Adaptive financial regulation and regtech: A concept article on realistic protection for victims of bank failures. *Duke Law Journal*, *66*(3), 567.

Belanche, D., Casaló, L. V., & Flavián, C. (2019). Artificial Intelligence in FinTech: understanding robo-advisors adoption among customers. *Industrial Management and Data Systems*, *119*(7). https://doi.org/10.1108/IMDS-08-2018-0368

Bolton, M., & Mintrom, M. (2023). RegTech and creating public value: Opportunities and challenges. *Policy Design and Practice*, pp. 1–17. https://doi.org/10.1080/25741292.2023.2213059

Buckley, R. P., Arner, D. W., Zetzsche, D. A., & Weber, R. H. (2020). The road to RegTech: The (astonishing) example of the European Union. *Journal of Banking Regulation*, *21*(1). https://doi.org/10.1057/s41261-019-00104-1

Buckley, R., & Webster, S. (2016). Fintech in developing countries: Charting new customer journeys. *Journal of Financial Transformation*, *44*(January).

Castri, S. D., Grasser, M., & Kulenkampff, A. (2018). Financial authorities in the era of data abundance: Regtech for regulators and Suptech solutions. *SSRN Electronic Journal*. https://doi.org/10.2139/ssrn.3249283

Chen, Y., kumara, E. K., & Sivakumar, V. (2021). Investigation of the finance industry on risk awareness model and digital economic growth. *Annals of Operations Research*. https://doi.org/10.1007/s10479-021-04287-7

Currie, W. L., Gozman, D. P., & Seddon, J. J. M. (2018). Dialectic tensions in the financial markets: A longitudinal study of pre-and post-crisis regulatory technology. *Journal of Information Technology*, *33*(4). https://doi.org/10.1057/s41265-017-0047-5

Deshpande, A. (2020). AI/ML applications and the potential transformation of Fintech and Finserv sectors. In *13th CMI Conference on Cybersecurity and Privacy – Digital Transformation – Potentials and Challenges, CMI 2020*. https://doi.org/10.1109/CMI51275.2020.9322734

Dubey, V., Sonar, R., Walimbe, R. S., & Mohanty, A. (2020). The role of CLOUD in FinTech and RegTech. *Annals of the Dunarea de Jos University of Galati. Fascicle I. Economics and Applied Informatics*, *26*(3). https://doi.org/10.35219/eai15840409130

Encompass Corporation. (2022). *Encompass named in FinTech Global's RegTech100 list for 2023*. Retrieved April 20, 2024, from https://www.encompasscorporation.com/press-releases/encompass-named-in-fintech-globals-regtech100-list-for-2023/#:~:text=Get%20in%20touch-,Encompass%20named%20in%20FinTech%20Global's%20RegTech100%20list%20for%202023, FinTech%20Global's%20RegTech100%202023%20list

Freij, Å. (2020). Using technology to support financial services regulatory compliance: Current applications and future prospects of regtech. *Journal of Investment Compliance*, *21*(2/3). https://doi.org/10.1108/joic-10-2020-0033

Gai, K., Qiu, M., Sun, X., & Zhao, H. (2017). Security and privacy issues: A survey on Fintech. *Lecture Notes in Computer Science (Including Subseries Lecture Notes in Artificial Intelligence and Bioinformatics)*, *10135 LNCS*. https://doi.org/10.1007/978-3-319-52015-5_24

Giudici, P. (2018). Fintech risk management: A research challenge for artificial intelligence in finance. *Frontiers in Artificial Intelligence*, *1*. https://doi.org/10.3389/frai.2018.00001

Goul, M. (2019). Services computing and regtech. *Proceedings - 2019 IEEE World Congress on Services, SERVICES 2019*. https://doi.org/10.1109/SERVICES.2019.00061

Guo, H., & Polak, P. (2021). Artificial intelligence and financial technology FinTech: How AI is being used under the pandemic in 2020. In *Studies in computational intelligence* (Vol. 935). https://doi.org/10.1007/978-3-030-62796-6_9

Gupta, R., Kukreja, G., Gupta, A., & Tyagi, L. (2021). Artificial intelligence fostering fintech: Emerging trends and use cases. *Communications in Computer and Information Science*, *1436 CCIS*. https://doi.org/10.1007/978-3-030-84842-2_5

Hasan, R., Ashfaq, M., & Shao, L. (2021). Evaluating drivers of fintech adoption in the Netherlands. *Global Business Review*. https://doi.org/10.1177/09721509211027402

Imam, T., McInnes, A., Colombage, S., & Grose, R. (2022). Opportunities and barriers for FinTech in SAARC and ASEAN countries. *Journal of Risk and Financial Management*, *15*(2). https://doi.org/10.3390/jrfm15020077

Ioannou, S., Wójcik, D., & Dymski, G. (2019). **Too-Big-To-Fail:** Why megabanks have not become smaller since the global financial crisis? *Review of Political Economy*, *31*(3). https://doi.org/10.1080/09538259.2019.1674001

Kavassalis, P., Stieber, H., Breymann, W., Saxton, K., & Gross, F. J. (2018). An innovative RegTech approach to financial risk monitoring and supervisory reporting. *Journal of Risk Finance*, *19*(1). https://doi.org/10.1108/JRF-07-2017-0111

Kurum, E. (2020). RegTech solutions and AML compliance: What is the future of financial crime? *Journal of Financial Crime*. https://doi.org/10.1108/JFC-04-2020-0051

Lee, J., Wewege, L., & Thomsett, M. C. (2020). Disruptions and digital banking trends. *Journal of Applied Finance & Banking*, *10*(6), 15–56.

Lootsma, Y. (2017). Blockchain as the Newest Regtech Application: The opportunity to reduce the burden of KYC for financial institutions. *Banking & Financial Services Policy Report*, *36*(8).

Lui, A., & Lamb, G. W. (2018). Artificial intelligence and augmented intelligence collaboration: Regaining trust and confidence in the financial sector. *Information and Communications Technology Law*, *27*(3). https://doi.org/10.1080/13600834.2018.1488659

Lukonga, I. (2018). Fintech, inclusive growth and cyber risks: Focus on the MENAP and CCA regions. *IMF Working Papers*, *18*(201). https://doi.org/10.5089/9781484374900.001

Lumpkin, S. (2010). Regulatory issues related to financial innovation. *OECD Journal: Financial Market Trends*, *2009*(2). https://doi.org/10.1787/fmt-v2009-art14-en

Malhotra, D., Saini, P., & Singh, A. K. (2022). How blockchain can automate KYC: Systematic review. *Wireless Personal Communications*, 122(2). https://doi.org/10.1007/s11277-021-08977-0

Matari, E. M. A., Mgammal, M. H., Alosaimi, M. H., Alruwaili, T. F., & Al-Bogami, S. (2022). Fintech, board of directors and corporate performance in Saudi Arabia financial sector: Empirical study. *Sustainability (Switzerland)*, *14*(17). https://doi.org/10.3390/su141710750

Mcquinn, A. (2019). Supporting financial innovation through flexible regulation. In *Information Technology & Innovation Foundation*.

Memminger, M., Baxter, M., & Lin, E. (2016). *Banking Regtechs to the rescue?* Bain & Company.
Miglionico, A. (2020). Automated regulation and supervision: The impact of RegTech on banking compliance. *European Business Law Review, 31*(4). https://doi.org/10.54648/eulr2020025
Miguel, A. F., & Algarvio, D. (2019). Bits and bytes of financial regulation: The Regtech environment. *International Journal of Business and Social Science, 10*(9). https://doi.org/10.30845/ijbss.v10n9a12
Novarlić, B., & Đurić, P. (2024). Enhancing comprehensive waste management in transition economies through green logistics: A case study of Bosnia and Herzegovina. *Journal of Intelligent Management Decision, 3*, 42–55.
Opoku-Afari, M., Abugre, J. A., & Oppong, K. A. (2022). Playing-catch up: SupTech and RegTech developments in Africa. In *The economics of banking and finance in Africa: Developments in Africa's financial systems* (pp. 745–794). Springer International Publishing. https://doi.org/10.1007/978-3-031-04162-4_22
Packin, N. G. (2018). RegTech, compliance, and technology judgment rule. *Chicago-Kent Law Review, 93*(1), 193–218.
Papantoniou, A. A. (2022). Regtech: Steering the regulatory spaceship in the right direction? *Journal of Banking and Financial Technology, 6*(1). https://doi.org/10.1007/s42786-022-00038-9
Plenk, M., Levant, I., & Bellon, N. (2019). How technology (or distributed ledger technology and algorithms like deep learning and machine learning) can help to comply with regulatory requirements. In *The impact of digital transformation and FinTech on the finance professional*. https://doi.org/10.1007/978-3-030-23719-6_14
RBI. (2019). *Opportunities and challenges of FinTech – Shri Shaktikanta Das, Governor, Reserve Bank of India – March 25, 2019 – Keynote Address Delivered at the NITI Aayog's FinTech Conclave*. Retrieved April 20, 2024, from https://www.rbi.org.in/commonman/english/Scripts/speeches.aspx?Id=2920.
Roy, B. S. (2019). How RegTech could help determine the future of financial services. In *The RegTech book*. https://doi.org/10.1002/9781119362197.ch8
Schizas, E., McKain, G., Zhang, B. Z., Garvey, K., Ganbold, A., Hussain, H., Kumar, P., Huang, E., Wang, S., & Yerolemou, N. (2020). The global RegTech industry benchmark report. *SSRN Electronic Journal*. https://doi.org/10.2139/ssrn.3560811
Sengupta, S., Kaulgud, V., & Sharma, V. S. (2011). *Cloud computing security–trends and research directions*. https://doi.org/10.1109/services.2011.20
Solms, J. V. (2021). Integrating regulatory technology (RegTech) into the digital transformation of a bank Treasury. *Journal of Banking Regulation, 22*(2). https://doi.org/10.1057/s41261-020-00134-0
Stewart, H., & Jürjens, J. (2018). Data security and consumer trust in FinTech innovation in Germany. *Information and Computer Security, 26*(1). https://doi.org/10.1108/ICS-06-2017-0039
Teichmann, F., Boticiu, S., & Sergi, B. S. (2023). RegTech – Potential benefits and challenges for businesses. *Technology in Society, 72*. https://doi.org/10.1016/j.techsoc.2022.102150
Thommandru, A., & Chakka, D. B. (2023). Recalibrating the banking sector with blockchain technology for effective anti-money laundering compliances by banks. *Sustainable Futures, 5*. https://doi.org/10.1016/j.sftr.2023.100107
Truby, J., Brown, R., & Dahdal, A. (2020). Banking on AI: Mandating a proactive approach to AI regulation in the financial sector. *Law and Financial Markets Review, 14*(2). https://doi.org/10.1080/17521440.2020.1760454
Tsang, C.-Y. (2019). From industry sandbox to supervisory control box: Rethinking the role of regulators in the era of fintech. *Journal of Law, Technology & Policy*.

Turki, M., Hamdan, A., Cummings, R. T., Sarea, A., Karolak, M., & Anasweh, M. (2020). The regulatory technology "RegTech" and money laundering prevention in the Islamic and conventional banking industry. *Heliyon*, *6*(10). https://doi.org/10.1016/j.heliyon.2020.e04949

Varga, D. (2017). Fintech, the new era of financial services. *Vezetéstudomány/Budapest Management Review*, *48*(11). https://doi.org/10.14267/veztud.2017.11.03

Villar, A. S., & Khan, N. (2021). Robotic process automation in the banking industry: A case study on Deutsche Bank. *Journal of Banking and Financial Technology*. https://doi.org/10.1007/s42786-021-00030-9

Yadav, Y. (2020). Fintech and international financial regulation. *SSRN Electronic Journal*. https://doi.org/10.2139/ssrn.3684821

Yang, D., & Li, M. (2018). Evolutionary approaches and the construction of technology-driven regulations. *Emerging Markets Finance and Trade*, *54*(14). https://doi.org/10.1080/1540496X.2018.1496422

Yang, Y.-P., & Tsang, C.-Y. (2017). Regtech and the new era of financial regulators: Envisaging more public-private-partnership models of financial regulators. *University of Pennsylvania Journal of Business Law*, *21*(2), 354.

Yerpude, S., Sood, K., & Grima, S. (2022). Blockchain-augmented digital supply chain management: A way to sustainable business. *Journal of Risk and Financial Management*, *16*(1), 7.

Yu, T. R., & Song, X. J. (2020). Big data and artificial intelligence in the banking industry. In *Handbook of financial econometrics, mathematics, statistics, and machine learning* (In 4 Volumes). https://doi.org/10.1142/9789811202391_0117

Zetzsche, D. A., Arner, D. W., Buckley, R. P., & Weber, R. H. (2019). The future of data-driven finance and RegTech: Lessons from EU Big Bang II. *SSRN Electronic Journal*. https://doi.org/10.2139/ssrn.3359399

Zetzsche, D. A., Buckley, R. P., Arner, D. W., & Barberis, J. N. (2017). Regulating a revolution: From regulatory sandboxes to smart regulation. *SSRN Electronic Journal*. https://doi.org/10.2139/ssrn.3018534

Chapter 14

The Influence of Artificial Intelligence on Personal and Corporate Finance: A Comprehensive Literature Review with Prospects for Future Research

Akansha Mer[a] *and Amarpreet Singh Virdi*[b]

[a]*Department of Commerce and Management, Banasthali Vidyapith, Tonk, Rajasthan, India*
[b]*Department of Management Studies, Kumaun University, Bhimtal (Nainital), Uttarakhand, India*

Abstract

Purpose: The surge in utilising big data, machine learning (ML), and artificial intelligence (AI) has significantly strengthened financial systems, enhancing their robustness, safety, and fairness. AI in finance is profoundly reshaping our lives. This study investigates AI's role in personal and corporate finance.

Methodology: A comprehensive literature review was conducted to examine studies on the application of AI in personal and corporate finance.

Findings: The financial services sector is undergoing an AI-led transformation, leveraging technologies such as deep learning, collaborative filtering, support vector machines, automation, robotic assistance, and AI-based predictive modelling. In personal finance, AI delivers personalised insights, automates procedures, detects fraud, and enhances financial literacy. It empowers individuals to manage their finances more effectively by tracking expenditures, aiding in budget management, and setting and monitoring financial goals. In corporate finance, AI aids in detecting and analysing credit risks, improving loan underwriting, and minimising financial risk.

Financial Landscape Transformation: Technological Disruptions, 253–268

doi:10.1108/978-1-83753-750-120251014

It also helps reduce financial crimes and enhances the financial performance of accounting firms. AI's role in bookkeeping, accounting, and financial management significantly benefits entrepreneurs, business executives, investors, and bankers involved in starting and growing organisations.

Practical Implications: In personal finance, AI enhances financial planning, automates transactions, improves credit scoring, and strengthens fraud detection. In corporate finance, AI facilitates advanced risk management, precise financial forecasting, cost reduction through automation, and optimised investment strategies.

Keywords: Artificial Intelligence and finance; ML and banking; corporate finance; personal finance; robots; banking; literature review; future research direction

JEL Codes: D14; O16; G20; G21

Introduction

High computer power, quick algorithm evolution, and, most crucially, the enormous amount of data collected worldwide are the factors that led to the breakthrough in artificial intelligence (AI), which is currently witnessing a significant acceleration. Devices powered by machine learning (ML) and AI are becoming more prevalent in our daily lives. The decision-makers stand to gain significantly from adopting AI in financial technology (FinTech). One of the domains where AI has been used more heavily is finance (Biallas & O'Neill, 2020). A more resilient, safe, and equitable financial system is now possible by using big data, ML, and AI. With time, the financial services (FS) industry has increasingly relied on new technology due to compelling commercial advantages, demand from tech-savvy consumers, and improved customer service. Financial institutions utilise AI-powered technologies like support vector machines (SVMs), deep learning, data analytics, and ML to streamline laborious human processes and increase operational efficiency (Mer & Virdi, 2022). As emerging technologies like AI and machine intelligence continue to push the boundaries of what is feasible, customer expectations are also increasing (Khan & Mer, 2023). How individuals and organisations manage their finances is changing due to AI. Credit risk may be predicted and minimised thanks to analytics-based collection methods and creative lending solutions with data-driven insights. These changes significantly impact financial inclusion and access.

AI plays a role in organisations by lowering costs and increasing productivity (Mer, 2023; Mer & Srivastava, 2022; Mer & Virdi, 2023a). AI has handled numerous works relating to personal and corporate finance that are financial. Financial institutions are also implementing AI to enhance security and transparency in payment systems, fraud detection and prevention, and identity verification to comply with regulatory duties relating to anti-money laundering and know your customers. Personalised experiences that foster consumer and small business owners' trust can be redefined and restored with AI. The benefits of AI in banking, such as fraud detection, task automation, and personalisation of services, have enabled round-the-clock client support and cost savings (Mer et al., 2024). Many individuals believe that AI-based quantitative investment strategies will eventually replace traditional investment management methods due to the widespread use of this technology in recent years. The ability of customers to obtain loans can be improved by applying ML models in credit evaluation and decision-making based on alternative data. Most AI applications in banking are now found in a small number of backend services, such as stock forecasting and credit rating by giant investment banks or credit scoring by credit card issuers, which are both traditionally highly computerised (Jadhav et al., 2016).

FinTech companies are heavily utilising AI in several areas of the banking sector. Corporate and retail financing, for instance, tailor-made goods, virtual assistant for customer relations, credit reporting but also credit risk management judgement, loan losses predicting the future, anti-money laundering, fraud tracking and sensing, customer support, Natural Language Processing (NLP) for sentiment analysis; investment management (automated financial, management of financial assets, regulatory compliance, sentiment analysis). The public sector and financial regulators are both using AI in RegTech and SuperTech initiatives, which is significant.

Against this backdrop, the study investigates the following:

(i) The role of AI in personal finance
(ii) The role of AI in corporate finance

Methodology

Literature Review

Prior qualitative and quantitative investigations were carefully analysed for the comprehensive literature review.

Sources of Data

The data sources are secondary, sourced from journals, magazines, newspapers, and reports issued by renowned organisations such as Gartner, Deloitte, etc.

Relevant Keywords

Among the pertinent keywords used to find research articles are AI, AI, machine learning, ML, data analytics, big data, robotics, natural language processing, NLP, Human Resources, finance, personal finance, and corporate finance. For a thorough literature review, articles published between 1999 and 2023 addressing AI in corporate and personal finance were resorted to.

Selection Criteria

The papers for the study were identified through screening and using eligibility criteria. The first stage was to identify articles from keywords and reference work. The second stage was to screen those articles that were duplicates, published before 1999, and not in a personal and corporate finance context. Finally, the remaining articles were included for literature review and meta-synthesis.

Initially, the authors identified 141 papers for the current chapter. Finally, 42 articles became part of the current study. The process of selecting 42 out of 170 articles went through a rigorous process. First, out of the 170 articles identified initially, 148 were identified from selected keywords, and 22 were identified from reference work (the authors screened the reference list of all the papers identified as qualified for synthesis). Secondly, 34 duplicate articles were removed in the identification stage – after which 38 more articles were excluded at the screening stage from 107 studies left. The 38 articles were excluded for the following reasons: 16 articles were published before 1999, 22 needed to be in the context of personal and corporate finance. Thirdly, 27 articles were excluded as they were not in the AI context. Thus, 42 studies were found eligible by full text after the screening stage. These 42 articles were included for review of literature and meta-synthesis.

AI in Personal Finance

Personal finance concerns how households handle their money and use the surrounding environment to fulfil their requirements (Maude, 2010). It includes things like budgeting, spending, investing, planning for taxes and retirement, among other things. The administration of one's money, including saving and investing, is known as personal finance. Financial planning for retirement, taxes, and estates is included, as well as banking, insurance, mortgages, and investments. Personal financial choices impact a household's wealth level, financial stability, and likelihood of long-term wealth accumulation. Personal financial decisions affect how well-off and financially secure a household is and how likely it is to build wealth over time. Since customers are ravenous for financial independence, the ability to regulate one's financial health is pushing the adoption of AI in personal finance.

The effectiveness and quality of financial management can both be increased by AI technology (Mer & Virdi, 2023b). People need to save money, for instance, for their retirement. The ability to invest and save differs between nations, income levels, age groups, and levels of economic uncertainty. This is crucial to keep in mind. 'Personal finance' refers to various activities, including utilising or obtaining financial products such as credit cards, insurance, mortgages, and many other investment forms. India has been at the forefront of adopting cutting-edge technologies, and its FS industry has evolved.

Robo-advisors are AI tools for algorithmic trading based on technical and fundamental analysis and portfolio rebalancing based on client profile data (Tokic, 2018). Any offering of recommendations and best practices derived from the analysis of big and open data in many areas of personal finance, including investments, tax management, consumption, savings, and debt-management decisions, is referred to as robo-advising (D'Acunto & Rossi, 2023).

Before the development of FinTech, most decisions on personal finances were made without a clear grasp of the economic issues at hand, the options available, or how those options would affect the decision-makers future wealth. The general need for more financial literacy among consumers exacerbated this. The newcomers, whether fintechs, tech behemoths, or neobanks, are all consumer-focused, technology-driven businesses utilising disruptive technologies to create appealing offers for their clients. The expanding use of data analytics – particularly employing AI/ML approaches and 'alternative data' – to personalise and automate consumer FS is a prominent trend under FinTech 2.0, which is relevant to the growth and regulation of consumer financial privacy. Modern Portfolio Theory (MPT), which is based on an ideal portfolio for a particular investor's risk appetite, is the foundation for the majority of the leading robo-advisory models that can be found in today's AI-driven technological world (Faloon & Scherer, 2017; Gomber et al., 2017). Robo advisers are computerised interfaces that lead investors through an entirely automated process of investing advisory, starting with assessing financial goals, analysing customers' risk profiles, and concluding with managing the entire portfolio. Conversational interfaces, or so-called AI-enabled 'chatbots', have emerged due to recent developments in AI and NLP (Davenport et al., 2020; Thomaz et al., 2020). These systems use a retrieval-based dialogue system to mimic the features of human-to-human conversations.

Indian financial institutions use AI-powered technologies to automate labour-intensive processes, lower operational expenses, and create new revenue opportunities. Machines have already been assigned to several mundane duties. Financial institutions are using AI to strengthen security and transparency in systems for payment fraud detection and prevention as well as for identity verification in order to comply with regulatory obligations related to anti-money laundering (AML) and know-your-customer (KYC). Innovative lending solutions with data-driven insights are making it possible to predict and reduce credit risk in addition to analytics-based collection methods. The impact of these modifications on financial inclusion and access is substantial. With the help of cutting-edge technologies like collaborative filtering, SVMs, deep learning, automated manual chores, and chatbots, the FS sector, which is typically the global bellwether industry, has begun on an AI-led transformation journey.

AI has completely changed how people manage their finances by providing tailored insights, automated processes, fraud detection, and financial literacy. However, it's essential to consider its capabilities and moral ramifications before adopting it as the standard for personal finance. Personal finance is only one of the numerous industries where it has altered the playing field. AI is transforming personal finance management and allowing people to take control of their financial futures. According to Jha (2023), AI is used in the personal finance industry in the following areas:

1. Budgeting

AI might analyse a person's spending patterns and suggest ways to cut back or save money. Additionally, it can help consumers set and track financial goals like retirement savings or property purchases.

2. Financial Literacy

People may improve their financial literacy through AI and ML, improving financial outcomes. AI is a technology that is becoming increasingly important in personal finance. Fraud detection, personalised advice, and process automation are all possible with it. In addition, it can help with goal-setting, financial monitoring, and budget management. With the development of technology, AI's role in managing personal money will only grow. AI can speed up laborious tasks and improve and supplement human intelligence (Jha, 2023). Financial assistants powered by AI are available to users for budgeting and saving. By learning about customers' needs and spending habits, these programmes help stop impulsive purchases. Users can track their spending using AI applications, which also learn from spending patterns. As a result, the apps might use predictive analytics to guide users in making prudent financial decisions. Information on personal finances is accessible through the following apps (Sarmah, 2019):

1. Cleo

Cleo is a Messenger financial assistant that uses AI to help users manage their money. Users can also send money to Facebook Messenger pals by connecting their bank accounts. Cleo can also be instructed to set aside a certain amount of spare change for the user's savings after the user specifies how much change is acceptable. Users can ask Cleo questions like if they have enough money to purchase a specific item or if they can afford a coffee, and the assistant will research the graphs and data-driven insights to respond.

2. Eva Money

Eva Money is an available personal finance aid for iOS and Android apps. The software supports AI, voice, and chat. It improves overall financial well-being and employs conversational intelligence to answer financial queries in an informed manner. Another characteristic of this programme is its ability to integrate all accounts with the app. The best approaches to optimise cash back, save money, raise credit scores, etc., can then be suggested.

3. MintZip

MintZip is a fintech app with AI that provides end-to-end financial solutions. The main 'Misa' product from MintZip, an AI-based financial companion run by Conversational AI, is also included in the app. The business claims that Misa is the most potent financial chatbot in existence. It considers factors like behavioural and financial sciences and continually updates its expertise to offer responses matching each user's financial position.

4. Olivia.ai

A free financial assistant app called Olivia uses AI and behavioural economics. In essence, this programme searches for patterns in how a person spends money. It then uses these patterns to create strategies that help individuals spend less while making money on the same goods. In addition, Olivia designs projects for its clients based on their regions of greatest need.

5. Wisely

Another AI-powered tool for saving money, Wizely, allows users to choose between a Flexi and Savings Plan, allowing them to save money incrementally. It also asserts to be the first digital piggybank application in India. Wizely's primary technologies are AI and ML. The platform delivers an adaptive learning method with its AI and ML algorithms, making it easier for customers to save.

FS companies should develop AI-powered financial assistants to strengthen their ties with clients. AI assistants are more accessible to contact than human agents because they can answer quickly, 24/7/365. As a result, these applications provide clients with a better experience than conventional customer care approaches. The advantages of AI in personal finance are as follows:

1. Better management of money.
2. Better security of finances.
3. Business management.

Personal financial choices significantly impact a family's ability to accumulate wealth over time, leave bequests to their children, and, among other things, prevent the psychological discomfort that a potential financial crisis may cause. These choices are crucial to a household's well-being and financial stability. According to Collardi (2012) and Maude (2010), personal banking refers to how households handle their finances and adapt the environment to meet their needs. Since customers hanker after financial freedom, the ability to manage one's financial health is what is pushing the usage of AI in personal finance.

In the financial sector, AI is centred on devices that can perceive and interpret tasks and take the necessary actions to accomplish those goals. The application of AI in personal finance is illustrated by several specific use cases, including robo-advice for investments, credit scoring (loan sector), fraud detection (insurance), etc. In portfolio management and investing platforms, high degrees of automation and efficiency improvements brought about by AI are particularly apparent (Palmiéa et al., 2020). AI could be utilised, for instance, to promote profitable growth through customer acquisition and retention through increased personalisation (King et al., 2021). One defining and distinctive feature of fintech that makes it a transformational force in human history is the use of massive and open data to inform individual financial decisions and disrupt the obstacles people must overcome to make personal finance decisions. Fintech applications also have an impact on how individuals make financial decisions (Virdi & Mer, 2023). It is known as 'robo-advising' when they generate financial lessons from the growth of vast and open data that they may transmit in real-time to decision-makers utilising mobile devices.

AI's ability to recognise and stop fraud and cyberattacks is one of the most critical business uses in the banking industry. Customers need secure bank accounts. AI can analyse patterns and identify abnormalities that humans might otherwise overlook. For banks, enhancing customer satisfaction is essential (Mer et al., 2022). Technologies that are AI-powered can provide users with highly tailored user experiences.

As a result of intelligent voice and chatbots, the way banks connect and communicate with their clients is changing. Today's retail buyers are less devoted to brands and more eager to evaluate pricing and user experiences to get the best bargain. They assume that banks would look out for their financial stability, go above and beyond banking to address needs connected to lifestyle and ensure data security and openness. Fintechs, technology behemoths, or neobanks – all new entrants – are customer-focused, technology-driven firms that leverage disruptive technologies to develop compelling offers for their clients. A significant trend under FinTech 2.0 that is highly relevant to developing and regulating consumer financial privacy is the rising use of data analytics, particularly the use of AI/ML methods and 'alternative data' to personalise and automate consumer FS. As society has grown more networked, digitised, and datafied, the amount of data consumers generate has rapidly expanded (Mayer-Schönberger & Cukier, 2013). Financial marketing, client identity verification, anti-money laundering/fraud control, financial counselling, credit scoring, and underwriting are just a few of the consumer finance applications where data analytics, mainly using AI/ML and alternative data, is becoming more and more well-liked (Bholat et al., 2020). A credit scoring algorithm includes risk variables and their weights, or the proportion of each risk element contributing to the subject's low credit (Bumacov et al., 2017). Big Data, AI, and NLP can be used to combat self-reported bias and greenwashing. AI may help banks enhance client interactions by supplying them with various innovative business methods. With the help of AI, the bank could track client portfolios and provide counselling and direction through customer analytics (Boobier, 2020).

AI in Corporate Finance

Corporate finance is the term used to describe the financial operations necessary to manage a firm. Corporate finance is the study of 'how corporations handle funding sources, capital structuring, accounting, and investment decisions', according to Investopedia. It relates to managing a company's assets and obligations, prudent budgeting, and raising money to satisfy company goals and objectives via debt and stock. The three primary facets of corporate finance are 'capital budgeting (e.g., for investing in company projects), capital financing (deciding how to fund projects/operations), and working capital management (managing assets and liabilities to operate efficiently)' (Hayes, 2024).

Corporate finance investments and transactions are a major form of business activity that significantly impacts industry sectors and national and regional economies.

Because it can more accurately identify and analyse credit issues, AI significantly impacts corporate finance. ML and other AI technologies can reduce financial risk and enhance loan underwriting for businesses aiming to grow. By enhancing fraud detection and spotting unusual conduct, AI may help reduce financial crime. The use of AI in bookkeeping, accounting, and financial management for businesses has benefits beyond boosting the bottom line for accounting firms; it also has advantages for business owners, executives, investors, bankers, and other parties engaged in starting and expanding organisations. In order to assess the potential hazards of financial irregularities within the firms, Wyrobeck (2020) studied the annual financial statements using an AI-based model.

Corporate finance comprises accounting and auditing and is a critical component of operations, governance, and regulation. Corporate finance is undergoing a paradigm shift from rule- and corporate-based accounting and auditing services, information management, and governance to individualised mobile and cloud financing and financing based on personal digital devices. Creating a division or department to oversee those financial tasks is usual. For example, a large corporation may need to decide between selling shares and issuing bonds to obtain additional funds (Al-Ansi et al., 2024; Novarlic et al., 2024).

Investment banks could advise the business on these issues and aid in marketing the securities (Kurt, 2024). A significant form of commercial activity that significantly impacts industry sectors, national economies, and regional economies is investing in and conducting transactions involving corporate finance. Corporate finance is significantly impacted by AI's improved ability to recognise and analyse credit concerns. ML and other AI advancements may improve loan underwriting and lower financial risk for companies looking to expand. AI may lessen financial crime by improving fraud detection and identifying odd behaviour. Investment banks could advise the business on these issues and aid in marketing the securities (Kurt, 2024). A significant form of commercial activity that significantly impacts industry sectors, national economies, and regional economies is investing in and conducting transactions involving corporate finance. Corporate finance is significantly impacted by AI's improved ability to recognise and analyse credit concerns. For businesses aiming to grow, ML and other AI advances may enhance loan underwriting and reduce financial risk. Financial crime may be reduced thanks to AI, which makes it easier to spot fraud and strange conduct. AI is also utilised to analyse the risk related to accounting processes, including workload imbalance, inconsistent accounting practises, unsuccessful and untimely journal processing approvals, and the efficacy and quality of accounting processing (Yerpude et al., 2022).

Leaders in financial planning and analysis (FP&A) should consider implementing five of the most important AI use cases for their roles, according to Gartner, Inc. 23 corporate finance AI application scenarios were examined by Gartner specialists to determine the types of processes that an autonomous finance organisation with a forward-thinking culture will employ (Gartner, 2022). Gartner has recognised the top five corporate finance scenarios:

1. Demand/Revenue Forecasting.
2. Anomaly and Error Detection.
3. Decision Support.
4. POC Revenue Forecasting.
5. Cash Collections.

Utilising internal and external data sources, models project demand and related revenue across several factors, including business unit, product line, client type, and region. In anomaly detection, ML models highlight transactions or balances that may be inaccurate or inconsistent with accounting standards. Another element of a comprehensive system is real-time analysis while data is being entered. This keeps errors out of the workflow and saves money on costly downstream modifications. When using alternative data values, ML prediction algorithms are employed to foretell outcomes based on existing data. Models with fictional data can forecast the results of various options. ML models anticipate the percentage-of-completion metrics (such as hours, cost, units, weight, etc.) to predict POC income and the overall work required to finish the project. ML models are used to anticipate when customers will pay invoices in order to make proactive collection efforts before payments become past due. The estimates from these models are used by employees who work in collections to focus their efforts on at-risk accounts. Expected cash collections also improve ML-driven cash flow forecasting.

According to a study from 2020 by Zhang et al., the capital cost (CC) of open-pit mining projects may be precisely forecasted using a unique AI model. Ant colony optimisation (ACO) and deep neural network (DNN) algorithms are combined in a unique way to form the 'ACO-DNN' algorithm. The variables MineAP (annual mine production), SR (stripping ratio), MillAP (annual production of the mill), RMG (reserve mean grade), and LOM (life of mine) were used in this model to account for the CC of open-pit mining projects. Various simple and complex artificial neural networks (ANN) were constructed to estimate the CC of 74 copper mining projects. The findings of this study showed that the DNN models were superior to the straightforward ANN models in forecasting the CC for open-pit mining projects. The precision of forecasting models was significantly improved using the ACO algorithm.

Debt and equity, the two main elements of the capital structure, provide information to investors in the company that they need to make investment decisions. Pao (2008) discovered that ANN and RMSE values outperformed other regression models when evaluating and predicting debt ratios. In light of this, it was suggested that ANNs can capture various nonlinear impacts in the financial industries.

According to Yoon (2020), a cloud system gathers and produces accounting data. To assist in decision-making, big data analytics and AI, including robotic process automation (RPA) and ML, can be used to provide more insightful and pertinent accounting data. Blockchain technology increases the bar for accounting data by ensuring its dependability and openness. This study aims to provide direction to other organisations considering a shift of a similar nature by illustrating how Korean companies have incorporated new technologies into their accounting practices. This study aims to assist firms considering technology adoption in changing their accounting process, with evidence from Korea.

Roszkowska (2021) delved into the audit-related causes of financial scandals and made recommendations for how new technology might be able to provide solutions. This study looks at the factors that encourage financial statement fraud and analyses certain fintech advancements that enhance the dependability of financial data for equities investment. The findings show that solutions built on blockchain, the Internet of Things, smart contracts, and AI each have unique features and can successfully address various problems related to financial reporting and auditing. Together, they can increase the veracity of the information in financial statements and radically change how firms are conducted.

Numerous data must be processed and analysed to do accounting, which might result in errors, blunders, and manipulation opportunities. Data can be stored more efficiently if it is wholly ordered and interoperable. Blockchain technology can be compared to a 'distributed database that is organised as a list of ordered blocks, where the committed blocks are immutable' (Casino et al., 2019). Blockchain is a hypothetical accounting-based system that treats data flows as transactions. Unlike traditional accounting software, blockchain allows for the maintenance of well-structured data that is easily retrieved and kept.

Due to the continuity, irrevocability, and irreversibility properties of blockchain ledgers, management can successfully restrain itself from falsifying the books (by creating fictitious transactions, changing records, employing backdating options, etc.). Due to the transparency of blockchain-based accounting systems, forensic accountants may find it simple to access and probe major related-party transactions (Dai & Vasarhelyi, 2017), and external auditors may benefit from already validated, accurate data (Deloitte, 2016).

Effective implementation of good governance can be facilitated by combining financial management with e-budgeting (Gamayuni & Hendrawaty, 2020). In this respect, smart budgeting is a methodical process that gathers necessary data and uses algorithmic models to produce a budget. Smart budgeting might provide a wide range of scenarios and offer helpful projections to help in decision-making using historical data and creative algorithms (Gil-Garcia et al., 2014).

Discussion

The study aims to achieve two objectives: (a) The role of AI in personal finance and (b) the role of AI in corporate finance. Since AI can foresee and assess loan risks more accurately, it benefits corporate finance. For companies looking to increase their value, AI advances like ML can improve loan underwriting and reduce financial risk. Additionally, AI can reduce financial crime through sophisticated fraud detection and uncover anomalous activity as firm accountants, analysts, treasurers, and investors concentrate on long-term growth.

Adopting AI approaches can increase operational workflow efficiency by lowering investment managers' back-office costs, automating reconciliations, and accelerating processes. This would reduce friction (costs associated with direct and indirect transactions) and improve performance overall by reducing noise (irrelevant features and information) in decision-making (Blackrock, 2019). Asset managers and other institutional investors also use AI to improve risk management. It enables the daily, cost-effective monitoring of hundreds of risk parameters and the modelling of portfolio performance across various market and economic scenarios. Credit Score with AI Support An engine can produce a good decision.

Wyrobeck (2020) used an AI-based model to analyse the annual financial records and assess the likelihood of financial irregularities within the enterprises. These discrepancies might be linked to financial frauds, which do not always affect the annual financial records. The algorithm employed to identify scam trends learnt to do so based on data unrelated to the behaviours being studied. Businesses that operate unfairly often have larger gross profits than those that operate honestly. Furthermore, dishonest companies typically stop operating, have little liquidity, and carry a significant debt load.

Implication

Banks can apply AI to ensure the legitimacy of the transactions (Mer & Virdi, 2021). For creating applications that comprehend user preferences in personal finance, ML methods (such as collaborative filtering, deep learning, unsupervised clustering, and k-nearest neighbours) have become the go-to approach within AI. For many companies in the finance sector, the introduction of AI has given them a competitive edge (Park et al., 2016). Financial businesses need to be able to dispel clients' concerns and improve their impressions of financial solutions powered by AI if they want to see growth in the use of AI in personal and corporate finance. With its exact decision support for enterprise strategy management and enterprise risk management based on past and future data, AI plays a significant role in executing comprehensive budgets, cost control, project management, and capitalisation investment decisions. According to international auditing standards, auditors must assess the risk of bankruptcy while planning an audit and revise the audit report if the risk is still present at the end of the audit. The entity will remain in existence for a sufficient period is a fundamental presumption underlying corporate financial reporting. A business occurrence called corporate financial distress costs society money. It may cause financial loss to shareholders, creditors, workers, and suppliers. Accordingly, one of the most significant issues today is the ability to predict financial health. Use AI in the form of Radial Basis Function Networks (RBF), Multi-Layer Perceptrons (MLPs), Self-Organising Feature Maps (SOFM) using MLP, and SVM neural architecture used to predict the financial health of businesses.

Future Research Direction

As regards future research work on the role of AI in personal finance, studies can be conducted on ethical considerations and mitigating bias in AI driven financial decision making. Second, studies can be conducted on understanding the factors impacting users' adoption of AI in finance. This will help in enhancing user engagement. Third, advanced personalisation techniques in AI can also be explored to tailor financial advice based on individual needs. Fourth, the effect of AI tools on financial literacy can be assessed for enhancing users' decision-making skills. Fifth, since data security and privacy are important in the context of finance, therefore, research can be conducted on robust AI methods for safeguarding users' data. Sixth, probing the long-term effect of AI on financial wellbeing can also be conducted.

As regards future research on corporate finance, studies can be conducted on integrating AI technologies with legal systems to enhance efficiency. Furthermore, the AI's role in risk management and regulatory compliance can be analysed.

Conclusion

The rapid advancement of AI has been crucial to the digital transformation of businesses, the provision of financial products and services, and consumer behaviour. Implementing ML models in the financial sector has been encouraged, particularly by the appearance and widespread use of many alternative data based on consumer purchase patterns and financial conduct. AI interventions have entirely changed how average customers who lack specialised knowledge may comprehend and resolve even the most complex personal finance problems. It can deliver precise results significantly superior to human labour (Duan et al., 2019). AI-based solutions offer several benefits, and in addition to identifying fraud and determining a person's creditworthiness, they are also used to follow regulations in both personal and corporate finance.

References

Al-Ansi, A. M., Garad, A., & Ryabtsev, V. (2024). Intelligent risk analysis of investment projects in the extractive industry. *Journal of Industrial Intelligence*, *2*(1), 42–53.

Biallas, M., & O'Neill, F. (2020). Artificial intelligence innovation in financial services. *International Finance Corporation*, *85*(6), 1–8.

Bholat, D. et al. (2020). The impact of COVID-19 on machine learning and data science in UK banking. *Bank of England Quarterly Bulletin 2020 Q4*. Available at SSRN: https://ssrn.com/abstract=3945570

Blackrock. (2019). *Artificial intelligence and machine learning in asset management Background*. Retrieved January 1, 2024, from https://www.blackrock.com/corporate/literature/whitepaper/viewpoint-artificial-intelligence-machine-learning-asset-management-october-2019.pdf

Boobier, T. (2020). *AI and the future of banking*. John Wiley & Sons Ltd.

Bumacov, V., Ashta, A., & Singh, P. (2017). Credit scoring: A historic recurrence in microfinance. *Strategic Change*, *26*(6), 543–554.

Casino, F., Dasaklis, T. K., & Patsakis, C. (2019). A systematic literature review of blockchain-based applications: Current status, classification and open issues. *Telematics and Iinformatics*, *36*, 55–81.

Collardi, B. F. (2012). *Private banking: Building a culture of excellence*. John Wiley & Sons.

D'Acunto, F., & Rossi, A. G. (2023). New frontiers of robo-advising: Consumption, savings, debt management, and taxes. In A. Capponi & C. A. Lehalle (Eds.), *Machine learning in finance: A guide to contemporary practice* (pp 9–32). Cambridge University Press.

Dai, J., & Vasarhelyi, M. A. (2017). Toward blockchain-based accounting and assurance. *Journal of Information Systems*, *31*(3), 5–21.

Davenport, T., Guha, A., Grewal, D., & Bressgott, T. (2020). How artificial intelligence will change the future of marketing. *Journal of the Academy of Marketing Science*, *48*(1), 24–42.

Deloitte. (2016). *Blockchain technology. A game-changer in accounting?* Retrieved May 7, 2023, from www2.deloitte.com/content/dam/Deloitte/de/Documents/Innovation/Blockchain_A-game-changer-in-accounting.Pdf

Duan, Y., Edwards, J. S., & Dwivedi, Y. K. (2019). Artificial intelligence for decision making in the era of big data – Evolution, challenges, and research agenda. *International Journal of Information Management*, *48*, 63–71.

Faloon, M., & Scherer, B. (2017). Individualisation of Robo advice. *Journal of Wealth Management*, *20*(1), 30–36.

Gamayuni, R. R., & Hendrawaty, E. (2020). E-Planning, E-budgeting and the quality of government institution performance accountability system in Indonesia. *Talent Development & Excellence*, *12*(1s), 218–225.
Gartner. (2022, October). *Gartner identifies 5 top use cases for AI in corporate finance*. Retrieved April 13, 2023, from https://www.gartner.com/en/newsroom/press-releases/2022-10-13-gartner-identifies-5-top-use-cases-for-ai-in-corporate-finance
Gil-Garcia, J. R., Helbig, N., & Ojo, A. (2014). Being smart: Emerging technologies and innovation in the public sector. *Government Information Quarterly*, *31*, I1–I8.
Gomber, P., Koch, J.-A., & Siering, M. (2017). Digital finance and FinTech: Current research and future research directions. *Journal of Business Economics*, *87*(5), 537–580.
Hayes, A (2024). *Retrieved from corporate finance definition and activities*. https://www.investopedia.com/terms/c/corporatefinance.asp#:~:text=Corporate%20finance%20has%20three%20main%20areas%3A%20capital%20budgeting%2C,a%20company%27s%20investments%20and%20endeavors%20will%20be%20financed.
IDC. (2020). *Worldwide Spending on Artificial Intelligence Is Expected to Double in Four Years, Reaching $110 Billion in 2024, According to New IDC Spending Guide*. https://www.idc.com/getdoc.jsp?containerId=prUS46794720
Jadhav, S., He, H., & Jenkins, K. (2016). An academic review: Application of data mining techniques in finance industry. *International Journal of Soft Computing and Artificial Intelligence*, *4*(1), 79–95. http://iraj.in/journal/IJSCAI/volume.php?volume_id=258.
Jha, K. (2023). *AI has transformed money management but it's too early to call it the undisputed king of personal finance*. Retrieved April 15, 2023, from https://mintgenie.livemint.com/news/personal-finance/what-does-the-term-portability-mean-in-an-insurance-policy-mintgenie-explains-151673886321156
Khan, F., & Mer, A. (2023). Embracing artificial intelligence technology: Legal implications with special reference to European Union initiatives of data protection. In K. Sood, B. Balusamy & S. Grima (Eds.), *Digital transformation, strategic resilience, cyber security and risk management. contemporary studies in economic and financial analysis* (Vol. 111B, pp. 31–55). Emerald Publishing Limited.
King, M. R., Timms, P. D., & Rubin, T. H. (2021). Use of big data in insurance. In D. Kurt, *Handbook of technological finance* (pp. 669–700). *The Palgrave*. Retrieved April 10, 2023, from https://www.investopedia.com/ask/answers/what-is-finance/
Kurt, E. (2024). Asymmetric effects of monetary policy on firms. *Journal of Money, Credit and Banking*.
Maude, D. (2010). *Global private banking and wealth management: The new realities* (Vol. *610*). John Wiley & Sons.
Mayer-Schönberger, V., & Cukier, K. (2013). *Big data: A revolution that will transform how we live, work, and think*. John Murray.
Mer, A. (2023). Artificial Intelligence in Human Resource Management: Recent Trends and Research Agenda. In E. Thalassinos, G. G. Noja, T. V. Stamataopoulos, T. Vasiljeva & T. Volkova (Eds.) , *Digital transformation, strategic resilience, cyber security and risk management. Contemporary Studies in Economic and Financial Analysis* (Vol. 111B, pp. 31–55). Emerald Publishing Limited.
Mer, A., Singh, A. P., Khan, F., Khati, K., & Joshi, D. (2022, December). Behavioural intention to adopt mobile banking by millennials: Empirical evidence from India. In *Congress on smart computing technologies* (pp. 205–220). Springer Nature Singapore.
Mer, A., Singhal, K., & Virdi, A. S. (2024). A review of the role of artificial intelligence in banking and stock market trading. In Taneja et al. (Eds.), *Finance Analytics in Business: Perspectives on Enhancing Efficiency and Accuracy* (pp. 175–198). Emerald Publishing.
Mer, A., & Srivastava, A. (2022). Employee engagement in the new normal: Artificial intelligence as a buzzword or a game changer? In Tyagi et al. (Eds.), *The adoption and*

effect of artificial intelligence on human resources management, Part 7A (pp. 15–46). Emerald.

Mer, A., & Virdi, A. S. (2021). Human resource challenges in NGOs: Need for sustainable HR practices. *World Review of Entrepreneurship, Management and Sustainable Development, 17*(6), 818–837.

Mer, A., & Virdi, A. S. (2022). Artificial intelligence disruption on the brink of revolutionising HR and marketing functions. In S. Balamurugan, S. Pathak, A. Jain, S. Gupta, S. Sharma, & S. Duggal, (Eds.), *Impact of artificial intelligence on organisational transformation* (pp. 1–19). Wiley.

Mer, A., & Virdi, A. S. (2023a). Navigating the paradigm shift in HRM practices through the lens of artificial intelligence: A post-pandemic perspective. In *The adoption and effect of artificial intelligence on human resources management, Part 7A* (pp. 123–154). Emerald.

Mer, A., & Virdi, A. S. (2023b). Modelling millennials' adoption intentions of E-banking: Extending UTAUT with perceived risk and trust. *FIIB Business Review, 23197145211052614.*

Novarlić, B., & Đurić, P. (2024). Enhancing comprehensive waste management in transition economies through green logistics: A case study of Bosnia and Herzegovina. *Journal of Intelligent Management Decision, 3*, 42–55.

Palmiéa, M., Wincenta, J., Paridace, V., & Caglard, U. (2020). The evolution of the financial technology ecosystem: An introduction and agenda for future research on disruptive innovations in ecosystems. *Technological Forecasting and Social Change, 151*, 119779. https://doi.org/10.1016/j.techfore.2019.119779.

Pao, H. (2008). A comparison of neural network and multiple regression analysis in modelling capital structure. *Expert Systems with Applications, 35*(3), 720–727.

Park, J., Ko, C. Y., Jung, H., & Lee, Y. S. (2016). Managerial ability and tax avoidance: Evidence from Korea. *Asia-Pacific Journal of Accounting & Economics, 23*(4), 449–477.

Roszkowska, P. (2021). Fintech in financial reporting and audit for fraud prevention and safeguarding equity investments. *Journal of Accounting & Organizational Change, 17*(2), 164–196. https://doi.org/10.1108/JAOC-09-2019-0098

Sarmah, H. (2019). *5 most popular AI-powered personal finance apps*. In Endless Origins. Retrieved April 15, 2023, from https://analyticsindiamag.com/5-most-popular-ai-powered-personal-finance-apps/

Thomaz, F., Salge, C., Karahanna, E., & Hulland, J. (2020). Learning from the dark web: Leveraging conversational agents in the era of hyper-privacy to enhance marketing. *Journal of the Academy of Marketing Science, 48*(1), 43–63.

Tokic, D. (2018). BlackRock Robo-advisor 4.0: When artificial intelligence replaces human discretion. *Strategic Change, 27*(4), 285–290.

Tufano, P. (2009). Consumer finance. *Annual Review Financial Economics, 1*(1), 227–247.

Virdi, A. S., & Mer, A. (2023). Fintech and banking: An Indian perspective. In N. Naifar, & A. Elsayed (Eds.), *Green finance instruments, FinTech, and investment strategies: Sustainable portfolio management in the Post-COVID Era* (pp. 261–281). Springer International Publishing.

Wyrobeck, J. (2020). Application of machine learning models and artificial intelligence to analyse annual financial statements to identify companies of unfair corporate culture. *Procedia Computer Science, 176*, 3037–3046.

Yerpude, S., Sood, K., & Grima, S. (2022). Blockchain-augmented digital supply chain management: A way to sustainable business. *Journal of Risk and Financial Management, 16*(1), 7.

Yoon, S. (2020). A study on the transformation of accounting based on new technologies: Evidence from Korea. *Sustainability, 12*(20), 8669.

Zaki, A. (2023, April). *5 Ways ChatGPT will impact corporate finance*. Retrieved April 13, 2023, from https://www.cfo.com/technology/artificial-intelligence/2023/04/chatgpt-corporate-finance-technology-ai-consulting-talent/

Zhang, H., Nguyen, H., Bui, X. N., Nguyen-Thoi, T., Bui, T. T., Nguyen, N., … Moayedi, H. (2020). Developing a novel artificial intelligence model to estimate the capital cost of mining projects using deep neural network-based ant colony optimisation algorithm. *Resources Policy*, *66*, 101604.

Chapter 15

Regulatory Technology (RegTech) Landscape of Bangladesh: Policies and Practices

S. M. Sohrab Uddin[a], *Mohammad Osman Goni*[b] *and Tasnim Ara Hossen*[c]

[a]*Department of Finance, University of Chittagong, Chattogram, Bangladesh*
[b]*Maslin Capital Limited, Dhaka, Bangladesh*
[c]*Brac-Micro Finance, Dhaka, Bangladesh*

Abstract

Purpose: This study examines the regulatory technology (RegTech) policies and practices in Bangladesh, highlighting barriers due to the slow adoption of RegTech and identifying opportunities amid the growing state of financial technology (FinTech).

Need for the Study: In response to the escalating complexity and volatility of regulatory requirements after the 2008 global financial crisis (GFC), RegTech has emerged worldwide. It harnesses the power of cutting-edge technologies to automate compliance, monitor regulatory changes, and provide real-time risk assessments. The development of RegTech solutions in developing countries is still in its nascent stages, and Bangladesh seems to be no exception.

Methodology: This study employs a secondary data-based research design, collecting data from the annual reports of the Bangladesh Financial Intelligence Unit (BFIU) and various commercial banks from 2017 to 2021. The data analysis employs descriptive statistics and content analysis to measure FinTech growth and assess the effectiveness of RegTech policies adopted by banks.

Financial Landscape Transformation: Technological Disruptions, 269–285

Published under exclusive licence by Emerald Publishing Limited
doi:10.1108/978-1-83753-750-120251015

Findings: The study found a 657% increase in registered users from 2014 to 2022, with transactions rising from BDT104.83 billion to BDT961.33 billion. Bangladesh has enacted strong policies against illicit financial activities, indicating that it is in the early RegTech 2.0 stage focusing on regulatory compliance.

Practical Implications: The analysis reveals that Bangladesh's lag in RegTech adoption, which exacerbates money laundering and suspicious transactions due to the increased use of FinTech. Regulatory authorities should enhance technology, enforce policies, and raise awareness to detect financial non-compliance.

Keywords: Anti-money laundering; Bangladesh Financial Intelligence Unit; global financial crisis; know-your-customer; RegTech 3.0; regulatory changes and suspicious transactions reporting

JEL Code: G38

Introduction

Following the 2008 Global Financial Crisis (GFC), the financial sector has witnessed a notable evolution driven by significant progress in technological innovation and regulatory revisions (Anagnostopoulos, 2018). Financial Technology, popularly known as FinTech, has shifted the paradigm to complex technology-based financial products, bringing a revolutionary change in the financial system. It has fundamentally transformed the industry, leading to a new and evolving landscape significantly different from the past (Machkour & Abriane, 2020). In light of these changes, there is a need for regulatory changes to adapt to the new models and to foster effective coordination for attaining the desired benefit from the adoption of FinTech (Arner et al., 2017; Machkour & Abriane, 2020).

In response to the escalating complexity and volatility of regulatory requirements in the aftermath of the GFC, the development of regulatory technology (RegTech) has emerged in different parts of the world (Teichmann et al., 2023). As the financial sector has been confronted with a plethora of regulatory changes, there has been an increased compliance burden, particularly about the ever-evolving Anti-money Laundering (AML) and know-your-customer (KYC) regulations (Utami & Septivani, 2022). These regulatory requirements present formidable challenges to businesses as traditional regulatory compliance methods become inadequate, resource-intensive, and costly. To address these challenges, RegTech solutions have been developed by capitalizing on cutting-edge technologies such as Artificial Intelligence (AI), Machine Learning, and Blockchain to automate compliance procedures, oversee regulatory changes, and furnish real-time assessments of compliance risks (Gurung & Perlman, 2018). The incorporation of these advanced technologies highlights the commitment of financial institutions in developed countries to improve their regulatory compliance processes through the adoption of such innovative technologies. Nevertheless, digitizing compliance procedures represents a step-by-step evolution toward a more effective and efficient regulatory framework (Arner et al., 2016). RegTech adoption in developed countries is called RegTech 3.0 (KPMG, 2018).

The development of RegTech solutions in developing countries is still in its nascent stages (Gurung & Perlman, 2018). Bangladesh is no exception since most financial entities depend on manual procedures to ensure compliance with regulatory obligations. The RegTech in Bangladesh has primarily focused on AML and countering the financing of terrorism (CFT) compliance. However, there has been a growing awareness of the potential benefits of RegTech, and some institutions have already started to embrace these solutions. The Government's Information and Communication Technology (ICT) Division recently published a national blockchain strategy to achieve the Sustainable Development Goals (SDGs) by 2030. Bangladesh Bank, the country's central bank, also published different circulars and guidelines that strengthen the RegTech compliance system, though Bangladesh needs to catch up in automated supervision. Only a few financial institutions have incorporated software solutions for Customer Due Diligence (CDD) and transaction monitoring. Similarly, various RegTech solutions, including electronic know-your-customer (E-KYC) verification, online payment processing systems, and transaction monitoring, have yet to be implemented entirely in Bangladesh. However, aligned to build Smart Bangladesh, a team of blockchain specialists will be required in the future. Bangladesh also needs to implement blockchain or distribution ledger technology in the future of FinTech and RegTech.

Considering the present status of RegTech worldwide, this study attempts to evaluate the landscape of RegTech policies and practices in Bangladesh with particular emphasis on the banking sector by analyzing different FinTech and RegTech variables, which remain undisclosed in the existing available literature. Furthermore, potential opportunities will be highlighted considering the burgeoning state of FinTech implemented by the financial sector.

The chapter is structured into four segments. The second segment presents a review of the relevant literature. Section three describes the data and methodology employed in this study. The fourth segment highlights the findings and analysis. The last segment offers concluding remarks based on the findings.

Literature Review

The 2008 GFC catalyzed the implementation of regulatory measures and the greater adoption of technological advancement within the financial sector, aiming to prevent future similar events (Teichmann et al., 2023; Utami & Septivani, 2022). However, the FinTech is not entirely free from risk. Financial institutions that embrace FinTech face significant vulnerability regarding technology-related risks (Utami & Septivani, 2022). For instance, the 1987 stock market crash, known as "Black Monday," highlighted the interconnectedness of the global markets through technology. Consequently, circuit breakers were implemented to slow down the pace of price fluctuations, prompting the regulators to establish collaborative mechanisms. In the same way, the GFC in 2008 adversely affected the bank's profitability and competitiveness, followed by subsequent regulations that led to unprecedented compliance costs, which, in turn, resulted in limited access to credit (Arner et al., 2017). Moreover, the adoption of FinTech by banks has rendered them susceptible to other risks, including the ever-present threat of money laundering (Utami & Septivani, 2022).

Afterward, there is a growing need for the development of RegTech. It is a type of technology that assists organizations in effectively managing their regulatory and compliance obligations by determining the effects of regulations on various aspects such as products and services, business models, operational procedures, and control measures. It also helps manage and mitigate financial and non-financial risks, facilitate compliance documentation, and implement compliant business systems and data management practices (Butler & O'Brien, 2019). Furthermore, according to Zabelina et al. (2018), RegTech is a collection of technologies that support organizations in meeting changing legal requirements while providing dependable, secure, and cost-effective solutions for financial institutions to improve their efficiency. Arner et al. (2017) and KPMG (2018) also stated that RegTech is a fast-growing field that utilizes advanced technologies to improve regulatory compliance outcomes through real-time monitoring, analytics, and automation of key compliance processes. According to them, the progression of RegTech can be delineated into the following three developmental phases. A summary of the above three stages of RegTech evolution is outlined below (Fig. 1).

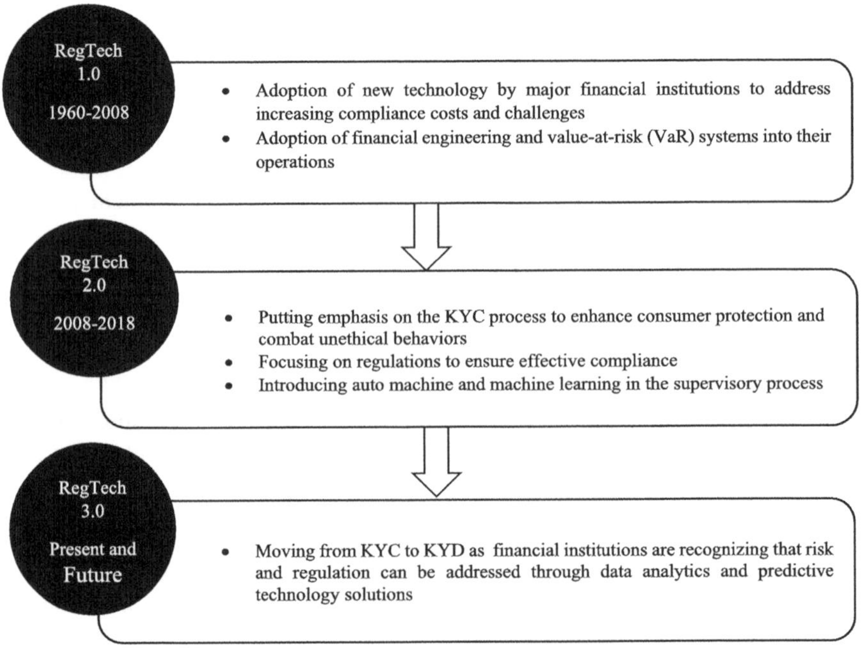

Fig. 1. Evolution of the RegTech. *Source*: Constructed by the authors.

- RegTech 1.0 indicates the pre-GFC era when financial entities began to adopt innovative techniques for observing and evaluating risks connected with particular policies or procedures. This period has marked the beginning of the development of some of the quantitative risk management practices commonly used today. Arner et al. (2017) stated that the financial industry and regulators were overly confident in their risk management proficiency using a quantitative information technology framework at the start of the 21st century. This overconfidence was particularly evident in the Basel II Capital Accord, which placed too much reliance on financial institutions' internal risk management systems. However, this approach was proven to be flawed during the GFC, leading to a loss of confidence in RegTech. RegTech 1.0 also had limitations in monitoring public securities markets, specifically detecting unusual behavior like insider trading. Regulators depended on trade surveillance systems managed by the securities exchanges to spot such behavior and investigate misconduct. However, as seen during the GFC, these systems had limitations, as they could not detect transactions that occurred off the exchange, such as those done through Electronic Communication Networks (ECN) and dark pools.
- RegTech 2.0 is the phase of technological innovation in the financial industry, which was prompted by the aftermath of the GFC. This phase is characterized by a focus on addressing the challenges of compliance, reporting, and processes as financial market participants and regulators seek to alleviate the increased regulatory burden, costs, and complexity (Johansson et al., 2019). KPMG (2018) also stated that technological solutions in RegTech 2.0 have primarily concentrated on enhancing consumer protection and discouraging unethical behaviors by focusing on KYC measures. New technologies like AI and deep learning are examples of the potential of RegTech 2.0 to automate consumer protection, market supervision, and prudential regulation. By leveraging these technologies, regulators can enhance their capabilities to identify and avert illicit financial activities (Arner et al., 2017). Also, RegTech 2.0 holds promise in mitigating the regulatory risks that were evident prior to the GFC.
- The financial industry is poised for the next phase of technological innovation (Brando, 2019), RegTech 3.0, which involves a shift from "KYC" to "Know Your Data (KYD)." In this stage, financial institutions use data analytics and technology to predict risks with advanced predictive algorithms (Johansson et al., 2019; KPMG, 2018).

As one of the early adopters of RegTech applications, the United Kingdom Financial Conduct Authority (FCA) pointed out four ways to adopt RegTech in 2015: regulatory expertise, support for FinTech and RegTech ecosystem, acceptable standards, and overcoming barriers related to innovation. The Monetary Authority of Singapore (MAS) has also utilized RegTech strategies to promote the growth of Singapore's FinTech industry, specifically focusing on digital identification, E-KYC, data governance, and innovation platforms. In the same way, the Security and Futures Commission of Hong Kong is exploring the application of data analysis tools to detect instances of market misconduct and suspicious trading behaviors (Arner et al., 2022).

Automating reporting and compliance processes has brought numerous benefits to regulatory practices today. This trend has facilitated significant cost savings for industries while providing regulators with superior monitoring capabilities. Consequently, real-time and proportionate regulatory regimes that can identify risks and enable more efficient compliance with regulations are emerging. In this regard, Turki et al. (2020) stated that adhering to AML regulations, monitoring customer transactions, and completing the necessary procedures for customer onboarding was complex, resource-intensive, and time-consuming in the past.

Gurung and Perlman (2018) inferred that the adoption of RegTech is likely to bring about notable transformations to the processes and systems of central banks in developing nations by utilizing the automation of reporting procedures, the acquisition of granular data, the generation of new streams of information, the enhancement of predictive and algorithmic supervision capabilities, and the integration of internal processes. Tertychnyi et al. (2022) stated that governments across the world combat money laundering by introducing measures to prevent such illegal activities, including automated monitoring systems and the timely detection of such activities. Chen et al. (2018) mentioned that machine learning technology enables banks to monitor transactions more effectively, using more advanced systems, controls, and practices. In addition, a study conducted in Indonesia showed that transaction monitoring and cost and time efficiency significantly prevent money laundering (Utami & Septivani, 2022). Another study by Meiryani et al. (2022) on Indonesian banks revealed that leveraging RegTech can result in cost savings, increased efficiency, and improved monitoring, reporting, and compliance regarding regulations for preventing non-compliant financial activities.

Data and Methodology

This study employs a research design based on secondary data collected from the Bangladesh Financial Intelligence Unit (BFIU) annual reports of Bangladesh Bank and various private commercial banks spanning 2017 to 2021. The descriptive statistics, circulars, and publications of Bangladesh Bank are analyzed. Various indicators, such as the number and amount of transaction growth, are used in this study to identify the development of FinTech. Several variables, including reporting of E-KYC compliance, software used to detect non-compliant transactions, AML compliance, employee training, suspicious transactions reporting (STR), cash transaction report (CTR), and system check inspection of banks, are adopted for assessing the effectiveness of the RegTech policies.

Findings and Analysis

RegTech Policies in Bangladesh

After analyzing the journey of RegTech 1.0, it has been found that RegTech in Bangladesh has been primarily driven by the need to comply with regulatory requirements. In 1997, Bangladesh was one of the first countries to join the

Asia-Pacific Group on Money Laundering (APG), but it was not until 2002 that a formal framework for the AML and CFT regime was established. The government set up a central task force and seven regional task forces, headed by the Deputy Governor of Bangladesh Bank, to combat money laundering and illegal hundi (an informal system used for transferring money) activities. In April 2002, Bangladesh passed the Money Laundering Prevention Act (MLPA), becoming the first country in the South-Asian region to have such legislation, revised later in 2012. In June 2002, the Anti-Money Laundering Department (AMLD) was established to implement and enforce the MLPA provisions. These actions demonstrate the government's commitment to address money laundering and terrorist financing and to establish a robust AML/CFT framework.

It is also evident that Bangladesh was rated as a non-compliant by the World Bank and International Monetary Fund (IMF) in 2002–2003 after the first and second round mutual evaluations due to its relatively new AML journey and failure to meet standards by the Financial Action Task Force (FATF). Although efforts were made to address deficiencies, the country received a non-compliant rating in the 2008–2009 APG evaluation, resulting in the inclusion in the International Cooperation Review Group (ICRG) process made by the FATF in October 2010. Finally, Bangladesh achieved compliant status in 2014–2015 after APG's third round of evaluation.

Bangladesh Bank ensured the implementation of BASEL III by 2019, which introduced the new RegTech stage, RegTech 2.0. Anti-Terrorism Act (ATA), Mobile Financial Services (MFS) guidelines, MFS Regulation, and E-KYC are the core legal frameworks based on which non-compliant financial activities are monitored. Furthermore, the goAML system, a comprehensive software program created by the United Nations Office on Drugs and Crime (UNODC) for reporting financial activity, was initiated in 2014. Fig. 2 makes a chronological display of various regulatory frameworks introduced in Bangladesh during the period 2002–2023.

As mentioned earlier, BIFU oversees the financial institutions' implementation of the regulations. It has kept up its efforts to build the information technology infrastructure required for the unit to operate effectively and efficiently. The goAML software has been installed to facilitate electronic reporting and computer-assisted analysis of CTR and STR. Additionally, it has set up an information system to maintain and update all the data and create the necessary reports

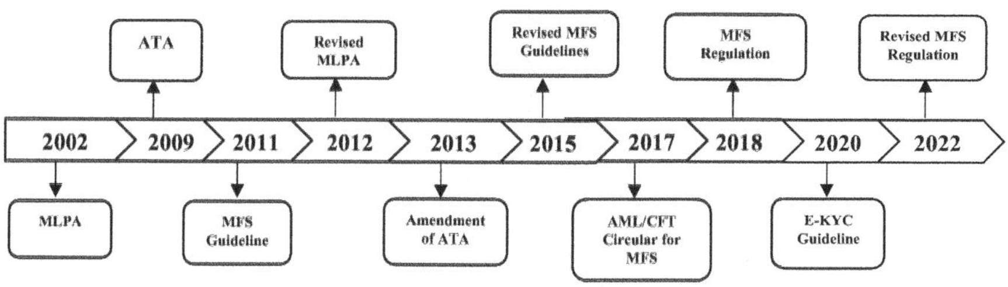

Fig. 2. Regulatory progression in Bangladesh. *Source*: Constructed by authors.

to add value to the RegTech development in Bangladesh. Moreover, to strengthen collaboration with foreign associates, BFIU has entered into Memoranda of Understanding (MoUs) with various countries' Financial Intelligence Units (FIUs). Recently, BFIU has emphasized enhancing CDD measures by obtaining more customer information, which will broaden RegTech development. BFIU can also exercise the power to suspend transactions and freeze an account of a reporting agency under section 15, sub-section 1(b) of MLA in case of any discrepancy. The critical aspects of the guidelines provided by BFIU are provided in Table 1. On the other hand, a summary of the E-KYC guidelines is documented in Table 2.

Table 1. Key Aspects of BFIU Guidelines.

Aspects	**Summary**
Reporting to BFIU	• Reporting institutions must immediately report any suspicious transactions to Bangladesh Bank. • Banks must submit various reports to Bangladesh Bank without delay, including STRs, CTRs, internal assessment reports, and an independent compliance system. • STR reported to the Central Compliance Unit (CCU) should be documented or recorded electronically.
Record keeping	The firm's records should cover: • relevant information about customers • transaction records • reports generated from internal sources, as well as reports received from external entities • the report provided by CCU • documentation of training sessions and compliance monitoring efforts
CDD	• In October 2001, the Basel Committee on Banking Supervision (BCBS) published an extensive document titled "CDD for banks," addressing deficiencies observed in KYC procedures worldwide. • The legislative and regulatory CDD requirements imposed on banks aim to make money laundering or terrorist financing activities within the banking industry more difficult. • Enhanced CDD measures go beyond the basic requirements of collecting and verifying customer information. These measures may include obtaining information about the customer's business activities, assets, and connections to other individuals or organizations. It also includes more frequent updates of customer information.

Table 1. (Continued)

Aspects	Summary
Automated mechanism of UNSCR	• Banks should use a system that allows them to identify any listed individuals or businesses before developing a business relationship with them. Banks should use automated screening methods to identify and monitor account onboarding and foreign exchange transactions to prevent any listed persons or entities from using the official financial channel. The banks should periodically check the United Nations website for updated lists and retain and maintain a digital record of all identified individuals and businesses. • They shall conduct routine checks on the specified parameters, such as transactional reviews, to see if any of the people or organizations designated by the relevant UNSCR Committee have any funds. Installing this automated UNSCR mechanism will pave the way for RegTech development.

Source: Constructed by authors.

Table 2. Summary of E-KYC Guidelines.

Aspects	Summary
Scope	• This guideline exclusively applies to individuals and does not extend to legal entities or organizations. • The applicability of the requirements outlined in this guideline depends on the risk profiles associated with financial institution customers. • It relies on the utilization of biometric authentication for identification purposes. • This guideline does not apply to clients classified as legal persons or arrangements. For such clients, KYC and CDD procedures will be carried out according to the regulations outlined in the MLPA 2012, the ATA 2009, and the MLP Rules 2019. • If technical difficulties prevent successful E-KYC attempts, the traditional KYC method should be employed to verify the individual's identity.
Objective	• The primary goal of promoting E-KYC is to enable fast customer onboarding by verifying their identity through digital methods. In addition, E-KYC can help institutions reduce costs and expand their customer base more efficiently than traditional methods.
E-KYC process	• The E-KYC module consists of simplified E-KYC and regular E-KYC, which are used to identify and authenticate customers' identities, store their KYC profiles digitally, and assess customer risk ratings using digital methods.

(*Continued*)

Table 2. (Continued)

Aspects	Summary
	• In the traditional KYC process, customers must fill out a physical KYC form and provide photo identification, signatures, and other necessary documents. This process is entirely manual. • On the other hand, E-KYC, which is conducted electronically, allows reporting organizations to perform customer onboarding quickly by recording in digital form, taking the customer's photo on the spot, and instantly authenticating their identification data, such as ID number, biometric information, and address proof. Transaction authentication can also be accomplished by utilizing e-signatures and biometric information.
Applicability	• E-KYC is exclusively relevant to documents relating to individuals with valid national identity (NID). In contrast, individuals lacking NID and legal entities or arrangements must follow periodic KYC norms as directed by BFIU. The type of E-KYC verification required will vary depending on the amount of money involved in the transaction and the level of risk associated with the customer. This guideline applies to all financial institutions authorized by the Bangladesh Bank.

Source: Constructed by authors.

RegTech Practices in Bangladesh

The rapid progression of FinTech necessitates a corresponding progression of RegTech to manage regulatory compliance in this digital era effectively. For this reason, the picture of recent FinTech development has been drawn. In this study, several registered users and the total number of transactions under MFS were considered to show the growth of FinTech in Bangladesh, as shown in Table 3. It has been found that the number of MFS users has been accelerating over the years. The point-to-point growth rate shows that the MFS beneficiary is growing at an increasing rate. The growth rate was 71% between 2021 and 2022, which has been the highest in the field of MFS. In the same way, the volume of transactions is also increasing as the amount in 2022 reached BDT 961 billion from BDT 167 billion in 2015.

In compliance with section 25(1)(d) of the MLPA, 2012, and section 16(1) of the ATA, 2009, financial entities are obligated to proactively present STR based on their discernment and apprehension of potential AML and CFT risks. Table 4 shows that the STR reached 8,571 in 2021–2022 and 1,094 in 2014–2015. Due to the COVID-19 effect, both STR and CTR were comparatively lower. However, the STR increased by 62.33% between 2020–2021 and 2021–2022. This increase in STR is alarming as it indicates accelerated fraudulent activities. The adoption of developed technology can assist in identifying STR more effectively and accurately.

Moreover, to assess reporting organizations' compliance with the regulations and guidelines outlined in the MLPA 2012 and ATA 2009, a system check inspection is carried out by BIFU. The inspection aims to monitor the efficiency of the

Table 3. Trend of MFS in Bangladesh.

Items	2015	2016	2017	2018	2019	2020	2021	2022
Number of registered users	31.85 (26%)	41.08 (29%)	58.8 (43%)	67.519 (15%)	79.51 (18%)	99.34 (25%)	111.47 (12%)	190.78 (71%)
Total amount of transactions	167.45 (60%)	216 (29%)	286 (32%)	321.05 (12%)	406.48 (27%)	565.57 (39%)	711.73 (26%)	961.33 (35%)

Source: Bangladesh Bank (2022).
Notes: The figures in the parenthesis represent the growth rate. The number of registered users is BDT million, and the total number of transactions is BDT billion.

Table 4. Historical Receipt of STR.

Year	2014–2015	2015–2016	2016–2017	2017–2018	2018–2019	2019–2020	2020–2021	2021–2022
STR	1,094	1,687	2,357	3,078	3,573	3,675	5,280	8,571
% change	76.17	54.20	39.72	30.59	16.08	2.85	43.67	62.33

Source: BFIU (2022).

Table 5. System Check Inspection by BIFU.

Bank	2014–2015	2015–2016	2016–2017	2017–2018	2018–2019	2019–2020	2020–2021	2021–2022
Head offices	56	0	57	26	23	24	23	29
Branches	213	56	57	54	49	40	29	37
Total	269	56	114	80	72	64	52	66
NBFI								
Head offices	21	22	5	20	2	10	3	8
Branches	9	10	5	10	0	10	1	12
Total	30	32	10	30	2	20	4	20

Source: BFIU (2022).

AML and CFT systems. Table 5 illustrates the status quo of system check inspection of banks and NBFIs conducted by BIFU. While the number of AML and CFT system inspections for banks and NBFIs increased in 2021–2022 compared to 2020–2021, it remains significantly lower than the number of inspections conducted in 2014–2015. Again, the system inspection conducted on the head offices and branches of banks and NBFIs still needs to be higher than the number of banks and NBFIs in Bangladesh. The decreased frequency of AML/CFT system inspections indicates a potential need for more emphasis on the review process for AML/CFT policy and compliance. This could have negative consequences, including the inability to effectively adhere to RegTech compliance and a potential increase in non-compliant financial activities.

Table 6 shows that 39 out of 49 banks reported their AML and CFT compliance. Though all banks must establish and sustain robust and comprehensive programs to implement AML and CFT rules, 20.41% of the scheduled banks still need to report compliance activities.

Table 7 reports the implementation of different RegTech variables essential to combating AML activities. It shows that 33 banks reported their E-KYC compliance in 2020 and 2021, respectively, whereas 16 did not report their E-KYC-related data in 2020 and 2021. The implementation of training, software, STR, and CTR measures has also been consistently reported by many banks each year. The number of non-reporting banks regarding software adoption and CTR is increasing, whereas training and STR are decreasing. Although the banking sector has taken steps to comply with the RegTech, evidenced by different RegTech variables, there is room for improvement in reporting and transparency, as many banks still need to report their RegTech compliance.

As section 23(1) (a) of the MLPA, 2012 grants the BFIU the right to acquire CTR from reporting organizations, banks, and NBFIs are obliged to submit CTR to BFIU monthly on the cash deposits or withdrawals for any value of BDT 1 million or more in an account in a single day. Table 8 shows that the number and volume of CTR transactions by banks are increasing every year, which directly assists in identifying the suspected transactions. The table also revealed that the CTR was comparatively lower (the number of transactions was BDT

Table 6. Reporting of RegTech by Banks.

Particulars	State-Owned Commercial Bank	Listed Conventional Commercial Bank	Non-Listed Conventional Commercial Bank	Islamic Bank
Reported	6	19	7	7
Not reported	0	4	3	3
Total	6	23	10	10

Source: Constructed by authors.

Table 7. Implementation of RegTech Variables by Banks.

Year	E-KYC	Training	Software	STR	CTR
2017	29(11)	23(22)	19(26)	15(28)	19(25)
2018	31(16)	25(22)	19(28)	17(30)	22(24)
2019	32(16)	26(22)	20(28)	15(33)	22(26)
2020	33(16)	25(24)	19(30)	17(32)	22(27)
2021	33(16)	26(23)	19(30)	18(31)	21(28)

Source: Authors' calculation.

Note: The figures in the parenthesis represent the number of non-reported banks.

Table 8. Reporting of CTR by Banks.

Year	2014–2015	2015–2016	2016–2017	2017–2018	2018–2019	2019–2020	2020–2021	2021–2022
Number of transactions	3.66	12.7	13.98	14.7	19.24	16.14	20.57	36.89
Volume of transactions	8,141	8,734	10,090	10,527	21,987	11,719	14,438	21,113

Source: BFIU (2022).

Note: The number of transactions is in BDT million, and the volume is in BDT billion.

16.14 million, and the volume of transactions was BDT 11,719 billion) in 2019–2020. The decrease can be attributed to the effect of COVID-19. Interestingly, this starts to increase in the subsequent years.

Thus, according to the findings above, Bangladesh has achieved significant adoption of RegTech policies, but it needs to catch up in implementing them effectively. Some financial institutions need to ensure proper reporting, and the supervision by authorities needs to be improved as the number of STRs is increasing daily. This calls for more effective supervisory activities to reduce such activities. Moreover, even though all the financial institutions, including MFS providers, are registered with the goAML system, only a few possess strong technological support and database systems that enable complete RegTech compliance.

Based on the findings, Fig. 3 depicts a brief status quo. Bangladesh is currently in the initial stage of RegTech 2.0, as automated supervision has yet to be fully implemented. Therefore, it cannot be categorized as being in the stage of RegTech 3.0. However, it is projected that by 2030, Bangladesh will adopt blockchain technology to control and manage money laundering activities.

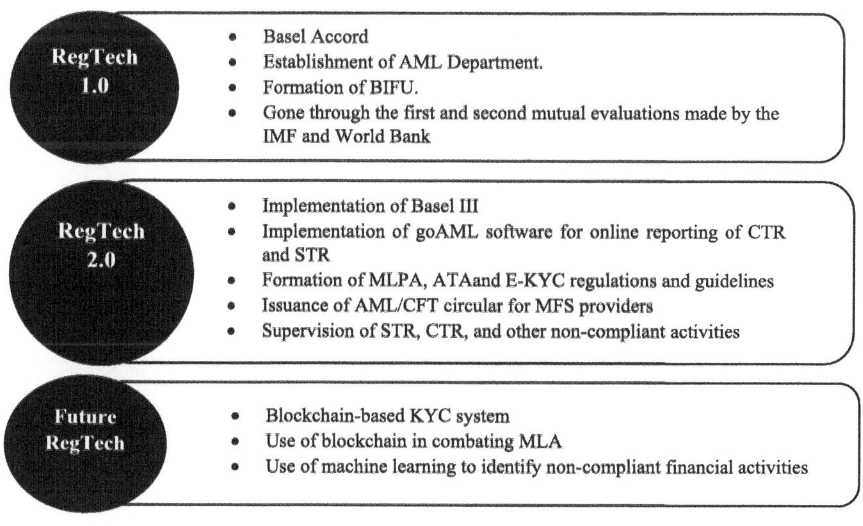

Fig. 3. Summary of RegTech adoption in Bangladesh. *Source*: Constructed by authors.

This implementation is supposed to bring about significant changes in the field of RegTech in Bangladesh.

Finally, the RegTech landscape of Bangladesh is shown in the following flow chart (Fig. 4). This flow chart considers some important RegTech indicators

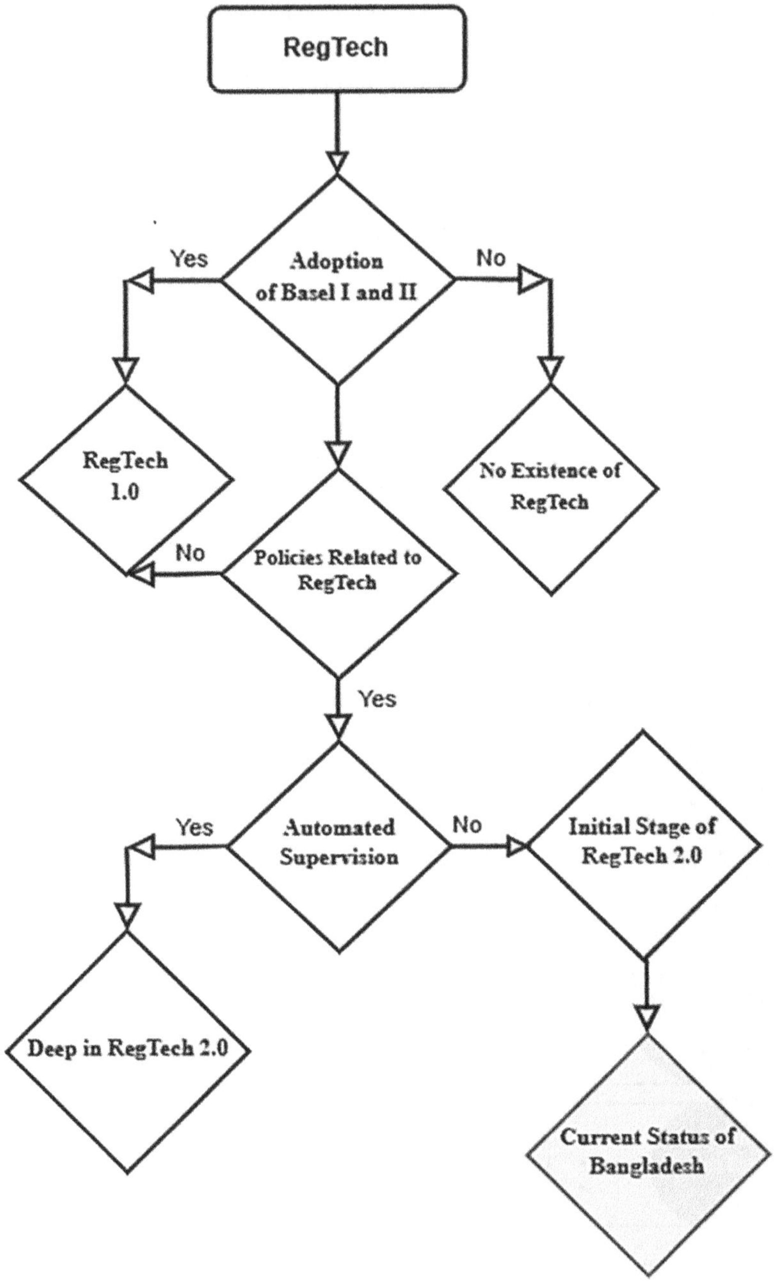

Fig. 4. Flow Chart to Understand the Current Status of RegTech Adoption in Bangladesh. *Source*: Constructed by authors.

at every stage. Bangladesh has adopted the BASEL accord and advanced to RegTech 1.0. In the next step, it is necessary to observe the existence of any policy relating to RegTech. If the answer is no, it will be considered that the country is still in the RegTech 1.0 stage. As in Bangladesh, there are some policies related to RegTech, and it is clear that Bangladesh has moved toward RegTech 2.0. Of course, RegTech 2.0 involves the use of regulatory compliance and the use of technology to ensure improved supervision (Arner et al., 2017). Thus, countries without automated supervision cannot go deep into the RegTech 2.0 stage. In the case of Bangladesh, financial institutions are adopting advanced technology to supervise compliance. Hence, Bangladesh still needs to be moved to the deep stage of RegTech 2.0. Adopting cutting-edge technology like blockchain to supervise compliance can improve RegTech's status.

Conclusion

RegTech is rapidly evolving, constantly advancing, and developing in response to the changing regulatory landscape and emerging technological advancements. Companies should effectively implement technologies in a dynamic regulatory environment to tackle compliance difficulties, including complexity and cost. RegTech solutions can help companies stay ahead of new regulations and cyber threats.

In this regard, this study aimed to evaluate the landscape of RegTech policies and practices in Bangladesh to identify the current state of RegTech adoption compared to the global perspective. Several RegTech variables were used in this study to achieve this goal. It has been found that E-KYC, MLPA, ATA, and AML/CFT circulars for MFS providers are the principal regulations formulated in Bangladesh to combat fraudulent financial activities. The regulatory authority is actively working to bring more regulations to implement RegTech.

It is also evident that the total number of STRs is increasing because of the continuous improvement in regulatory supervision. This number can be checked in the best possible manner if the cutting-edge technology can be used for supervision in the future. However, the reporting of the implementation of RegTech variables by banks could be better. Therefore, BFIU needs to play an influential role in addressing the issue. Furthermore, the system checks inspection results show that the AML/CFT inspection is shallow, which can be regarded as one of the causes of raising potential non-compliant activities by financial institutions. Apart from this, the CTR is on an increasing trend. Organizations need to be aware of the reporting of CTR and are required to adopt innovative technology so that they can reduce money laundering and other non-compliant activities.

It is also clear that regulatory compliance in Bangladesh is gradually improving, and at present, it belongs to the early stage of RegTech 2.0, which primarily focuses on regulatory compliance. However, the greatest challenge in adhering to RegTech compliance lies in adopting more technology. Also, detecting money laundering and suspected transactions can prove formidable in today's intricate Fintech landscape. Thus, it is recommended that the regulatory authority take effective initiative to develop advanced RegTech to keep pace with the growth of

FinTech. Otherwise, detecting non-compliant financial activities in the coming days will be challenging.

Due to the limitations of the data's availability, this study excludes financial intermediaries in the capital market, insurance companies, and other companies authorized by the Bangladesh Bank. Therefore, based on the availability and collection of such data, further research opportunities lie in this topic.

References

Anagnostopoulos, I. (2018). Fintech and regtech: Impact on regulators and banks. *Journal of Economics and Business*, *100*, 7–25.

Arner, D. W., Ahmed, S. M., & Gazi, S. (2022). Building regulatory and supervisory technology ecosystems: For Asia's financial stability and sustainable development. *Available at SSRN*.

Arner, D. W., Barberis, J. N., & Buckley, R. P. (2016). The emergence of RegTech 2.0: From know your customer to know your data.

Arner, D. W., Barberis, J., & Buckley, R. P. (2017). *FinTech and RegTech in a nutshell, and the future in a sandbox*. CFA Institute Research Foundation.

Bangladesh Bank. (2022). *Mobile financial services comparative summary*. Bangladesh Bank.

BFIU. (2022). *Annual Report 2021-2022*, Bangladesh Financial Intelligence Unit (BFIU.

Brando, M. C. (2019). The adoption of a EU Regulatory Sandbox on the Way to RegTech 3.0. *Mercato Concorrenza Regole* (3), 547–577.

Butler, T., & O'Brien, L. (2019). Understanding RegTech for digital regulatory compliance. In T. Lynn & J. G. Mooney (Eds.), J *Disrupting finance: FinTech and strategy in the 21st century* (pp. 85–102). Palgrave Macmillan.

Chen, Z., Van Khoa, L. D., Teoh, E. N., Nazir, A., Karuppiah, E. K., & Lam, K. S. (2018). Machine learning techniques for anti-money laundering (AML) solutions in suspicious transaction detection: A review. *Knowledge and Information Systems*, *57*, 245–285.

Gurung, N., & Perlman, L. (2018). Use of Regtech by Central Banks and its impact on financial inclusion. *Available at SSRN 3285985*.

Johansson, E., Sutinen, K., Lassila, J., Lang, V., Martikainen, M., & Lehner, O. (2019). Regtech – A necessary tool to keep up with compliance and regulatory changes. *ACRN Journal of Finance and Risk Perspectives, Special Issue Digital Accounting*, *8*, 71–85.

KPMG. (2018). *There's a revolution coming, Embracing the challenge of RegTech 3.0*. https://assets.kpmg.com/content/dam/kpmg/uk/pdf/2018/09/regtech-revolution-coming.pdf

Machkour, B., & Abriane, A. (2020). Industry 4.0 and its implications for the financial sector. *Procedia Computer Science*, *177*, 496–502.

Meiryani, M., Soepriyanto, G., & Audrelia, J. (2022). Effectiveness of regulatory technology implementation in Indonesian banking sector to prevent money laundering and terrorist financing. *Journal of Money Laundering Control*.

Teichmann, F., Boticiu, S., & Sergi, B. S. (2023). RegTech–Potential benefits and challenges for businesses. *Technology in Society*, *72*, 102150.

Tertychnyi, P., Godgildieva, M., Dumas, M., & Ollikainen, M. (2022). Time-aware and interpretable predictive monitoring system for Anti-Money Laundering. *Machine Learning with Applications*, *8*, 100306.

Turki, M., Hamdan, A., Cummings, R. T., Sarea, A., Karolak, M., & Anasweh, M. (2020). The regulatory technology "RegTech" and money laundering prevention in Islamic and conventional banking industry. *Heliyon*, *6*(10), e04949.
Utami, A. M., & Septivani, M. D. (2022). Regulatory Technology (RegTech): The solution to prevent money laundering in Indonesia. *Telaah Bisnis*, *23*(1), 86–98.
Zabelina, O., Vasiliev, A., & Galushkin, S. (2018). Regulatory Technologies in the AML/CFT. *KnE Social Sciences*, 394–401.

Websites

https://www.bfiu.org.bd/pdf/pub/annual/2021-2022.pdf
https://www.bfiu.org.bd/pdf/pub/annual/2015-2016.pdf
https://www.bb.org.bd/en/index.php/financialactivity/mfsdata

Chapter 16

InsurTech: Digital Transformation of the Insurance Industry

Shakil Ahmad[a], *Rejaul Karim*[b], *Nargis Sultana*[c] *and Reshma Pervin Lima*[d]

[a]*School of Business, University of Creative Technology Chittagong, Bangladesh*
[b]*Department of Business Administration, Varendra University, Bangladesh*
[c]*Department of Finance and Banking, Comilla University, Bangladesh*
[d]*Department of Accounting, Mawlana Bhashani Science and Technology University, Bangladesh*

Abstract

Introduction: The insurance industry is undergoing constant transformation to keep up with the demands of digitally savvy consumers. "Insur-Tech" refers to using technological breakthroughs in the insurance sector to boost competition, innovate new products, increase customer happiness, and improve operational operations. Insurance technology has many potential applications across the complete product lifecycle, from initial research and development to post-contract administration, back-office processes and risk management.

Purpose: This chapter discusses the insurance industry's current and potential future state with the emergence of insur-tech. The objective is to explore the emergence of new-age technologies in the insurance industry and the challenges faced in their implementation.

Methodology: Researchers conducted an extensive literature review and analyzed recent news articles to explore the digital transformation of the insurance industry through InsurTech. The literature review encompassed

Financial Landscape Transformation: Technological Disruptions, 287–299

Published under exclusive licence by Emerald Publishing Limited
doi:10.1108/978-1-83753-750-120251016

academic journals, industry reports, and relevant books to provide a theoretical framework and historical context. Concurrently, researchers examined news articles from reputable sources to capture current developments, real-world applications, and emerging trends. This dual approach allowed researchers to assess the role of digital innovations on the insurance.

Findings: The findings reveal how large and continuing databases impact the operational processes and general insurance markets, facilitating the acquisition of optimal policyholder behavior and speeding up claims processing. This chapter delves into how AI improves traditional insurance processes, spanning from the first point of contact to claims processing and how potential changes brought about by blockchain technology.

Keywords: Insurance; innovation; Insur-Tech; digital transformation; artificial intelligence; blockchain; big data

JEL Codes: G22; O33

Introduction

Rapid technological progress has compelled individuals to embrace the digital era, significantly affecting customer behavior, processing methods, information handling, and various other issues. The transition to the digital age has brought about substantial changes in companies' economies and working environments, impacting how individuals work. The effects of digitization are considered the fourth wave of industrialization, which will profoundly reshape the commercial landscape. Hence, the duration of a company's operation hinges on its capacity to address the novel challenges posed by digitization (Apdillah et al., 2022). "Digital transformation" is a word used to describe a change in the operating environment or internal use of digital technology within an organization, affecting roles, offerings, and how business is performed. Promoting digital transformation will boost the adoption of diverse digital technologies in company operations. Consequently, the firm gains many benefits. The advent of digital technology enables the development of novel business models while simultaneously improving and supplementing existing products and services. Companies must invest in developing information technology architecture to take advantage of the tools and services offered by digitalization (Parviainen et al., 2017). Undoubtedly, the insurance business must modernize its processes and adopt digital transformation. The increasing aggregate insurance premiums and density pattern demonstrate India's growing need for life insurance coverage. One contributing element to the rising insurance penetration in India is the digitalization of the insurance business. Indian consumers strongly desire to buy digital insurance goods, especially those provided by financial technology and electronic commerce (Alt et al., 2021). Insur-tech is the outcome of the digital transformation of the insurance industry. Insur-tech offers digital insurance aggregators, digital agents, online claims features, and marketplaces. It also incorporates big data, blockchain, and the Internet of Things (IoT) to enhance these services (Uyun et al., 2020).

The Digitization of Insurance Industry

Insurance organizations must have an integrated digitization strategy to address changes in consumer behavior effectively. The author's research, conducted through a survey, emphasizes seven essential factors necessary for a successful shift to digital technology. Subsequently, it presents a systematic approach to creating a digitalization strategy. Another author comparably assesses the insurance industry, observing the emergence of new business models, reduced market entry barriers, and accelerated innovation cycles. Insurance companies should prioritize five key factors, including a clear vision for digitization, to tackle the challenges of the modern digital business landscape (Jafarizadeh et al., 2013). The remarkable development of digital ecosystems in the insurance industry is emphasized, explicitly focusing on expanding three categories: comprehensive service providers, interconnected devices, and personalized distribution segments. Consumer expectations, technology adoption, and legislation accelerate the spread of the ecosystem. The distribution, underwriting, and claims administration sectors subsequently emphasize the possible risks to insurers. The research yielded five strategic action points. Insurance businesses must evaluate the risks and probabilities they face, offer services within their capabilities, and establish an operational approach that fosters innovation. They should also form strategic partnerships and experiment with new ideas on a modest scale before expanding rapidly (Dupont, 2019).

Most insurance managers lack comprehension of "digitization" and its impact on their industry. The chapter discusses how insurers can utilize digitalization to make their corporate operations more efficient, change how they engage with consumers, and generate and utilize data for artificial intelligence (AI) systems (Ansi et al., 2024; Novarlic et al., 2024). Digitization can cause changes in the products, marketing, price, service, distribution, and claims offered by credible insurers. To maintain a competitive edge, it is necessary to have a well-executed digital transformation plan and roadmap. Digitization has disrupted the value chain, highlighting the risk of organizations falling behind if they pay attention to these issues. Insurance businesses must formulate a digital strategy and anticipate future operations to find investment initiatives within and outside the company. Additionally, they must foster a culture that promotes digital thinking (Riikkinen et al., 2018).

Deloitte examines the impact of technology on the insurance sector by identifying ten key themes and classifying them as either disrupters or facilitators. Subsequently, he discusses eight contemporary technological trends that have the potential to influence the insurance industry imminently. The mentioned terms are software-defined everything, ambient computing, dimensional marketing, Chief Integration Officer (CIO), renaissance, amplifying intelligence, and IT worker

(Deloitte, 2015). Feilmeier offers other perspectives on the impact of technology in the digital transformation of the insurance sector. He identifies five technical factors that cause changes in company structures. These variables encompass big data, mobile devices, social engagement, cloud computing, and the IoT. The insurance business will implement new requirements for worker credentials and data security in response to the rise of these factors (Feilmeier, 2016).

Furthermore, the World Economic Forum's research identified three potential applications for smart contracts and the corresponding blockchain technology in the insurance industry. Intelligent contracts can accelerate the claims management process by utilizing data from external sources and executing predefined computer-coded procedures. Furthermore, the digitization of company activities leads to a reduction in operating costs. Furthermore, blockchain technology can facilitate the identification of suspicious behavior and improve risk assessments by retaining historical claim data. Furthermore, the chapter delineates three essential conditions for using smart contracts in the insurance industry (World Economic Forum, 2016).

The traditional model may face danger in the future due to the emergence of a new digital model. Agents will need to readjust whenever carriers start engaging more directly with customers. Various communication channels will be available, encompassing face-to-face interactions, telephone conversations, online platforms, and video conferencing. In the coming decade, automation will substantially influence the insurance industry. Full-time positions may be consolidated or substituted by a maximum of 25%. The functions that will experience the most significant impact are those related to administrative support and operations (Yerpude et al., 2022).

Additionally, there will be emerging career roles that require stringent qualifying criteria. These pertain to teams specializing in data analysis, support for marketing and sales in digital channels, and people with expertise in digital technologies. Therefore, locating and cultivating workers will be vital for the prosperity of insurance companies (McKinsey, 2013).

Role of Insurance in the Insurance Life Cycle

By leveraging insurance technology, insurance companies can digitally transform many stages of the insurance product life cycle. InsurTech can be utilized in every insurance service life cycle aspect, such as product development, underwriting, distribution platforms, administration, and claims processing (Wilamowicz, 2019). The adoption of InsurTech can be categorized by examining the steps of the insurance cycle and how current technology benefits insurance firms and clients. InsurTech plays several functions in the insurance product cycle:

Pre-contract Stage – InsurTech has a substantial impact during the pre-contract period. Digital services can provide potential clients with practical answers to their challenges. This can manifest as online comparison tools that aid users in finding the most cost-effective or competitive insurance choices. Other InsurTech companies provide comprehensive services encompassing the entire insurance process, including helping customers choose appropriate insurance products, handling claims and insurance management, and aiding consumers in effectively managing their insurance portfolios. Insurance goods can be sold using online platforms, including enhanced digital infrastructure, self-service websites, chatbots, and other features. This study will employ a fusion of technologies, such as AI, big data, machine learning (ML), and the IoT (Lin & Chen, 2020).

Product Development – InsurTech has a substantial impact during the pre-contract period. This point could facilitate the advancement of business-provided insurance products, such as intelligent contract-enabled airline delay insurance products that allow for automatic payments based on data collected via the internet on-aircraft delays. Emerging use-based insurance companies offer ad hoc temporary insurance tailored to the consumer's use of the insured property. Consequently, there could be a reduction in total insurance expenses and a more customized insurance policy (Ahmad et al., 2024).

Post Contact – InsurTech can reduce the expense of filing an insurance claim by simplifying and optimizing the claims procedure. This can be accomplished by developing a platform that connects insured persons, auto repair businesses, and insurance companies, facilitates the evaluation of disaster claims, and connects patients with physicians and insurance companies. This service aims to enhance clients' overall experience and streamline the claim procedure. Claim settlement is crucial in determining client involvement with insurance products (Agarwal et al., 2022).

Back Office Operation – Employing InsurTech can enhance the efficiency of insurance companies' administrative tasks, including underwriting, risk management, and regulatory compliance. InsurTech can enhance insurers' ability to assess customer risk profiles more precisely using advanced data analytic tools and comprehensive big data analyses. For example, due to the perception that men tend to drive more recklessly than women in the same age group, conventional risk profiling methods usually lead to young men paying higher prices for car insurance than women of the same age. Consequently, personalized information can provide sufficient knowledge to produce a high-quality service tailored to each customer's requirements (Rajput & Ahmad, 2022).

Risk Control – InsurTech can improve risk management and loss assessment to reduce moral hazard once the insurance has been issued. Running an insurance provider or insurance broker can significantly benefit from this advantage. For example, some InsurTech companies have developed tools to assess the risks that individual drivers bring to the safety of vehicle fleets or are utilizing smartphone telematics to track clients' driving behavior. Enhanced risk assessment allows the insurer to effectively weigh the factors in selecting whether to provide coverage, resulting in improved decision-making. Similarly, InsurTech can enhance the efficiency of the loss adjustment process by ensuring better customer care at the claims stage. Life insurance companies commonly employ technological solutions to encourage specific healthy behaviors among clients, leading to improved health and reduced risk for the insured. Insurers can use technology to conduct know-your-customer

("KYC") verifications, detect fraudulent activities, and streamline compliance with anti-money laundering requirements. Blockchain technology has been employed specifically to address insurance fraud, improve identity management, track the origin and ownership of assets, and facilitate the exchange of fraud information across insurance providers. Technology can also assist insurance organizations in making better-informed investment decisions (Raj et al., 2021).

The Role of AI in the Insurance Process

Insurance companies have already begun employing AI tools to analyze vast amounts of unprocessed data and make informed decisions. ML, AI, and big data are crucial in enhancing business operations and ensuring high levels of client pleasure.

AI in the Underwriting Process: AI swiftly supplants alternative technologies as the prevailing set of tools for underwriters. AI technology enables underwriters to assimilate and comprehend more data, enhancing their ability to forecast the underwriting process more precisely. An underwriter uses AI to improve the accuracy of premium calculations, hence reducing loss ratios. Example 1: Historically, yearly car insurance rates have been determined as a set sum. While a telematics device may influence the rates, you are ultimately charged based on real-time usage and its corresponding pricing. This gadget sends temporary data between the covered vehicle and the insurer's central management system. Insurance businesses employ AI technology to develop a flexible and ongoing pricing structure (Azzopardi & Cortis, 2013). Example 2: In the standard life insurance underwriting process, inquiries are made to anticipate the future life events of the proposer(s). AI now partners with life insurance companies to generate quotes using face analytics. This method combines sensory analytics with a possible investigation. To obtain a quote, the client must provide a self-portrait photograph. The technology will utilize the picture to assess the subject's physiological characteristics and ascertain their lifespan, well-being, and disease vulnerability. This system analyses several face characteristics in the uploaded photo to offer underwriters information like predicted age, BMI, and smoking indication. These will provide more comprehensive and reliable information about a person's lifespan (Solutions, 2017) compared to the traditional questions on life insurance application forms. Insurance companies have also begun implementing AI in accident and health insurance. Insurance corporations are gaining vital information about their consumers' physical health through advanced technology, such as embedded sensors and AI-powered wearable devices.

AI in the Claims Management Process – AI is supplanting conventional claims. Case 1: In Japan, an AI system deployed a group of 30 individuals tasked with calculating refunds for policyholders (McCurry, 2017). Case 2: A property insurance company has created an automated claims procedure that streamlines the process of making a new claim. Intelligent applications pose a broad query to the policyholder to collect fundamental information about the asset. The policyholder can use the smartphone camera to record evidence of the claim, accurately identifying the damaged item without completing a claim form. The AI will examine the provided data and apply 18 anti-fraud algorithms. Clear and easy-to-understand claims are promptly granted, while complex claims are forwarded to the human staff of the complaints department for evaluation. Technology is being used to emphasize and streamline the oversight of intricate claims. Case 3: Utilizing aerial drone photos to document substantial property damage and determining the magnitude of the damage through image analytics. Insurance organizations have transitioned from relying on skilled humans to utilizing AI to investigate specific fraud trends (Cognizant, 2017).

AI in Client Interaction – The insurance sector is often seen as the leader in customer service innovation. Even with this perception, a few insurance businesses developed and incorporated chatbots into their regular business operations, similar to other industries. Chatbots like those seen on Facebook Messenger are AI technology designed to replicate customer service agents. They engage in conversations with both existing and new clients. A robot would initiate dialogue with clients by assessing their requirements and identifying the insurance products that would best suit their needs. Insurance companies have recently adopted chatbot technology to offer immediate insurance policy pricing through messaging networks. This chatbots can recommend the most suitable insurance package to customers based on their needs (Chuadhry, 2023).

The Role of DLT in the Insurance Process

Distributed ledger technology (DLT) presents prospects for transformative shifts in the insurance industry. Existing insurers can benefit from DLTs in their operations and establish competitive peer-to-peer (P2P) insurance networks.

Improving Current Process – DLTs, through identity verification, can enhance an insurer's evaluation and KYC standards (Mainelli & Smith, 2015). These benefit entities, individuals, and information that have experienced alterations or a sequence of custody. The total number of claims filed for the same occurrence may be reduced due to DLT. Example 1: In the event of a travel delay, the insured or policyholder cannot submit several complaints for the same incident. Consider a scenario where a DLT is employed to transmit financial and medical transactions. Upon receiving the policyholder's consent, the insurer can determine the expense of health insurance without requiring the policyholder to fill out any more documentation. In addition, constructing models using personalized data and external data evaluation enables prompt adjustments to policy and price. This helps to reduce the time required for insurance services. Example 2: DLT is currently employed in crop insurance. Automated coverage could be achieved if claims are resolved only based on meteorological conditions, without needing a physical inspection, as Lorenz et al. (2016) stated. DLTs offer advantages for claims handling that extend beyond complex insurance procedures. Implementing an intelligent contract might lead to an instant reimbursement once the components are delivered after an automobile damage claim (Lorenz et al, 2016).

P2P Insurance – As the distance between people decreases, using P2P insurance practices is likely to become increasingly common. This can potentially revolutionize the insurance industry by disrupting specific types of coverage, similar to how Uber/Grab and AirBnB have entirely transformed their industries. Illustration 1: If the flight is canceled, group insurance coverage can be created by ten individuals, with each person contributing Rs. 10 toward the expenses. The individuals would go through the joining procedure, paying an annual charge of Rs. 10. If the P&I Club arrangement determines that this amount is insufficient, they would be expected to contribute further monies. For example, when two participants have filed claims, the total expenditure would amount to Rs. 200. Consequently, each member would be required to contribute an extra Rs. 10 to cover these costs. If no legal action is taken, the participants will divide the profit of Rs. 100 equally among themselves. In addition, we are contemplating using DLTs within a comparable P2P system. This would involve incorporating reinsurance to ensure sufficient coverage in cases where the total premiums are insufficient to meet claims. If the reserves are inadequate to cover the claims, this will eliminate the need to raise capital (Mainelli & Gunten, 2014).

The Role of Big Data in the Insurance Process

Today, data is increasingly recognized as a significant asset, leading enterprises to shift their focus toward it. This "phenomenon" in the financial services sector can be attributed to the observation that earlier insurance models are becoming more flexible by incorporating the increasing influx of data from several diverse sources. Telematics, wearable devices, and the IoT are three technologies that significantly impact the insurance industry.

Telematics – It is crucial to guarantee that insurance companies collect sufficient premiums by appropriately pricing their services. Automobile insurers have traditionally assessed the probability of policyholders making an accident claim by considering factors such as the age and gender of drivers, their postcodes, the type of their vehicles, and their history of complaints. These rating elements can predict the likelihood of a claim being submitted. Example 1: Teenage drivers are classified as high-risk individuals and are subject to higher insurance rates than middle-aged drivers. The current pricing structure needs to be revised due to its failure to account for the exceptional driving ability exhibited by particular youngsters. Pricing should be detached and distinct from the specific vehicle they own or their age. Telematics technology devices can identify many driving factors such as location, day of the week, driving frequency, mileage and behavior in hazardous areas, acceleration rates, speed, and braking patterns. The previously incarcerated policyholders can now be freed from their attributes, such as age, and demonstrate their worth as cautious drivers who pose an acceptable level of risk and are unlikely to be involved in an accident or make a subsequent claim (Barbara, 2017). These parameters can be considered in a more precise and personalized pricing model.

Wearable Technology – Although wearable gadgets such as the Apple Watch are commonly worn on the wrist, innovation has now led to the generation of vast amounts of data from various sensors integrated into devices that extend to fashion accessories like apparel, jewellery, and shoes. Like telematics, these technological advancements are becoming accessible, and insurance companies are improving their pricing models by utilizing the influx of new data. Wearables can gather various types of biometric data during exercise, including recorded walks, duration of sitting, and miles cycled. They can also measure cardiac metrics such as heart rate, rhythm fluctuations, electrocardiogram readings, and blood pressure. Additionally, wearables can track sleep information, including total sleep time and sleep quality, body temperature, skin galvanic response, sugar levels, and even exposure to contaminants. Wearable devices, such as telematics, enable insurers to identify or at least approach the underlying causes of the insured individual more accurately (Zeya et al., 2023).

Internet of Things – The IoT refers to a network of tangible items equipped with sensors and connectivity, enabling them to transport and share data. Applications of the IoT include monitoring intelligent household devices, such as evaluating water and air quality. The impact of IoT on the market is significant, and forecasts suggest that by 2020, there will be up to 30 billion IoT objects, and the industry will be valued at $7.1 trillion (Nordrum, 2016). The IoT also facilitates the accessibility of several data sources pertinent to the insurance sector, much like telematics and wearables do. Smart home devices enable insurance companies to adopt a more proactive approach to risk management. An IoT smart home sensor collects data and offers the potential for a novel kind of customer interaction. Example 1: Before substantial harm occurs, the policyholder may receive notification of a leak problem using real-time data from a water pressure monitoring sensor (Hsu & Lin, 2016).

Enabling Factors for InsurTech in Emerging Markets

Undoubtedly, the insurance industry in emerging nations has significant potential for expansion, and the utilization of technology-driven business models and ensure-tech will play a vital role in facilitating this growth. In emerging nations, in contrast to mature markets, individuals usually initiate their life or health insurance coverage, particularly those with lower incomes, rather than starting with vehicle, renters, or property insurance (Holliday, 2019; Sultana et al., 2023). The subsequent characteristics are essential for insur-tech to have a significant influence:

Compulsory Motor Third-Party Liability Insurance and automobile insurance are essential for pedestrians injured in car accidents. Furthermore, insurance disseminates insurance information and serves as a platform for insurance companies to introduce new products. Taxation of the market should be avoided to incentivize and acknowledge responsible driving.

Financial literacy – This issue is not limited to emerging markets; it is prevalent in other countries. Many individuals and proprietors of small businesses need more awareness regarding the potential hazards they are exposed to. This lack of awareness increases the likelihood of losing all their accumulated savings in the event of an illness or a catastrophic incident such as a fire or a flood. InsurTech can assist by offering online guidance and education, gamification, contact centers, chatbots, and other related technologies. Nevertheless, literacy should commence within the confines of the classroom since this enables kids to acquire knowledge about borrowing, saving, and other viable options for amassing and safeguarding wealth early in their education. Furthermore, both banks and microfinance institutions are engaged in this.

Biometric ID – Implementing this measure can effectively mitigate fraud, preventing an increase in insurance premiums for loyal customers, particularly in health insurance. Although it may be deemed redundant, evidence from India and certain African countries demonstrates that this identification process effectively reduces the obstacles to developing improved insurance solutions.

Access to mobile networks and WIFI – Although several applications can store and transmit data at a later time, it is crucial to have access to a dependable network or WIFI connection at least once daily. For example, the parametric program ACRE Africa allows farmers to replant crops if there has been no rainfall for 21 days after the initial planting. The payment to the farmer for new seeds relies on mobile banking via M-PESA, while the program activation requires a mobile connection using the unique code found on the seed packet.

Payment mechanisms – Mobile payment alternatives for premiums and claims enhance efficiency, reduce costs, and mitigate the potential for fraudulent activities.

Digital signature – While moist signatures may cause delays and incur additional costs, they are ultimately unnecessary. We recommend that authorities embrace digital signatures as society increasingly transitions to a digital and mobile-oriented environment. This can be achieved by leveraging KYC data from alternative sources such as banks or mobile telecommunication networks (MTN).

Regulation for different models – As mentioned earlier, many insurance companies start as managing general agents before eventually becoming full-stack insurers. The government should acknowledge the concept of Managing General Agent (MGA) in numerous developing countries. Recognizing and efficiently regulating different business models employed by insurance businesses, MGAs, brokers, agents, and price comparison websites is crucial. Ensuring sufficient protection while promoting innovation is essential, despite customers often needing to be aware of the distinctions. The United Kingdom, with its extensive track record in insurance regulation, is a prime illustration of a comprehensive policy (Akter et al., 2018).

Conclusion

Insurance businesses are often perceived as needing to be faster to embrace new technology. According to Cortis et al. (2019), insurance companies allocate 50% to 70% of their IT budget to operations expenses rather than research and development (R&D). The transformative power of big data in the insurance industry was apparent. The advancements in AI have facilitated the utilization of vast amounts of data from many sources, like telematics, wearables, and the IoT.

This enables the production of highly personalized goods for consumers. These data sources are also starting to uncover a distinct customer relationship, enabling the insurer to engage with policyholders more profoundly. The sector is expected to undergo significant and lasting changes due to the continued influence of big data in the foreseeable future. The insurance sector is currently experiencing disruption from DLTs, the IoT, and AI. The extent and nature of the disturbance that will occur is still uncertain. As digital innovation in the insurance market progresses, InsurTechs will assume a more prominent position. Regular evaluation of insurance performance is essential for attaining long-term economic growth. To enhance future performance, digital insurance must be guided appropriately (Sultana et al., 2023).

References

Agarwal, S., Bhardwaj, G., Saraswat, E., Singh, N., Aggarwal, R., & Bansal, A. (2022, February). Insurtech fostering automated insurance process using deep learning approach. In *2022 2nd International conference on innovative practices in technology and management (ICIPTM)* (Vol. 2, pp. 386–392). IEEE.

Ahmad, S., Saxena, C., Islam, S., & Karim, R. (2024). Impact of Insur-Tech on the premium performance of insurance business. *SN Computer Science*, *5*(1), 138–147.

Akter, R., Ahmad, S., & Islam, M. S. (2018). CAMELS model application of non-bank financial institution: Bangladesh perspective. *Academy of Accounting and Financial Studies Journal*, *22*(1), 1–10.

Alt, M. A., Săplăcan, Z., Benedek, B., & Nagy, B. Z. (2021). Digital touchpoints and multichannel segmentation approach in the life insurance industry. *International Journal of Retail & Distribution Management*, *49*(5), 652–677.

Apdillah, D., Panjaitan, K., Stefanny, N. T. P., & Surbakti, F. A. (2022). The global competition in the digital society 5.0 era: The challenges of the younger generation. *Journal of Humanities, Social Sciences and Business*, *1*(3), 75–80.

Al-Ansi, A. M., Garad, A., & Ryabtsev, V. (2024). Intelligent risk analysis of investment projects in the extractive industry. *Journal of Industrial Intelligence*, *2*(1), 42–53.

Azzopardi, M., & Cortis, D. (2013). Implementing automotive telematics for insurance covers of fleets. *Journal of Technology Management & Innovation*, *8*(4), 59–67.

Barbara, C., Cortis, D., Perotti, R., Sammut, C., & Vella, A. (2017). The European insurance industry: A PEST analysis. *International Journal of Financial Studies*, *5*(2), 14–31.

Chuadhry, S. A. (2023). Exploring the nexus: employee maturity, customer interaction, and client satisfaction in the AI-Driven Software Industry of Pakistan. *Annals of Artificial Intelligence and Data Sciences*, *1*(01), 12–22.

Cognizant. (2017). *Cognizant and measure partner to deliver a dramatic business impact for insurers using drones*. Retrieved June 2, 2024, from Cognizant Solution Overview [PDF Document] (fdocuments.in).

Cortis, D., Debattista, J., Debono, J., & Farrell, M. (2019). InsurTech. *Disrupting Finance: FinTech and Strategy in the 21st Century*, *8*(4), 71–84.

Deloitte. (2015). *Tech Trends 2015: An insurance industry perspective*. Retrieved June 2, 2024, from deloitte.com

Dupont, B. (2019). The cyber-resilience of financial institutions: Significance and applicability. *Journal of Cybersecurity*, *5*(1), 13–27.

Feilmeier, M. (2016). *Digitalisierung, Big Data und andere digitale Techniken in der Versicherungswirtschaft*. Retrieved June 2, 2024, from DAV_Kompass_Ausgabe2_web.pdf (aktuar.de)

Holliday, S. (2019). *How InsurTech can close the protection gap in emerging markets*. World Bank Document.

Hsu, C. L., & Lin, J. C. C. (2016). An empirical examination of consumer adoption of Internet of Things services: Network externalities and concern for information privacy perspectives. *Computers in Human Behavior*, *62*(4), 516–527.

Lin, L., & Chen, C. (2020). The promise and perils of InsurTech. *Singapore Journal of Legal Studies*, *20*(2), 115–142.

Lorenz, J. T., Münstermann, B., Higginson, M., Olesen, P. B., Bohlken, N., & Ricciardi, V. (2016). Blockchain in insurance—Opportunity or threat. *McKinsey & Company*, *1–9*. Retrieved June 2, 2024, from the-digital-insurer.com

Jafarizadeh, A. A., Fathi, Z., & Hasanpour, E. (2013). Identifying and prioritizing the factors affecting customer loyalty to a brand (Case study: insurance industry). *European Online Journal of Natural and Social Sciences*, *2*(3), 348–363.

Mainelli, M., & Von Gunten, C. (2014). Chain of a Lifetime: How blockchain technology might transform personal insurance. Retrieved June 2, 2024, from SSRN: https://ssrn.com/abstract=3676416

Mainelli, M., & Smith, M. (2015). Sharing ledgers for sharing economies: An exploration of mutual distributed ledgers (aka blockchain technology). *Journal of Financial Perspectives*, *3*(3), 12–26.

McCurry, J. (2017). A Japanese company replaces office workers with artificial intelligence. *The Guardian*, *5*.

McKinsey. (2013). *Agents of the future: The evolution of property and casualty insurance distribution*. Retrieved June 2, 2024, from mckinsey.com

Nordrum, A. (2016). Popular internet of things forecast of 50 billion devices by 2020 is outdated. *IEEE Spectrum*, *18*(3), 223–236.

Novarlić, B., & Đurić, P. (2024). Enhancing comprehensive waste management in transition economies through green logistics: A case study of Bosnia and Herzegovina. *Journal of Intelligent Management Decision*, *3*, 42–55.

Parviainen, P., Tihinen, M., Kääriäinen, J., & Teppola, S. (2017). Tackling the digitalization challenge: How to benefit from digitalization in practice. *International Journal of Information Systems and Project Management*, *5*(1), 63–77.

Raj, R., Dixit, A., Saravanakumar, D., Dornadula, A., & Ahmad, S. (2021). Comprehensive review of functions of blockchain and crypto currency in finance and banking. *Design Engineering*, *21*(9), 3649–3655.

Rajput, S., & Ahmad, S. (2022). Challenges and opportunities in creating digital insurance business in Bangladesh. *International Journal of Early Childhood Special Education*, *14*(5), 6690–6693.

Riikkinen, M., Saarijärvi, H., Sarlin, P., & Lähteenmäki, I. (2018). Using artificial intelligence to create value in insurance. *International Journal of Bank Marketing*, *36*(6), 1145–1168.

Solutions, L. (2017). *Lapetus solutions launches new data collection initiative to support the global expansion of its predictive technologies*. Custom AI Analytical Services.

Sultana, N., Lima, R. P., & Ahmad, S. (2023, April). Enabling technologies for human development in developing countries: A bibliometric analysis on Insur-Tech. In *2023 International conference on computational intelligence, communication technology and networking (CICTN)* (pp. 396–400). IEEE.

Sultana, N., Rahman, K. S., Lima, R. P., & Ahmad, S. (2023, May). Financial technology and competitive landscape in the banking industry of Bangladesh: An exploratory focus. In *International conference on emergent converging technologies and biomedical systems* (pp. 225–241). Springer Nature Singapore.

Uyun, A., Sekarhati, D. K. S., Amastini, F., Nefiratika, A., Shihab, M. R., & Ranti, B. (2020, October). Implication of InsurTech to implementation IT decision domain perspective: The case study of insurance XYZ. In *2020 6th International Conference on Computing Engineering and Design (ICCED)* (pp. 1–6). IEEE.

Wilamowicz, A. (2019). The great FinTech disruption: InsurTech. *Banking & Finance Law Review*, *34*(2), 215–238.

World Economic Forum. (2016). *The future of the financial infrastructure*. Retrieved June 2, 2024, from weforum.org

Yerpude, S., Sood, K., & Grima, S. (2022). Blockchain-augmented digital supply chain management: A way to sustainable business. *Journal of Risk and Financial Management*, *16*(1), 7.

Zeya, F., Sultana, N., Rahman, K. S., & Ahmad, S. (2023, October). Digital transformation adoption in the insurance sector of Bangladesh: A quantitative study from the perspective of insurer. In *2023 4th IEEE global conference for advancement in technology (GCAT)* (pp. 1–5). IEEE.

Chapter 17

FinTech: A New Financial Revolution

S. M. Ashraful Alam[a], *Rozina Akter*[b], *Sadia Noor Khan*[c] *and Shakil Ahmad*[d]

[a]*Department of Management Information System, Begum Rokeya University, Bangladesh*
[b]*Department of Business Administration, Daffodil International University, Bangladesh*
[c]*Department of Banking and Insurance, Dhaka University, Bangladesh*
[d]*School of Business, University of Creative Technology Chittagong, Bangladesh*

Abstract

Introduction: The bank plays a significant role in financial intermediation and serves as market-makers and agents. The emergence of new financial technology, commonly known as "FinTech", is anticipated to revolutionize these industries. FinTech encompasses technological advancements in the financial sector to enhance consumer satisfaction, streamline operational procedures, create novel products, and foster greater competition.

Purpose: The primary aim is to discuss the banking industry's current and potential future state with the emergence of financial technology. The specific objective is to explore the emergence of new-age technologies in the banking industry and the challenges faced in their implementation.

Methodology: A qualitative method is employed to analyze the FinTech landscape. Researchers conducted an extensive literature review and analyzed recent news articles to explore the banking industry's digital transformation through FinTech. The literature review encompassed academic journals, industry reports, and relevant books to provide a theoretical framework and

Financial Landscape Transformation: Technological Disruptions, 301–316

Published under exclusive licence by Emerald Publishing Limited
doi:10.1108/978-1-83753-750-120251017

historical context to capture current developments, real-world applications, and emerging trends.

Findings: The evolution and impact of financial technology on the global economic landscape have been explored. It highlights how FinTech innovations, such as blockchain, artificial intelligence, and mobile payments, have revolutionized traditional banking, enhancing efficiency, accessibility, and security. It discusses regulatory challenges and the need for a balanced approach to foster innovation while ensuring consumer protection. The findings underscore FinTech's potential to drive economic growth and the importance of continuous adaptation to evolving technological trends.

Keywords: Finance; banking; innovation; FinTech; InsurTech; Regteh; Crowd Funding; P2P lending; online payment

JEL Codes: G21; O33

Introduction

The banking industry has tried to stay abreast of financial and technological changes. However, in the last decade, it has undergone significant disruption due to the introduction of advanced technology and essential changes in consumer preferences. Furthermore, the banking industry had to adapt to implementing stricter financial laws due to the financial crisis 2008. The financial crisis revealed the banking industry's problems with excessive leverage and inadequate capital. Financial institutions bear greater responsibility and incur higher expenses to adhere to more rigorous financial laws. Consequently, banks were incentivized to prioritize adherence to regulations rather than developing new ideas or advancements. FinTech encompasses various innovative technology and digital advancements in the financial sector and its operations. FinTech provides financial services and solutions by using advanced technologies such as Distributed Ledger Technology (DLT), Machine Learning (ML), Artificial Intelligence (AI), Internet of Things (IoT), and application programming interfaces (Gogia & Chakraborty, 2022).

FinTech companies depend on state-of-the-art technology to offer innovative financial services that more effectively meet the needs and habits of modern customers. Moreover, these companies are constructed on innovative business strategies that enable them to broaden the availability of their services. The distinctive features and rapid growth of FinTechs have disrupted the financial system, namely the banking industry. Established players are facing severe competition from FinTechs. They view FinTechs as a menace and must modify their strategy to sustain their presence in the financial sector. FinTechs' innovative solutions strive to provide customers with a broader array of financial services and providers, user-friendly interfaces, rapid transaction processing, and enhanced transparency. Experienced professionals in the financial business are facing competition from emerging rivals who are not only automating their operations but also making investments in financial technology companies or collaborating with them. Implementing this approach may expand their customer base and leverage state-of-the-art technology without substantially changing their infrastructure (Ahmad & Saxena, 2022).

The phrase "FinTech," a neologism made up of the words "financial" and "technology," denotes the interaction between new technological advancements and the established practices of the financial sector. FinTech encompasses various technological advancements, including distributed ledger technology, cryptocurrency, robo-advice, equity crowd-funding, online marketplace lending, and machine learning. Companies that attempt to increase the flexibility and efficiency of financial solutions by using new technologies are referred to as being in the fintech sector (Gomber et al., 2018). Fintech firms are typically technical start-ups that offer customers a wide range of services and work to strengthen their position in the industry by contending with established banks and other financial institutions. FinTech comprises financial innovators and disruptors who provide appointed financial intermediaries with less flexibility, efficiency and opportunity. When referring to established financial institutions that employ innovation to grow their businesses, fintech is called "sustaining fintech", where new enterprises use IT to contend with established financial institutions by offering new financial services (Blakstad & Allen, 2018).

Evolution of Financial Technology

Technology and innovation have always substantially impacted the expansion of the financial sector. The Automatic Teller Machine (ATM) was introduced in the late 1960s as a replacement for traditional bank branches and tellers. In the 1970s, the first digital stock trading was promoted on stock exchange floors. Financial institutions began adopting new information technologies (IT) in the 1980s. The models of e-commerce and the Internet were introduced in the 1990s. Over the past six decades, notable breakthroughs have occurred in invention. The technological and financial innovations of the past few decades have profoundly impacted the economic environment, influencing the development of products and services as well as regulatory matters (Arner et al., 2016).

Financial diplomats have consistently sought and embraced innovations to satisfy their clientele. 1987 marked the start of a new age in finance, characterized by digital transactions between economic players and their clients globally. The processes of globalization and digitization drove this shift. Financial institutions adopted computerized trading systems to mitigate rising risks in the financial industry. Banks have established Information Technology infrastructures to facilitate their internal business operations and client interactions. Since the emergence of the Internet, most banks have wholly digitized their internal operations and connections with the public and retail clients (Arner et al., 2015; Sultana et al., 2023).

The financial services sector transformed in the 1990s due to the increasing prevalence of the Internet and subsequent technological improvements. They ignited the rise of electronic finance (e-finance), encompassing diverse economic activities such as banking and stock trading conducted through electronic channels. The rapid progress of the smartphone user population played a crucial role in the emergence of the mobile finance industry in the 2000s, facilitating the introduction of various e-finance services such as mobile banking and payment. The convergence of electric finance, the Internet, artificial intelligence, and big data analytics has significantly contributed to the growth of FinTech, especially in the aftermath of the 2008 financial crisis (Giglio, 2022).

Following the global financial crisis, newly founded businesses and existing technology corporations ventured into the banking sector. They commenced offering financial solutions and services directly to companies and end customers. Historically, FinTech consisted of established and regulated financial institutions that utilized new technologies to provide financial services and products. The global economic recession 2008 served as a significant impetus for the emergence of FinTech 3.0. Consequently, we promptly examined how the crisis expedited the advancement and success of FinTech in the financial industry (Ashta & Biot-Paquerot, 2018).

Divers of Financial Technology

Supply-side factors – Supply drivers incentivize individuals to participate in the financial market by introducing novel products or services. This encompasses factors such as continuous technological progress, the regulatory framework, revolutionary innovations, and the overall macroeconomic conditions. As mentioned, technology has consistently played a crucial role in advancing the financial industry. ATMs, the Internet, electronic finance, digital banking, and mobile payments are notable instances of significant technological progress. Technological improvements can significantly change the financial system's concentration, contestability, and composition (Ikeo, 2021).

Technological advancements enable new or unorthodox vendors to challenge established market leaders by offering products or services that bypass regulations. This often leads to increased competition, reduced market dominance of weaker players, and lower prices, ultimately reducing market concentration. Regarding contestability, technology can reduce the initial costs for new rivals and facilitate their entry into the market. Consequently, the outcome is less ability for the established players to set prices. Technology can reduce financial services' disintegration, alter service providers' composition, and lead to numerous activities not subject to regulatory oversight (Hill, 2018; Zeya et al., 2023).

Regulation, encompassing regulatory and supervisory prerequisites alterations, often catalyzes financial innovation. The 2008 financial crisis compelled authorities to strengthen the existing legislation, resulting in significant changes to the economic incentives for both incumbent corporations and new entrants. The banking industry's standards became more rigorous, resulting in banks discontinuing the provision of low-value loans and shifting their focus away from short-term financing. To protect the system of financial intermediaries, consumers, and banks, banks are now required to comply with more rigorous requirements. Implementing the new law imposed stricter regulations on banks, limiting their ability to cater to the needs of a diverse clientele (Al-Ansi et al., 2024; Novarlić & Đurić, 2024).

Consequently, this created an opportunity for emerging financial entities to surpass the established market leaders in providing financial products and services to individuals and enterprises. Often, one innovation can trigger the emergence of another innovation, initiating an "innovation spiral" that leads to a systematic sequence of significant advancements. Innovation is a contributing component as it enables the generation of later inventions (Hasan et al., 2021).

Demand side factors – A financial diplomat can develop and provide diverse services when considering demand. However, a crucial condition for achieving success is a significant market demand for these offerings. The impetus for financial innovation originates from customer preferences and behaviors. Due to technological advancements and widespread internet usage, the behaviors of both consumers and organizations have undergone significant changes. This has an impact on their everyday routines and the functioning of banks. Customers increasingly expect quick access to financial services that align with their other internet activities. They seek more efficient, tailored, and user-friendly financial solutions than previous options (Claessens et al., 2018; Yerpude et al., 2022).

The consumer base for fintech services is predominantly composed of younger generations due to their distinct behaviors compared to their parents and grandparents. Unlike traditional banks and financial organizations, which often cater to the general public, younger individuals seek personalized solutions. Moreover, younger cohorts exhibit excellent proficiency in utilizing contemporary technologies, rendering them the primary demographic for FinTech ventures. Financial institutions must fulfill the expectations of younger customers seeking more creative and interactive financial goods and services despite FinTech solutions being already famous in this age (Frost, 2020).

The Emergence of Fintech Companies

While numerous studies also examine factors that facilitated the establishment of FinTech businesses, the main drivers of the phenomenon are demand-side and supply-side issues. These issues encompass critical technological and economic factors that contribute to the creation and success of FinTech firms. These factors can be categorized into nine groups: finance, payments, risk management, asset management, insured techs or insurance technology (Ahmad & Saxena, 2022), loyalty programs, regh-tech or regulatory technology, exchanges and other commercial activities. The study is based on four primary hypotheses and focuses on establishing FinTech business in 55 countries between 2006 and 2014 (Christopher & De Vries, 2020).

Initially, the process of creating FinTech start-ups is made more accessible by the presence of highly developed economies and financial markets. Given that many start-ups necessitate substantial finance to initiate and sustain their business models, entrepreneurs can more readily obtain these resources if conventional capital markets are robustly established. Moreover, there is a higher probability that individuals will require innovative financial tools and fresh services in developed economies, especially in major financial markets with excellent prospects for advancement and digitalization. The availability of the latest technologies in the market is another incentive. Technological progress is essential for bringing innovative ideas and disrupting the financial sector. FinTech enterprises necessitate technological enhancements to fulfill the requirements of emerging clientele by implementing expedited payment systems, streamlined operations, improved information interchange, and reduced financial activity expenses. To facilitate the provision of FinTech solutions, the nation's economy needs to have an existing infrastructure that can support the latest technology. The third component in advancing FinTech pertains to the characteristics of the financial industry (Kang et al., 2016). The financial crisis 2008 significantly impacted the short-lived surge in FinTech start-ups for various reasons. Following the issue, there was a decline in confidence in banks, which facilitated the emergence of FinTechs to disrupt the cycle of distrust and mitigate the decline in financial stability.

Benefits of Financial Technology

Financial innovations are developed to rectify market flaws or inefficiencies and provide societal benefits by resolving at least one of those faults. FinTech seeks to broaden the reach of financial services globally by improving financial inclusion, especially in emerging and developing countries where digital or traditional services are not yet broadly accessible. FinTech offers specialized financial products and services to enhance financial inclusion. FinTech may provide customers with benefits that surpass traditional incumbents, who frequently adopt a mass-market approach. The advantages encompass enhanced quality and user experience, specialized merchandise, easy service access, and cost-effective solutions. FinTech leverages big data to analyze the preferences of individual clients and offers customized tools (Vučinić, 2020).

FinTech enterprises prioritize their clients' demands, requirements, and attitudes, as clients have the final say in decision-making and seek interactive and adaptive services. FinTech enables credit and other financial institutions to enhance their operational efficiency by reducing costs, accelerating service delivery, expanding their customer base through improved financial inclusion, and reducing expenses related to regulatory compliance. Unlike traditional financial institutions, FinTech companies are not constrained by rigid regulations, complex IT systems, or physical branch networks. As a result, they can reduce banking costs associated with physical branches, complex processes, and rigorous industry regulations. In addition, due to the stricter criteria imposed after the 2008 financial crisis, banks often have to decline credit applications from small- and medium-sized enterprises (SMEs). FinTech firms can address these deficiencies. This is possible since most FinTech lending institutions utilize alternative data and credit risk assessment methodologies to increase access to loans for previously underserved consumers, such as younger individuals, less lucrative businesses, smaller enterprises, and minority-owned companies (Vijai, 2019).

These advancements provide stability to the credit market and assist FinTech companies in avoiding the two main risks associated with banking activities: excessive borrowing and mismatched timeframes for repayments. Banks function as mediators by accepting deposits from depositors, providing loans to borrowers, and facilitating depositors' access to liquidity. However, it is essential to note that these operations can sometimes lead to bank runs, which have historically caused crises (Abdul-Rahim et al., 2022). FinTech companies facilitate direct connections between individuals who save money and individuals who borrow money through online lending platforms. FinTech has the potential to benefit the financial sector more comprehensively by providing innovative digital services, improving transparency, and optimizing the efficiency of information dissemination. The FinTech rebellion has caused a substantial transformation in the financial industry and the operations of conventional financial providers. (i) It has changed how companies are organized, how banks work, and how clients can access new options. (ii) It provides new personalized banking services and products by using big data. (iii) Startups in the financial technology sector have replaced certain activities that banks traditionally did (Haqqi & Suzianti, 2020).

Challenges of Financial Technology

Due to the reliance on digitalization, networked IT systems, and data exchange among several parties, digital finance has increased its vulnerability to cyberattacks. Due to the growing availability of financial networks and technologies, mainly through open platforms such as the Internet and mobile devices, it is necessary to strengthen preventative measures against online threats. In the event of a breach of cyber security systems, institutions will face legal, operational, and reputational risks, as well as financial damages. This also undermines long-term trust in digital solutions, constraining rates of acceptance. A coordinated surge of attacks might reduce the availability of money in the market and put the financial stability of economic participants at risk. Cyber security exemplifies the necessity of regulating FinTech since it has increased the vulnerability of the financial industry to potential dangers (Rajput & Ahmad, 2022; Sultana et al., 2023).

FinTech projects have posed substantial legal challenges and encountered resistance from traditional economic actors in adopting innovative technology. The upcoming pages will examine the connection between FinTech and regulation. However, numerous FinTech activities and companies emerge and function outside the traditional regulatory framework. FinTechs benefit from increased flexibility, faster execution, and reduced subservience costs. However, this also poses challenges for regulators in monitoring these activities, leading to decreased coordination between the financial services industry, FinTech businesses, and regulatory officials (Suryono et al., 2020).

Traditional financial institutions have encountered numerous challenges due to the emergence of FinTech. Regarding the advancement of digital transformation through the FinTech revolution, established companies have limited strategic alternatives to combat new entrants. FinTech companies gain a competitive advantage by embracing innovations. Financial diplomats want to be early adopters by enhancing the skills of their information technology teams and motivating their personnel to embrace contemporary work habits. This may also involve directly acquiring FinTech start-ups or financial products and services from FinTech enterprises, although the latter option is rare. Despite the potential advantages the acquisition could bring to established players in the financial sector, conventional corporations seem resistant to incorporating a new entity into their existing infrastructure (Das, 2019).

An alternative is collaborating with FinTech companies to develop innovative services and convert stagnant client relationships into more interactive ones. Since incumbents can offer their services to third parties in unsealed formats and FinTech companies require partners well-versed in the financial industry to market their services, cooperation between them can be mutually beneficial. Conventional financial institutions employ this strategy to establish relationships with FinTech startups and leverage their distribution networks and customer base. Imputed acts as a service design platform by offering unbranded products to FinTechs through this digital approach, enhancing their ability to adapt to changing user requirements. The sole risk of this approach is that FinTech companies with direct consumer interactions might have a platform offering financial products (Lee & Shin, 2018). Ignoring the risks and challenges, the absence of innovative financial technology would heighten the risk of becoming complacent and technologically outdated compared to other countries. Technological improvements can erode the competitive advantage of financial institutions, rendering their economic environment non-competitive in the global financial market.

Regulation of Financial Technology

The regulators aim to achieve financial stability, effective oversight, equitable competition, and the growth of the financial market in the financial sector. Before formulating a pertinent regulation, supervisors must assess a technology's benefits and potential uses. Regulators should revise their procedures and policies to support FinTech's growth better, as these emerging enterprises are rapidly developing and presenting a significant challenge to established incumbents. Regulators should refrain from creating excessive obstacles for new entrants by excessively safeguarding established companies. Increased regulation can foster innovation and enhance competition within the financial sector. In addition, authorities should prioritize emerging FinTech enterprises by implementing less burdensome restrictions than older ones (Akter et al., 2019).

Typically, newcomers in the financial business are exempt from the stringent regulations and requirements implemented after the 2008 global economic crisis, which may lead to security concerns owing to inadequate information protection. The decisions made by regulators directly and indirectly impact the competition between incumbent businesses and new entrants in the financial market. The main goal of the regulatory framework is to provide equal treatment for all economic participants while promoting a dynamic, competitive, and safe financial sector. To maintain stability in the financial system, laws should be implemented to ensure equitable treatment of all participants and prevent competition among them. In addition, regulators must focus on the incentives offered to market intermediaries and how these incentives can influence the decisions and behavior of participants (Buchak et al., 2018).

Regulators need help recognizing the parallelism between the demands of identified individuals and the necessity to supervise the emergence of new financial diplomats. Authorities often impose increasingly stringent limitations on established players because of their familiarity with their operations and objectives. However, they tend to be more receptive to new companies that participate in innovative activities and provide unfamiliar services, even though the associated risks still need to be addressed. Effective regulation should facilitate financial innovation, enable incumbents to endure, and promote robust competition. Multiple contributors provide ideas and guidance to assist rule-makers in accomplishing these aims. Legislation should facilitate fair competition among players, regardless of whether they utilize innovative technology or offer traditional solutions, and eliminate obstacles to the growth of new entrants. Furthermore, the regulatory system must ensure fair treatment of all participants, considering their characteristics and actions (by the notion of a level playing field). Regulators should prioritize safeguarding financial system users as they are vulnerable to unforeseen risks (Taylor et al., 2020).

Implications of Financial Technology for Banking System

FinTech companies generally concentrate on consumer finance, lending, and payment systems. They have created innovative technology and tools, such as peer-to-peer funding platforms, crowd-funding markets, robo-advisors, and machine learning software, which enable them to identify and fulfill clients' demands for customized, cost-effective, and user-friendly financial solutions. Peer-to-peer lending solutions facilitate direct lending between lenders and borrowers without bank intermediation. This allows customers and businesses to deal with small enterprises, such as SMEs or younger businesses. These platforms utilize algorithms, big data analytics, and non-conventional consumer information to reduce intermediation costs and evaluate borrowers' credit risk (Eva et al., 2018).

While banks still dominate the business, FinTech's payments sector has grown significantly. Bitcoin and other digital currencies have the potential to disrupt traditional payment methods. Blockchain technology enables the creation of digital currency and facilitates the validation of transactions by verifying them against blocks of records, eliminating the need for intermediaries such as banks. These systems enable the implementation of several potential economic enhancements and allow for the establishment new currencies without relying on the government or a trustworthy intermediary. A significant development in the financial sector has been the implementation of blockchain technology, which enhances transaction transparency and provides mechanisms to protect clients' privacy (Raj et al., 2021).

Machine-learning and robo-advisor systems can hinder the usual functions of banks by providing investment advice without the typical conflicts between investors and human advisors. The emergence of robo-advice in the FinTech industry challenges traditional financial advisory services. Robo-advice employs algorithms and models to ascertain optimal investing strategies for clients and offers online portfolio management services. Robo-advisors are automated internet services providing portfolio allocation and virtual financial guidance (Chen, 2020). The following principal fintech instruments are discussed:

1. ***Payment systems*** – Conventional payment systems are intricate and costly due to the involvement of numerous agents, instruments, institutions, and processes. Payment systems have consistently undergone transformations, technological progress, and inventive developments to improve their functionality in clients' best interests. The emergence of nonbank digital firms, the enhancement of payment infrastructures, the elimination of obstacles in international money transfers, and the digitization of traditional banking activities pose a danger to the existing payments landscape (Chiu, 2017).

   Nonbank fintech companies are increasingly acquiring market share in the payment system, intensifying the pressure on traditional banks. They are attracting important customers away from banks, reducing fees for local transactions, and promoting electronic payments as a preferred alternative to checks and cash. To successfully rival nonbank competitors and meet evolving client demands, banks must also adjust to new services, digital channels, and technology offered by nonbank entities. The inclusion of nonbank entities impacts both domestic and international payment systems. Thus far, banks have yet to make much effort to resolve the obstacles associated with foreign money transfers or payments, even though these hurdles are expensive for customers. FinTech companies and tools aim to overcome the challenges of international payments, such as the absence of traceability and transparency and the long processing time, by shifting from consumer-to-consumer (C2C) to business-to-business (B2B) payment systems (Kang, 2018).

   Utilizing blockchain-based cryptocurrencies such as Bitcoin can be an effective means of reducing expenses and accelerating international transactions. However, it is essential to note that the volatility of blockchain-based instruments and their lack of reliability may undermine their positive influence on the payment system. Significant developments in transaction banking are driving the growth of digital changes in customers' payments and commercial banking. As customers and individuals become more familiar with faster and cheaper prices in the retail industry, they will seek similar services in transactional banking for their enterprises. The advancements in financial technology (FinTech) inside the payments system provide customers with efficient and automated operations. This is made possible through mobile devices and the availability of more extensive possibilities to collect information and data on consumer preferences and attitudes. Technological advancements that offer these advantages have the potential to threaten existing payment systems, especially those reliant on credit cards (Khiaonarong & Goh, 2020).

2. ***Deposit and lending functions*** – Conventional retail banks provide deposit and loan services but face intense competition from FinTech startups and enterprises. Commercial banks take deposits from account holders and subsequently offer a return on those deposits. Subsequently, they generate loans for clients by utilizing the funds they had previously accumulated, for which they receive a distinct interest rate. Banks utilize credit scores to assess the risk profiles of borrowers to determine loan availability and interest rates. They can detect individuals who are inclined to take risks or are cautious about taking risks, as well as individuals who are likely to borrow with low or high levels of risk (Akter et al., 2018).

   Despite the traditional dominance of established banks in deposits and loans, financial technologies have emerged in this sector and gained increasing popularity in the previous decade. In 2016, FinTech companies accounted for 33.3% of all non-secured consumer loans in the US. These loans are projected to increase by 20% annually over the next five years. The quick growth and widespread adoption of alternative financing solutions have considerably impacted the consumer credit industry, especially retail banking. The FinTech lending business differs from traditional banking due to the need for physical infrastructure, bankers, and branches. However, it facilitates the same type of monetary transfer that conventional commercial banks engage in, which involves moving funds from individuals who save money to individuals who borrow money. Historically, banks have served as intermediaries between depositors and borrowers in loan transactions. They provide loans to borrowers using the funds deposited by savers in the bank, and in return, they offer clients interest on their accounts. Conversely, FinTech lenders establish a direct connection between savings and borrowers. They do not provide loans; instead, the funds are provided by investors or partner banks (Savoie & Hoffman, 2018).

   The author observed that two potential consequences are inherent in all probable scenarios. Investors opting for FinTech lending platforms as short- and medium-term investment options may lead to a decrease in the conventional deposits and investment products provided by banks and financial institutions. This could weaken the capital ratio and result in a reduction in the size of the balance sheet. Furthermore, the dispersion of clients' credit and savings portfolios across multiple alternative platforms with different reporting standards and procedures may pose a more significant challenge for banks in consistently assessing their customers' creditworthiness (Balyuk et al., 2020).

3. ***P2P lending*** – Peer-to-peer lending is the predominant FinTech lending model for consumer finance. The term "peer-to-peer" describes a direct relationship between two participants, bypassing the need for an intermediary. The distinguishing feature of this innovation is the organic matching of lenders and borrowers through online lending platforms. In peer-to-peer

lending, individuals seeking loans access the website, make loan requests and provide information regarding their present financial situation, including their income and existing credit lines. Both individual and institutional investors can make their investments alone, as part of investment groups, or through automated processes. Typically, lenders need to provide total funding for a loan. Instead, they may redistribute funds among borrowers who receive financing only if investor bids surpass a specific threshold. Lending platforms apply an interest rate on loans depending on the borrower's risk score, provided sufficient bids exist (Najaf et al., 2022).

Information asymmetry impacts peer-to-peer lending systems and creates a principal-agent problem between borrowers and investors. Consequently, lenders want to obtain as much precise information on borrowers as possible. Conversely, borrowers may intentionally hide certain aspects of their identity to secure a loan with a low-interest rate. To mitigate the information imbalance, peer-to-peer networks require borrowers to disclose specific information about their financial circumstances. Investors are given the borrower's economic characteristics, such as credit ratings, information on annual income and expenses, property ownership, and the debt-to-income ratio, in a general manner. P2P lenders assess the creditworthiness of borrowers before proceeding with the pricing and screening procedures. Investors evaluate loans by utilizing a range of distinctive algorithms and accessing additional regional and financial data that banks may need access to. Initially, P-2-P lending had inexperienced investors serving as lenders. However, the substantial expansion of this invention enticed institutional investors, who possess a strategic advantage and expertise in understanding the credit market's conditions and characteristics (Rusadi & Benuf, 2020).

Finally, peer-to-peer lending platforms significantly reduce the expenses associated with evaluating potential borrowers by employing automated algorithms to determine the interest rates and assess the creditworthiness of loan applicants. P2P lenders can evaluate minor loans that banks usually decline because of their low profitability, as all aspects of the application, verification, and payment procedure are automated.

4. ***Crowd Funding*** – Crowd funding is a FinTech invention that can potentially disrupt the banking sector, although less significantly than cutting-edge payment systems and FinTech lending. Crowdfunding has emerged as an alternative means of obtaining funding for entrepreneurial ventures instead of depending on venture capital or other traditional forms of financing. Crowd financing is a unique form of fundraising that has emerged due to the growth of the Internet. It combines elements of microfinance and crowdsourcing. Crowd fundraising is an online method where business owners can openly request and collect the required funds through donations or by offering rewards or voting privileges (Ma & Liu, 2017).

   Crowdfunding collects funds for a project or a new business venture from numerous online contributors. Increasing a modest amount of money from a large pool of contributors is feasible. The utilization of online platforms and the subsequent reduction in transaction costs can generate substantial amounts of wealth. Through the Internet, it is now possible to directly connect funders with individuals or entities seeking financial support without intermediaries. Crowdfunding is an essential means of obtaining finance, especially for business owners of start-ups whose credit crunch hinders access to funds from banks (Harris & Wonglimpiyarat, 2020).

Crowdfunding has the potential to pose a threat to commercial banks in the realm of FinTech lending. This is because it can serve specific consumer categories that traditional financial institutions usually overlook. Banks are adapting the business models of crowdfunding platforms to offer tailored and specialized solutions to meet the needs of minor loan applicants. Crowdsourcing innovation carries inherent risks. The primary concern lies in its ability to overcome critical difficulties, such as more skill and comprehension to conduct a thorough investigation, challenges related to information imbalance, sufficient monitoring, and a suitable exit strategy for investors. Despite a few cases of prosperous equity crowdfunding, the industry as a whole presently needs a historical record to assess its ability to generate value for both investors and entrepreneurs (Rizwan & Mustafa, 2022).

Conclusion

Conventional banks utilize modern technology to compete with FinTech firms and ensure their financial stability despite the limitations imposed by rigorous legislation. FinTech firms may challenge the traditional banking system due to their ability to offer personalized services to meet consumers' needs and preferences. Provide more flexible and innovative financial solutions due to less strict regulation. They compete in the exact location of traditional banks but need help to cater to the needs of clients and businesses. Assumed control of duties and obligations that were before exclusive to financial institutions. Conclusively, FinTech activities can be categorized into five types of financial services: clearing and settlement, deposits and lending, payments, insurance, investment management, capital raising and market assistance. For example, the payment category encompasses sophisticated payment alternatives like mobile payment systems. P2P transfers, cryptocurrencies, deposits, crowd financing, crowd lending, and microcredit solutions all fall under the category of lending activities (Rana et al., 2023).

References

Abdul-Rahim, R., Bohari, S. A., Aman, A., & Awang, Z. (2022). Benefit-risk perceptions of FinTech adoption for sustainability from bank consumers' perspective: The moderating role of fear of COVID-19. *Sustainability*, *14*(14), 83–97.

Ahmad, S., & Saxena, C. (2022, May). Artificial intelligence and blockchain technology in the insurance business. In Y. Singh, C. Verma, I. Zoltán, J. K. Chhabra & P. K. Singh (Eds.), *The international conference on recent innovations in computing* (pp. 61–71). Springer Nature Singapore.

Akter, R., Ahmad, S., & Islam, M. S. (2018). CAMELS model application of non-bank financial institution: Bangladesh perspective. *Academy of Accounting and Financial Studies Journal*, *22*(1), 1–10.

Akter, R., Ahmad, S., Kulsum, U., Hira, N. J., Akhter, S., & Islam, M. S. (2019). A study on the implementation of Basel III: Bangladesh perspective. *Academy of Strategic Management Journal*, *18*(6), 1–10.

Al-Ansi, A. M., Garad, A., & Ryabtsev, V. (2024). Intelligent risk analysis of investment projects in the extractive industry. *Journal of Industrial Intelligence*, *2*(1), 42–53.

Arner, D. W., Barberis, J., & Buckey, R. P. (2016). FinTech, RegTech, and the reconceptualization of financial regulation. *Northwestern Journal of International Law & Business*, *37*(2), 371–384.

Arner, D. W., Barberis, J., & Buckley, R. P. (2015). The evolution of Fintech: A new post-crisis paradigm. *Georgetown Journal of International Law*, *47*(4), 127–141.

Ashta, A., & Biot-Paquerot, G. (2018). FinTech evolution: Strategic value management issues in a fast-changing industry. *Strategic Change*, *27*(4), 301–311.

Balyuk, T., Berger, A. N., & Hackney, J. (2020). *What is fueling FinTech lending? The role of banking market structure*. Retrieved June 2, 2024, from https://ssrn.com/abstract=3633907 or http://dx.doi.org/10.2139/ssrn.3633907

Blakstad, S., & Allen, R. (2018). *FinTech revolution* (pp. 121, 132). Springer.

Buchak, G., Matvos, G., Piskorski, T., & Seru, A. (2018). Fintech, regulatory arbitrage, and the rise of shadow banks. *Journal of Financial Economics*, *130*(3), 453–483.

Chen, K. C. (2020). Implications of Fintech developments for traditional banks. *International Journal of Economics and Financial Issues*, *10*(5), 227.

Chiu, I. H. (2017). A new era in fintech payment innovations? A perspective from the institutions and regulation of payment systems. *Law, Innovation and Technology*, *9*(2), 190–234.

Christopher, L. A., & De Vries, M. (2020). Selecting a scaled agile approach for a fin-tech company. *South African Journal of Industrial Engineering*, *31*(3), 196–208.

Claessens, S., Frost, J., Turner, G., & Zhu, F. (2018). *Fintech credit markets worldwide: size, drivers and policy issues*. Retrieved June 2, 2024, from bis.org

Das, S. (2019). *Opportunities and challenges of FinTech. Keynote Address Delivered at NITI Aayog's Fin-Tech Conclave, New Delhi*. Retrieved June 2, 2024, frombis.org

Eva, S. A., Islam, M. S., Shariar, M. S., Akter, R., & Ahmad, S. (2018). Board of directors structure and bank's performance: Evidence from Bangladesh. *Journal of Academy of Business and Economics*, *18*(2), 29–44.

Frost, J. (2020). *The economic forces driving fintech adoption across countries. The technological revolution in financial services: how banks, fintech and customers win together*. Retrieved June 2, 2024, from https://ssrn.com/abstract=3515326

Giglio, F. (2022). Fintech: A literature review. *International Business Research*, *15*(1), 80–85.

Gogia, J., & Chakraborty, D. (2022). Open banking: A revolution in the Tech-Fin industry. *International Journal of Electronic Banking*, *3*(2), 100–120.

Gomber, P., Kauffman, R. J., Parker, C., & Weber, B. W. (2018). On the fintech revolution: Interpreting the forces of innovation, disruption, and transformation in financial services. *Journal of Management Information Systems*, *35*(1), 220–265.

Haqqi, F. R., & Suzianti, A. (2020, June). Exploring risk and benefit factors affecting user adoption intention of fintech in Indonesia. In *Proceedings of the 3rd Asia Pacific conference on research in industrial and systems engineering* (pp. 13–18).

Harris, W. L., & Wonglimpiyarat, J. (2020). Dynamics of crowdfunding and FinTech challenges. *International Journal of Business Innovation and Research*, *23*(4), 501–514.

Hasan, R., Ashfaq, M., & Shao, L. (2021). Evaluating drivers of fintech adoption in the Netherlands. *Global Business Review*, *9*(3), 126–139.

Hill, J. (2018). *Fintech and the remaking of financial institutions*. Academic Press. https://doi.org/10.1016/C2016-0-03863-9

Ikeo, K. (2021). New risks from Fintech (2) financial system destabilization. *The Economics of Fintech, 12*(5), 199–210.

Kang, J. (2018). Mobile payment in Fintech environment: Trends, security challenges, and services. *Human-Centric Computing and Information Sciences, 8*(1), 1–16.

Kang, Y. M., Lee, Y. G., Kwon, H. J., Han, K. S., & Chung, H. S. (2016). A study on the information security system of fin-tech business. *Journal of Convergence Society for SMB, 6*(2), 19–24.

Khiaonarong, T., & Goh, T. (2020). FinTech and payments regulation: An analytical framework. *Journal of Payments Strategy & Systems, 14*(2), 157–171.

Lee, I., & Shin, Y. J. (2018). Fintech: Ecosystem, business models, investment decisions, and challenges. *Business Horizons, 61*(1), 35–46.

Ma, Y., & Liu, D. (2017). Introduction to the special issue on Crowdfunding and FinTech. *Financial Innovation, 3*(1), 1–4.

Najaf, K., Subramaniam, R. K., & Atayah, O. F. (2022). Understanding the implications of FinTech Peer-to-Peer (P2P) lending during the COVID-19 pandemic. *Journal of Sustainable Finance & Investment, 12*(1), 87–102.

Novarlić, B., & Đurić, P. (2024). Enhancing comprehensive waste management in transition economies through green logistics: A case study of Bosnia and Herzegovina. *Journal of Intelligent Management Decision, 3*, 42–55.

Raj, R., Dixit, A., Saravanakumar, D., Dornadula, A., & Ahmad, S. (2021). A comprehensive review of functions of blockchain and cryptocurrency in finance and banking. *Design Engineering*, 3649–3655.

Rajput, S., & Ahmad, S. (2022). Challenges and opportunities in creating digital insurance business in Bangladesh. *International Journal of Early Childhood Special Education, 14*(5), 6690–6693.

Rana, S., Das, S., Shikder, S., & Ahmad, S. (2023). Industry 5.0: Sustainable development in Bangladesh. *International Journal of Engineering Applied Sciences and Technologies, 8*(1), 106–111.

Rizwan, A., & Mustafa, F. (2022). Fintech attaining sustainable development: An investor perspective of crowdfunding platforms in a developing country. *Sustainability, 14*(12), 7114.

Rusadi, F. A. R. P., & Benuf, K. (2020). Fintech peer-to-peer lending as a financing alternative for developing MSMEs in Indonesia. *Legality: JurnalIlmiahHukum, 28*(2), 232–244.

Savoie, R., & Hoffman, P. (2018). Marketplace lending and Fintech. *The Business Lawyer, 73*(2), 509–516.

Sultana, N., Lima, R. P., & Ahmad, S. (2023, April). Enabling technologies for human development in developing countries: A bibliometric analysis on Insur-Tech. In *2023 International conference on computational intelligence, communication technology and networking (CICTN)* (pp. 396–400). IEEE.

Sultana, N., Rahman, K. S., Lima, R. P., & Ahmad, S. (2023, May). Financial technology and competitive landscape in the Banking Industry of Bangladesh: An exploratory focus. In *International conference on emergent converging technologies and biomedical systems* (pp. 225–241). Springer Nature Singapore.

Suryono, R. R., Budi, I., & Purwandari, B. (2020). Challenges and trends of financial technology (Fintech): A systematic literature review. *Information, 11*(12), 590.

Taylor, M. C. R., Wilson, C., Holttinen, E., & Morozova, A. (2020). *Institutional arrangements for Fintech regulation and supervision* (pp. 1–19). International Monetary Fund. Google Books.

Vijai, C. (2019). FinTech in India – Opportunities and challenges. *SAARJ Journal on Banking & Insurance Research (SJBIR). 8.*

Vučinić, M. (2020). Fintech and financial stability potential influence of FinTech on financial stability, risks and benefits. *Journal of Central Banking Theory and Practice*, *9*(2), 43–66.

Yerpude, S., Sood, K., & Grima, S. (2022). Blockchain-augmented digital supply chain management: A way to sustainable business. *Journal of Risk and Financial Management*, *16*(1), 7.

Zeya, F., Sultana, N., Rahman, K. S., & Ahmad, S. (2023, October). Digital transformation adoption in the insurance sector of Bangladesh: A quantitative study from the perspective of insurer. In *2023 4th IEEE Global Conference for Advancement in Technology (GCAT)* (pp. 1–5). IEEE.

Index

Printed and bound by CPI Group (UK) Ltd, Croydon, CR0 4YY

15/09/2026

14962489-0007